Virtue Epistemology

MIT Readers in Contemporary Philosophy

Virtue Epistemology

Contemporary Readings

edited by John Greco and John Turri

The MIT Press
Cambridge, Massachusetts
London, England

MIT Press books may be purchased at special quantity discounts for business or sales promotional use. For information, please email special_sales@mitpress.mit.edu or write to Special Sales Department, The MIT Press, 55 Hayward Street, Cambridge, MA 02142.

This book was set in Stone Serif and Stone Sans on InDesign by Asco Typesetters, Hong Kong. Printed and bound in the United States of America.

Library of Congress Cataloging-in-Publication Data

Virtue epistemology : contemporary readings / edited by John Greco and John Turri.
    p. cm. — (MIT readers in contemporary philosophy)
Includes bibliographical references and index.
ISBN 978-0-262-01787-9 (hardcover : alk. paper) — ISBN 978-0-262-51780-5 (pbk. : alk. paper)
1. Virtue epistemology. I. Greco, John. II. Turri, John.
BD176.V56   2012
121—dc23   2011046883

10   9   8   7   6   5   4   3   2   1

Contents

Introduction

John Greco and John Turri

Virtue epistemology is by now a broad and varied field. Also by now, there are various helpful overviews of the field available, some of which are included in this volume (see especially Battaly, chapter 1, and Baehr, chapter 2).[1] This introduction will not provide another. Rather, we will begin with a brief characterization of what virtue epistemology is (section 1), and then briefly describe some of the topics that are treated in this volume (section 2). Some of these are topics that have occupied epistemology in general, while others are raised by virtue epistemology in particular. We end with a summary of the selections that have been collected here (section 3).

1   What Is Virtue Epistemology?

Virtue epistemology begins with the premise that epistemology is a normative discipline and that, accordingly, a central task of epistemology is to explain the sort of normativity that knowledge, justified belief, and the like involve. A second premise of virtue epistemology is that a focus on the intellectual virtues is essential to carrying out this central task. In these respects, virtue epistemology is conceived on an analogy with virtue ethics: in both fields, a focus on the virtues is taken to be central to the explanation of an important normative domain.

One way to characterize virtue epistemology is in terms of a thesis about the direction of analysis. In virtue ethics, the thesis is that moral properties in general may be explained in terms of the moral properties of persons. Person-level moral excellences (moral virtues) are fundamental, and other moral properties are to be explained in terms of them. In virtue epistemology, the thesis is that epistemic properties in general may be explained in terms of the epistemic properties of persons. In this case, person-level intellectual excellences (intellectual virtues) are fundamental. In virtue ethics, for example, the rightness of actions is to be explained in terms of the

moral virtues of actors, rather than the other way around. In virtue epistemology, the justification of beliefs is to be explained in terms of the intellectual virtues of believers, rather than the other way around.

A different way to understand virtue epistemology, still on the analogy
with virtue ethics, is in terms of a weaker characterization. While not endorsing the thesis about direction of analysis described above, some virtue
epistemologists advocate a focus on the virtues nonetheless. Motivations
for such a focus are varied. Some claim that a focus on the intellectual
virtues helps us to make progress on traditional problems in epistemology,
even if not by way of a traditional analysis of epistemic properties. Others
claim that a focus on the virtues broadens and enriches epistemology,
either by raising new questions or by returning us to older ones. For example, a focus on the virtues provides a good entry into questions about
intellectual agency and about the relationships between intellectual and
moral agency. Alternatively, a focus on the virtues can return us to questions about understanding and wisdom that have been long neglected in
the field. Some strands in virtue epistemology, then, look to expand or
reorient epistemology in general, sometimes in radical ways. This constitutes yet another analogy with virtue ethics, which did as much for moral
philosophy in the latter part of the twentieth century.

Before moving to a discussion of topics in section 2, we note one more
way in which discussions of virtue epistemology vary. Namely, different
virtue epistemologists have tended to think of the intellectual virtues in
different ways. First, some think of the intellectual virtues as cognitive
abilities or powers, such as reliable perception, sound memory, and sound
reasoning. Others, however, think of the intellectual virtues as character
traits, such as open-mindedness, intellectual courage, or intellectual honesty, and so as more closely analogous to the moral virtues. At times, discussions on this topic have been framed as if epistemologists are here
disputing a substantive issue: What are the intellectual virtues *really* like, or
what is the *right* way to think of the intellectual virtues? Nowadays, however, most virtue epistemologists are happy to agree that there are at least
two kinds of intellectual virtue, or intellectual excellence. One's focus on
powers or on traits will be determined by one's theoretical interests.

2   Some Questions in Epistemology and Virtue Epistemology

When Ernest Sosa first introduced the notion of intellectual virtue into the
contemporary literature, his topic was *the structure of knowledge*, and more
specifically the debate between foundationalism and coherentism. Founda-

tionalist theories propose that knowledge is structured like a pyramid, with a firm foundation supporting the remaining edifice. Coherentist theories propose that knowledge is structured like a raft, held together by relations of mutual support, and with no piece in the structure more fundamental than others. Sosa's proposal was that his virtue theory preserves the truth in both pictures: On the one hand, intellectual powers such as perception and introspection are sources of knowledge in virtue of their reliable access to relevant truths. Such powers are "foundational" in that they are not reasoning powers, and therefore generate knowledge that is not inferred from knowledge that is evidentially more fundamental. The Pyrrhonian regress is thereby avoided. But coherence, too, is a virtue, Sosa argues. More exactly, coherence-seeking reason is an intellectual power that, in our world, gives reliable access to the truth and therefore counts as an intellectual virtue. Moreover, coherence-seeking reason can give rise to *understanding* and, in particular, understanding regarding the source of belief in intellectual virtue. Accordingly, intellectual virtue is self-supporting in a way that a full resolution of the Pyrrhonian problematic demands.

Sosa's early discussions already contained suggestions about *the nature of knowledge*, or what knowledge *is*. This is the age-old question of Plato's *Theaetetus*, and aims to explain the difference between knowledge and mere opinion. A popular theme in virtue epistemology is that knowledge is true belief from intellectual virtue. More exactly, in cases of knowledge, S believes the truth *because* S's belief is produced by intellectual virtue. A number of the selections in this volume put forward this sort of view. Hence,

Greco: S knows *p if and only if* S believes the truth (with respect to *p*) because S's belief that *p* is produced by intellectual ability. (Greco, chapter 4)

Sosa: Belief amounts to knowledge when it is apt: that is to say, when its correctness is attributable to a competence exercised in appropriate conditions. (Sosa, chapter 8)

Turri: Knowledge is adept belief . . . you know Q just in case *your truly believing* Q manifests your cognitive competence. (Turri, chapter 6)

Riggs: S knows that *p* iff: (1) S believes *p*, (2) *p* is true, (3) S is sufficiently deserving of credit for the fact that she has come to hold a true belief in this instance . . . S's coming to hold a true belief in this instance is the product of S's actual abilities. (Riggs, chapter 13)

An adequate theory of knowledge ought to explain the difference between knowing and not knowing—between cases that amount to knowledge and cases that do not. A working assumption among episte-mologists is that knowledge is well formed in a way that mere opinion is not. For example, it has been proposed that knowledge must be based on good evidence, or epistemically responsible, or perhaps "epistemically jus-tified." In any case, an adequate theory ought to explain this normative dimension to knowledge, or the way in which knowledge is well formed and mere opinion is not.

Another working assumption is that *knowledge cannot be true by accident*, at least not in the relevant sense of "accident." For example, in Gettier cases the subject has a true belief, and even a true belief that seems well formed in the sense of being justified, or epistemically responsible, or based on good evidence. Nevertheless, S's believing the truth seems "too lucky" to count as knowledge. The Lottery Problem and skeptical problems also sug-gest that knowledge must exclude luck in some important sense. Accord-ingly, an adequate theory ought to explain how knowledge is incompatible with luck or accident, and in what sense.

Virtue theories try to meet these demands, proposing that the difference between knowledge and opinion is to be explained in terms of intellectual virtue. What makes knowledge good or well formed, the idea goes, is that it is produced by intellectual virtue. This same feature, moreover, explains how and why knowledge is incompatible with luck or accident. The main idea is this: knowledge is incompatible with luck in the way that credit-worthy success in general is incompatible with luck. Knowledge is a kind of achievement, or creditworthy success, and so relates to luck as do achieve-ments in general.

One objection to this account is that it is too weak. In particular, Duncan Pritchard (chapter 5) argues that the account does not rule out the sort of luck that is involved in Gettier cases and barn facade cases. Pritchard also objects that the account is too strong—some kinds of knowledge, for ex-ample testimonial knowledge, seem not to require the sort of virtuous for-mation that the theory says is required. Jennifer Lackey (chapter 14) has put the objection in the form of a dilemma: Either the virtue condition is to be interpreted strongly, in which case it rules out too much, including some cases of testimonial knowledge and innate knowledge, or the virtue condition can be interpreted weakly, but then it will be too weak to do the proposed work regarding Gettier cases and the like. Virtue theorists have tried to respond in various ways.

We said that knowledge has a normative dimension, and that an ade-quate theory of knowledge ought to explain its nature. A closely related question regards *the value of knowledge*. It is generally assumed that we value knowledge more than mere opinion, and even more than true opinion. But why should that be so, especially if true opinion has the same practical value that knowledge does?

Questions about the value of knowledge go back at least to Plato's *Meno*, but recently they have come back to the fore in epistemology. One reason for the renewed interest is the rise of reliabilist theories, which seem especially vulnerable to the value problem. According to generic reliabilism, knowledge is superior to mere true opinion because knowledge is reliably formed. But Linda Zagzebski (chapter 7) has argued that this provides an inadequate explanation of knowledge's value over true belief. In general, she argues, having been reliably produced does not add value to something. For example, a good cup of espresso is not more valuable in virtue of having been produced by a reliable espresso machine.

A number of authors have argued that virtue epistemology offers an elegant solution to the value problem, or the problem of explaining the value of knowledge over true belief. First, we may return to the distinction marked above between merely lucky success and success from ability. Only in the latter case do we have success that is creditable to the agent, in virtue of its production through agent ability or competence. In other words, we have an achievement or accomplishment. The proposal, then, is that knowledge is a kind of achievement, and thereby has the value of achievements in general. More specifically, the value of knowledge over mere true belief is an instance of something more general: the value of achievement over merely lucky success.

The solution is elegant but has problems nonetheless. First, it is only as good as its major claim—that knowledge is a kind of success from ability. Second, the proposal raises further questions about epistemic value. Is epistemic value "monistic," so that the value of knowledge is always parasitic on the value of true belief? And if so, does the present solution really avoid the problem of the *Meno*, or the "swamping" problem raised for reliabilist theories above?[2] Another problem: Is true belief always valuable, even when idiosyncratic or trivial? And if not, can the value of knowledge really be explained in terms of the value of true belief? These are questions about epistemic value for epistemology in general, but pressing for virtue epistemology in particular.

Another issue that has occupied epistemology in general, and that is treated in some of the essays collected here, regards *the scope of knowledge*. Questions about the scope of knowledge are directly related to skeptical arguments, which seek to show that knowledge's scope is limited in some important way. A standard kind of skeptical argument is *Cartesian*. This sort of argument challenges our knowledge of the external world by invoking skeptical possibilities that are incompatible with what we take ourselves to know. It is impossible to rule out the possibility that we are dreaming, the argument goes, or that we are victims of a deceiving demon. Another standard kind of skeptical argument is *Pyrrhonian*. This is the sort of argument that occupies foundationalism and coherentism, as we saw above. It invokes the regress of reasons, and argues that belief must be founded on vicious regress, dogmatic assumption, or question-begging circle. Some of the essays in this volume engage these skeptical problems and try to offer virtue-theoretic solutions. Most notably, the selections from Sosa (chapter 8) engage different versions of the Cartesian dream argument. And as is well known, Sosa's accounts of animal and reflective knowledge are developed with Pyrrhonian challenges in mind.

Likewise, John Greco's accounts of ability and intellectual ability are developed with Cartesian skepticism in mind. Greco (chapter 4) argues that abilities in general are dispositional properties: to say that S has the ability to achieve result R is to say that S has a disposition or tendency to achieve R across some *range of relevantly close worlds*. More exactly, we will be interested only in worlds where, among other things, S has the relevant physical constitution and S is in some relevant set of conditions and environment. A perceptual ability, for example, would be a disposition to form true perceptual beliefs across some range of relevantly close worlds—worlds where S is physically constituted as in the actual world, and where S is in conditions and an environment that are relevant to the kind of perceptual task in question. The important point in this context is that skeptical scenarios often invoke irrelevant conditions and environments. For example, presumably there is no close world where I am a brain in a vat or the victim of a deceiving demon. But then those sorts of worlds are irrelevant to determining whether my perceptual beliefs in the actual world are from ability.

This general approach comes with problems, of course. Perhaps most importantly, the approach must be filled in with an adequate account of which worlds count as relevantly close. Sosa does this in terms of what is normal and appropriate to the ability in question, whereas Greco relativizes to practical interests. In each case, however, the account of intellectual ability is informed by considerations about abilities or competences in general. This is as it must be, if such an account is to have explanatory power—that is, if it is to *explain* what makes a world relevantly close, as opposed to offering ad hoc stipulation.

Here we note a recurring theme in virtue epistemology: that knowledge is an instance of a more general normative phenomenon—that of success through virtuous (able, competent) agency—and that we make progress in epistemology by invoking the more general relations among agency, virtue, luck, and credit. By locating epistemic issues within this more general normative domain, we gain insight into the dynamics that drive epistemology's problems. By exploiting the relations that hold across the domain, our theories gain in explanatory power. That, in any case, is a recurring theme. Questions about how that theme should play in its details, and to what extent it is successful, are taken up by the essays that follow.

As we have already seen, some virtue epistemologists confront skepticism head-on, viewing it as an opportunity to help clarify what exactly knowledge requires. But some virtue epistemologists think that *avoiding* a confrontation with skepticism can be illuminating as well. For example, Zagzebski (chapter 16) points out that progress on some philosophical questions tends to come only once we are "ready to put skeptical worries aside." Indeed, she claims, modern epistemology has been partly "stultified" by an obsession with skepticism and its attendant focus on certainty and justification. The consequence is that we have neglected other important epistemic categories, such as understanding and wisdom.

The suggestion that we look beyond a confrontation with skepticism is not, as Zagzebski notes in her discussion, unprecedented in the history of Western epistemology. But some recent trends in virtue epistemology represent a more radical departure from traditional themes. For instance, Jonathan Kvanvig (chapter 17) argues that virtue epistemologists ought to break free of the Cartesian paradigm of individualistic epistemology and embrace a historical and social perspective on cognition, from which perspective the full import of the intellectual virtues becomes apparent. And Miranda Fricker (chapter 15) makes the case that virtue epistemology is suited to help us understand the political dimensions of knowledge through an examination of the habits involved in the consumption of testimony.

Nevertheless, even when virtue epistemology appears at its most iconoclastic, just beneath the surface we find connections with deep trends in the history of Western philosophy. For instance, Fricker's discussion owes a debt to John McDowell's theory of normativity, which draws explicitly on Aristotle's ethics, focusing on the role of culture in initiating humans into the distinctively rational activities of basing beliefs and actions on reasons, the assessment of reasons, criticism, and so on. A similar approach informs Zagzebski's and, especially, Kvanvig's discussions as well.

It turns out, then, as it does in so much of philosophy, that what was old is new again. We gain a fresh perspective on the prospects and possibilities of epistemology by revisiting the ancient roots of virtue theory in the

Western tradition. Contemporary virtue epistemology is an exciting and dynamic field with a rich tradition to draw upon in order to help address epistemological questions, both old and new.

3   Summary of Chapters[3]

A.   Overviews of the Field

In "Virtue Epistemology," Heather Battaly provides an admirable overview of virtue epistemology, which also introduces new ways of thinking about the field and makes a suggestive proposal that advances the debate over the correct definition of knowledge. Battaly first distinguishes virtue epistemology from belief-based epistemology. Belief-based epistemology focuses on properties of beliefs—such as whether they fit the evidence, fulfill epistemic obligations, or are reliably produced—and treats these as primary. Conventional analytic epistemology is belief-based. By contrast, virtue epistemology focuses on agents and their intellectual traits, treats these as primary, and aims to explain other epistemic notions, such as justification or knowledge, in terms of them. Battaly also distinguishes two strands of virtue epistemology: the *theory* and *anti-theory* strands. Virtue theories aim to define knowledge and justified belief, just as conventional analytic epistemology does, except that it treats agents and their virtues as primary. Virtue anti-theories eschew "formulaic" definitions and instead focus on the virtues "in their own right." Battaly also suggests combining virtue reliabilist and virtue responsibilist approaches to generate a "unified theory of knowledge." This is motivated by the observation that virtue responsibilism is better suited to explaining "high-grade" knowledge, whereas virtue reliabilism is better suited to explaining "low-grade" knowledge and solving the Gettier problem. The introduction to section II presents an enlightening list of questions facing any theory of intellectual virtues, which can be used to generate a nuanced and helpful taxonomy of the field.

In "Four Varieties of Character-based Virtue Epistemology," Jason Baehr presents a fourfold taxonomy of "responsibilist" or "character-based" virtue epistemologies and assesses each variety. Character-based virtue epistemology treats intellectual virtues as refined intellectual traits, such as intellectual courage and open-mindedness. Within the character-based camp, conservative views appeal to intellectual virtues to engage traditional epistemological questions about the nature and scope of knowledge. Strong conservative views propose that the virtues will feature centrally and fundamentally in answers to the traditional questions. Weak conservative views envision a more modest, secondary but still notable role for virtues. Autonomous views appeal to intellectual virtues to blaze new trails in epistemology. Radical autonomous views aim to replace and eliminate traditional epistemological questions. Moderate autonomous views aim only to add questions to the agenda. Baehr argues in favor of the moderate conservative and weak autonomous varieties, and lists some ways to fruitfully develop these research programs.

B.   The Nature of Knowledge

In the selections from *A Virtue Epistemology*, Sosa marshals two principal resources to explain the nature of knowledge and respond to a form of skepticism. The first resource is the "AAA" model of performance assessment. A performance is *accurate* if it achieves its aim, *adroit* if it manifests relevant competence or skill, and *apt* if it is accurate because adroit. Sosa treats belief as an intellectual performance whose aim is truth, and defines knowledge as apt belief; that is, belief that is true because competent. Although apt beliefs might typically also be safe beliefs—a safe belief is one that would not have easily been false, at least when held on the basis that it actually is held—Sosa denies that safety is absolutely required for aptness. Safety and aptness can come apart. This allows Sosa to respond to skeptical doubts which take as their starting point the nearby possibility that we might be dreaming in sleep.[4] This nearby possibility might render our perceptual beliefs unsafe, but does not render them inapt. The second resource is the distinction between animal and reflective knowledge. Whereas animal knowledge is apt belief, reflective knowledge is "apt belief aptly noted"; that is, knowing that you know. Sosa employs this distinction to handle objections to his response to dreaming skepticism.

In "The Nature of Knowledge," Greco proposes that you have knowledge if and only if you believe the truth because your belief is produced by intellectual ability. He then develops this thesis in the context of three themes: that knowledge attributions are somehow context sensitive; that knowledge is intimately related to practical reasoning; and that one purpose of the concept of knowledge is to flag good sources of information. Wedding these themes to the proposed account, Greco argues, helps to explain a wide range of cases, including barn facade cases and standard Gettier cases. It also helps to answer some important objections, including the generality problem for reliabilism, and the charge that virtue theories cannot explain testimonial knowledge.

In "Apt Performance and Epistemic Value," Pritchard contests Sosa's theory of knowledge as apt belief, arguing that apt belief is neither necessary nor sufficient for knowledge. It is not sufficient because apt performance is, but knowledge is not, compatible with the sort of luck on display in typical Gettier cases and in fake-barn cases. It is not necessary because knowledge based on testimony need not involve apt performance on the hearer's part (see Lackey's paper in the section "Credit and Luck"). Pritchard suggests that these results motivate a shift to "anti-luck virtue epistemology," which appends a safety condition to standard virtue-theoretic accounts of knowledge. There are two fundamental and independent intuitions about knowledge that Pritchard says his proposal vindicates. First, that knowledge involves true belief due to ability. Virtue epistemologists privilege this intuition. Second, that knowledge precludes luck. Those who favor safety, sensitivity, reliability, or similar requirements privilege this intuition. Pritchard proposes an account that respects both of these intuitions, by identifying knowledge with safe true belief produced by cognitive ability.

In "Manifest Failure," John Turri argues that the basic insight behind virtue-theoretic definitions of knowledge can be strengthened by paying close attention to the metaphysics of dispositions. The key move is to highlight the distinction between, on the one hand, an outcome happening merely because of a disposition, and on the other, an outcome manifesting a disposition. This is a perfectly general distinction that applies to all dispositions, not just intellectual ones. *That the subject forms a true belief is* often the outcome of inquiry. You gain knowledge when, and only when, such an outcome manifests your intellectual dispositions or abilities. Knowledge is true belief manifesting intellectual ability, or what Turri calls "adept belief." Turri concludes that virtue epistemology has the resources to solve the Gettier problem once and for all.

C. Epistemic Value

In "The Search for the Source of Epistemic Good," Zagzebski argues for several theses about the value of knowledge. First, she argues that reliabilism cannot solve the value problem, which is the problem of explaining what makes knowledge better than mere true belief. This is because reliabilists understand knowledge to be reliably produced true belief, and *being reliably produced* does not add any value to a true belief, just as good espresso is not more valuable for having been made by a reliable espresso machine. Indeed, a similar inability affects internalist theories that claim that justification's value is merely instrumental to truth. To properly solve the value problem, Zagzebski argues, we must recognize that knowledge has value independently of anything "external" to it. She suggests thinking of knowledge as a properly motivated "act" or "state of the agent" for which the agent earns credit. Proper motivation adds value. For belief, proper motivation is love of truth.

In "Knowing Full Well," Sosa amplifies the AAA-model of performance assessment we met with earlier, distinguishing first-order from second-order performances. He employs this distinction to explain the normativity involved in assessing not only belief but also the suspension of judgment. The normativity of belief is that of apt performance more generally—that is, performances that succeed due to the agent's skill or competence. The normativity of suspending judgment is that of "meta-apt" performances more generally. Specifically, it is the sort of normativity involved in assessing an agent's decision to proceed, or to not proceed, with a first-order performance. Knowledge is more valuable than mere true belief because it is an apt performance, and not successful merely through luck. A "fully apt" performance is not only apt, but also apt because meta-apt. Reflective knowledge fits into this picture by contributing to fully apt belief.

In "Can Virtue Reliabilism Explain the Value of Knowledge?," Berit Brogaard argues that Zagzebski and others overlook an important category of non-instrumental extrinsic value, which would allow generic reliabilists to account for the value of knowledge without adverting to intellectual virtues or virtuous motivation. The non-instrumental or "final" value of something can be enhanced by its relation to something external to it, such as, for example, the source that produced it. Additionally, if virtue epistemologists cannot locate a principled distinction between belief-producing processes that are "grounded in the agent's virtuous abilities and those that are not," then they are no better positioned than generic reliabilists to adequately solve the value problem. Here Brogaard refines the problem of "strange and fleeting processes" that virtue reliabilists have used as a cudgel against generic reliabilists, and trains it on virtue-reliabilism.

In the selections from "Epistemic Normativity," Stephen Grimm argues that "teleological accounts" of epistemic value, which consider true belief to be the ultimate epistemic value, suffer from a potentially serious defect, and then considers whether Sosa's theory of epistemic value provides a way to remedy it. Grimm argues that Sosa's theory fails because it cannot account for the "binding," "non-optional," "reason-giving force" of epistemic evaluation. The main problem with Sosa's account, Grimm contends, is that it allows epistemic value to be only relatively, non-categorically valuable.

In "Knowledge and Final Value," Pritchard asks whether the thesis that knowledge is an intellectual achievement can properly explain knowledge's distinctive value. After arguing that intellectual achievement is neither necessary nor sufficient for knowledge, Pritchard asks what can be salvaged from the virtue-epistemological program. Again we encounter the two "master intuitions" about knowledge discussed above: the ability intuition and the anti-luck intuition. Whereas virtue epistemologists tend to think that properly satisfying the ability intuition will suffice to satisfy the anti-luck intuition, Pritchard argues that this is false. Instead, the anti-luck intuition "imposes a distinct constraint" on a theory of knowledge. Pritchard argues that his own anti-luck virtue epistemology satisfies both master intuitions and explains knowledge's value.

D. Credit and Luck

In "Knowledge as Credit for True Belief," Greco argues that knowledge is true belief for which you deserve credit, and supplements this with a theory of intellectual credit; to wit, you deserve intellectual credit for believing the truth only if your reliable cognitive character is "an important and necessary part" of the causal explanation of your true belief. Recognizing that knowledge ascriptions have an illocutionary force—namely, that of crediting someone for believing the truth—helps resolve the lottery problem and Gettier problems. In lottery cases, the salience of reliable character is trumped by chance. In Gettier cases, the salience of reliable character is trumped by abnormality—that is, by something odd or unexpected in the way that S comes to have a true belief. Greco ends by arguing that this account of knowledge solves the value problem as well.

In "Why Epistemologists Are So Down on Their Luck," Wayne Riggs notes that there is virtual unanimity among epistemologists that knowledge excludes luck, and then asks, why *does* knowledge exclude luck? He argues that the best explanation for this is that knowledge is "credit-worthy true belief," or in other words, "an accomplishment," wherein it is not "inadvertent" that your abilities produce your true belief. This view also solves the value problem, since an accomplishment (in this case, knowledge) is more valuable than lucky success (in this case, mere true belief). Riggs also offers a partial account of luck and credit to complement his theory of knowledge. An event is lucky for you only if it was not the product of your abilities, or you inadvertently caused it to happen. And you deserve credit for an event only if it is not lucky for you that it occurred.

In "Knowledge and Credit," Lackey reviews and responds to objections to her critique of "the credit thesis," which she advanced in an earlier influential paper.[5] The credit thesis says that knowledge requires deserving credit for getting at the truth; this is a popular view among virtue epistemologists. Lackey produced what she took to be a counterexample to the credit thesis. The case involves Morris, who just arrived in Chicago. He asks "the first adult passerby that he sees" for directions to the Sears Tower. The stranger knows the city very well and gives Morris impeccable directions, which Morris accepts as accurately locating the tower. Lackey argues that Morris knows where the tower is, but does not deserve credit for his true belief. Rather, the passerby deserves credit for Morris gaining a true belief. This problem threatens to generalize, because Morris's belief is a fairly typical testimonial belief. Lackey goes on to consider a revised credit thesis, which pertains only to "first-hand" knowledge, rather than second-hand knowledge through testimony. She thinks this revised credit thesis is also false, adducing as evidence the possibility of innate knowledge, as well as a case of reliably produced, virus-induced true belief. In "Knowledge and Credit," Lackey responds to objections from Riggs, Greco, Pritchard, and Sosa. In the end, Lackey believes that the credit thesis faces a fundamental dilemma: *either* it requires too much for a subject to deserve credit, in which case it results in skepticism about testimonial knowledge, *or* it requires too little for a subject to deserve credit, in which case it cannot solve the Gettier problem.

E. Visions for Epistemology

In "Epistemic Injustice and a Role for Virtue in the Politics of Knowing," Fricker offers a fascinating study of the role played by intellectual traits in assessing testimony. Fricker's focus is the "epistemic injustice" suffered by the less powerful and marginalized, which is the result of improperly formed "testimonial sensibility" on the part of hearers. The vice of testimonial injustice is a disposition to improperly assign less credibility to someone's testimony, often based on their social status (e.g., gender, ethnicity, class). The virtue of testimonial justice is a disposition to remain aware of and resist your prejudices from interfering with your estimation of someone's testimony. A properly formed testimonial sensibility displays "reflexive critical openness to the words of others," which is the result of socialization and training, especially emotional training. Here Fricker draws on the work of John McDowell, whose epistemology is in turn modeled explicitly on Aristotle's virtue ethics. Fricker's discussion contains detailed case studies from literature, in particular *To Kill a Mockingbird* and *The Talented Mr. Ripley*. These provide examples of culpable and non-culpable testimonial injustice.

In "Recovering Understanding," Zagzebski draws inspiration from the history of epistemology and conjectures that work on *understanding* will take center stage as epistemologists renounce their post-Cartesian preoccupation with skepticism and its attendant narrow focus on certainty and justification. Understanding is closely tied to mastering a skill, is holistic rather than directed at a single proposition, involves nonpropositional representations, and is a property of persons rather than belief states. Virtue epistemology is uniquely suited to explain understanding, she argues, because its account of understanding will be structurally similar to its account of knowledge. Roughly, we need only exchange a propositional object for a nonpropositional one, and exchange the virtues aimed at truth for those, as of now poorly understood, aimed at understanding. Zagzebski proposes that understanding is cognizing "nonpropositional structures of reality," and that it is "impossible to understand without understanding that one understands."

In the selections from *The Intellectual Virtues and the Life of the Mind*, Kvanvig argues that we ought to abandon the Cartesian perspective in epistemology, according to which "the deepest epistemological questions concern the isolated intellect," focusing narrowly on individual time-slices of individual thinkers and their individual beliefs. Kvanvig advises us to instead take the "genetic" and "social" aspects of cognition seriously, including the history of an individual's intellect, the education she received, the habits she has developed, her role models, and the ways information is organized and communicated in her community. Rather than ask whether some isolated proposition is justified for her, we should ask how she was trained as an inquirer and whether she knows how to properly gather and assess information. The virtues, and the virtuous exemplar, play a central role in this new epistemological vision, underwriting our assessment of individual and collective cognitive activities, intellectual training, and the social organization of information.

Notes

1. Inline references are to chapter numbers in this volume. See also Linda Zagzebski, "Virtue Epistemology," *Routledge Encyclopedia of Philosophy*; Jason Baehr, "Virtue Epistemology," *Internet Encyclopedia of Philosophy*; John Greco and John Turri, "Virtue Epistemology," *Stanford Encyclopedia of Philosophy*; John Turri and Ernest Sosa, "Virtue Epistemology," *Oxford Bibliographies Online*.

2. So called because the value of true belief "swamps" the value of reliably formed belief. See Jonathan Kvanvig, *The Value of Knowledge and the Pursuit of Understanding* (Cambridge University Press, 2003).

3. We note that we have not included selections from Sosa's and Zagzebski's early work in virtue epistemology. This is because lessons from that early work have been thoroughly assimilated in the later literature.

4. As Sosa notes, skeptical arguments often invoke "far off" possibilities of illusion, such as that one is a brain-in-a-vat, or the disembodied victim of a Cartesian demon. Here Sosa considers the more "nearby" possibility that one is simply fooled by a dream in normal sleep.

5. Jennifer Lackey, "Why We Don't Deserve Credit for Everything We Know." *Synthese* 158 (2007), 27–42.

A   Overviews of the Field

1 Virtue Epistemology

Heather Battaly*

Abstract

What are the qualities of an excellent thinker? A growing new field, virtue epistemology, answers this question. Section I distinguishes virtue epistemology from belief-based epistemology. Section II explains the two primary accounts of intellectual virtue: virtue-reliabilism and virtue-responsibilism. Virtue-reliabilists claim that the virtues are stable reliable faculties, like vision. Virtue-responsibilists claim that they are acquired character traits, like open-mindedness. Section III evaluates progress and problems with respect to three key projects: explaining low-grade knowledge, high-grade knowledge, and the individual intellectual virtues.

In 1980, analytic epistemology was abuzz with proposed solutions to the Gettier problem, responses to skepticism, newly minted objections to a variety of internalist and externalist theories of justification, and enthusiastic criticisms of foundationalism and of coherentism. Debates over competing analyses of knowledge and justification raged. Enter Ernest Sosa's "The Raft and the Pyramid," in which the notion of intellectual virtue made its bold contemporary debut. There, Sosa drew the then iconoclastic conclusion that the notion of intellectual virtue could resolve the debate between foundationalists and coherentists. The exploration of intellectual virtue has since become a diverse and increasingly well-established field that has earned its own classification, virtue epistemology, (and its own blog).[1] It has attracted attention largely because it hopes to solve or avoid some of the problems that have shaped the trajectory of traditional analytic epistemology. Whether virtue epistemology succeeds in resolving or avoiding

Reprinted from Heather Battaly, "Virtue Epistemology," *Philosophy Compass* 3 (2008): 639–663.

any of the aforementioned problems is open for debate. But, even if it ultimately fails in this endeavor, it might still provide an illuminating perspective on both traditional and new issues in the field. In section I, I contrast virtue epistemology with belief-based epistemology, identifying two types of virtue epistemology: virtue theory, and virtue anti-theory. Section II explains the two main accounts of intellectual virtue: virtue-reliabilism and virtue-responsibilism. Section III evaluates virtue epistemology's progress and problems with respect to three important projects: explaining low-grade knowledge, high-grade knowledge, and the individual intellectual virtues and vices.

I   What Is Virtue Epistemology?

How does virtue epistemology differ from traditional analytic epistemology? Traditional analytic epistemology has focused on analyzing knowledge and epistemic justification, and has generated a plethora of competing analyses of each of these two concepts. To illustrate, leading rival analyses of justification have claimed that beliefs are justified when they are (for instance): in accordance with one's epistemic obligations (Chisholm), supported by one's evidence (Conee and Feldman), produced by a reliable process (Goldman, *Epistemology and Cognition*), or based on adequate grounds (Alston). Rival analyses of knowledge have claimed (for example) that knowledge is undefeated justified true belief (Lehrer and Paxson); that knowledge requires one's belief to track the truth (Nozick); or that the standards for knowledge shift with changes in context (Cohen). Though they have little else in common, all of the aforementioned views are versions of belief-based epistemology. In *belief-based epistemology*, beliefs are the primary objects of epistemic evaluation, and knowledge and justification, which are evaluations of beliefs, are the fundamental concepts and properties in epistemology. In contrast, in *virtue epistemology*, agents rather than beliefs are the primary objects of epistemic evaluation, and intellectual virtues and vices, which are evaluations of agents, are the fundamental concepts and properties. Specifically, virtue epistemology takes intellectual virtues and vices—types of agent-evaluation—to be more fundamental than justification, knowledge, or any other type of belief-evaluation; whereas belief-based epistemology takes justification and knowledge—types of belief-evaluation—to be more fundamental than the intellectual virtues and vices, or any other type of agent-evaluation. The belief-based epistemologies mentioned above do not make a point of addressing the epistemic evaluation of agents or the intellectual virtues. But if they had, they would have made agent-evaluation subordinate to belief-evaluation by explaining the virtues in terms of knowledge or justification. For instance, a belief-based epistemologist might define an intellectual virtue to be a disposition to attain justified beliefs, and define justified beliefs to be those that accord with one's epistemic obligations. In sum, virtue epistemology differs from traditional analytic epistemology because the former takes intellectual virtues to be more fundamental than knowledge and justified belief, and the latter does the reverse (Battaly, "Teaching Intellectual Virtue").[2]

There are two different ways in which virtue epistemologists take the intellectual virtues to be more fundamental than knowledge and justified belief. (1) Some construct *theories* which define or otherwise ground knowledge and justified belief in terms of the intellectual virtues. (2) Others, *anti-theorists*, shun formulaic connections between the virtues and knowledge, but argue that the intellectual virtues are the central concepts and properties in epistemology and warrant exploration in their own right.

I.A   Virtue Theories

Virtue *theories* in epistemology are analogous in structure to virtue theories in ethics. Ethical theories systematically explain the connections between right and wrong acts, good and bad states of affairs, and the moral virtues and vices. *Virtue theories* in ethics define or explain act evaluations in terms of the moral virtues and vices, rather than the other way around. For example, in *On Virtue Ethics*, Rosalind Hursthouse explains right action in terms of the moral virtues as follows: "An action is right iff it is what a virtuous agent would characteristically . . . do in the circumstances" (Hursthouse 28). Analogously, epistemological theories systematically explain the connections between knowledge and justified and unjustified beliefs, epistemically good and bad states of affairs, and the intellectual virtues and vices. *Virtue theories* in epistemology define or explain belief evaluations in terms of the intellectual virtues and vices, rather than the other way around. As Sosa suggests in "The Raft and the Pyramid," in an "epistemology of intellectual virtues," "primary" epistemic evaluation attaches to the intellectual virtues themselves, and "secondary" evaluation attaches to "particular beliefs" because of "their source in intellectual virtues" (189). Ernest Sosa and Linda Zagzebski are the two most prominent virtue theorists in epistemology. In *Ernest Sosa and His Critics*, *A Virtue Epistemology*, and several papers in *Knowledge in Perspective*, Sosa argues that knowledge requires true belief that is produced by an intellectual virtue.[3] In her ground-breaking 1996 book, *Virtues of the Mind*, Linda Zagzebski contends that both knowledge and justified belief are grounded in the intellectual virtues. In her words, a justified belief is 'what a person who is motivated by intellectual virtue, and who has the understanding of his cognitive situation a virtuous person would have, might believe in like circumstances' (241). Knowledge is belief that results from acts of intellectual virtue (271).

What is the appeal of epistemic virtue theories? First, advocates of virtue theory have argued that it can resolve some of the key debates in traditional analytic epistemology. With this end in mind, both Sosa and Zagzebski have proposed solutions to the Gettier problem, and provided accounts of low-grade perceptual knowledge. Second, Zagzebski has argued that her virtue theory can also address an important type of knowledge that has been neglected by traditional analytic epistemology. Thus, she intends her analysis of knowledge to apply both to low-grade perceptual knowledge *and* high-grade knowledge, the latter of which requires active inquiry on the part of the agent, and arguably includes scientific and moral knowledge. In short, virtue theory is attractive because it simultaneously pursues knowledge on multiple fronts. *If* virtue theory were to succeed in grounding these two different sorts of knowledge in one or another sort of intellectual virtue, then it will have supplied a (more-or-less) unified theory of knowledge.

Does virtue theory succeed in any of these endeavors? In section III, I argue that Zagzebski's view of low-grade perceptual knowledge and her reply to the Gettier problem do not succeed. But, the branch of virtue theory that is grounded in Sosa's work fares better on this front: it offers a valuable (albeit contestable) account of low-grade perceptual knowledge—the credit theory—and a potentially promising (albeit contestable) reply to the Gettier problem.[4] The branch of virtue theory that is grounded in Zagzebski's work clearly fares better than the credit theory on the second front: Zagzebski provides an illuminating and much-needed (though, again, contestable) account of high-grade knowledge. In sum, the strengths and weaknesses of each branch of virtue theory complement those of the other. Together, the two branches of virtue theory, with their respective strengths on different fronts, are taking positive steps toward a (more-or-less) unified theory of knowledge.

I.B Virtue Anti-theories

One need not construct a systematic theory to be a virtue epistemologist. One can take the intellectual virtues to be the central concepts and properties in epistemology but deny that knowledge and justified belief can be systematically defined in terms of the virtues. This approach is analogous to *anti-theory* in ethics, which focuses on the moral virtues but denies that there are necessary and sufficient connections between the moral virtues and right action (Clarke and Simpson). For anti-theorists in virtue epistemology, exploring the intellectual virtues is the most important epistemological project, even though it won't yield systematic connections to knowledge or justification. To illustrate, in *Epistemic Responsibility*, Lorraine Code argues that epistemology is centered on the intellectual virtue of epistemic responsibility, but explicitly denies that there is any "easy calculus" or systematic theory that could define knowledge in terms of the virtues. In her words, "theor[ies] of intellectual virtue" cannot "provide a decision-making scale against which specific knowledge claims can be measured for validity" (63).

There are two main types of virtue anti-theory: virtue-eliminativism and virtue-expansionism. Virtue-eliminativism and virtue-expansionism have two key features in common. First, they are virtue epistemologies (as opposed to belief-based epistemologies): they focus on the virtues. Second, they deny that knowledge and justified belief can be systematically defined in terms of the virtues. This makes them anti-theories. The primary difference between virtue-eliminativism and virtue-expansionism is that the former argues that epistemological projects other than explorations of the virtues should be eliminated: we should abandon discussions of knowledge and justification, and replace them with analyses of the virtues. In contrast, the latter, virtue-expansionism, argues that there is room in epistemology both for analyses of the intellectual virtues and for analyses of knowledge, even though there won't be systematic connections between these projects. Expansionists are pluralists who argue that there are multiple projects in epistemology that warrant exploration, the most important of which is analyzing the virtues. But, on their view, a focus on the virtues does not warrant abandoning other worthwhile projects, like analyses of knowledge and justification. In other words, expansionists intend to widen the parameters of what counts as epistemology so that there is space for focusing on the virtues; whereas eliminativists intend to narrow those parameters, thus forcing a shift to the virtues. Jonathan Kvanvig argues for virtue-eliminativism in *The Intellectual Virtues and the Life of the Mind*. Kvanvig contends that knowledge and justified belief cannot be reduced to the intellectual virtues; nor can the virtues be reduced to knowledge or justified belief. Instead, the virtues compose an independent part of "the cognitive ideal" (150, 157, 169). There, he maintains that traditional "S knows that p" epistemology is unsuited for exploring the virtues, and even suggests that it should be eliminated and replaced by a virtue-centered approach.

Virtue-expansionism is currently a growth-industry in virtue epistemology. Arguably, Christopher Hookway, Miranda Fricker, and Robert C. Roberts and Jay Wood are all virtue-expansionists. Christopher Hookway argues that the goals of traditional analytic epistemology—explaining justification and knowledge—are too narrow and should be expanded to include the explanation of all types of epistemic evaluation. He contends that since the project of explaining the intellectual virtues falls under this broader goal, one can legitimately focus on that project without being compelled to tie one's analyses of the virtues to knowledge or justification. In *Epistemic Injustice*, Miranda Fricker maintains that traditional epistemology is not "conducive to revealing the ethical and political aspects of our epistemic conduct" (2). She sets out to expand epistemology so as to make room for such projects (not to jettison projects to which traditional epistemology is already conducive). Accordingly, she focuses on analyzing the vice of testimonial injustice, the virtue of testimonial justice, and their ethical and epistemological ramifications. Testimonial justice is (roughly) a disposition to neutralize one's prejudicial perception of speakers (92). Fricker argues that there are connections between this virtue and testimonial knowledge, but she seems to think that these connections are not the necessary and sufficient conditions found in virtue theories. For instance, she contends that knowledge sometimes fails to be transmitted from speaker to hearer because hearers lack testimonial justice; as when the jurors in *To Kill a Mockingbird* fail to neutralize their prejudicial perceptions of Tom Robinson, or Herbert Greenleaf in *The Talented Mr. Ripley* fails to neutralize his prejudicial perception of Marge. But, Fricker appears to stop short of systematically requiring testimonial justice for testimonial knowledge.[5] The goal of Robert Roberts's and Jay Wood's *Intellectual Virtues* is to offer epistemic guidance. Roberts and Wood explicitly deny that they are constructing formulaic theories of knowledge or virtue. They intend to offer a "broader and richer conception of . . . epistemic goods than has characterized recent epistemology" (30). With that end in mind, they provide extended analyses of seven intellectual virtues, and argue that some high-grade knowledge in the actual world requires virtue possession. The latter is not a conceptual claim, but a contingent one (see section III.B). Hookway, Fricker, and Roberts and Wood are all virtue epistemologists: they think that analyzing the intellectual virtues is the most important, or at least the most pressing, epistemological project. They are all virtue anti-theorists: each appears to think that knowledge cannot be systematically defined in terms of the virtues. Lastly, they are all virtue-expansionists: each seems to recognize a plurality of worthwhile projects in epistemology.

Virtue anti-theorists view epistemology as an evaluative discipline that need not be constrained by formulaic accounts of knowledge and justification. What is the appeal of virtue anti-theory? It is safe to say that its appeal is not primarily due to virtue-eliminativism. After all, virtue-eliminativism would have to show that the project of analyzing propositional knowledge is bankrupt. This just doesn't seem to be in the offing, for we appear to have low-grade perceptual knowledge; and even if we ultimately lack such knowledge, it would be worthwhile to find out why we lack it. But, virtue-expansionism is another story. It is appealing because it stands to open up the field to new projects. It carves out space to analyze individual intellectual virtues and vices, to provide advice about how to acquire the virtues, and to draw connections between epistemology and ethics. In section III, I evaluate Roberts and Wood's claim that some real-world knowledge requires the virtues. I also assess progress and problems with respect to anti-theorists' analyses of individual intellectual virtues and vices.

II What Are the Intellectual Virtues?

Virtue epistemologists all agree that the intellectual virtues are cognitive excellences, but disagree about what sort of cognitive excellences they are. One group—the *virtue-reliabilists*—led by Ernest Sosa and John Greco, has argued that the intellectual virtues are reliable faculties, the paradigms of which include sense perception, induction, deduction, and memory. Virtue-reliabilists adopt a concept of virtue according to which "anything with a function—natural or artificial—does have virtues" (Sosa, *Knowledge in Perspective* 271). Thus, virtues are the qualities of a thing that enable it to perform its function well. Knives and computers have virtues, and so do we. Since our primary intellectual function is attaining truths, the intellectual virtues are (roughly) whatever faculties enable us to do that, be they natural or acquired. In contrast, another group—the *virtue-responsibilists*—led by Linda Zagzebski and James Montmarquet conceives of the intellectual virtues as states of character, as "deep qualities of a person, closely identified with her selfhood," not as natural faculties, which are "the raw materials for the self" (Zagzebski 104). Both Montmarquet and Zagzebski explicitly reject Sosa's claim that reliable vision, memory, and the like count as intellectual virtues (Montmarquet 20, 35n4; Zagzebski 8–9, 104).[6] Virtue-responsibilists model their analyses of intellectual virtue on Aristotle's analysis of the moral virtues; i.e., they conceive of the intellectual

virtues as acquired character traits, for which we are to some degree responsible. Their paradigms of intellectual virtue include open-mindedness, intellectual courage, and intellectual autonomy.[7]

There are five primary questions that analyses of the intellectual virtues
should address. First, are the virtues natural or acquired? Second, does
virtue possession require the agent to possess acquired intellectually
virtuous motivations or dispositions to perform intellectually virtuous
actions? Third, are the virtues distinct from skills?[8] Fourth, are the virtues
reliable? Finally, fifth, what makes the virtues valuable? Are they instrumentally, constitutively, or intrinsically valuable? By way of preview,
virtue-reliabilists argue that the intellectual virtues are reliable faculties
that can be natural or acquired. Accordingly, virtue possession does not
require the agent to possess acquired intellectual motivations or dispositions to perform intellectual actions. The virtues that are acquired (rather
than natural) are like skills. Because all of the virtues are reliable, they are
(at the very least) instrumentally valuable as a means to truth. In contrast,
virtue-responsibilists argue that the intellectual virtues are character traits
that require acquired intellectual motivations and dispositions to perform
intellectually virtuous actions. Responsibilists differ over whether the virtues require reliability; and consequently differ over what makes them
valuable (if the virtues are not reliable, they must be valuable for some
other reason). Responsibilists often argue that the virtues are distinct from
skills.

II.A Virtue-Reliabilism

What are the qualities of an excellent thinker? Virtue-reliabilism begins
with the intuition that excellent thinking consists in reliably getting the
truth. Roughly, virtuous thinkers are reliable truth-producers; i.e., their faculties of sense perception, memory, induction, and deduction reliably produce true beliefs. The progenitor of virtue-reliabilism is process-reliabilism.
Process-reliabilism argues that a belief is justified if an only if it is produced
by a reliable belief-forming process. There are three main problems for
process-reliabilism: (1) the generality problem; (2) clairvoyancy cases,
which claim that reliability is not sufficient for justification; and (3) evil
demon cases, which claim that it is not necessary. In two papers in *Knowledge and Perspective*, Sosa develops his account of intellectual virtue with
the express purpose of solving these problems.[9] Sosa argues that the intellectual virtues are stable reliable faculties or competences. He takes vision,
hearing, memory, introspection, induction, and deduction to be the paradigmatic virtues.

There are five key features of Sosa's account, each of which answers one of the five questions above. First and foremost, the virtues are reliable. That is, they are dispositions to attain more true beliefs than false ones. Sosa points out that the reliability of a cognitive disposition does not require that it attain truths in highly unusual condition just as the reliability of one's car does not require that it start when submerged underwater (Sosa, *Knowledge in Perspective* 275; *Virtue Epistemology* 83–4). For instance, the reliability of the faculty of vision is not impugned by its failure to issue true beliefs about objects that are in the dark. Nor is it impugned by its failure to issue true beliefs about an object's very complex shape (e.g., chiliagon) or specific color (e.g., chartreuse). Rather, its reliability is indexed to conditions (C) in which one sees objects in good light, and to fields of propositions (F) that are about the object's basic shape, color, and so on. Accordingly, Sosa defines the virtue of vision as (roughly) a disposition to attain a preponderance of true beliefs about the basic colors and shapes of medium-sized objects (F), when one sees those objects nearby, without obstruction, and in good light (C) (*Knowledge in Perspective* 139).

Second, according to Sosa, the intellectual virtues can be natural or derived (*Knowledge in Perspective* 278). "Much of our intellectual competence comes with our brains, but much is due to learning" (*Virtue Epistemology* 86). Vision is a natural virtue; interpreting MRI films would be a derived virtue. The skills one acquires in critical thinking and logic courses would also be derived virtues. In short, the virtues can be, but need not be, acquired. Consequently, the third key feature is that the virtues do not require acquired intellectual motivations. Virtue-responsibilists have argued that the motivation to care appropriately about the truth is acquired. To acquire it, one must acquire a sufficient degree of desire for the truth, and learn which truths are appropriate objects of that desire (see section II.B). Sosa's natural virtues of vision, memory, induction, and deduction do not require any such motivation. After all, children possess the virtues of vision, memory, and the like, but do not yet possess any learned motivation to care appropriately about the truth. Nor, on Sosa's view, do the virtues require dispositions to perform intellectual actions. Intellectual actions are, roughly, acts that an agent intentionally performs in acquiring beliefs; e.g., generating hypotheses, searching for evidence, considering objections, giving reasons for a claim. The natural virtues of vision, and so on, do not require intentional acts on the part of the agent. Since vision, memory, and the like, will reliably produce true beliefs as long as they are functioning well (in an appropriate, non-demon environment), there is no need for the agent to perform intentional acts. She can get the truth without intentionally doing anything.

Sosa's early work in the field emphasized the natural virtues. But, the fourth key feature of his recent work is his emphasis on the analogy between virtues and skills. Sosa now regularly uses the terms 'virtue,' 'skill,' and 'competence' interchangeably, and often compares the intellectual virtues to the acquired skills of being a good archer and a good tennis player.[10] This shift in emphasis may well be fueled by a need to respond to the value problem (see section III). But, it is important to note that, whatever his current emphasis, Sosa still clearly intends the terms 'virtue' and 'competence' to apply to both natural faculties and acquired skills, intellectual or otherwise. In *A Virtue Epistemology*, he defines a competence as: "a disposition . . . with a basis resident in the competent agent . . . that would in appropriately normal conditions ensure (or make highly likely) the success of any relevant performance issued by it" (29). This definition is designed to include both performances that are intentional (e.g., shooting an arrow at a target) and competences that are acquired skills (e.g., being a good archer), and performances that are unintentional (e.g. forming a perceptual belief that a truck is coming toward you) and competences that are natural (e.g., good vision). It is also designed to range over different sorts of competences: intellectual, athletic, etc.

Fifth, in *Knowledge and Perspective*, Sosa argues that the virtues are instrumentally valuable (225). The virtues are valuable because they are reliable means to attaining truth, and truth is intrinsically (fundamentally) valuable. He has since argued that the virtues are not just instrumentally valuable, but also constitutively valuable.[11]

Like Sosa, John Greco argues that the intellectual virtues are stable reliable faculties that can be natural or acquired ("Virtues in Epistemology"; *Putting Skeptics in Their Place* 164–203). Sosa and Greco advocate different analyses of "internal justification"; i.e., a belief's being justified from the subject's own point of view. Their different treatments of internal justification lead to the only ostensible difference in their accounts of intellectual virtue: a weak motivation condition. Sosa argues that internal justification requires the subject to possess an epistemic perspective: the subject must believe that her lower-level belief is produced by an intellectual virtue. Greco contends that this requirement is too strong, and instead argues that the subject's beliefs need only be "produced by cognitive dispositions that the [subject] manifests when motivated to believe what is true" ("How to Preserve Your Virtue" 103). This prompts Greco to allow a weak motivation condition in his account of virtue. For Greco, an intellectual virtue is a well-motivated stable reliable faculty. The motivation in question is a motive to attain truths and avoid falsehoods. But, it is not a motivation that takes time and effort to acquire. Rather, it is our normal default position of trying to believe what is true. Greco emphasizes that "there is no strong motivation condition, no control condition" ("Virtues in Epistemology" 304). This clearly distinguishes his view from virtue-responsibilism.

II.B Virtue-Responsibilism

Virtue-responsibilism begins with the intuition that what makes an agent an excellent thinker are active features of her agency: actions, motivations, and habits over which she has some control and for which she is (to some degree) responsible. Unlike virtue-reliabilists, responsibilists think that only sentient beings can have virtues. They argue that the intellectual virtues, like the moral virtues, are acquired traits of character—acquired habits of intellectual action and intellectual motivation.

How does Montmarquet answer the five key questions above? First, he conceives of the intellectual virtues as acquired character traits. Second (and relatedly), he argues that the intellectual virtues require an acquired intellectual motivation. According to Montmarquet, the primary intellectual virtue, conscientiousness, is constituted by the motivation to attain truth and avoid falsehood. A person is conscientious when she is "*trying . . . to arrive at the truth and to avoid error*" (21). Unlike Aristotle, Montmarquet does not believe that "all men desire to know by nature" (Aristotle, *Metaphysics* 980a20). We can, and often do, lack the motivation for truth. Moreover, we can possess it and still fail to be intellectually virtuous overall. For instance, an agent might fervently seek the truth, but also emphatically believe that she has already attained it. This agent is conscientious but dogmatic. Montmarquet argues that to be virtuous overall, we must not only be conscientiousness, but possess three additional kinds of regulating virtues—the virtues of impartiality, sobriety, and intellectual courage—which regulate the desire for truth, and prevent it from producing dogmatism, enthusiasm, and cowardice. On Montmarquet's view, the motivation for truth can be felt too weakly or too strongly, and can be directed at inappropriate objects. To be intellectually virtuous overall, one must learn how to hit the mean with respect to one's motivation for truth; and to do that, one must acquire the regulating virtues.

The regulating virtues are acquired habits of appropriate action and motivation. To illustrate, Montmarquet thinks that the virtue of open-mindedness involves the tendency to overcome our initial inclination to dismiss unfamiliar ideas. To overcome this inclination, we must perform intellectual actions; specifically, we must seek out and consider alternative ideas. According to Montmarquet, to be open-minded, we must also be motivated to attain truth and, consequently, motivated to consider alternatives. He argues that open-mindedness, and the other regulative virtues, are widely thought to be reliable. Hence, those who desire truth will also want to entertain unfamiliar ideas. Thus, open-mindedness is an acquired habit of both motivation and action: the motivation to entertain alternatives, and the disposition to act in accordance with that motivation.

Third, though Montmarquet does not explicitly contend that the intellectual virtues are distinct from skills, his account is entirely consistent with this claim. He does explicitly argue that the intellectual virtues are entrenched habits (27). Since (arguably) habits are not skills, he could have gone on to claim that the virtues are not skills. Habits are not skills because though one can deliberately forego opportunities to perform skilled acts without thereby forfeiting one's skill, the same cannot be said of habits or of virtues. As Peter Goldie puts the point: "there is no 'holiday' from virtue as there is from skill" (351).

Fourth, Montmarquet argues that the intellectual virtues need not be reliable. Montmarquet claims that the virtues are thought to be reliable, and may even be reliable in the actual world. But, he explicitly denies what virtue-reliabilists assert: he thinks that the virtues do not require reliability. He argues as follows. Suppose that unbeknownst to us, a demon has manipulated our world so that true beliefs are, and have always been, best attained by the traits we call vices (e.g., dogmatism) rather than by the traits we call virtues (e.g., open-mindedness). He thinks that in this demon world, traits like open-mindedness will still be virtues even though they are unreliable because "the epistemic virtues are qualities that a truth-desiring person . . . would want to have" (30). In the demon world, truth-desiring people will still believe that open-mindedness and the other virtues are reliable, and will still want to acquire them. Fifth, for Montmarquet, what makes a trait a virtue is not its reliability, but its desirability to those who want truth. The virtues are valuable not because they are instruments for attaining truths, but because the motivation for truth is intrinsically valuable.

Zagzebski agrees that the intellectual virtues are acquired habits of action and motivation. But, unlike Montmarquet, she argues that the intellectual virtues require reliability. On her view, the intellectual virtues are enduring, acquired traits that require both an appropriate epistemic motivation, and reliable success in attaining the end of that motivation (137). Her list of intellectual virtues includes: open-mindedness, intellectual courage, intellectual autonomy, intellectual humility, and thoroughness.

First, she argues that agents merit praise for possessing the intellectual virtues. The virtues are qualities that are difficult to acquire. One might easily fail to attain them. Hence, agents who do attain the virtues warrant praise, and agents who do not (but could have) warrant blame. Since agents neither warrant praise for possessing natural faculties nor censure for failing to possess them, natural faculties are not virtues. Second, Zagzebski claims that skills are not virtues. She argues that virtues and skills are both acquired and both reliably achieve their ends. But, unlike virtues, skills need not be virtuously motivated.

Third, Zagzebski thinks that the intellectual virtues are acquired habits (dispositions) of appropriate motivation and appropriate action. On her view, the motivational component of each virtue is two-fold. Each virtue involves an underlying motivation for "cognitive contact with reality"; i.e., for truth, knowledge, or understanding (167). She focuses on the motivation for truth. This underlying motivation for truth generates the motivations that are distinctive of the individual intellectual virtues. So, like Montmarquet, she thinks that agents who are motivated to attain truths will be motivated to entertain alternative ideas (the motive distinctive of open-mindedness), to persevere when faced with opposition (the motive distinctive of intellectual courage), and so on. She, too, believes that we often lack sufficient motivation for the truth, and must acquire it via effort and training. Moreover, she contends that to be virtuous one must not only be appropriately motivated, one must also reliably succeed in attaining both ends of one's two-fold motivation. To illustrate, to be open-minded, one must be motivated to attain truth and motivated to entertain alternatives, and one must also be reliably successful at entertaining alternatives and reliably successful at attaining truth. Let's look at the first end: success at entertaining alternatives. In Zagzebski's words, to be open-minded, one must "actually be receptive to new ideas, examining them in an even-handed way" (177). That is, one must perform intellectual actions—e.g., entertaining alternatives—which hit the mean. Zagzebski thinks that open-mindedness, like many of the intellectual virtues, lies in a mean between a vice of excess and a vice of defect. The dogmatic person ignores alternatives she should consider; whereas the person we might label 'naïve' considers alternatives she should ignore. The open-minded person hits the mean in her intellectual actions—considering and ignoring alternatives appropriately. To illustrate, suppose that Jane is an open-minded police detective who is investigating the homicide of a prostitute in London. In forming a belief about the identity of the murderer, she considers various alternatives, each of which has a high probability of being true (e.g., one of the victim's clients, or her employer, did it). She does not ignore alternatives that are likely to be true, or consider alternatives that are highly likely to be false (e.g., the President of the United States did it) (Battaly, "Intellectual Virtue" 159).

Fourth, Zagzebski argues that the virtues require reliability. To be virtuous, one must be reliably successful in attaining both ends of the twofold motivation. One of those ends is truth. Accordingly, one cannot be intellectually virtuous unless one reliably attains truths. In sum, to be open-minded, one must be (1) motivated to attain truths and thus (2) motivated to entertain alternatives; (3) reliably successful at entertaining alternatives; and as a result (4) reliably successful at attaining truths. (Montmarquet endorses conditions (1) to (3), but not (4).) Zagzebski explicitly rejects Montmarquet's arguments for the claim that the virtues do not require reliability (184–94). In reply to his demon world argument, she claims:

> if it turned out that we were wrong about the truth-conduciveness of [open-mindedness], that trait would cease to be considered an intellectual virtue. What we would not do is . . . continue to treat it as an intellectual virtue and then go on to declare that intellectual virtues are not necessarily truth-conducive. (185)

According to Zagzebski, in these circumstances we would cease to consider open-mindedness a virtue because the value of the virtues derives partly from their truth-conducivity.

Lastly, she implies that the virtues may well be instrumentally, constitutively, and intrinsically valuable. They are instrumentally valuable insofar as they reliably produce true beliefs, or other goods. They are constitutively valuable insofar as they are constituents of *eudaimonia*—living well. And, they are intrinsically valuable insofar as the motivation for truth is intrinsically valuable.

So, who is correct—reliabilists or responsibilists? Which account of intellectual virtue is the 'real' account? I submit that there is no single 'real' account of intellectual virtue, and arguments to that effect will be unproductive. Both accounts are good; neither is more 'real' or 'correct' than the other. This is because the concept of intellectual virtue is vague. Though the concept entails that intellectual virtues are in some sense cognitively valuable, there is no definite answer as to which additional conditions are necessary or sufficient for its application. In other words, there is more than one good way to fill out the concept. Provided that both of the aforementioned ways of filling it out are equally legitimate, it would be mis-guided to argue over which of them is 'correct' (Battaly, "Thin Concepts to the Rescue").

Instead, we can acknowledge that both virtue-reliabilists and virtue-responsibilists succeed in identifying virtues. After all, one way to be an excellent thinker is to reliably get the truth: to have reliable faculties of vision, induction, deduction, and the like. Virtue-reliabilism explains the widespread intuition that good vision and memory and skills in critical thinking are cognitive excellences. Another way to be an excellent thinker is to possess virtuous motivations and perform virtuous actions: to have the character traits of open-mindedness, intellectual courage, and consci-entiousness. Virtue-responsibilism explains the widespread intuition that when it comes to active inquiry, we admire people who act appropriately and care about getting the truth. These are different sorts of intellectual virtues, with ties to different sorts of knowledge. In section III, I argue that virtue-reliabilism is better-suited for explaining low-grade knowledge, while virtue-responsibilism is better-suited for explaining high-grade knowledge. Treating the above accounts as complementary, rather than competitive, benefits both virtue-reliabilists and virtue-responsibilists.

III Progress and Problems

Here, I evaluate virtue epistemology's progress and problems with respect to three important projects: analyzing low-grade knowledge, high-grade knowledge, and the intellectual virtues and vices themselves. Low-grade knowledge, the paradigm of which is perceptual knowledge, is acquired passively. Arguably, one can't help but acquire visual knowledge when one's eyes are open, one's brain is functioning well, and one is in a well-lighted and otherwise appropriate environment. No intentional action on the part of the subject is required. Adult human beings share low-grade knowledge with children and, perhaps, other animals. In contrast, high-grade knowledge is acquired actively, rather than passively, as a result of intentional inquiry.[12] The paradigms of high-grade knowledge include sci-entific knowledge (e.g., that $E = mc^2$, that anthrax can be killed by cipro-floxacin), philosophical knowledge (e.g., that behaviorist theories of mind are false), evaluative and moral knowledge (e.g., that Candidate C will be the best President; that lying is wrong except in extreme circumstances), and, what we might call, 'investigative applied' knowledge (e.g., that the patient is infected with bacteria B; that suspect S committed the crime). One won't acquire high-grade knowledge simply by opening one's eyes in an appropriate environment; one must conduct an inquiry: roughly, generate an hypothesis, test it, search for confirming and disconfirming evidence, consider alternatives and objections, and so on.[13] Traditional analytic epistemology has focused on the valuable goal of analyzing low-grade knowledge. But, analyzing high-grade knowledge is also valuable, since much of our knowledge appears to be high-grade.

First, I contend that Zagzebski's virtue theory is too strong for low-grade knowledge, and fails to solve the Gettier problem. The credit theory of virtue-reliabilists, though not without its own problems, fares better on these fronts. Second, I argue that the credit theory is too weak for high-grade knowledge. Zagzebski's virtue theory, and anti-theories (though not without their own problems) fare better on this front. Finally, if anti-theorists are correct, the intellectual virtues and vices warrant exploration even if they cannot be systematically connected to knowledge. Hence, I conclude by examining progress and problems in anti-theorists' analyses of individual intellectual virtues and vices.

III.A Low-grade Knowledge and the Gettier Problem

Zagzebski argues that both low- and high-grade knowledge consist in beliefs that result from acts of intellectual virtue. In her words, "Knowledge is a state of belief arising out of acts of intellectual virtue" (271). An act of intellectual virtue is

an act that arises from the motivational component of [the virtue], is something a person with [the] virtue would . . . do in the circumstances, is successful in achieving the end of the . . . motivation, and is such that the agent acquires a true belief . . . through these features of the act. (270)

According to Zagzebski, knowledge does not require full-blown virtue possession. One can perform an act of, say, open-mindedness even though one lacks a settled disposition to consider alternative ideas. In short, the difference between an act of intellectual virtue and full virtue possession is the absence or presence of an entrenched habit or disposition to perform virtuous acts.

One major problem is that Zagzebski's analysis of low-grade knowledge is far too strong. Recall that for Zagzebski, to know, one must perform an act of intellectual virtue, and to do that latter, one must both act as the virtuous person would, and possess the motivational component of the virtue in question. But, according to Zagzebski, the motivational components of the virtues are acquired, and intellectual acts are voluntary. She argues that like morally virtuous motivations, intellectually virtuous motivations are acquired (in part) via practice and the imitation of exemplars. And, like morally virtuous acts, intellectually virtuous acts are voluntary. But, low-grade knowledge—e.g., the visual knowledge that a truck is bearing down on you—does not require an acquired motivation for truth or a voluntary intellectual act (virtuous or otherwise). If there is a truck bearing down on you, and your eyes are open and your visual faculties are functioning well, then you can't help but believe that a truck is bearing down on you. Greco and Baehr both agree with this objection. Greco argues that "you know there is a truck moving toward you independent of any control" ("Virtues in Epistemology" 296). Moreover, one need not be motivated to be "open-minded, careful, or the like. On the contrary, it would seem that you know that there is a truck coming toward you even if you are motivated *not* to be open-minded" (296, original emphasis). Likewise, Baehr contends that in cases of passive knowledge, "having certain motives or performing certain acts . . . are conspicuously absent" ("Character in Epistemology" 495). Thus, when the electricity in one's office suddenly shuts down, one "*automatically* or *spontaneously* form[s] a belief to the effect that the lighting in the room has changed" (494, original emphasis). Hence, Zagzebski's conditions are not necessary for low-grade knowledge.

Are her conditions sufficient for low-grade knowledge; specifically, has she solved the Gettier problem? Gettier argued that true justified belief is not sufficient for knowledge because justified beliefs can be true by accident. To illustrate, suppose that S has excellent evidence for her belief that Nogot owns a Ford (Nogot tells her he owns a Ford, and she sees him driving one). S then infers that someone in Nogot's office owns a Ford. It turns out that Nogot does not own a Ford (he was participating in an elaborate ruse), but someone else in Nogot's office—Havit—does own a Ford. S's belief that someone in Nogot's office owns a Ford is justified and ends up being true, but it is true by accident, and hence not knowledge. Zagzebski argues that Gettier problems arise for any theory of knowledge which claims that "knowledge is true belief plus something else that does not entail truth" (283). In her words: "since justification does not guarantee truth, it is possible for there to be a break in the connection between justification and truth but for that connection to be regained by chance" (284). Accordingly, she intends to immunize her analysis of knowledge against the Gettier problem by defining an act of intellectual virtue so that it *does* entail true belief. Recall that an act of intellectual virtue is such that "the agent acquires a true belief . . . through the [virtuous] features of the act" (270). In other words, if one arrives at a true belief because of luck, not because of one's virtuous motives and actions, then one has not performed an act of intellectual virtue, and hence, one's true belief is not knowledge. So, in reply to cases like Nogot, Zagzebski argues that S obtains a true belief that someone in Nogot's office owns a Ford by accident, not because of her virtuous motives or actions. Hence, S's belief that someone in Nogot's office owns a Ford does not arise from an act of intellectual virtue, and is not knowledge.[14]

The primary objection to Zagzebski's reply to the Gettier problem is that we can still construct Gettier-style counterexamples to her account of knowledge. Arguably, there will still be situations in which an agent performs an act of intellectual virtue but, because of luck, lacks knowledge. To adapt an excellent example from Jason Baehr, suppose that Brenda is a police detective in Los Angeles, who is investigating the homicide of an accountant who worked for a multi-billion dollar corporation.[15] Brenda cares about getting the truth, and consequently is motivated to consider alternative ideas about who committed the homicide and to take care in searching for and evaluating evidence. In short, she is virtuously motivated. Further, for the sake of simplicity, suppose that there are only two suspects: the CEO of the corporation, and the accountant's husband. The hard evidence reveals that the accountant's husband openly despised his wife. It also reveals that the accountant repeatedly concealed the corporation's income, that the federal government was conducting an investigation of the corporation's accounting practices, and that the fingerprints of the corporation's CEO were on the murder weapon. Suppose that the majority of the hard evidence points toward the CEO, and that Brenda is thus inclined to believe that the CEO committed the homicide. But, because she wants to get the truth and cares about considering alternative scenarios, she asks her team of detectives for their opinions. In seeking out their opinions, she does what the virtuous person would do. Unbeknownst to Brenda and her team, the corporation has brain-washed her team into believing that the accountant's husband committed the crime. So, when she consults them, they confidently claim that the husband did it, and contend that she has misinterpreted the hard evidence. After weighing her options, Brenda "out of an earnest openness to [her] colleagues' views and a keen awareness of [her] own fallibility" comes to believe that the accountant's husband committed the homicide (Baehr, "Character in Epistemology" 488). Brenda is correct; the husband did it. But, even though all of Zagzebski's conditions for knowledge are met—Brenda was virtuously motivated, did what the virtuous person would do, and attained a true belief because of these features of her act (if she hadn't performed an open-minded act then she wouldn't have arrived at a true belief)—Brenda does not seem to know that the husband did it.

The credit theory, an off-shoot of virtue-reliabilism, claims that an agent has knowledge if and only if she arrives at a true belief because her belief is produced by her intellectual virtues; i.e., stable reliable faculties like vision and memory.[16] Since she obtains a true belief because of her virtues, not because of luck, she deserves credit for believing the truth. On Greco's view, S has knowledge regarding p (e.g., the wall is white) if and only if: S believes the truth regarding p because her belief that p issues from an intellectual virtue (e.g., vision). If S obtains a correct belief because of her own virtues, she merits credit; if she obtains a correct belief as a result of luck, she does not. In Greco's words,

> to say that S's believing the truth is to her credit is to say that S's cognitive abilities, her intellectual virtues, are an important part of the causal story regarding how S came to believe the truth. It is to say that [they] are a particularly salient part, perhaps the most salient part, of the total set of relevant causal factors. ("Virtues in Epistemology" 310)

Similarly, according to Sosa, an agent has animal knowledge if and only if her belief is apt.[17] Subject S's belief is apt if it is: true, produced by an intellectual virtue, and S obtains the truth because her belief is produced by an intellectual virtue. In other words, in the case of apt belief, believing correctly is "attributable to a competence" of the subject; she does not arrive at a true belief by accident (Sosa, *Virtue Epistemology* 92).

Sosa's and Greco's accounts of low-grade knowledge have at least one clear advantage over Zagzebski's. The virtues that *they* require need not involve acquired intellectual motivations or voluntary intellectual actions. On their accounts, S knows that a truck is bearing down on her because her natural virtue of vision produces this true belief. S need not perform any action, or possess an acquired motive for truth. Granted, Sosa's and Greco's accounts of low-grade knowledge are still subject to the standard internalist objections.

Sosa and Greco use the credit theory to propose solutions to the Gettier problem and the value problem. In reply to cases like Nogot above, they argue that S does not arrive at a true belief because of her virtues—her virtues are not the most salient cause of her coming to have a true belief that someone in Nogot's office owns a Ford. Rather, luck is the most salient cause. S arrives at a true belief because, unbeknownst to her, someone else in the office—Havit—just happens to own a Ford. One objection to Sosa's and Greco's reply to the Gettier problem is that it may not be a clear advance on Goldman's causal reply (Goldman, "Causal Theory of Knowing"). In short, one might wonder whether Sosa's and Greco's reply is subject to 'fake barn' cases. Briefly, imagine that you are driving through a region that, unbeknownst to you, contains very few real barns and many barn facades (you are unable to distinguish between the two). You see what appears to be the side of a barn and form the belief "that is a barn." Your belief turns out to be true, because you happen to have seen one of the few real barns in the area; but, arguably, you do not know that what you have seen is a barn. Now, it seems that your belief meets Sosa's and Greco's conditions for knowledge: it is true, produced by the virtue of vision, and this virtue is a particularly salient cause (perhaps the most salient cause) of your coming to have a true belief. But, it is important to note that there are several potential ways for Sosa and Greco to reply to this objection, all of which they have pursued or are currently pursuing. First, Sosa (in particular) might argue that in the above case, you do have animal knowledge, what you lack is reflective knowledge (Sosa, *Virtue Epistemology* 32). Second, Greco (in particular) might argue that your virtue of vision is not the most salient cause of your coming to have a true belief. Rather, the most salient cause is luck—you just happened to look at one of the few real barns in the area. This reply requires further analysis of causation and salience. Third, they might add a safety requirement to their accounts of knowledge, which would, in turn, require further analysis of safety conditions.[18] In short, the credit theory's reply to the Gettier problem is potentially promising, but clearly requires further defense. Whether the credit theory will ultimately succeed in answering the Gettier problem is open for debate.[19]

The value problem claims that reliably produced true belief is not sufficient for knowledge (Zagzebski 301–4). This is because knowledge is more valuable than true belief, and the sum of the value of a true belief and the value of its being reliably produced falls short of the value of knowledge. The value of reliability is merely instrumental. Credit theories claim that the added value is supplied by the credit the agent deserves for arriving at the truth because of her virtues. Both Sosa and Greco argue that it is intrinsically valuable to believe the truth because of one's virtues. Knowledge (apt belief) is more valuable than true (accurate) reliably produced (adroit) belief because of this extra intrinsic value. Whether this reply succeeds will partly depend on whether the successful exercise of natural faculties and skills really is intrinsically valuable. Would such a claim imply that natural faculties and skills cannot be used for bad intellectual ends (e.g., believing whatever it is easiest to believe, or whatever makes one feel good)? If so, why couldn't they be used for bad ends?

III.B High-grade Knowledge

Unlike low-grade knowledge, high-grade knowledge is acquired actively as a result of intentional inquiry. At a minimum, high-grade knowledge requires the agent to perform voluntary intellectual actions. To illustrate, recall Brenda's attempt to determine who murdered the accountant, but this time, focus on necessary conditions for such knowledge. Since Brenda did not witness the murder, and she is not clairvoyant, she cannot acquire knowledge of the murderer's identity without performing intellectual actions. She must, say, search for and weigh evidence, formulate a hypothesis, entertain objections, consider alternatives, and follow through on leads. Baehr and Roberts and Wood suggest that much of our scientific, moral, historical, and anthropological knowledge is high-grade.[20] 'Investigative applied' knowledge, like that of police detectives, doctors, nurses, and economic forecasters, is also paradigmatically high-grade; hence such knowledge is not restricted to theoreticians or academics.

We have seen that the credit theory defines knowledge in terms of true beliefs that are produced by intellectual virtues. Though the credit theory is primarily interested in accounting for low-grade knowledge, we should consider how it fares with respect to the high-grade. Can Brenda acquire knowledge of the murderer's identity via the passive operation of her natural faculties of vision, memory, induction, and deduction? If she could, she would be superhuman—to us she would appear clairvoyant! Brenda's natural faculties will produce true beliefs about her surroundings, but she won't be able to identify the murderer unless she also performs intellectual actions. Though her reliable faculties are arguably necessary for high-grade knowledge, they are not sufficient. The key necessary component in high-grade knowledge is the performance of intentional actions, but we have seen that natural faculties do not require such acts. Credit theorists do allow for derived virtues, but they have not provided an analysis of them —they have not explained what, in addition to reliability, is required for derived virtues. Consequently, the credit theory is too weak to explain high-grade knowledge.

Virtue-responsibilism has at least one clear advantage over the credit theory in explaining high-grade knowledge: it is not too weak. Recall that for Zagzebski, knowledge requires an intellectual act: (1) that arises from virtuous motives; (2) is what the virtuous person would do; (3) that attains the ends of those motives; and (4) attains a true belief because of those virtuous motives and actions. Zagzebski is in a better position to explain high-grade knowledge because her analysis requires the agent to perform voluntary intellectual actions. On her view, for Brenda to know the

identity of the murderer, she must perform the actions that an intellectually virtuous person P would perform were P conducting such an investigation (condition 2). For Einstein to know that $E = mc^2$, he must perform the
actions that an intellectually virtuous person P would perform were P generating and testing such a hypothesis. Gettier problems aside, Zagzebski's
account of high-grade knowledge cannot be accused of being too weak. If
anything, its motivation condition (1) makes it too strong (see below).

Some responsibilists are virtue anti-theorists. As anti-theorists, they think
that knowledge cannot be systematically defined in terms of the intellectual virtues. So, unlike Zagzebski, they do not propose necessary and sufficient conditions for knowledge. But, this does not prevent them from
arguing that knowledge is sometimes contingently connected to the intellectual virtues. Thus, both Roberts and Wood and Battaly have argued that
in the actual world, high-grade knowledge sometimes requires virtuous
motivations and actions. Roberts and Wood claim that though reliable faculties may be sufficient for low-grade knowledge,

for interesting kinds of knowledge—self-knowledge in a deep moral sense, scientific knowledge, religious knowledge, complex historical knowledge—considerably
greater powers are needed: in particular, epistemic skills and virtues. (109)

For instance, they argue that Jane Goodall could not have acquired her
sophisticated knowledge of chimps without the virtues of courage, love of
knowledge, generosity, and practical wisdom. In their words: "certain traits
of character were necessary for the successful pursuit of Goodall's intellectual practices" (147). For instance, her love of animals motivated her to
"spend vast amounts of time . . . with them," which was "needed to garner
the animals' trust, which in turn made it possible for her to observe things
never before recorded by humans" (147). Roberts and Wood argue that
Goodall's love of animals is "at the same time a love of knowing about
[animals] in considerable, rigorous detail" and that "this love is an *epistemic
virtue*" (147, original emphasis).

In a similar vein, I have argued that knowing one's own sexual orientation sometimes requires the motivations and actions associated with
open-mindedness, intellectual autonomy, and care in gathering evidence.
Contemporary society pressures agents to believe that they are heterosexual. This pressure can cause non-heterosexual agents to ignore evidence,
employ wishful thinking, and jump to the conclusion that society favors.
Hence, some non-heterosexual agents, overwhelmed by this pressure, will
falsely believe that they are heterosexual. Combating this pressure requires
agents to perform intellectually virtuous actions—to entertain the possibil-

ity that they are not heterosexual, and to consider all relevant evidence. Performing these acts requires a sufficiently strong motivation for truth. Without sufficient motivation to get the truth, agents will succumb to the motivation to believe whatever it is easiest believe, or to believe whatever will make one feel safe or fit in. In short, sometimes one cannot acquire knowledge of one's own sexual orientation without possessing intellectually virtuous motivations and performing intellectually virtuous actions.

Though responsibilism fares better than the credit theory in explaining high-grade knowledge, it is still subject to two serious objections, both of which argue that the responsibilist views above are too strong. First, one might object that the responsibilist views above lead to skepticism about high-grade knowledge. For, those views claim that (some or all) high-grade knowledge requires virtue possession (Roberts and Wood) or the possession of virtuous motivations (Zagzebski; Battaly). And, according to responsibilists, virtues and virtuous motivations are difficult to acquire: children lack them, and so do many adults. Hence, skepticism threatens. In reply, responsibilists might argue that high-grade knowledge is difficult, but not impossible, to attain; and that this is as it should be. High-grade knowledge is harder to get than low-grade knowledge.

Second, and relatedly, one might object that although virtuous acts are required for high-grade knowledge, virtuous motives are not. After all, it seems that one could attain knowledge as a result of a virtuous act that one performs because of non-virtuous, or even vicious, motives. To illustrate, suppose that scientist S is motivated to believe whatever will get his name published in the trendy journals, or whatever will make him famous. This motivation leads S to conduct a thorough and careful investigation of a new topic in his field, which, in turn, results in S's coming to have several true beliefs about this topic. S is careful in gathering and evaluating evidence; hence, he arguably does what the intellectually virtuous person would do. Moreover, the true beliefs that S acquires as a result of his actions seem to constitute knowledge. But S's motive is not intellectually virtuous. In reply, responsibilists might argue that though S's *ulterior* motive (believing whatever will get his name in the trendy journals) is not virtuous, S is still motivated to attain the truth, and hence does attain knowledge.[21] But if S must value the truth intrinsically in order to possess intellectually virtuous motives, then this reply fails.

III.C Individual Intellectual Virtues
Anti-theorists argue that intellectual virtues and vices warrant exploration even if they cannot be systematically connected to knowledge.

Anti-theorists like Fricker and Roberts and Wood have just begun to analyze individual intellectual virtues and vices in greater depth. Fricker has
argued that the vice of testimonial injustice occurs when "prejudice causes
a hearer to give a deflated level of credibility to a speaker's word" (1). She
contends that in paradigmatic cases of testimonial injustice, the hearer is
prejudiced with respect to the speaker's social identity, for instance, her
gender or racial identity. Fricker discusses two such cases at length. First,
she argues that in *To Kill a Mockingbird*, white jurors fail to believe the
testimony of Tom Robinson, a black man accused of raping a white girl,
because of racial prejudice. Second, she argues that in *The Talented Mr.
Ripley*, gender prejudice causes Herbert Greenleaf to dismiss Marge's claim
that Ripley killed Greenleaf's son. Fricker argues that hearers may be unaware of their prejudices, and may even believe that they are not prejudiced. The virtue of testimonial justice is a critical awareness of, and
entrenched disposition to correct, one's prejudicial perception of speakers.
This virtue requires the motivation to make unprejudiced judgments, and
reliable success in neutralizing prejudiced judgments. Fricker allows for the
possibility that one's credibility judgments may be unprejudiced from the
start.

Fricker's is the first extended analysis of an individual intellectual vice.
As such, it prompts several important questions about the nature of intellectual vice. First, how difficult is it to possess an intellectual vice like testimonial injustice? Responsibilists have argued that it is difficult to acquire
the intellectual virtues. Are the intellectual vices also acquired, and if so,
are they just as difficult to acquire? If not, why not? Second, what makes an
intellectual vice bad? Are vices like testimonial injustice only instrumentally bad, or also intrinsically bad? Third, must an intellectually vicious
person have acquired vicious motivations? If so, what is the nature of those
motivations? Finally, are the virtue of testimonial justice and the vice of
testimonial injustice contraries or contradictories? Relatedly, is there conceptual space for intellectual *enkrateia* and intellectual *akrasia*?

Roberts and Wood have provided detailed analyses of seven virtues: love
of knowledge, firmness, courage and caution, humility, autonomy, generosity, and practical wisdom. They argue that these virtues are diverse. Some
are defined in terms of a distinctive motivation—e.g., love of knowledge—
others in terms of particular sorts of intellectual acts—e.g., courage. Love of
knowledge is an acquired motivation to desire knowledge that is significant, worthy, and relevant. One who possesses this virtue does not love all
truths equally; she does not desire trivial truths (e.g., about the Los Angeles

phone book). Rather, she desires truths that are significant "in the sense that other epistemic goods rest on them," worthy "in the sense that their objects are intrinsically important or bear on human *eudaimonia*," and relevant in the sense that they are connected to her life and interests (Roberts and Wood 160). To illustrate, jurors who love knowledge will want to know whether the defendant is guilty; while a biologist who possesses this virtue may well desire truths about the human genome. In contrast, courage does not require virtuous motives. According to Roberts and Wood, the courageous person's motive may be self-interested; he may act courageously "in an effort to forward his career or to make money; or his motive may even be evil" (217). Intellectual courage is a disposition to overcome fear (e.g., of criticism of our views) and act with aplomb in the face of intellectual dangers (e.g., defend our views appropriately). It lies in a mean between cowardice and recklessness.

Roberts and Wood's analysis raises several questions about the nature of the virtues. First, is courage always a virtue, or can it sometimes be a vice? Is courage a skill that can be possessed both by virtuous people and vicious people? Second, is there a distinction between full virtue possession and *enkrateia*? To illustrate, can one who possesses the virtue of love of knowledge simultaneously possess competing motivations (e.g., the motivation to believe whatever it is easiest to believe), or does the possession of competing motivations demonstrate that one is not fully virtuous? Finally, what are the connections between the moral and intellectual virtues? Are the intellectual virtues a subset of the moral virtues? Are there points at which the analogy between moral and intellectual virtue fails?

To sum up, I have argued that virtue-responsibilism and virtue-reliabilism complement each another. With respect to virtue theory, I have argued that though the credit theory fails to explain high-grade knowledge, it offers a valuable (albeit contestable) account of low-grade knowledge. Likewise, though Zagzebski's responsibilism fails to explain low-grade knowledge, it offers an illuminating (albeit contestable) account of high-grade knowledge. Finally, I have suggested that virtue anti-theory is opening up epistemology to valuable new projects.

Acknowledgment

I am grateful to Tamar Gendler, Merrill Ring, Clifford Roth, and an anonymous referee for comments on an earlier draft.

Notes

* Correspondence address: California State University, Fullerton, Hum 214, 800 N State College Blvd., Fullerton, CA 92834-6868, USA. Email: hbattaly@fullerton.edu.

1. See Guy Axtell's blog on virtue theory: ⟨http://janusblog.squarespace.com/⟩.

2. Also see two Web resources: Greco, "Virtue Epistemology"; Battaly, "What is Virtue Epistemology?".

3. In *Knowledge in Perspective*, see especially "Reliabilism and Intellectual Virtue" 131–45; "Knowledge and Intellectual Virtue" 225–44; and "Intellectual Virtue in Perspective" 270–93.

4. I do not compare the credit theory's solutions to those of belief-based epistemology, though I would applaud such research.

5. See her use of *To Kill a Mockingbird* (Fricker 23–9) and of *The Talented Mr. Ripley* (86–91); and her chapter 3 "Toward a Virtue Epistemological Account of Testimony."

6. See Montmarquet: "I do not follow ... the unrestricted kind of teleological approach of Ernest Sosa ... wherein any truth-conducive capacity, regardless of whether it is a personal quality, counts as an epistemic virtue" (35 n. 4).

7. Guy Axtell coined the terms 'virtue-reliabilism' and 'virtue-responsibilism.' See Axtell, *Knowledge, Belief, and Character* xiv–xix.

8. Aristotle argues that the moral virtues and practical wisdom are distinct from skills. See NE.1105a18–1105b4; NE.1140b20–1140b30.

9. See "Reliabilism and Intellectual Virtue" and "Intellectual Virtue in Perspective" in Sosa, *Knowledge in Perspective*; Greco's introduction to *Ernest Sosa and His Critics* xxii–xxiii. Each token belief-forming process (e.g., believing that there is a red plate on my desk at time t1 as a result of seeing it nearby and partly occluded) is an instance of many different process types (e.g., sense-perception, vision, vision of objects that are partly occluded, vision of nearby objects that are partly occluded, etc.). These process types will have different degrees of reliability. The generality problem challenges reliabilists to determine which process type is the relevant one. Sosa argues that the relevant process type is a virtue that is defined in terms of fields of propositions and conditions that can be "usefully generalized upon" both by the members of "the epistemic community" and by "the subject himself as he bootstraps up from animal to reflective knowledge" (Sosa, *Knowledge in Perspective* 284). Sosa argues that the new evil demon and clairvoyancy problems can be solved by indexing virtues to environments (288–290).

10. See Sosa, "Virtue Perspectivism"; "Place of Truth"; *Virtue Epistemology*.

11. Sosa, *Virtue Epistemology* 88. See also Sosa, "Replies" 320–1, where he argues that virtuously derived true belief is intrinsically valuable.

12. Once high-grade knowledge is acquired by one member of the community, it can be transmitted to others via testimony.

13. For Zagzebski's distinction between low- and high-grade knowledge, see Zagzebski 273–83.

14. James Summerford argues that beliefs like 'someone in Nogot's office owns a Ford' do arise from acts of intellectual virtue; and hence that Zagzebski's analysis of knowledge fails to avoid Gettier problems.

15. Baehr, "Character in Epistemology" 487–8.

16. See Greco, "Knowledge as Credit"; Riggs; Sosa, *Virtue Epistemology*.

17. In *A Virtue Epistemology*, Sosa argues that aptness is sufficient for animal knowledge; safety is not required. Sosa distinguishes animal knowledge from reflective knowledge. The former is apt belief that p. The latter is apt belief that the belief that p is apt.

18. Sosa endorses a safety requirement in, for instance, "Replies," but argues that safety is not required for knowledge in *A Virtue Epistemology*.

19. Should Greco or Sosa succeed in defending an analysis of causal saliency that solves the Gettier problem, Zagzebski's account of knowledge might also benefit. She might adopt their analysis as an explanation of her condition that the agent must acquire a true belief *through* the virtuous features of the act.

20. See Roberts and Wood; Baehr "Character, Reliability, and Virtue Epistemology."

21. This is Zagzebski's preferred reply. See Zagzebski 313–19.

Works Cited

Alston, William P. "An Internalist Externalism." *Epistemic Justification: Essays in the Theory of Knowledge.* Ithaca, NY: Cornell UP, 1989. 227–45.

Aristotle. *Metaphysics. The Complete Works of Aristotle.* Ed. Jonathan Barnes. Princeton, NJ: Princeton UP, 1984.

———. *Nicomachean Ethics.* Trans. David Ross. New York, NY: Oxford UP, 1992.

Axtell, Guy, ed. *Knowledge, Belief, and Character.* Lanham, MD: Rowman & Littlefield, 2000.

———. "Site Administrator." 2008 *JanusBlog: The Virtue Theory Discussion Forum.* 25 Apr. 2008 ⟨http://janusblog.squarespace.com/⟩.

Baehr, Jason S. "Character in Epistemology." *Philosophical Studies* 128 (2006): 479–514.

———. "Character, Reliability, and Virtue Epistemology." *The Philosophical Quarterly* 56 (2006): 193–212.

———. "Virtue Epistemology." *Internet Encyclopedia of Philosophy*, 2004. 9 May 2005. ⟨http://www.iep.utm.edu/v/VirtueEp.htm⟩.

Battaly, Heather D. "Intellectual Virtue and Knowing One's Sexual Orientation." *Sex and Ethics: Essays on Sexuality, Virtue, and the Good Life.* Ed. Raja Halwani. New York, NY: Palgrave, 2007. 149–61.

———. "Teaching Intellectual Virtues: Applying Virtue Epistemology in the Classroom." *Teaching Philosophy* 29.3 (September 2006): 191–222.

———. "Thin Concepts to the Rescue: Thinning the Concepts of Epistemic Justification and Intellectual Virtue." *Virtue Epistemology: Essays on Epistemic Virtue and Responsibility.* Eds. Abrol Fairweather and Linda Zagzebski. New York, NY: Oxford UP, 2001. 98–116.

———. "What is Virtue Epistemology?" 20th World Congress of Philosophy, 2000. 1 July 2005 ⟨http://www.bu.edu/wcp/Papers/Valu/ValuBatt.htm⟩.

Chisholm, Roderick M. *The Theory of Knowledge.* 3rd ed. Englewood Cliffs, NJ: Prentice Hall, 1989.

Clarke, Stanley G. and Evan Simpson, eds. *Anti-Theory in Ethics and Moral Conservatism.* Albany, NY: State U of New York P, 1989.

Code, Lorraine. *Epistemic Responsibility.* Hanover, NH: UP of New England, 1987.

Cohen, Stewart. "How to be a Fallibilist." *Philosophical Perspectives 2: Epistemology* (1988): 91–123.

Conee, Earl and Richard Feldman. *Evidentialism: Essays in Epistemology.* Oxford: Clarendon Press, 2004.

Fricker, Miranda. *Epistemic Injustice: Power and the Ethics of Knowing.* Oxford: Oxford UP, 2007.

Goldie, Peter. "Seeing What is the Kind Thing to Do: Perception and Emotion in Morality." *Dialectica* (2007): 347–61.

Goldman, Alvin I. "A Causal Theory of Knowing." *The Journal of Philosophy* 64 (1967): 357–72.

———. *Epistemology and Cognition.* Cambridge, MA: Harvard UP, 1986.

Greco, John. "How to Preserve Your Virtue while Losing Your Perspective." *Ernest Sosa and His Critics.* Malden, MA: Blackwell, 2004. 96–105.

———. "Introduction: Motivations for Sosa's Epistemology." *Ernest Sosa and His Critics.* Malden, MA: Blackwell, 2004. xv–xxiv.

———. "Knowledge as Credit for True Belief." *Intellectual Virtue: Perspectives from Ethics and Epistemology*. Eds. Michael DePaul and Linda Zagzebski. New York, NY: Oxford UP, 2003. 111–34.

———. *Putting Skeptics in Their Place*. New York, NY: Cambridge UP, 2000.

———. "Virtue Epistemology." *Stanford Encyclopedia of Philosophy*. 2004. 9 May 2005 ⟨http://plato.stanford.edu/entries/epistemology-virtue/⟩.

———. "Virtues in Epistemology." *The Oxford Handbook of Epistemology*. Ed. Paul K. Moser. New York, NY: Oxford UP, 2002. 287–315.

Hookway, Christopher. "How to be a Virtue Epistemologist." *Intellectual Virtue: Perspectives from Ethics and Epistemology*. Eds. Michael DePaul and Linda Zagzebski. New York, NY: Oxford UP, 2003. 183–202.

Hursthouse, Rosalind. *On Virtue Ethics*. New York, NY: Oxford UP, 1999.

Kvanvig, Jonathan L. *The Intellectual Virtues and the Life of the Mind: On the Place of Virtues in Epistemology*. Savage, MD: Rowman & Littlefield, 1992.

Lehrer, Keith and Thomas Paxson, Jr. "Knowledge: Undefeated Justified True Belief." *The Journal of Philosophy* 66 (1969): 225–37.

Montmarquet, James. *Epistemic Virtue and Doxastic Responsibility*. Lanham, MD: Rowman & Littlefield, 1993.

Nozick, Robert. *Philosophical Explanations*. Cambridge, MA: Harvard UP, 1981.

Riggs, Wayne. "Reliability and the Value of Knowledge." *Philosophy and Phenomenological Research* 64 (2002): 79–96.

Roberts, Robert C. and Jay Wood. *Intellectual Virtues: An Essay in Regulative Epistemology*. Oxford: Oxford UP, 2007.

Sosa, Ernest. *Knowledge in Perspective*. New York, NY: Cambridge UP, 1991.

———. "The Place of Truth in Epistemology." *Intellectual Virtue: Perspectives from Ethics and Epistemology*. Eds. Michael DePaul and Linda Zagzebski. New York, NY: Oxford UP, 2003. 155–79.

———. "The Raft and the Pyramid: Coherence versus Foundations in the Theory of Knowledge." *Midwest Studies in Philosophy* 5 (1980): 3–25. Reprinted in *Knowledge in Perspective*. New York, NY: Cambridge UP, 1991. 165–91.

———. "Replies." *Ernest Sosa and His Critics*. Ed. John Greco. Malden, MA: Blackwell, 2004. 275–325.

———. *A Virtue Epistemology: Apt Belief and Reflective Knowledge*. Vol. 1. Oxford: Oxford UP, 2007.

————. "Virtue Perspectivism: A Response to Foley and Fumerton." *Philosophical Issues* 5 (1994): 29–50.

Summerford, James. "Virtue Epistemology and the Gettier Problem." *The Southern Journal of Philosophy* 38 (2000): 343–53.

Zagzebski, Linda Trinkaus. *Virtues of the Mind: An Inquiry into the Nature of Virtue and the Ethical Foundations of Knowledge.* New York, NY: Cambridge UP, 1996.

2 Four Varieties of Character-Based Virtue Epistemology

Jason Baehr

Abstract

The terrain of character-based or "responsibilist" virtue epistemology has evolved dramatically over the last decade—so much so that it is far from clear what, if anything, unifies the various views put forth in this area. In an attempt to bring some clarity to the overall thrust and structure of this movement, I develop a fourfold classification of character-based virtue epistemologies. I also offer a qualified assessment of each approach, defending a certain account of the probable future of this burgeoning subfield.

The field of virtue epistemology has enjoyed remarkable growth over the last decade. Several international conferences drawing top scholars in epistemology and ethics have been held on the topic, a number of books and scores of articles have been published, and several new lines of inquiry have opened up. But these developments have yet to be accounted for in the literature in a systematic way.[1] This is problematic, among other reasons, because developments in the field have resulted in extreme theoretical diversity, such that it is no longer clear what exactly the term "virtue epistemology" picks out or what the defining tenets or commitments of this novel approach are supposed to be.

This confusion is evident in two recent characterizations of virtue epistemology. John Greco and Linda Zagzebski, both leading figures in the field, define "virtue epistemology" in terms of a thesis about the "direction of analysis" of certain basic epistemic concepts. Greco comments: "Just as virtue theories in ethics try to understand the normative properties of actions in terms of the normative properties of moral agents, virtue epistemology

Reprinted from Jason Baehr, "Four Varieties of Character-Based Virtue Epistemology," *The Southern Journal of Philosophy* 46 (2008): 469–502.

tries to understand the normative properties of beliefs [viz., knowledge and justification] in terms of the normative properties of cognitive agents" (2004, par. 1). Similarly, Zagzebski says that virtue epistemology is "a class of theories that analyse fundamental epistemic concepts such as justification or knowledge in terms of properties of persons rather than properties of beliefs" (1998, 617; cf. Axtell 2000, xiii). But even at the time these characterizations were written, they failed to account for the full range of views within the field. Several virtue epistemologists (for instance, Code 1987; Kvanvig 1992; Hookway 2003)—authors whom Greco and Zagzebski themselves describe as such—eschew any attempt to offer a virtue-based analysis of knowledge, justification, or any related concept. These authors focus instead on matters of intellectual character and virtue that are largely independent of more standard epistemological questions and issues. And in recent years, the field has continued to expand in this direction (see, for example, Hookway 2006 and Baehr 2006a, 2006b, and 2009).

In this paper, I offer an up-to-date account of virtue epistemology that sheds significant light on its basic structure, substance, and promise. I do so by developing a fourfold classification of approaches to virtue epistemology, together with an assessment of each approach.

There are, however, two limitations of the paper that must be noted up front. First, my concern is limited to *character*-based or "responsibilist" approaches to virtue epistemology. These are approaches that conceive of intellectual virtues as excellences of intellectual character like fairmindedness, open-mindedness, inquisitiveness, attentiveness, carefulness and thoroughness in inquiry, intellectual courage, honesty, and so forth, rather than as cognitive *faculties* or related abilities like vision, hearing, memory, introspection, and reason. While I will have occasion to say something brief about faculty-based or "reliabilist" approaches to virtue epistemology, they are not my immediate or central concern.[2] This is noteworthy given that some of the leading contributors to virtue epistemology proper (for example, Greco and Ernest Sosa) are proponents of a faculty-based approach. Nonetheless, the theoretical differences between the two approaches are significant enough, and my space here is limited enough, that I shall focus almost exclusively on character-based approaches. Fortunately, this is not a major liability, for the lot of character-based approaches is considerably more diverse than that of faculty-based approaches and therefore stands in greater need of a broad, systematic treatment. Moreover, character-based approaches represent a considerably more novel— and in the judgment of some a more *interesting*—innovation within epistemology.[3]

The second limitation is also related to the paper's scope but in a different way. For each of the four main approaches to character-based virtue epistemology, I identify the central challenge and go some way toward considering the likelihood of its being overcome. However, given the relatively broad scope of the paper, together with limitations of space, my assessment of the relevant views is necessarily less than exhaustive. Thus, while I shall take a stand regarding the plausibility of each of the four approaches, I do not consider debate on these matters entirely closed. My hope, however, is that by clarifying the structure of the field and offering a substantive preliminary assessment of its various elements, the paper nonetheless will prove to be an illuminating and much-needed contribution to the literature in virtue epistemology.

1   The Varieties Delineated

The initial basis for distinguishing between varieties of character-based virtue epistemology concerns how the authors of the relevant views conceive of the relationship between (1) the concept of intellectual virtue and (2) the problems or questions of traditional epistemology. By "traditional epistemology" I mean, roughly, epistemology in the Cartesian tradition, the central focus of which has been and remains the *nature, limits, and sources* of knowledge. Some of the topics and debates central to this tradition include global and local skepticism, the nature of perception, rationalism vs. empiricism, the problem of induction, the analysis of knowledge, foundationalism vs. coherentism, internalism vs. externalism, and the Gettier problem.[4] My claim is that we can begin to distinguish between varieties of virtue epistemology based on what these approaches imply concerning the relation between (1) and (2).

Some proponents of virtue epistemology regard an appeal to the concept of intellectual virtue as having the potential to "save the day" within traditional epistemology, for example, to solve (or in certain cases to *dissolve*) certain longstanding problems or debates in the field. These authors view the concept of intellectual virtue as meriting a *central* and *fundamental* role within traditional epistemology. One example is Zagzebski, who defends an analysis of knowledge according to which knowledge is, roughly, true belief produced by "acts of intellectual virtue" (1996, 264–73). She argues that conceiving of knowledge in this way not only yields a satisfactory account of the nature of knowledge, but also a way of undermining skepticism, resolving the tension between internalism and externalism, overcoming the Gettier problem, and more.[5] To be sure, this represents an extremely high view of the conceptual connection between intellectual virtue and traditional epistemology.

Other authors are less sanguine about (or just less interested in) any conceptual connections between intellectual virtue and traditional epistemology. These authors see reflection on the intellectual virtues as motivating fundamentally new directions and inquiries in the field: directions and inquiries that are largely *independent* of traditional concerns about the nature, limits, and sources of knowledge.[6] Hookway (2000; 2003), for instance, commends an approach to epistemology that focuses on the domain of *inquiry* rather than on individual *beliefs* or states of knowledge; and because intellectual character virtues like carefulness and thoroughness, sensitivity to detail, intellectual perseverance, and intellectual honesty often play a critical role in successful inquiry, he contends that such an approach will be a virtue-based one. Likewise, Robert Roberts and Jay Wood have recently defended an approach to virtue epistemology that focuses on *individual* intellectual virtues and makes little attempt to engage or "solve" the problems and questions of traditional epistemology. Their aim is rather to provide something like a "conceptual map" of virtuous intellectual character (2007, 23–30). Accordingly, they offer chapter-length analyses of several virtues, including love of knowledge, intellectual firmness, courage and caution, humility, autonomy, generosity, and practical wisdom.

This suggests an initial, broad distinction between two main varieties of character-based virtue epistemology: "conservative" approaches, which appeal to the concept of intellectual virtue as a way of engaging the epistemological tradition or mainstream, and "autonomous" approaches, which focus on matters of intellectual virtue in ways that are largely independent of the traditional quarry.

Each of the two main types of virtue epistemology can be subdivided, resulting in a total of four types. I begin by distinguishing two varieties of "conservative" virtue epistemology. According to Zagzebski's approach noted above, the conceptual connection between intellectual virtue and traditional epistemology is central and fundamental. But conservative virtue epistemologists need not adopt this strong of a stance: they need not regard an appeal to the concept of intellectual virtue as "saving the day" within or as properly transforming traditional epistemology. Instead, they might posit considerably weaker or peripheral conceptual connections between these two relata. For instance, I have argued in recent years that while the concept of intellectual virtue does *not* merit a central or fundamental role in an analysis of knowledge or any other traditional problem in epistemology (2006a), it does have a *background* or *secondary* role to play in connection with at least two major accounts of knowledge. I argue (2006b), first, that reliabilist accounts of knowledge must incorporate intellectual character virtues in their repertoire of "knowledge-makers," or traits that contribute to knowledge, and that doing so generates some difficult theoretical challenges. Second, I argue (Forthcoming) that evidentialist accounts of epistemic justification must incorporate a virtue-based *background* condition or constraint, according to which, if a person's agency impacts her "evidential situation," she must operate in a minimally virtuous way. I shall have more to say about these arguments below. The point at present is merely that a view like Zagzebski's is not the only alternative within "conservative" virtue epistemology, for while the arguments just noted are aimed at identifying conceptual links between intellectual virtue and traditional epistemology, these links are at most secondary or peripheral: they do not amount to giving the concept of intellectual virtue a "central or fundamental" role within traditional epistemology.[7]

In keeping with this distinction, I shall use the term "*Strong* Conservative VE" to refer to the view that the concept of intellectual virtue merits a central and fundamental role in connection with one or more traditional epistemological problems and "*Weak* Conservative VE" to refer to the view that while there are some notable conceptual connections between intellectual virtue and traditional epistemology, these connections are considerably less central, or more peripheral, than those posited by Strong Conservative VE. Again, Strong Conservative VE sees an appeal to the concept of intellectual virtue as having a major, transformative effect within traditional epistemology, while Weak Conservative VE posits considerably more modest connections between the two.

The second general type of character-based virtue epistemology identified above regards reflection on the intellectual virtues as occupying an epistemological niche outside of traditional epistemology; again, it views such reflection as motivating new and largely unaddressed questions about intellectual virtues and their role in the intellectual life—questions that nonetheless are broadly epistemological in nature. These "autonomous" approaches also admit of two types. Here the difference depends, not on the positive substance or direction of the approaches themselves, but on how they perceive their status vis-à-vis a more traditional approach to epistemology. "*Radical* Autonomous VE" says that an autonomous or independent concern with matters of intellectual virtue ought to *replace* or *supplant* traditional concerns. "*Moderate* Autonomous VE" views an independent virtue-based approach as properly *complementing* more traditional approaches[8] (see Figure A).

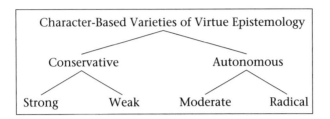

Figure A.

One natural motivation for Radical Autonomous VE is the sense that traditional epistemology is somehow fundamentally misguided or futile and that a more direct or independent concern with intellectual virtue holds the promise of a more vital theoretical alternative. One example of Radical Autonomous VE along these lines is Jonathan Kvanvig's 1992 book *The Intellectual Virtues and the Life of the Mind.*[9] Kvanvig argues that the notion of intellectual virtue should be the focus of epistemology, but that the belief-based, synchronic framework of traditional epistemology cannot accommodate such a focus (more on this argument below); consequently, he calls for a rejection of the traditional framework and the issues and questions central to it. Kvanvig's preferred, more diachronic and socially oriented framework begins with a conception of "human beings in terms of potentialities in need of socialization in order to participate in communal efforts to incorporate bodies of knowledge into corporate plans, practices, rituals, and the like for those practical and theoretical purposes that ordinarily characterize human beings" (1992, 169). Central to this framework are several questions and issues an adequate treatment of which, he claims, will give a major role to the concept of intellectual virtue. These include questions about how "one progresses down the path toward cognitive ideality," the significance of "social patterns of mimicry and imitation" and "training and practice" in human intellectual formation, the acquisition of the sort of "know-how" involved with searching for and evaluating explanations (170–73), the relative merits of different kinds of epistemic communities and the bodies of knowledge these communities generate (176), and the evaluation of "structured chunks" of information (vs. discrete propositions, 182–86). Because of the fundamental role that Kvanvig's proposed approach gives to the concept of intellectual virtue, and because he intends it as a *replacement* for traditional epistemological projects and concerns, this approach represents a clear instance of Radical Autonomous VE.[10]

Defenders of *Moderate* Autonomous VE agree that reflection on intellectual virtue and its role in the intellectual life can form the basis of an epistemological research program that is largely independent of traditional epistemology. But they do not regard this program as a replacement for traditional epistemology; instead they envision it existing alongside or as *complementing* a more traditional approach. Put another way, defenders of Moderate Autonomous VE insist merely that epistemology proper is not *reducible to* or *exhausted by* traditional epistemology, and that the borders of traditional epistemology ought to be *expanded* to make room for a more immediate or independent concern with intellectual virtues. One representative sample of Moderate Autonomous VE is Lorraine Code's *Epistemic Responsibility* (1987). According to Code, epistemic responsibility can be understood as an excellence of intellectual *character*, indeed, as the *chief* intellectual character virtue. But Code does not appeal to the notion of epistemic responsibility in an effort to formulate an analysis of knowledge or any other familiar epistemic concept. In fact she thinks (for reasons similar to Kvanvig's) that the basic categories and focus of traditional epistemology obscure what is philosophically most interesting about the intellectual virtues (1987, 63–64, 253). She aims instead to "develop a perspective in theory of knowledge that is neither analogous in structure nor in functional capacity to [the traditional perspective], but that sees a different set of questions as central to epistemological inquiry" (13). This perspective "turns questions about, and conditions for, epistemic responsibility into focal points of explication and analysis" (3).

I began in this section by delineating two general types of character-based virtue epistemology: conservative and autonomous. I have shown that each of these two general types admits of two subtypes. Strong Conservative VE is the view that there are major, substantive connections between intellectual virtue and traditional epistemology, that the concept of intellectual virtue stands to "save the day" within or to transform traditional epistemology. Weak Conservative VE is the view that the conceptual connections between intellectual virtue and traditional epistemology, while genuine, are more secondary or less central. Radical Autonomous VE is the view that an autonomous or independent concern with intellectual virtue ought to *replace* traditional epistemological concerns. Moderate Autonomous VE is the view that an autonomous or independent approach is a proper *complement* to traditional epistemology.

Finally, it is worth reiterating that these categories are inspired by the range of views that *have actually been developed and defended in the virtue epistemology literature.*[11] The point of the classification, again, is to shed light on what is at first glance an extremely diverse and even disorienting philosophical literature. I take it, then, that inasmuch as the classification covers the full range of relevant views (to my knowledge there are no contributions to the virtue epistemology literature that fail to fit into one of the four relevant categories), it stands to advance our understanding of the basic structure and content of character-based virtue epistemology in a substantive and much-needed way.

2   Evaluating the Varieties

The aim of this paper is not merely to illuminate the relevant terrain. It is also to provide at least an initial *assessment* of the four main approaches to character-based virtue epistemology. I turn now to this task. I begin with a consideration of the two more ambitious approaches and argue that neither appears to be very promising. I shall then turn to consider the prospects of the remaining two approaches, arguing that both appear to have considerable plausibility. As noted earlier, while these assessments are necessarily limited in scope and depth, they are revealing enough to shed valuable light on the probable viability of each approach, and thus on the probable future of character-based virtue epistemology as a whole.

2.1   Strong Conservative VE

Strong Conservative VE says that the concept of intellectual virtue can form the basis of a solution to one or more problems in traditional epistemology. For this to happen, however, it appears that the concept of intellectual virtue must occupy a central role in a viable *analysis* of knowledge, and more specifically, that something like an exercise of intellectual virtue must be an *essential* or *defining* feature of knowledge.[12] This is because traditional debates about the nature, structure, and limits of knowledge are debates about the necessary or essential features of knowledge, such that if an exercise of intellectual virtue is not among these features, the concept of an intellectual virtue is unlikely to figure prominently in a solution to any of these problems.[13] Consider, for instance, the problem of skepticism about the external world. Nonskeptical responses to this problem attempt to show that some of our beliefs about the external world do actually qualify as knowledge, that is, that they satisfy the necessary (and sufficient) conditions for knowledge. The concern here is *not* with any properties or features that the beliefs in question instantiate only sometimes or occasionally. Thus if an exercise of intellectual virtue is not a necessary feature of knowledge, a concern with the relevant traits apparently will be of minimal relevance to dealing with the skeptical challenge.[14] A similar point can be made in connection with the debate between foundationalists, coherentists, and others about the underlying structure of epistemic justification. Here again the concern is with the *essential* features of justification, and in particular, with whether these features should be conceived along foundationalist, coherentist, or other lines; it is not with any *incidental* features of justification. So again, it is difficult to see how the concept of an intellectual virtue might figure prominently in a response to any traditional epistemological problems without also forming the basis of a plausible analysis of knowledge.[15] This in turn suggests that the central challenge facing Strong Conservative VE is to show that something like an exercise of intellectual virtue is an essential feature of knowledge.

The most straightforward way of evaluating Strong Conservative VE, then, is to consider whether it is possible to acquire knowledge *absent* an exercise of intellectual virtue, for if it is, then an exercise of intellectual virtue is not a necessary or defining feature of knowledge. One obvious reason for thinking that knowledge is indeed possible apart from an exercise of intellectual virtue is that otherwise, the class of knowers would be limited (implausibly) to the class of intellectually virtuous agents: a person lacking in intellectual virtue could not be said to know *anything* (even, for instance, that she has hands or that two plus three equals five). Defenders of Strong Conservative VE have taken measures to get around this objection. Zagzebski, for instance, stops short of requiring that to have knowledge a person must actually *be* intellectually virtuous. She requires merely that the person possess the *motives* and perform the *actions* characteristic of an intellectually virtuous person (and that the person reach the truth as a result of these motives and actions).[16] This is possible even where the relevant motives and actions do not arise from a *settled disposition* or *character trait* on the part of the agent.

But even for an attenuated position like Zagzebski's, a serious problem remains, for we also appear to be capable of knowing many things absent any virtuous intellectual motives or actions. Right now, for instance, I seem to know that there is (or at least seems to be) a computer monitor before me, that I do not have a headache, that music is playing in the background, that the room smells of freshly ground coffee, that today is Tuesday, that I have been working for at least an hour this morning, and much more. And none of this putative knowledge appears to have involved even a momentary or fleeting manifestation of any virtuous motives or actions.[17]

Zagzebski does more than any other defender of Strong Conservative VE to accommodate knowledge of this sort, which she refers to as "low-grade" knowledge.[18] While her discussion suggests more than one possible reply,[19] I shall focus here on what is apparently her preferred response, which is also, to my mind, the prima facie most plausible one. Zagzebski suggests that while intellectually virtuous motives and actions *seem* to be absent from low-grade knowledge, they are in fact present and operative at a certain "low" or subconscious level. She says that in cases of simple perceptual knowledge, for instance, an intellectually virtuous person is characteristically guided by a "presumption of truth," which she describes as an intellectual *attitude*, and that it is plausible to think that this motive is also possessed by ordinary cognizers under similar conditions (1996, 280–81). To add to this suggestion, let us suppose that in the cases in question, virtuous and nonvirtuous agents alike also possess something like a low-level *desire* for truth. For instance, it might be said that when I form the belief that there is a ceramic mug on the desk before me, this process is guided by an *interest* in knowing what is on the table before me together with a basic *willingness* to trust that my senses are not deceiving me. The suggestion, then, is that in cases of low-grade knowledge, the beliefs in question do in fact arise from virtuous motives and actions and thus that a virtue-based account of knowledge can accommodate them.

I will not dispute that in a range of the cases in question, certain low-level intellectual motives or actions may be operative, that is, that the relevant beliefs are not always the product of strictly brute or mechanical cognitive processes. Nonetheless, I find it implausible, first, to characterize the motives or actions in question as *virtuous*—to think of them as *characteristic* of intellectual *virtue*. As Zagzebski herself suggests, these motives and actions are entirely pedestrian: they are routinely manifested by mediocre cognitive agents and by young children (and possibly, she says, by animals). Moreover, she characterizes a *failure* to manifest such actions and motives as a rather extreme kind of intellectual *paranoia* (1996, 280). Character virtues, on the other hand, are typically thought to pick out a comparatively high and distinguished level of personal excellence: something that is not possessed by the average cognitive agent or by young children (and certainly not by animals!). Thus to the extent that our concern is whether something resembling an exercise of intellectual virtue is necessary for knowledge, the suggested line of response to the problem of low-grade knowledge appears unpromising.

An even more serious problem is that inasmuch as certain low-level motives or actions (whether virtuous or not) are operative in these cases, it seems clear that they do not stand in the required *causal* relation to the *truth* of the relevant beliefs. As Zagzebski and others have noted, a plausible virtue-based account of knowledge must require, not only that a known belief be true and that it have its origin in intellectually virtuous motives or actions, but also that the *truth of the belief itself* be attributable to the relevant motives and actions.[20] Consider my belief that music is presently playing in the background. While it is possible that this belief involves the sort of low-level intellectual motives or actions described above, surely these are not the primary *cause* of the *truth* of my belief that music is playing. Rather, the primary or salient reason my belief is true is that I have good *hearing*, that my auditory faculty is in good working order. A similar point can be made in connection with many other instances of perceptual knowledge: the *truth* of my belief that there is a computer monitor before me or that the aroma of coffee is in the air, for instance, is explainable, not in terms of any intellectual motives, actions, or effort on my part, but rather in terms of the standard, brute or relatively untutored operation of one or more of my sensory modalities.[21]

It appears, then, that this response to the problem of low-grade knowledge is unsuccessful. One further consideration reinforces this conclusion. I have been assuming that in the cases in question, certain minimal or low-level intellectual motives or actions are operative. But this concession is too generous, for there appear to be cases of low-grade knowledge that are unaccompanied by *any* genuine motives or actions. These are cases in which the agent in question is *passive* with respect to the belief in question. Suppose, for instance, that as I sit working at my desk late one night, the electricity suddenly shuts off, causing the room immediately to go dark. As a result, I *immediately* and *automatically* form a corresponding belief. I am *overcome* by knowledge of the change in lighting. This knowledge simply *dawns* on me (see Baehr 2006a). By all appearances, this is a case in which I do not manifest any relevant intellectual motives or actions. I do not, even at a "low" or subconscious level, *seek* the truth about the state of affairs in question. Nor is plausible to think I am "trusting my senses" in the relevant, motivational sense. And yet surely I come to *know* that the lighting in the room has changed. Moreover, cases like this are not few and far between: they include knowledge that, for instance, a loud sound has just occurred or that one presently has a severe headache or is feeling nauseous. Again, knowledge of this sort seems not to involve or implicate the knower's agency in any significant way.[22]

I have examined the central challenge facing Strong Conservative VE and have found the most natural and prima facie plausible response to this challenge to be unsuccessful. Thus, this assessment, while falling short of a comprehensive or exhaustive critique of Strong Conservative VE, provides at least some initial reasons for thinking that the prospects of this approach are grim.

2.2   Radical Autonomous VE

I turn now to consider the second of the two more ambitious varieties of character-based virtue epistemology. As a version of *autonomous* virtue epistemology, Radical Autonomous VE endorses a theoretical concern with or focus on intellectual virtue that is independent of the traditional preoccupation with questions about the nature, limits, and sources of knowledge. What distinguishes this approach from *Moderate* Autonomous VE is its claim that an independent virtue-based research program should *replace* traditional epistemology: that traditional epistemological projects and pursuits should be *rejected* in favor of a virtue-based approach.

Radical Autonomous VE faces two main challenges, one positive and the other negative. The *positive* challenge is that of making good on the claim that there are indeed substantive philosophical questions and issues that are distinct from the questions of traditional epistemology but that nonetheless can form the basis of an alternative approach to the discipline. Because this is also the central challenge for Moderate Autonomous VE, I shall postpone a discussion of it to the section on Moderate Autonomous VE below. The *negative* challenge for Radical Autonomous VE is that of showing that an independent theoretical focus on intellectual virtue is not just an interesting and promising *complement* to traditional epistemology but, rather, that the epistemological enterprise should be entirely *reoriented* in this direction (that epistemologists should *jettison* the questions and issues of traditional epistemology).

Clearly the defender of Radical Autonomous VE is in a difficult dialectical position. Why think that an independent, virtue-based epistemological research program (assuming, for the moment, that there can be such a thing) should merit the lion's share of attention in epistemology? Why think that traditional epistemology should be *abandoned* in favor of an alternative, virtue-based approach? Given the seriousness of this challenge, it is not too surprising that to date there is only one systematic and fully worked out defense of Radical Autonomous VE in the literature. This is Kvanvig's *The Intellectual Virtues and the Life of the Mind* (1992).[23]

Kvanvig's argument for the negative component of Radical Autonomous VE is not easy to pin down. At points, it looks as if he simply begins with the (intuitive?) premise that the intellectual virtues should be the focus of epistemology and proceeds to argue that the traditional epistemological framework cannot accommodate this focus and so should be abandoned (see, for instance, 1992, vii–x and 186–87). Elsewhere, and more plausibly, his argument appears to be grounded in a certain meta-epistemological requirement, according to which "[w]hat we really want from an epistemologist is an account of the cognitive life of the mind that addresses our cognitive experience and helps us understand how to maximize our potential for finding truth and avoiding error" (vii). By Kvanvig's lights, traditional epistemology fails badly on this score. He argues that it generates a conception of the cognitive life by "cementing together the time-slice accounts of justification and knowledge for each moment of an individual's life" and that the result is a conception that is "removed from the ordinary concerns of . . . human cognizers." He likens traditional epistemology to "a maze of complexities surrounding the analysis of knowledge and justification from which no route into the promised land seems possible" (167, vii). According to Kvanvig, this defect could be remedied if epistemologists were to turn their attention to matters of intellectual virtue. For this reason, he spends several chapters examining whether and how the concept of intellectual virtue might figure into the landscape of traditional epistemology (see chs. 2–5). But based in part on the sorts of objections raised against Strong Conservative VE above, he eventually concludes that the synchronic, belief-based framework of traditional epistemology leaves no room for the relevant kind of concern with intellectual virtue. This in turn leads him to the conclusion that traditional epistemology should be abandoned in favor of an independent or autonomous virtue epistemology.[24]

While interesting and provocative, Kvanvig's argument does not ultimately warrant the repudiation of traditional epistemology. First, it is doubtful that the meta-epistemological condition he endorses is a genuine *requirement* on any plausible epistemology. Surely one important goal of epistemology is simply to provide an accurate and illuminating account of the basic nature and structure of knowledge, that is, to deepen our reflective *understanding* of this concept. However, if a particular theory of knowledge clearly fares well with respect to this goal, but not with respect to Kvanvig's desideratum, presumably it would be hasty and unfortunate to dismiss this theory as an epistemological failure.[25] Put another way, if a given account of knowledge goes a considerable way toward capturing the essential nature or structure of knowledge, this by itself would seem to make it epistemologically worthwhile. It is not essential that the theory *also* have the kind of practical value that interests Kvanvig.[26] If this is right, then even if traditional theories of knowledge fail to satisfy Kvanvig's meta-epistemological requirement, this does not justify a wholesale rejection of these theories.

A second problem with Kvanvig's argument concerns the premise that traditional epistemology completely fails to serve the relevant practical end, that it fails to "address our cognitive experience" and to give us a better idea of "how to maximize our potential for finding truth and avoiding error" (1992, vii). This claim is also too strong. Why think that an accurate and well-constructed (even if still technical or theoretical) account of knowledge or justification would not be of use to a person striving for the epistemic good? Indeed, surely some of the more plausible and sophisticated accounts of knowledge and justification in the literature have *something* to offer in the way of practical insight or usefulness. This is true of some of the better accounts of epistemic reliability and proper function, of various doxastic and evidential principles, and of the so-called basing relation (to name just a few). These accounts function, not merely to uncover the basic nature and structure of their subject matter, but also to provide some guidance or instruction relative to achieving the epistemic good. This is reminiscent of Aristotle's famous claim that a person with an informed and accurate conception of *eudaimonia* or happiness is, like an archer with a focused view of his target, considerably more likely to achieve this state than a person with an uninformed or inaccurate conception (*NE*, book 1, ch. 2 [1094a]). Likewise, achieving the *epistemic* good can be facilitated by the possession of a robust and illuminating conception of this good, even if the conception in question is abstract or technical. I am not suggesting, of course, that familiarity with traditional theories of knowledge is *necessary* for epistemic success but, rather, that such an understanding can contribute at least to some extent to this goal and, thus, that traditional epistemology is not entirely void of the sort of value that interests Kvanvig.

It appears, then, that Kvanvig's argument for the negative and defining tenet of Radical Autonomous VE is unsuccessful. This does not, of course, guarantee the failure of Radical Autonomous VE as a whole, for in principle, any number of reasons might be given for abandoning traditional epistemology. Moreover, it is worth noting that I concur with Kvanvig on the point that one desideratum of an approach to epistemology is the kind of practical or action-guiding significance he identifies, and that traditional theories would be even more successful or worth taking seriously if they were stronger in this regard. My point, once more, is simply that this is not a *requirement* of an approach to epistemology (and that even if it were, this requirement would be satisfied at least to some extent by several traditional theories). Accordingly, while my critique of Kvanvig's argument does not spell doom for Radical Autonomous VE at large, it does, I take it, illustrate an important point, namely, that Radical Autonomous VE shoulders a daunting argumentative burden. Again, its defenders must demonstrate, not just that traditional questions and projects are merely *part* of what matters from an epistemological standpoint but, rather, that they do not matter at all.[27] Therefore, until such a project has been carried out, and carried out in a way that at least leaves open the possibility of an alternative, virtue-based approach to epistemology, the prospects of Radical Autonomous VE are bound to appear questionable at best.[28]

2.3   Weak Conservative VE

We have examined two of the four main varieties of character-based virtue epistemology and have found that their prospects do not appear to be very good. I turn now to examine the other two varieties. As the names suggest, Weak Conservative VE and Moderate Autonomous VE are considerably less ambitious than their "strong" or "radical" counterparts. It is not too surprising, then, that their prospects turn out to be considerably better. My focus in this section is Weak Conservative VE, which is the view that there are some conceptual connections between intellectual virtue and the subject matter of traditional epistemology, even if not connections that warrant giving the concept of intellectual virtue a central or fundamental role within traditional epistemology. I shall attempt to illustrate what I take to be the promise of Weak Conservative VE by briefly reiterating some recent arguments that, if compelling, amount to a vindication of this approach's central thesis.

As noted earlier, I have argued recently (2006b; 2009) that the concept of intellectual virtue deserves at least some kind of role in connection with two prominent accounts of the nature of knowledge or epistemic justification. The first of these accounts is reliabilism, which says that knowledge is, roughly, true belief produced by reliable or truth-conducive cognitive traits. The traits that reliabilists have in mind tend to be highly mechanistic and impersonal: they include things like vision, hearing, memory, and introspection.[29] I think that reliabilists are right to regard such traits as the basis of epistemic reliability, but only with respect to limited "fields" of propositions (propositions about the appearance of one's immediate surroundings, say) and within limited environments (for example, "normal" environments with good lighting). That is to say that when in the relevant environments, reaching the truth about the relevant subject matters requires little more than properly functioning faculties of the sort just mentioned; it requires little more than good "cognitive mechanics." I think that reliabilists are mistaken, however, to think that such traits are the basis of epistemic reliability with respect to *all* propositional fields and environments, including some that pertain to the most valued and sought after forms or instances of knowledge.[30] Reaching the truth about philosophical, scientific, mathematical, historical, moral, or religious reality, for example, or reaching the truth in circumstances or environments in which doing so requires overcoming significant obstacles, does not (in the typical case) depend primarily on one's having perfect vision, an excellent memory, or the like; rather, it depends, we might say, on one's having a *will* of a certain sort: for example, on one's being *motivated* to reach the truth, or on one's possessing certain intellectual *character* virtues like carefulness and thoroughness in inquiry, attentiveness, determination, open-mindedness, and fair-mindedness. These traits are the vehicle or basis of epistemic reliability with respect to the sorts of propositions and environments just noted.[31] The claim, then, is that to the extent that reliabilists fail to include intellectual character virtues in their repertoire of reliable traits or "knowledge-makers," they are unable to account for the status of much of the knowledge that is most important to us as human beings.

If this is correct, then the concept of intellectual virtue has at least some role to play within a reliabilist account of knowledge. It is not, for reasons already noted, the *focal* point of such an account. It is, however, necessary for understanding one form or dimension of this focal point, that is, one form or dimension of epistemic *reliability*. Finally, it is worth noting that the conceptual connection in question has certain theoretical reverberations. As I explain in much more detail in "Character, Reliability, and Virtue Epistemology" (2006b), the inclusion of intellectual character virtues in reliabilism's repertoire of "knowledge-makers" generates several new and challenging theoretical questions and problems. These questions arise mainly from certain structural differences between intellectual character virtues, on the one hand, and the more mechanistic, faculty virtues, on the other. And these are questions with which any plausible reliabilist account of knowledge must reckon.

Evidentialism offers an account of epistemic justification that is typically characterized as a competitor of a reliabilism.[32] According to evidentialism, a person is justified in believing a given claim just in case (roughly) her evidence supports this claim.[33] This view is vulnerable to criticism based on cases in which a person's belief is supported by her evidence but only because the person has failed to inquire with respect to the relevant subject matter, has inquired in a shoddy and superficial way, or is presently ignoring or suppressing potential defeaters to her belief (Baehr 2009). Imagine, for instance, a person whose evidence supports her belief that long-term exposure to secondhand smoke has no negative consequences for her health, but only (due, say, to acute anxiety about health-related matters) because she has shown extreme tunnel vision, denial, and self-deception in her thinking and inquiry about this issue. While this person's belief may satisfy the evidentialist's condition for justification, her belief intuitively is unjustified.

Because the explanation for this person's lack of justification apparently lies with her manifestation of various intellectual *vices* (inattentiveness, carelessness and hastiness in inquiry, an unwillingness to consider counterevidence, etc.), one solution for the evidentialist would be to incorporate a condition according to which justification supervenes on a belief that fits a person's evidence only if this person has exercised certain intellectual *virtues* in the formation or maintenance of this belief. But for reasons noted earlier in connection with Zagzebski's defense of Strong Conservative VE, making virtuous agency a *necessary* condition or precondition for justification would be a mistake. For again, there are cases of "passive knowledge," in which the agent (qua agent) is uninvolved with the formation of her belief. A more plausible solution is for the evidentialist to adopt a virtue-based *constraint* or *proviso*: one that applies or is binding only with respect to the sorts of cases in question. Accordingly, evidentialists might hold that a person is justified in believing a given claim just in case this claim is supported by her evidence—*provided* that, if the person's agency makes a salient contribution to her evidence concerning the belief in question, she functions in a manner consistent with intellectual virtue (again, see Baehr Forthcoming for more on this point). If this argument is compelling, it represents a second way in which the concept of intellectual virtue bears upon a traditional account of knowledge without occupying center stage in or forming the conceptual basis of the account.

This brief reiteration of the relevant arguments is intended to illustrate what the positive substance of Weak Conservative VE might amount to. The arguments demonstrate how the concept of intellectual virtue might figure into the landscape of traditional epistemology in a certain background, secondary, or peripheral way. Moreover, I take it that the arguments have sufficient prima facie plausibility to warrant some optimism about the prospects of Weak Conservative VE, or at least to justify taking seriously the *possibility* of such an approach. And of course there is little reason to think that the connections identified above are the *only* potential points of contact between the concept of intellectual virtue and the positions and debates central to traditional epistemology.[34] We may conclude that while Strong Conservative VE is unpromising, the prospects of Weak Conservative VE are considerably better.

2.4   Moderate Autonomous VE

I noted earlier that the *positive* challenge for Radical Autonomous VE is identical to the *central* challenge for Moderate Autonomous VE. Again, defenders of both views advocate a virtue-based approach to epistemology that is largely independent of traditional epistemology. But the question naturally arises: if the focus of such an approach is *not* the nature, sources, and limits of knowledge, then what exactly is it? The reply that the focus is, say, "the intellectual virtues and their role in the cognitive life considered in their own right," while perhaps indicative of a viable and interesting research program, is not sufficient in this context, for it says next to nothing about the positive theoretical *substance* of the approach: nothing about the specific issues, questions, problems, puzzles, etc., responses to which might constitute its theoretical basis. Indeed it leaves open the possibility that there are *not* any (or many) such issues or questions: that when reflection on the intellectual virtues is divorced from traditional considerations, these traits are of little or no philosophical or epistemological significance. Defenders of either version of autonomous virtue epistemology must, then, be explicit about the positive theoretical focus of the virtue-based approach they endorse. I shall refer to this as the "theoretical challenge."

This challenge may not seem to pose a very serious threat to the viability of an autonomous virtue epistemology. But when one looks at some of the seminal attempts to defend a version of Moderate Autonomous VE, this appearance dissipates. While clearly embracing its defining tenets, several principal defenders of Moderate Autonomous VE either fail to be very specific about the positive theoretical focus of their proposed approaches or go about specifying issues or questions that (for one reason or another) fail to have much epistemological traction.[35] For instance, much of Code's *Epistemic Responsibility* (1987) is devoted to discussions that have no immediate bearing on matters of intellectual virtue or whose bearing is tenuous enough that it is unclear how the relevant issues and questions could form the basis of a virtue-based alternative to traditional epistemology. This applies to her lengthy (and often interesting) discussions of metaphysical realism (1987, ch. 6), literature as a source of knowledge about cognitive well-being (chs. 2 and 8), doxastic voluntarism (ch. 4), and similarities between epistemic and moral evaluation (ch. 3). Moreover, when Code does squarely address issues like the basic nature and structure of intellectual virtues, her discussion is often surprisingly thin. Consider the following passage, which is not atypical: "How, then, are we to *delineate more precisely the nature of intellectually virtuous character?* . . . Intellectually virtuous persons value knowing and understanding how things really are. They resist the temptation to live with partial explanations where fuller ones are attainable; they resist the temptation to live in fantasy or in a world of dream or illusion, considering it better to know, despite the tempting comfort and complacency a life of fantasy or illusion (or one well tinged with fantasy or illusion) can offer" (58–59; my italics; for similar passages, see 61–66, 131–44, and 172–77). Characterizations like this, while perhaps accurate as far as they go, can lead even the open-minded reader to wonder whether there is really much for epistemologists to talk about in connection with intellectual virtue. They suggest that an understanding of intellectual virtue may be more or less a matter of common sense.[36]

A related point can be made in connection with some of Hookway's work discussed above. While Hookway is considerably more reflective about the theoretical requirements of a genuine, virtue-based alternative to traditional epistemology,[37] his discussions of such an alternative at times exhibit some similar limitations. We saw above that central to Hookway's argument for a version of Moderate Autonomous VE is the idea that the notion of intellectual virtue should figure prominently in the practice of "epistemic evaluation." The reason, again, is that when making such evaluations, our concern is not merely *beliefs*, but also cognitive *deliberations* and *inquiries*; and in these domains, success or failure often turns on whether the person in question possesses various excellences of intellectual character. Thus, Hookway concludes, if we are to offer reasonably "thick" and accurate assessments of our cognitive deliberations and inquiries, we shall have to appeal to the concept of intellectual virtue.

I do not wish to dispute the validity of Hookway's argument. Rather, my concern is that it is unclear what bearing it is supposed to have on the enterprise of *epistemology*, virtue epistemology or otherwise. Cognitive evaluation is primarily a *practical* affair: it is engaged in by ordinary cognitive agents in ordinary cognitive situations. It is not principally an activity undertaken by the epistemologist *qua* epistemologist. To be sure, epistemologists sometimes offer "epistemic evaluations" in the sense that they construct theories of knowledge and justification that can then be applied in the assessment of individual beliefs. But Hookway does not endorse a virtue-based analysis of justification or any other familiar epistemic concept. Instead, his point is apparently that an accurate and illuminating assessment of various cognitive phenomena will necessarily appeal to the language and concepts of intellectual virtue. But how is this insight supposed to form the basis of anything like an alternative, virtue-based epistemological research program? What would the governing issues, questions, problems, etc., be on such an approach? Put another way, what *work* is there for epistemologists to do in light of Hookway's argument?[38]

My claim is *not* that the discussions of Code, Hookway, or others are entirely bereft of any hints or suggestions concerning the possible theoretical or philosophical substance of a virtue-based alternative to traditional epistemology. (Indeed, as I explain below, I think the discussions of both Code and Hookway at times point in some promising directions.) It is rather that the discussions in question are not sufficiently explicit or convincing on this score and that, consequently, their proposed "alternatives" to traditional epistemology come off looking questionable.[39]

While the "theoretical challenge" is genuine, it is not insurmountable. Indeed, there are good reasons to think that it can be overcome. Some of these reasons are evident in other contributions to the virtue epistemology literature. Others pertain to issues and questions that to date have received scant if any treatment. In the remainder of this section, I shall briefly enumerate several theoretical issues or projects that, when taken together, warrant at least some optimism about the possibility of a relatively autonomous, virtue-based epistemological research program.[40] Again, the challenge is to identify philosophical issues and questions surrounding the intellectual virtues that might form the basis of a virtue-based epistemological research program that is independent of a more traditional program: issues and questions that might occupy proponents of Moderate Autonomous VE.

Several challenging and broadly epistemological questions arise with reflection on the precise *nature* of an intellectual virtue. Here the central question is what *makes* the relevant character traits intellectual virtues. This question has been answered in several ways, all of which have at least some plausibility, but which ultimately appear to be incompatible. Julia Driver (2000, 2003) argues that a trait is an intellectual virtue just in case it is epistemically reliable or truth-conducive. It seems reasonable to think that many of the traits we regard as intellectual virtues (for example, intellectual carefulness, thoroughness, attentiveness, fairness, etc.) are reliable in this sense; and since it also seems plausible to regard any reliable or truth-conducive trait as an "intellectual virtue" in some sense, Driver's proposal has at least some initial promise. But this is not the only account of intellectual virtue available. Montmarquet (1993, 2000), for example, maintains that the traits in question are intellectual virtues on account of certain of their internal or psychological features considered *in their own right*. This includes a *desire* for truth or knowledge, which Montmarquet and others regard as *intrinsically* valuable.[41] An account of this sort has the advantage of being able to explain the apparent personal worth or value associated with the traits in question, that is, the fact that these traits seem to make their possessor a good or better *person*. This feature of intellectual virtues is difficult to account for on a model which (like Driver's) says that intellectual virtues (as such) are strictly *instrumentally* valuable. A third account weds the two just noted. Zagzebski argues that a trait is an intellectual virtue just in case it is reliable *and* involves an intrinsically valuable motive (1996, 168–83).[42] Despite its conciliatory tone, this mixed or hybrid account has the (problematic) appearance of trying to bring together two very different sorts of value (one instrumental, the other intrinsic; one impersonal, the other personal) under a single, univocal concept of intellectual virtue. The problem lies not with the possibility that a single trait might *be* both instrumentally and intrinsically valuable but, rather, with the idea that such a trait might be an intellectual *virtue* in a single and univocal sense: that it might satisfy the conditions of just one, rather than two separate, concepts of intellectual virtue.[43] Mixed accounts also run the risk of inheriting any defects internal to either of the accounts they are attempting to integrate. It appears, then, that the answer to the question of what ultimately *makes* the relevant character traits intellectual virtues is far from obvious.

A related set of issues focuses directly on the (alleged) *reliability* of the intellectual virtues. We just noted that many of the traits commonly regarded as intellectual virtues seem to be reliable. But this is not so obvious with respect to other putative virtues: for instance, intellectual integrity, autonomy, and originality. It is much less clear whether these traits tend in a systematic way to help their possessor reach the truth and avoid error. Moreover, virtually none of the traits commonly regarded as intellectual virtues is reliable when possessed in *isolation*. An intellectually careful but dogmatic and closed-minded person, for instance, is unlikely to acquire a preponderance of true beliefs. This suggests that the intellectual virtues are "unified" in a reasonably strong sense, which in turn raises questions about how, if at all, they are to be *individuated*. For example, if reliability is a defining feature of an intellectual virtue, but none of the relevant traits taken by itself is reliable, in what sense can these traits really be considered intellectual virtues? This problem is magnified by the fact that even when taken as a whole, the traits in question are reliable only if combined with properly functioning cognitive *faculties* (for example, good eyesight, a good memory, etc.). A final problem arises from certain counterfactual considerations. Montmarquet (1993) and others (Swank 2000; Dancy 2000; Baehr 2007) envision a person who bears all the internal marks of intellectual virtue, and who, from her own internal (and reasonable) perspective, is extremely cognitively successful. Owing to the work of a Cartesian demon, however, this person is in fact extremely *unreliable*. According to the authors in question, such a person should still be regarded as intellectually virtuous. If they are correct, this presents a further obstacle to the initially attractive view that reliability is a defining feature of an intellectual virtue. Thus the sense (if any) in which intellectual virtues are reliable, and the implications this has for the individuation of intellectual virtues and related matters, is also something that merits further thought and reflection from "autonomous" virtue epistemologists.

Other relevant issues and questions arise with reflection on the internal *structure* of an intellectual virtue. According to Zagzebski, the fundamental psychological requirement of any intellectual virtue is a *motivation* for truth and related cognitive goods (1996, 166–68). While something like this requirement is plausible, intellectual virtues seem essentially to have a certain *cognitive* or *doxastic* component as well.[44] This is suggested by some of the work of virtue ethicists on the moral virtues. John McDowell (1979), for instance, characterizes moral virtue as fundamentally involving a kind of moral *perception*. And Julia Annas (2005) gives the notion of practical *reason* a central place in her account of moral virtue. These requirements are arguably complementary and plausible. And it is reasonable to think that intellectual virtues might exhibit an analogous internal structure. This underscores several important questions concerning the structure of an intellectual virtue, none of which has been very widely discussed by virtue epistemologists or other philosophers. For instance, what is the full *range* of psychological states essential to intellectual virtue? What is the precise nature of these states? And how exactly are these states related to each other?[45]

Several related questions concern the *ends* or *goals* proper to intellectual virtue. First, what ultimately motivates an intellectually virtuous person? According to one fairly standard view (Montmarquet 1993), the proper aim or end of all intellectual virtues is *truth*. But Zagzebski (2001) and Wayne Riggs (2003) have recently argued to the contrary that the fundamental aims of intellectual virtue extend beyond truth and knowledge, and include such "higher end" cognitive values as understanding and insight. It is also important to consider *whose* cognitive success or well-being might be the intentional object of an intellectual virtue. It is easy to get the impression from the literature that an intellectually virtuous person is always *egoistically* motivated, for the intellectual virtues are usually characterized in relation to the context of personal *inquiry*, where the goal is typically the inquirer's *own* acquisition of true beliefs. But surely the intellectual virtues are applicable to other contexts as well. They are relevant, for instance, to the domains of teaching, reporting, and public debate. In these areas, the goal of an intellectually virtuous person is likely to be *others'* acquisition of various cognitive goods.[46] Very little work has been done to explore these alternative applications of intellectual virtue or what they indicate about the intrinsic aims or goals of intellectual virtue.[47]

Some of the recent work of Robert Roberts and Jay Wood suggests a considerably different type of focus and methodology that might profitably be pursued by a proponent of autonomous virtue epistemology. Instead of focusing on the general concept of intellectual virtue, Roberts and Wood give their attention primarily to the nature and structure of *individual* virtues.[48] As noted above, they devote entire chapters of their recent book *Intellectual Virtues: An Essay in Regulative Epistemology* (2007) to analyses of virtues like intellectual firmness, courage and caution, autonomy, generosity, and humility.[49] And again, their aim in these chapters is not to identify the necessary and sufficient conditions for the relevant traits but, rather, to offer a "conceptual map" of the characterological dimension of cognitive flourishing (2007, 23–30). The result is several rich, well-illustrated, and illuminating philosophical profiles of individual intellectual virtues.

The work of Roberts and Wood illustrates a general, recognizably Aristotelian methodology that can be applied to virtually any intellectual virtue with worthwhile philosophical results. For any virtue *V*, the following sorts of questions might be addressed: What are the basic actions, feelings, attitudes, motives, judgments, etc., characteristic of *V*? What is it to perform these actions, have these feelings, etc., in the right way, at the right time, toward the right person, and so forth? How does *V* differ from closely related intellectual virtues? (For example, in the case of open-mindedness, how is this virtue distinct from, say, intellectual empathy or fairness?) Which vices, if any, correspond to *V*? And how exactly are they related to *V*? Which domains of the intellectual life (for instance, inquiry, teaching, or public debate) does *V* bear on most directly? Which epistemic goods does it deliver? And how does it do so? This method is philosophically fruitful, both for the light it can shed on the nature and structure of individual virtues, but also because it can help shore up and illustrate some of the more general or fundamental philosophical questions surrounding intellectual virtue (for instance, whether there is a univocal concept of intellectual virtue that "covers" all putative instances of intellectual virtue[50]).

A final general area of potential inquiry begins with the plausible assumption that there are fixed and generic dimensions of the cognitive life that make certain fairly systematic and traceable demands on an agent's intellectual character. These include dimensions associated with, say, mastering challenging subject matter, inquiring in the face of threats to one's well-being, evaluating testimony, collaborating with others in intellectual ventures, engaging an intellectual opponent or adversary, teaching a difficult subject matter, or motivating an audience to care about a particular idea or body of knowledge. It is plausible to think that success or failure in these and related domains depends in substantial and systematic ways on the extent to which one exercises one or more intellectual virtues (to follow through with a threatening but important inquiry, one needs intellectual courage and perseverance; to carry out a joint intellectual venture, one needs to be intellectually open, attentive, and adaptable; etc.). This suggests an additional method for investigating the intellectual virtues from a broadly epistemological standpoint. For a given intellectual domain *D*, we might ask: What is the general structure of *D*? What sorts of character-relevant demands does success in *D* typically involve? Which virtues are relevant to meeting these demands? How are they relevant? How do they contribute to success in *D*?[51]

A fine example of this sort of inquiry is some recent work by Miranda Fricker. In a recent essay (2003), and in an even more recent book (2007), Fricker examines the role of intellectual character in the evaluation of testimony. She is concerned in particular with certain sorts of *injustices* that tend to occur in this domain (for example, where a person's word or opinion is not taken seriously because of her gender, race, or accent). Fricker makes clear that the injustices in question admit of a definite, discernable structure, and argues convincingly that the proper corrective is a certain "testimonial sensibility" partly constituted by an intellectual virtue she labels "reflexive critical openness" (2003, 8–11, 17–19). Fricker's work in this area reveals some of the subtle, complex, but ultimately systematic and traceable ways in which the intellectual virtues are related to cognitive success. As such, it is a model of the sort of inquiry that a defender of an autonomous virtue epistemology might profitably undertake.[52]

This canvassing of various issues and questions pertaining to intellectual virtue suggests five broad themes or categories that might constitute the theoretical focus of a plausible version of Moderate Autonomous VE: (1) The fundamental *nature* of an intellectual virtue (What exactly *makes* the traits in question intellectual virtues? Is there just a single "right answer" to this question?); (2) The fundamental *structure* of an intellectual virtue (Which psychological states are essential to intellectual virtue? How are they related to each other? What is the range of potential aims or goals associated with intellectual virtue?); (3) Relations *among* intellectual virtues (On what sorts of configurations of virtues does reliability supervene? To what extent are the intellectual virtues "unified"? How can they be individuated? Are there any "master" or "executive" intellectual virtues?); (4) The relation of intellectual virtues to *other* dimensions or elements of the intellectual life or character (Which virtues pertain to which dimensions of the cognitive life? How do they do so? What *general* or *systematic* connections between various virtues or groups of virtues, on the one hand, and various cognitive domains, on the other, can be identified? How are intellectual virtues related to intellectual *vices*? Do intellectual virtues represent a "mean" between a corresponding vice of deficiency and vice of excess?); and (5) The internal structure and application of *individual* intellectual virtues (How are we to understand what appear to be structurally unique virtues like intellectual integrity or wisdom? Or, for any virtue, what are the essential psychological ingredients of that virtue? And what is it to manifest or instantiate these ingredients in the right way, at the right time, toward the right person, etc.?).

The aim of identifying these various avenues of inquiry has been to offer support for the idea that there are indeed issues and questions for virtue epistemologists to talk about in connection with the intellectual virtues, even after they give up trying to "solve" one or more problems within traditional epistemology. Cursory as it has been, I take it that the discussion warrants at least some optimism—hopefully even some *enthusiasm*—about the prospects of Moderate Autonomous VE. Because of its direct or immediate focus on the matters of intellectual character, such an approach might properly be dubbed "character epistemology."[53]

3   Conclusion

I have delineated four main varieties of character-based virtue epistemology and have found that two of the four face formidable challenges: Strong Conservative VE on account of its commitment to the idea that something like an exercise of intellectual virtue is an essential feature of knowledge; and Radical Autonomous VE on account of its contention that traditional epistemology should be *repudiated* in favor of an autonomous, virtue-based approach. A more promising alternative to the former, we have found, is Weak Conservative VE, which, instead of trying to give the concept of intellectual virtue a "central and fundamental" role in connection with traditional epistemology, sees this concept as occupying a mere "secondary" or "peripheral" role in this context. And a more promising alternative to Radical Autonomous VE is Moderate Autonomous VE, according to which an independent concern with intellectual virtues and their role in the intellectual life offers a suitable *complement* to traditional epistemology. While the approaches of Weak Conservative VE and Moderate Autonomous VE are still largely undeveloped, they seem likely to represent the way of the future within character-based virtue epistemology.[54]

Notes

1. The last systematic account of the literature in virtue epistemology, published more than a decade ago, was Guy Axtell's "Recent Work in Virtue Epistemology" (1997).

2. The terms "virtue responsibilist" and "virtue reliabilist" originate, respectively, with Code 1987 and Axtell 1997. Some examples of virtue reliabilism are Greco 2000 and Sosa 1991 and 2007.

3. See, for example, Blackburn 2001, in which he characterizes a faculty-based virtue epistemology as little more than a revamped reliabilism.

4. For an overview and representative sample of traditional epistemology see Bon-Jour 2002. Some other topics or debates that might reasonably be included under the "traditional" rubric include contextualism and infinitism. Though these issues have come to the fore in epistemology more recently than the issues just listed, they (as well as others) are still aimed at addressing or "solving" the traditional epistemological questions. At any rate, as will become clear shortly, it is not important for drawing the relevant fourfold distinction that the line between traditional and non-traditional epistemology be drawn too sharply.

5. See, for example, Zagzebski 1996, 279–81, 291–95, 329–34. Guy Axtell (2008) and Abrol Fairweather (2001) are also supportive of giving the concept of intellectual character virtue a significant role in an account of knowledge. Axtell, however, does not *define* the notion of intellectual virtue as a certain type of *character* trait; instead he endorses a "thinner" conception of intellectual virtue that incorporates both character virtues *and* faculty virtues.

6. The two sorts of approaches are not strictly mutually exclusive, since one might, like Zagzebski (1996) apparently does, think that there are major conceptual connections between intellectual virtue and traditional epistemology *and* that matters of intellectual virtue are epistemologically interesting in their own right.

7. Another way to put the point is that the arguments in question do not assert or presuppose that an exercise of intellectual virtue is a *defining* feature of knowledge. I shall have more to say about this in my assessment of Zagzebski's account of knowledge below.

8. I use the terms "moderate" and "radical," rather than "weak" and "strong," both because they provide a more accurate description of the relevant views and to mark

the fact, noted above and elaborated on below, that the basis of the distinction between the two types of autonomous virtue epistemology is significantly different than that between the two types of conservative virtue epistemology.

9. While ultimately stopping short of calling for a total repudiation of traditional epistemology, Code (1987), Roberts and Wood (2007), and Hookway (2003) also, and for reasons similar to Kvanvig's, flirt with Radical VE.

10. At times, Kvanvig's position regarding the status of traditional epistemology is somewhat less clear (see, for instance, 1992, 171). However, at several other points (for instance, 150, 158, 168, 170, and 187), he seems clearly to be calling for the rejection of traditional epistemology. At any rate, the actual content of his argument (discussed below) is such that, if valid, it apparently eliminates any motivation for traditional epistemology.

11. As this suggests, other ways of carving up the relevant terrain may be possible (including ways that might somehow "in principle" seem to make more sense). But again, my concern is to shed some light on the field of virtue epistemology *in its present stage of development*.

12. Or of epistemic *justification*, but since justification is commonly thought to be a (and indeed the *relevant*) ingredient of knowledge, I shall limit my attention here to whether an exercise of intellectual virtue is essential to knowledge.

13. This might be put by saying that traditional debates are about the *concept* of knowledge and thus about its essential or defining features. But as some of the recent work of Bob Roberts and Jay Wood (2007, chs. 1–2) shows, it is possible to clarify or shed light on the concept of knowledge without limiting one's attention to (or even focusing primarily on) its essential features.

14. An apparent counterexample to this may be Hookway 2003, in which Hookway attempts to show that the concept of intellectual virtue is relevant to the problem of skepticism but *without* claiming that this concept merits a place in an analysis of knowledge. While I cannot develop the point here, I will simply note that the skeptical problem that concerns Hookway is *not* the traditional one: by his own admission, Hookway is not, for instance, trying to show that it is possible for us to have non-question-begging reasons for some of our beliefs about the external world. Thus, despite its value in other respects, Hookway's discussion is unlikely to be of much interest to a traditional skeptic.

15. And indeed, for some of the traditional questions (for example, those concerning the fundamental *sources* of knowledge), it is not at all clear how the concept of an intellectual virtue could form the basis of an answer even if knowledge *could* plausibly be defined in terms of intellectual virtue.

16. This is essentially what is involved with the performance of "acts of intellectual virtue." See Zagzebski 1996, 279, for a development of this point.

17. Of course on a broader conception of intellectual virtue—for example, one that includes intellectual or cognitive *faculties*—these cases might be easily accounted for. But our concern is with the intellectual *character* virtues, that is, with intellectual virtues conceived as excellences of personal character (rather than as cognitive faculties).

18. See especially Zagzebski 1996, 277–83. It is not easy to tell, however, just what Zagzebski thinks *makes* something an instance of low-grade knowledge (for example, whether this is a function of the content of the relevant propositions, the processes by which the beliefs in question are formed, or something else). But since it is easy enough to agree on paradigm cases, we need not settle this issue here.

19. Two other replies suggested by her discussion are, very briefly, as follows. First, Zagzebski sometimes (1996, 262f) seems tempted to bite the bullet and deny that the cases in question amount to genuine knowledge. This is extremely problematic, however, given that the cases in question have seemed to epistemologists for centuries to be among the *clearest* and *least controversial* cases of knowledge. (Note that this does *not* amount to saying that they are *paradigm* cases of knowledge [cf. 69 and 278], for the notion of a "paradigm" case in this context has a normative dimension that the notion of a "clear" or "uncontroversial" case does not; the former, but not the latter, presumably represents the upper normative boundary of human cognition.) Second, Zagzebski's discussion sometimes (279–80) suggests that a true belief counts as knowledge just in case it was formed in a way that an intellectually virtuous person might form it under similar conditions. The implication is that because such persons presumably form beliefs of the relevant sort *without* manifesting any virtuous actions or motives, the cases in question turn out to count as knowledge on her view. Aside from the fact that this represents a major departure from her original position (according to which virtuous motives and actions *are* a requirement for knowledge), this alternative position remains problematic. When intellectually virtuous persons form beliefs in the relevant, mechanistic way, they do not do so *qua* virtuous persons (again, they do not manifest any virtuous motives or actions). The result is that nothing pertaining to the notion of intellectual virtue explains why the beliefs in question count as knowledge, which in turn reveals that the modified position is not genuinely *virtue*-based.

20. This condition is necessary, among other reasons, for dealing adequately with the Gettier problem. See Zagzebski 1996, 283–98, Greco 2003, and Sosa 2007. On a related note, it is in fact unclear, in the cases in question, whether the relevant low-level motives or actions stand in the required causal relation even to the relevant *beliefs*. It is one thing for the motives and actions to *present*; it is another for them (vs. the person's cognitive machinery, say) to be the *source* or *cause* of the belief (much less of the *truth* of this belief).

21. In response, it might be claimed that what Zagzebski is really trying to offer is something like an analysis of "higher grade" or "reflective" knowledge, which ex-

cludes simple perceptual knowledge and the like. But this response does not appear capable of rescuing Strong Conservative VE. The main reason is that there does not appear to be a univocal, pretheoretical concept of "higher grade" or "reflective" knowledge that is likely to admit of a virtue-based analysis. The notion of "reflective knowledge" does have some currency in the epistemological literature (and, I take it, some traction in common sense). See, for instance, Sosa 1991. However, on standard ways of thinking about what, in general, such knowledge amounts to, it appears possible to acquire reflective knowledge absent any intellectually virtuous motives and actions (or at least absent these things playing the required causal role vis-à-vis the *truth* of the known belief). Suppose that reflective knowledge requires having a "reflective perspective" on the known belief and that this amounts to something like having good evidence or reasons in support of this belief. (While this is not precisely Sosa's account, I think it is an accurate description of the general sort of knowledge of which Sosa offers a more precise and slightly differently focused analysis.) It seems quite possible that one might, say, follow a simple chain of reasoning in support of a certain belief and thus have good evidence for this belief and yet not be manifesting any excellences of intellectual *character*. It appears, then, that Zagzebski's conditions do not map onto any univocal and pretheoretical concept of "higher grade" or "reflective" knowledge, and thus they cannot vindicate Strong Conservative VE on this account.

22. It might be wondered whether beliefs like this are in fact the product of an entrenched perceptual *habit* that might at some level involve virtuous motives or actions. This may very well be the case for certain *spontaneous* perceptual beliefs. An expert birdwatcher, for instance, might *automatically* and *reflexively* form a belief about the identity of a passing bird that we would be prepared to count as knowledge; and this process or event might involve virtuous agency at some level—either in the process itself (spontaneous or automatic as it is) or in the initial formation of the corresponding perceptual habit. But this sort of case is very different from the "lights out" case just considered. While in cases like that of the birdwatcher just noted, there is no temptation to characterize the relevant perceptual process or event (the formation of the birdwatcher's belief) as *brute*, this *is* a plausible characterization of the sort of cognitive process or processes involved with the "lights out" and other related cases. This suggests that while both types of belief are formed spontaneously, whatever type of perceptual habit may be involved with the kind of case at issue does *not* involve any virtuous motives or actions.

23. As indicated earlier, several authors flirt with Radical Autonomous VE but ultimately stop short of endorsing it, opting instead for a version of Weak Autonomous VE. This includes Roberts and Wood (2007) and Hookway (2003).

24. For a sketch of this alternative approach, see Kvanvig 1992, 170–88.

25. I am assuming, uncontroversially I hope, that this represents a genuine possibility: that is, it is possible for a theory of knowledge to fare well relative to the goal of

facilitating understanding without faring well relative to the practical standard that interests Kvanvig.

26. As I explain below, I am not denying that the theory in question would be even *better* if it were to satisfy Kvanvig's condition. That is, I am not denying that this condition represents a genuine theoretical *desideratum* but, rather, that it is a theoretical *requirement*.

27. This problem is exacerbated by the fact that it takes very little in the way of philosophical or theoretical commitment to motivate a considerable range of traditional epistemological issues and questions. While I cannot develop the point in any detail here, the basic idea is that a concern with true belief, taken together with the fact that we lack immediate or unproblematic access to whether our beliefs are in fact true, motivates a further concern with the notion of good *evidence* or good epistemic *reasons* (the latter being our best indication of the truth or probable truth of our beliefs). Reflection on the notion of good epistemic reasons, however, gives rise to a number of difficult, and characteristically *traditional*, epistemological questions: What is the underlying or logical structure of such reasons? Are any of our beliefs (including those about the external world) really supported by such reasons? What are the fundamental *sources* of such reasons? Etc. This again is meant to underscore the fact that it takes relatively little to motivate a substantial segment of traditional epistemology, which in turn underscores the formidable character of the central challenge facing Radical Autonomous VE (for again, this approach insists that traditional epistemology is unmotivated and should be abandoned).

28. It should also be kept in mind that the negative challenge in question is only half the battle for Radical Autonomous VE. It also faces a certain positive challenge, which I get to below.

29. See, for instance, "Epistemic Folkways and Scientific Epistemology" in Goldman 1992 or Sosa 1991.

30. That reliabilists *do* suggest as much seems clear both from what they say and from what they fail to say about the relevant character virtues. See Baehr 2006b for a development of this point.

31. This does not mean that well-functioning cognitive faculties are irrelevant; indeed, as I argue in 2006b, intellectual character virtues typically manifest themselves in the operation of cognitive faculties. The point is rather that in the cases in question, an agent's success at reaching the truth is to be explained in terms of a manifestation of her intellectual virtues (where this may very well involve the operation of certain faculties) rather than the brute or untutored operation of the faculties themselves. Put another way, the *seat* of the agent's reliability is her intellectual character virtues.

32. The two need not exclude each other, since one might identify forming/maintaining beliefs in accordance with the available evidence as the relevant form

of reliability. For a representative sample of evidentialism, see Conee and Feldman 2004.

33. I am characterizing evidentialism as a thesis about justification rather than knowledge. But with the addition of a truth (and perhaps an anti-Gettier) condition, it can easily be adapted to a thesis about knowledge.

34. See, for example, John Turri's "Believing for a Reason." Guy Axtell's recent account of knowledge (2008) also strikes me as rightly regarded as a contribution to Weak Conservative VE. Axtell defends a virtue-based account of knowledge, but he does not *define* the notion of an intellectual virtue as a *character trait*. Nonetheless, intellectual character virtues, along with faculty virtues, *do* count as intellectual virtues and thus can contribute to knowledge on his view. His account is not a version of Strong Conservative VE, however, because he does not give the concept of an intellectual character virtue as such the central or fundamental role in the account.

35. As I explain in more detail below, this lack of traction can be due to any number of factors: the questions or issues may be more or less a matter of common sense; they may be amenable strictly or primarily to empirical inquiry; or they may be the proper subject matter of some other philosophical discipline like ethics. Where any of these possibilities obtains, the relevant issues and questions will fail to support an alternative, virtue-based approach to *epistemology*, for the content of epistemology exceeds that of common sense, is not (unlike cognitive science, say) exclusively or primarily empirical, and is distinct from (even if closely related to) that of ethics.

36. For a related worry concerning whether Code successfully outlines a genuine epistemological *alternative*, see BonJour 1990.

37. See especially Hookway 2003.

38. An analogous point can be made about Hookway's discussion (2001) of the connection between intellectual virtue and epistemic *akrasia* noted earlier. I think Hookway is entirely correct to suggest that the possession of various intellectual character virtues is the proper antidote to the relevant kind of weakness of the will. What he fails to make sufficiently clear, however, is what bearing this should have on the practice of *epistemology*. He does not make clear enough why the proper response to his argument (by an epistemologist or anyone else) should not be simple *concession* or *agreement*, with little further discussion or inquiry or debate to be had on the matter.

39. Two other discussions and a possible diagnosis are worth noting. First, I think Kvanvig (1992), while sensitive to the need to outline a positive theoretical research program, fails to make good on the claim that the program in question will be genuinely or deeply *virtue*-based. See, for instance, the sorts of questions he says are central to his proposed alternative on p. 176. For several of these questions, it is difficult to see why an answer would involve any appeal to intellectual virtue. Second,

Montmarquet (1993) defends a virtue-based account of doxastic justification that he claims is essential for an adequate understanding of *moral* responsibility. Montmarquet himself acknowledges that the concept of justification that interests him is different from the concept that interests epistemologists. Accordingly, his analysis comes off looking more like the proper subject matter of *ethics* than of epistemology. A possible *diagnosis* of the failure of at least some autonomously minded virtue epistemologists to overcome the "theoretical challenge" (including Code and Hookway) is that they assume, hastily, that because the traits in question are of *practical* epistemic significance, they must also be of *epistemological* significance. See, for instance, Hookway 2001, 200, and Code 1987, 26–27. But this, it seems to me, is an invalid inference. Epistemology is a *philosophical* or *theoretical* discipline. It trades in various challenging questions, problems, puzzles, etc., that arise with philosophical reflection on the cognitive life. However, the mere fact that something is helpful for reaching the truth does not by itself show that this thing will be amenable to distinctively philosophical inquiry. I think a similar error is made in some of the virtue ethics literature. See Louden 1997 for a similar point.

40. Some of these issues and questions are discussed in Baehr 2006a.

41. Dancy 2000 suggests a similar account. Kvanvig 1992, ch. 6, and Zagzebski 1996 also contain related discussions.

42. See Lahroodi 2006 for a partial defense of mixed and "externalist" or consequentialist accounts of intellectual virtue.

43. Thus it may be that Driver and Montmarquet are offering analyses of different, but equally legitimate, concepts of intellectual virtue and that Zagzebski is attempting to run these concepts together into a single analysis.

44. There are, however, resources in the virtue ethics literature that might be used to mount an argument against this claim. See, for instance, Arpaly 2002 and Driver 2001. This disagreement reinforces the point that there are genuine philosophical questions or challenges associated with trying to get a handle on the internal structure of an intellectual virtue.

45. A further possibility worth considering is that the concept of intellectual virtue is not fully determinate or univocal to begin with, in which case there may not be any general or univocal "right answers" to these questions. Both Battaly 2001 and Roberts and Wood 2007 suggest something like this position.

46. A related question is whether intellectual virtues must be possessed by individuals, or whether they can also be possessed by social groups. For a discussion of this and issues related to the social dimension of intellectual virtue, see Lahroodi 2007b.

47. One exception is Roberts and Wood 2003 and 2007. These authors characterize the intellectual virtues as bearing on the acquisition, maintenance, transmission, and application of knowledge. And they discuss some of the nonegoistic applica-

tions of intellectual virtue in rich detail. See, for example, their discussion of intellectual generosity (2007, ch. 11). Jason Kawall (2002) also argues convincingly that intellectual virtues are not strictly egoistic.

48. Another good example of this general approach is Lahroodi and Schmitt 2008, in which the authors offer an account of the virtue of curiosity.

49. These authors refrain from drawing a sharp distinction between intellectual and moral virtues, but their concern here is with the application of the traits in question to the *intellectual* life.

50. See Roberts and Wood 2007 for a defense of the claim that there is no such concept.

51. Such a project would overcome the "theoretical challenge" discussed above given that the connections in question are indeed *broad* and *systematic* and that they are not simply a matter of *common sense*. I take it that both of these assumptions are plausible. If developed in more detail, some of what Hookway or Code say in support of a virtue-based approach to epistemology (see Hookway 2001 and 2003 and Code 1987) might be viewed as motivating inquiries of this sort.

52. Another fine example is Battaly 2006, in which Heather Battaly examines various systematic ways in which intellectual virtues bear on and can be cultivated in the context of classroom instruction.

53. See Baehr 2006a. A final point is that while such an approach would be closely aligned with virtue ethics, it would be a mistake to regard this approach as a version of ethics *rather than* epistemology, while the relevant issues and questions are not about the nature, sources, and limits of knowledge per se, they are concerned with personal character as it relates, both intentionally and causally, to distinctively epistemic ends like knowledge, truth, rationality, and understanding. This by itself appears sufficient for regarding these issues as proper to epistemology broadly conceived. As these remarks suggest, however, I see no reason to deny that this may be an area in which epistemology and ethics *overlap*.

54. I am grateful to several individuals and audiences for helpful comments and discussion on earlier drafts of this paper. These include Guy Axtell, John Greco, Bob Roberts, Jay Wood, and Linda Zagzebski, as well as audience members at the 2005 Southern California Philosophy Conference and a Loyola Marymount University departmental colloquium at which earlier versions of the paper were read.

Bibliography

Annas, Julia. 2005. Virtue ethics. In *The Oxford companion to ethical theory*, ed. David Copp, 515–36. Oxford: Oxford University Press.

Anscombe. 1958. Modern moral philosophy. *Philosophy* 33:1–19.

Arpaly, Nomy. 2002. *Unprincipled virtue.* Oxford: Oxford University Press.

Audi, Robert. 2001. Epistemic virtue and justified belief. In Fairweather and Zagzebski 2001, 82–97.

Axtell, Guy, ed. 1996. Epistemic virtue-talk: The reemergence of American axiology? *Journal of Speculative Philosophy* 10:172–98.

———. 1997. Recent work on virtue epistemology. *American Philosophical Quarterly* 34:1–26.

———. 2000. *Knowledge, belief, and character.* Lanham, MD: Rowman and Littlefield.

———. 2007. Two for the show: Anti-luck and virtue epistemologies in consonance. *Synthese* 158:363–83.

———. 2008. Expanding epistemology: A responsibilist approach. *Philosophical Papers* 37:51–87.

———. 2008. Virtue theoretic responses to skepticism. *The Oxford handbook on skepticism,* ed. John Greco. Oxford: Oxford University Press, 557–580.

Baehr, Jason. 2004. Virtue epistemology. *Internet encyclopedia of philosophy,* ed. James Feiser, URL = ⟨http://www.iep.utm.edu/v/VirtueEp.htm⟩.

———. 2006a. Character in epistemology. *Philosophical Studies* 128 (3): 479–514.

———. 2006b. Character, reliability, and virtue epistemology. *The Philosophical Quarterly* 56 (223): 193–212.

Baehr, Jason. 2007. On the reliability of moral and intellectual virtues. *Metaphilosophy* 38:457–71.

———. 2009. Evidentialism, vice, and virtue. *Philosophy and Phenomenological Research* 78:545–567.

Battaly, Heather. 2001. Thin concepts to the rescue: Thinning the concepts of epistemic justification and intellectual virtue. In Fairweather and Zagzebski 2001, 98–116.

———. 2006. Teaching intellectual virtues. *Teaching Philosophy* 29:191–222.

Blackburn, Simon. 2001. Reason, virtue, and knowledge. In Fairweather and Zagzebski 2001, 15–29.

BonJour, Laurence. 1990. Review of Lorraine Code's *Epistemic Responsibility. The Philosophical Review* 99:123–27.

———. 2002. *Epistemology: Classic problems and contemporary responses.* Lanham, MD: Rowman and Littlefield.

Brady, Michael, and Duncan Pritchard, eds. 2003. *Moral and epistemic virtues.* Oxford: Blackwell.

Chisholm, Roderick. 1966. *Theory of knowledge*. Englewood Cliffs, NJ: Prentice-Hall, Inc.

Code, Lorraine. 1984. Toward a 'responsibilist' epistemology. *Philosophy and Phenomenological Research* 65:29–50.

———. 1987. *Epistemic responsibility*. Andover, NH: University Press of New England.

Conee, Earl, and Richard Feldman. 2004. *Evidentialism: Essay in epistemology*. Oxford: Oxford University Press.

Dancy, Jonathan. 2000. Supervenience, virtues, and consequences. In Axtell 2000, 73–86.

DePaul, Michael, and Linda Zagzebski, eds. 2003. *Intellectual virtue: Perspectives from ethics and epistemology*. Oxford: Oxford University Press.

Driver, Julia. 2000. Moral and epistemic virtue. In Axtell 2000, 123–34.

———. 2001. *Uneasy virtue*. Cambridge: Cambridge University Press.

———. 2003. The conflation of moral and epistemic virtue. In Brady and Pritchard 2003, 101–16.

Fairweather, Abrol, and Linda Zagzebski, eds. 2001. *Virtue epistemology*. Oxford: Oxford University Press.

Fairweather, Abrol. 2001. Epistemic motivation. In Fairweather and Zagzebski 2001, 63–81.

Fricker, Miranda. 2003. Epistemic justice and a role for virtue in the politics of knowing. *Metaphilosophy* 34 (1): 154–73.

———. 2007. *Epistemic injustice*. Oxford: Oxford University Press.

Goldman, Alvin. 1992. *Philosophy meets the cognitive and social sciences*. Cambridge, MA: MIT Press.

Greco, John. 2000. *Putting skeptics in their place*. New York: Cambridge University Press.

———. 2003. Knowledge as credit for true belief. In DePaul and Zagzebski 2003, 111–24.

———. 2004. Virtue epistemology. *Stanford encyclopedia of philosophy*, ed. Edward Zalta, URL = ⟨http://plato.stanford.edu/archives/win2004/entries/epistemology-virtue/⟩.

Greco, John, and Ernest Sosa, eds. 1999. *The Blackwell guide to epistemology*. Oxford: Blackwell.

Hookway, Christopher. 2000. Regulating inquiry: Virtue, doubt, and sentiment. In Axtell 2000, 149–60.

Hookway, Christopher. 2001. Epistemic *Akrasia* and epistemic virtue. In Fairweather and Zagzebski 2001, 178–99.

———. 2003. How to be a virtue epistemologist. In DePaul and Zagzebski 2003, 183–202.

———. 2006. Reasons for belief, reasoning, virtues. *Philosophical Studies* 130:47–70.

Kawall, Jason. 2002. Other-regarding intellectual virtues. *Ratio* 15:257–75.

Kvanvig, Jonathan. 1992. *The intellectual virtues and the life of the mind.* Savage, MD: Rowman and Littlefield.

———. 2003. *The value of knowledge and the pursuit of understanding.* Cambridge: Cambridge University Press.

Lahroodi, Reza. 2006. Evaluational internalism, epistemic virtues and the significance of trying. *Journal of Philosophical Research* 31:1–20.

———. 2007a. Evaluating need for cognition: A case study in naturalistic epistemic virtue theory. *Philosophical Psychology* 20:227–45.

———. 2007b. Collective epistemic virtues. *Social Epistemology* 21:281–97.

Lahroodi, Reza, and Frederick F. Schmitt. 2008. The epistemic value of curiosity. *Educational Theory* 58:125–48.

Louden, Robert. 1997. On some vices of virtue ethics. In *Virtue Ethics*, ed. Daniel Statman. Washington, DC: Georgetown University Press.

McDowell, John. 1979. Virtue and reason. *The Monist* 62:331–50.

Montmarquet. 1993. *Epistemic virtue and doxastic responsibility.* Savage, MD: Rowman and Littlefield.

———. 2000. An 'internalist' conception of intellectual virtue. In Axtell 2000, 135–48.

Riggs, Wayne. 2003. Understanding 'virtue' and the virtue of understanding. In DePaul and Zagzebski 2003, 203–26.

Roberts, Robert, and Jay Wood. 2003. Humility and epistemic goods. In DePaul and Zagzebski 2003, 257–79.

———. 2007. *Intellectual virtues: An essay in regulative epistemology.* Oxford: Oxford University Press.

Solomon, David. 2003. Virtue ethics: Radical or Routine? In DePaul and Zagzebski 2003, 57–80.

Sosa, Ernest. 1991. *Knowledge in perspective.* Cambridge: Cambridge University Press.

———. 2007. *A virtue epistemology: Apt belief and reflective knowledge*. Oxford: Oxford University Press.

Steup, Matthias, ed. 2001. *Knowledge, truth, and duty*. Oxford: Oxford University Press.

Swank, Casey. 2000. Epistemic vice. In Axtell 2000, 195–204.

Turri, John. Unpublished. "Believing for a reason."

Zagzebski. 1996. *Virtues of the mind*. Cambridge: Cambridge University Press.

———. 1998. Virtue Epistemology. *Routledge Encyclopedia of Philosophy*, ed. Edward Craig. London: Routledge, 617–21.

———. 1999. What Is Knowledge? In Greco and Sosa 1999, 92–116.

———. 2001. Recovering Understanding. In Steup 2001, 235–54.

B The Nature of Knowledge

3   Selections from *A Virtue Epistemology: Apt Belief and Reflective Knowledge*, Volume 1

Ernest Sosa

A VIRTUE EPISTEMOLOGY

When an archer takes aim and shoots, that shot is assessable in three respects.

First, we can assess whether it succeeds in its aim, in hitting the target. Although we can also assess how accurate a shot it is, how close to the bull's-eye, we here put degrees aside, in favor of the on/off question: whether it hits the target or not.

Second, we can assess whether it is adroit, whether it manifests skill on the part of the archer. Skill too comes in degrees, but here again we focus on the on/off question: whether it manifests relevant skill or not, whether it is or is not adroit.

A shot can be both accurate and adroit, however, without being a success creditable to its author. Take a shot that in normal conditions would have hit the bull's-eye. The wind may be abnormally strong, and just strong enough to divert the arrow so that, in conditions thereafter normal, it, would miss the target altogether. However, shifting winds may next guide it gently to the bull's-eye after all. The shot is then accurate and adroit, but not accurate *because* adroit (not sufficiently). So it is not apt, and not creditable to the archer.[1]

An archer's shot is thus a performance that can have the AAA structure: accuracy, adroitness, aptness. So can performances generally, at least those that have an aim, even if the aim is not intentional. A shot succeeds if it is aimed intentionally to hit a target and does so. A heartbeat succeeds if it helps pump blood, even absent any intentional aim.

Reprinted selections from Ernest Sosa, *A Virtue Epistemology: Apt Belief and Reflective Knowledge*, vol. 1 (Oxford: Oxford University Press, 2007), 22–43 and 101–112.

Maybe all performances have an aim, even those superficially aimless, such as ostensibly aimless ambling. Performances with an aim, in any case, admit assessment in respect of our three attainments: accuracy: reaching the aim; adroitness: manifesting skill or competence; and aptness: reaching the aim *through* the adroitness manifest. The following will be restricted to performances with an aim.

Some acts are performances, of course, but so are some sustained states. Think of those live motionless statues that one sees at tourist sites. Such performances can linger, and need not be constantly sustained through renewed conscious intentions. The performer's mind could wander, with little effect on the continuation or quality of the performance.

Beliefs too might thus count as performances, long-sustained ones, with no more conscious or intentional an aim than that of a heartbeat. At a minimum, beliefs can be assessed for correctness independently of any competence that they may manifest. Beliefs can be true by luck, after all, independently of the believer's competence in so believing, as in Gettier cases.

Beliefs fall under the AAA structure, as do performances generally. We can distinguish between a belief's accuracy, i.e., its truth; its adroitness, i.e., its manifesting epistemic virtue or competence; and its aptness, i.e., its being true *because* competent.[2]

Animal knowledge is essentially apt belief, as distinguished from the more demanding reflective knowledge. This is not to say that the word "knows" is ambiguous. Maybe it is, but distinguishing a kind of knowledge as "animal" knowledge requires no commitment to that linguistic thesis. Indeed, despite leaving the word "knows" undefined, one might proceed in three stages as follows:

(a) affirm that knowledge entails belief;

(b) understand "animal" knowledge as requiring apt belief *without* requiring *defensibly* apt belief, i.e., apt belief that the subject aptly believes to be apt, and whose aptness the subject can therefore defend against relevant skeptical doubts; and

(c) understand "reflective" knowledge as requiring not only apt belief but *also* defensibly apt belief.

There you have the core ideas of the virtue epistemology to be developed in the remaining lectures.

One other idea has also been part of virtue epistemology, that of the *safety* of a belief. This too is a special case of an idea applicable to performances generally. A performance is safe if and only if not easily would it then have failed, not easily would it have fallen short of its aim. What is required for the safety of a belief is that not easily would it fail by being false, or untrue. A belief that p is *safe* provided it would have been held only if (most likely) p.

By contrast, someone's belief that p is *sensitive* if and only if were it not so that p, he would not (likely) believe that p.

Surprisingly enough, such conditionals do not contrapose. Suppose that if it were so that p, then it would be so that q. It might seem to follow that if it were *not* so that q, then it would *not* be so that p. After all, if it were *not* so that q while it was still so that p, it *would* then be so that p *without* it being so that q. How then could it be that if it were so that p, it would be so that q? It is thus quite plausible to think that such conditionals contrapose, as do material conditionals; plausible, but still incorrect. If water now flowed from your kitchen faucet, for example, it would then be false that water so flowed while your main house valve was closed. But the contrapositive of this true conditional is false.

Accordingly, a belief can be safe without being sensitive. Radical skeptical scenarios provide examples. Take one's belief that one is not a brain in a vat fooled by misleading sensory evidence into so believing. That belief is safe without being sensitive. We can thus defend Moorean common sense by highlighting the skeptic's confusion of safety with sensitivity. Although our belief that we are not radically fooled is not sensitive, it is still safe, since not easily would that belief be false. Radical scenarios are ones that not easily would materialize.

That defense against radical skepticism is soon halted by beliefs that seem unsafe while still amounting to knowledge. I am hit hard and suffer excruciating pain, perhaps, believing on that basis that I am in pain. But I might very easily have suffered only a slight glancing blow instead, experiencing only discomfort, while still believing myself to suffer pain. This might have been due to priming, perhaps, or to hypochondria. Nevertheless, I do know I suffer pain when the pain is excruciating, surely, even if my belief is unsafe because I might too easily have so believed in the presence of discomfort that was not really pain.

What knowledge requires is hence not outright safety but at most basis-relative safety. What is required of one's belief, if it is to constitute knowledge, is at most its having some basis that it would not easily have had unless true, some basis that it would (likely) have had only if true. When

your belief that you are in pain is based on your excruciating pain, it satisfies this requirement: it would not easily have been so based unless true, it
would (likely) have been so based only if true. And this is so despite its *not*
being safe outright, since you might too easily have believed that you were
in pain while suffering only discomfort and not pain.

A belief that p is *basis-relative safe*, then, if and only if it has a basis that
it would (likely) have only if true. By contrast, a belief that p is *basis-relative
sensitive* if and only if it is based on a basis such that if it were false that p,
then not easily would the believer believe that p on that same basis.

More plausibly, then, what is properly required for knowledge is basis-
relative safety, rather than outright safety.

The radical skeptic claims, about some epistemologically crucial beliefs,
that they have no basis they would lack if false. If you were deceived based
on radically misleading experience, for example, you would still believe
that you were *not* so deceived, and there need be no basis that you now
have for that belief which you would then lack.

In so reasoning, the skeptic restricts us to bases for belief that are purely
internal and psychological, by contrast with those that are external. Otherwise, his main premise would collapse. If we allow external bases, then the
brain in a vat will no doubt lack some basis that sustains our ordinary belief
that we are normally embodied. The skeptic's internalist assumption has of
course been challenged in recent years, but here I will grant it for the sake
of argument. I wish to explore a different line of defense, a virtue epistemology that is compatible with but not committed to content or basis externalism. Part of the interest of this line of defense may indeed derive from
the fact that it does *not* depend on such externalism.

What then is the alternative defense? It proceeds as follows:

(a) reject the skeptic's requirement of outright sensitivity, and even his
requirement of basis-relative sensitivity;
(b) point out the intuitive advantage, over such sensitivity requirements,
enjoyed by corresponding safety requirements;
(c) suggest that the plausibility of the sensitivity requirements derives from
the corresponding safety requirements so easily confused with them
through failure to appreciate that strong conditionals do not contrapose;
(d) conclude that the skeptic does not refute common sense, nor does he
even locate a paradox within common sense, since we are commonsensi-
cally committed at most to basis-relative safety, and not to basis-relative
sensitivity; for, our belief that we are not radically deceived—as in a brain-

in-a-vat or evil-demon scenario—is basis-relative safe, though not basis-relative sensitive.

Although quite plausible against radical scenarios, that defense falls short against the one traditional scenario that does not depend on remote possibilities, namely the dream scenario. That scenario is most useful to the skeptic on the orthodox conception according to which the episodes of consciousness that we undergo in our dreams are ones that we thereby really undergo, while we dream. I have challenged that orthodox conception in my first lecture, while proposing that dreaming is much more like imagining than like hallucinating. But let us here set aside that challenge, in order to explore an alternative solution to the problem of dreams, one with its own distinctive interest and more directly in line with our virtue epistemology.

I would like to confront dream skepticism directly, without presupposing the imagination model. Indeed, let us initially grant to the skeptic the orthodox conception required for the dream-based attack. How might a virtue epistemology help thwart that attack?

Return first to our archer's shot. There are at least two interesting ways in which that shot might fail to be safe: I mean, two ways in which that archer might then too easily have released that arrow from that bow aimed at that target while the shot failed. The following two things might each have been fragile enough to deprive that shot of safety: (a) the archer's level of competence, for one, and (b) the appropriateness of the conditions, for another.

Thus (a) the archer might have recently ingested a drug, so that at the moment when he aimed and shot, his blood content of the drug might too easily have been slightly higher, so as to reduce his competence to where he would surely have missed. Or else (b) a freak set of meteorological conditions might have gathered in such a way that too easily a gust might have diverted the arrow on its way to the target.

In neither case, however, would the archer be denied credit for his fine shot simply because it is thus unsafe. The shot is apt and creditable even if its aptness is thus fragile. What is required for the shot to be apt is that it be accurate because adroit, successful because competent. That it might too easily have failed through reduced competence or degraded conditions renders it unsafe but not inapt.

So we have seen ways in which a performance can be apt though unsafe. Moreover, a performance might be safe though inapt. A protecting angel with a wind machine might ensure that the archer's shot would hit the bull's-eye, for example, and a particular shot might hit the bull's-eye through a gust from the angel's machine, which compensates for a natural gust that initially diverts the arrow. In this case the shot is safe without being apt: it is not accurate *because* adroit.

In conclusion, neither aptness nor safety entails the other. The connection that perhaps remains is only this. Aptness requires the manifestation of a competence, and a competence is a disposition, one with a basis resident in the competent agent, one that would in appropriately normal conditions ensure (or make highly likely) the success of any relevant performance issued by it. Compatibly with such restricted safety, the competence manifest might then be fragile, as might also the appropriate normalcy of the conditions in which it is manifest.

The bearing of those reflections on the problem of dreams is now straightforward. True, on the orthodox conception dreams do pose a danger for our perceptual beliefs, which are *un*safe through the nearness of the dream possibility, wherein one is said to host such a belief on the same sensory basis while dreaming. However, what dreams render vulnerable is only this: either the perceptual competence of the believer or the appropriate normalcy of the conditions for its exercise.

The dreamer's experience may be fragmentary and indistinct, so that his sensory basis may not be quite the same as that of a normal perceiver. Recall Austin's "dreamlike" quality of dreams,[3] and Descartes' idea that dreams are insufficiently coherent.[4] However, the dreamer's reduced or lost competence may blind him to such features of his experience, features that would enable him to distinguish dreaming from perceiving. Sleep might render one's conditions abnormal and inadequate for the exercise of perceptual faculties. The proximate possibility that one is now asleep and dreaming might thus render fragile both one's competence and also, jointly or alternatively, the conditions appropriate for its exercise. That is how the possibility that one is asleep and dreaming might endanger our ordinary perceptual beliefs. But this is just one more case where safety is compromised while aptness remains intact.

Ordinary perceptual beliefs might thus retain their status as apt, animal knowledge, despite the possibility that one is asleep and dreaming. Ordinary perceptual beliefs can still attain success through the exercise of perceptual competence, despite the fragility of that competence and of its required conditions. However unsafe a performer's competence may be, and however unsafe may be the conditions appropriate for its exercise, if a performance does succeed through the exercise of that competence in its proper conditions, then it is an apt performance, one creditable to the performer. Knowledge is just a special case of such creditable, apt performance. Perceptual knowledge is unaffected by any fragility either in the knower's competence or in the conditions appropriate for its exercise. The knower's belief can thus remain apt even if unsafe through the proximity of the dream possibility.

Despite how plausible that may seem intuitively, we soon encounter a problem. You see a surface that looks red in ostensibly normal conditions. But it is a kaleidoscope surface controlled by a jokester who also controls the ambient light, and might as easily have presented you with a red-light+white-surface combination as with the actual white-light+red-surface combination. Do you then know the surface you see to be red when he presents you with that good combination, despite the fact that, even more easily, he might have presented you with the bad combination?

Arguably, your belief that the surface is red is an apt belief, in which case it amounts to knowledge, or so it does according to our account. For you then exercise your faculty of color vision in normal conditions of lighting, distance, size of surface, etc., in conditions generally appropriate for the exercise of color vision. Yet it is not easy to insist that you therefore *know* that surface to be red.

If forced to retreat along that line, our solution to the problem of dreams will be undone. For we will not be able to insist that, despite the proximity of the dream possibility, perceptual beliefs are nonetheless apt and therefore knowledge. Apt they may still be, but no longer clearly knowledge. Of course, we could still fall back to the imagination model, but our solution directly through a virtue epistemology would have vanished.

Recall, however, our distinction between two sorts of knowledge, the animal and the reflective. Any full account would need to register how these are matters of degree. For present purposes, however, the key component of the distinction is the difference between apt belief *simpliciter*, and apt belief aptly noted. If K represents animal knowledge and K^+ reflective knowledge, then the basic idea may be represented thus: $K^+p \leftrightarrow KKp$.

That is a distinction worth deploying on the kaleidoscope example. The perceiver would there be said to have apt belief, and animal knowledge, that the seen surface is red. What he lacks, we may now add, is *reflective* knowledge, since this requires apt belief that he aptly believes the surface to be red (or at least it requires that he aptly take this for granted, or assume it or presuppose it, a qualification implicit in what follows).

Why should it be any less plausible to think that he aptly believes that he aptly believes than to think that he aptly believes *simpliciter*? Well, what competence might he exercise in believing that he aptly so believes, and how plausible might it be to attribute to that competence his being right in believing that he aptly believes?

What, for example, is the competence we exercise in taking the light to be normal when we trust our color vision in an ordinary case? It seems a kind of default competence, whereby one automatically takes the light to be normal absent some special indication to the contrary. And that is presumably what the kaleidoscope perceiver does, absent any indication of a jokester in control. So, we may suppose him to retain that competence unimpaired *and* to exercise it in taking for granted the adequacy of the ambient light, so that he can aptly take the surface to be red. Since the belief that he believes aptly is a *true* belief, and since it is *owed* to the exercise of a competence, how then can we suppose it not to be itself an apt belief? Well, recall: the requirement for aptly believing is not just that one's belief be true, and derive from a competence. The requirement is rather that one believe *correctly* (with truth) through the exercise of a competence in its proper conditions. What must be attributable to the competence is not just the belief's existence but its correctness.

Here now is a premise from which I propose to argue:

C.   For any correct belief that p, the correctness of that belief is attributable to a competence only if it derives from the exercise of that competence in appropriate conditions for its exercise, and that exercise in those conditions would not then too easily have issued a false belief.

Consider now the kaleidoscope perceiver's belief that he aptly believes the seen surface to be red. We are assuming that the competence exercised in that meta-belief is a default competence, one which, absent any specific indication to the contrary, takes it for granted that, for example, the lights are normal. Because of the jokester in control, however, the exercise of that competence might then too easily have issued a false belief that the lights are normal. Given principle C, therefore, we must deny that the truth of our perceiver's belief that he aptly believes the surface to be red is *attributable to his relevant competence*. There being no other relevant competence in view, we must deny that the perceiver *aptly* believes that he aptly believes the surface to be red. Nor can the perceiver then have animal knowledge that he has animal knowledge that the surface is red. And that is why the perceiver then lacks reflective knowledge of the color of that surface.

What shall we now say of the problem of dreams? If it is analogous to the kaleidoscope problem, then, although we can defend our perceptual beliefs as apt, we must surrender to the dream skeptic their status as reflectively defensible. We can defend our perceptual beliefs as cases of animal knowledge, but must relinquish any claim to the higher status of reflective knowledge. Surrender seems hasty, though; let's retreat and reconsider.

The problem of dreams arises for any ordinary case of perceptual knowledge through the fact that the subject might too easily have believed just as he does in that instance, although his belief and its sensory basis would have been housed in a dream. Too easily, then, might any ordinary perceptual belief have had its same basis while false.

Although ordinary perceptual beliefs *are* thus rendered unsafe, we responded, they can remain apt even so, and hence knowledge of a sort, of the animal sort. What is endangered by the dream possibility is only our perceptual competence or the presence of appropriate conditions for its exercise. But this poses no danger to the aptness of beliefs yielded by perceptual competence in appropriately normal conditions, and only aptness is required for animal knowledge, not safety.

However, the kaleidoscope case puts that response in doubt. What seems there endangered is one's perceptual competence or the conditions for its exercise, yet we are strongly drawn to claim that although one's belief is apt it is not knowledge.

It helps to distinguish between animal and reflective knowledge, between apt belief *simpliciter*, and apt belief aptly noted. That distinction helps us defend the kaleidoscope perceiver's knowledge as a case of *animal* knowledge. We thus implicitly suggest that he has knowledge of a sort, animal knowledge, while lacking knowledge of another sort, reflective knowledge. So, if we apply our reasoning about that case to the problem of dreams, the consequence will be that perceptual knowledge generally falls short of the reflective level. The skeptic wins.

If common sense is to prevail, based on our virtue epistemology, we must see how, in ordinary perceptual belief, one can aptly presuppose, or take it for granted, that the relevant competence and conditions are in place. But the aptness of any such presupposition would require that it be correct because of a competence exercised in the conditions in which it is exercised. And the relevant competence seems nothing more than a default competence of assuming ourselves awake whenever conscious, absent any specific indication to the contrary. But the ease with which we might have gone wrong by so presupposing on such a basis is proportional to the proximity of the dream possibility, and that is really too close for comfort. So we would have to conclude that our getting it right when we ordinarily believe ourselves awake is not attributable (sufficiently) to the exercise of our default competence. That is the conclusion to which we are led by reasoning from principle C above. We do not get it right through competence in presupposing ourselves awake, since the supposed competence that we exercise, in its proper conditions, might too easily lead us astray.

That is where we are led if we take our cue, for ordinary perception in general, from the kaleidoscope example. In that example, we retain animal knowledge because we seem clearly enough to exercise our color vision in its normal conditions (of distance, lighting, size of surface, etc.). There we fall short of reflective knowledge, however, because the jokester precludes the aptness of our implicit confidence that our perceptual belief is apt. His being in control makes it too easy for us to be confident in that default way, in normal conditions for the exercise of our perceptual competence, while still mistaken. So when, as it happens, we are right, not mistaken, this cannot be attributed to the exercise of our default competence as a success derived from it.

It might well be thought that the presence of the jokester makes our conditions abnormal for presupposing that the light is good. But in so presupposing we must then fall short of aptness, in either of two ways. Perhaps we fall short because, although we presuppose that the light is good, in appropriate conditions for doing so, nevertheless, our correctness still cannot be credited to our default competence, in its proper conditions. Given the jokester's presence, we might too easily so presuppose, in such conditions, and still get it wrong. Alternatively, we fail because the conditions for the exercise of our default competence are already spoiled by the very presence of the jokester. Either way, we then fail aptly to presuppose that the light is good, since we fail to presuppose correctly *through* the exercise of a competence in its appropriate conditions.

Is the case of ordinary perception alike in those crucial respects? That is not so clear. Among the things we must take for granted in attaining ordinary perceptual knowledge is that we are awake. What is our basis if any for so presupposing? Is it simply our being conscious? Plausibly it is, at least on the orthodox conception of dreams. In our dreams we are awake, and on the orthodox conception we thereby believe accordingly, while we dream. Plausibly, then, our basis when we take ourselves to be awake is simply being conscious. And what are the conditions appropriate for the exercise of this competence? Here it is less clear what to say.

Do we retain when dreaming our normal competence to tell when we are awake? No, sleep would seem to deprive us of normal competence to discern features of our experience that would show to someone awake that it was just a dream (if it is possible to inspect the contents of a dream while awake, which seems implied by the phenomenon of lucid dreaming).[5] Again, Austin spoke of a "dreamlike" quality, and Descartes of a certain lack of coherence. Suppose the orthodox conception is right, so that in dreaming we have real experiences, and respond to them with real beliefs, including the belief that one is awake. Perhaps we take for granted that we are awake whenever we are conscious. If our basis for so assuming is just being conscious, then the pertinent competence might too easily lead us astray in any ordinary situation, since in any ordinary situation, despite the proximity of the dream possibility, we would still assume ourselves to be awake on the same basis: namely, that of being conscious.

If we reason thus, however, we must then take back our claim that we can know ourselves to be in pain when we suffer excruciating pain, even if, through priming or hypochondria, we might easily have believed ourselves to suffer pain while it was only discomfort. We must take back that claim to know, for we can no longer claim the excruciating pain to be the relevant basis for our belief. After all, we would have believed ourselves to be in pain whether the pain had been excruciating or not. So the real basis for the belief is some more determinable experience of which excruciating pain is only one determinate.

Suppose we resist such reasoning. Despite the fact that we would have believed ourselves in pain even when suffering only discomfort, we might argue, still there is some sense in which the excruciating pain is in all its intensity a cause and a basis of our belief that we are in pain. If so, then we open the way for a similar response to the problem of dreams. "Even if we would have believed ourselves awake had we simply been conscious," we could now say, "this does not take away the richer basis that we enjoy in waking life for the belief that one is awake." Now we could appeal, with Austin, to the vividness and richness of wakeful experience, and with Descartes to its coherence, as part of the basis for our belief that we are awake.

Of course, it may be that dreams pose a problem for the safety of ordinary perceptual knowledge in two ways. First, the phenomenological content of dreams may simply be different from that of waking life, in the ways suggested by Austin and Descartes.[6] So, the dreams you commonly undergo may very rarely if ever really be intrinsically much like wakeful experience in content. Second, being asleep may impair your competence to discern features relevant to whether it is a dream or waking life. So, the way in which you tell things in a dream—as when in dreaming you implicitly assume that you are awake and perceiving things—is not the competent way in which you do so in waking life. This may be because you do not have the same experiential basis, since the dream basis would fall short in respect of vividness, richness, or coherence. Alternatively, and compatibly, it may be because even if your experience in a dream could match ordinary waking experience in those respects, nevertheless your competence to take such respects into account would be so impaired when asleep that it would not matter. You would take yourself to be awake so long as you were conscious, regardless of how vivid, rich, or coherent your experience might or might not be.

Neither dream-involving threat to the safety of our perceptual beliefs is a threat to their aptness, however, since both would endanger only our normal competence to form perceptual beliefs. And we have seen how this can leave aptness unaffected.

The first lecture proposed an imagination model of dreams, as a way to block the skeptic's conclusion that dreams endanger ordinary perceptual beliefs. A further argument was still required for the further claim that our perceptual beliefs do normally rise above the animal level to a higher reflective level. And this led to a surprising pairing of our knowledge that we are awake with our knowledge of the *cogito*.

This second lecture proposes a virtue epistemology that distinguishes between aptness and safety of performance generally, and of belief in particular, which enables a further solution to the problem of dreams, beyond the imagination model. On this supplementary solution, dreams preclude the safety of our perceptual beliefs, but not their aptness, which is all they need in order to constitute animal knowledge.

In summary, some skeptics find a paradox at the heart of common sense. They argue that to know something requires that you believe it sensitively, in that had it been false you would not have believed it; or at least that you believe it on a basis such that had it been false you would not have so believed it. A first step in response is to replace any such sensitivity requirement with one of safety, which a belief satisfies by having a basis that a belief would likely have only if it were right. A belief can thus be safe without being sensitive, which comports with the fact that subjunctive conditionals do not contrapose. Though more adequate than the sensitivity requirement, this requirement of safety is still inadequate. For we still face the skeptic's paradox, given that dreams are a common enough fact of life, unlike the usual run of outlandish skeptical scenarios. The special threat from dreams is that they seem to render our ordinary perceptual beliefs unsafe. Too easily might we have so believed on a similar enough basis in a dream, while our belief was false.

I have offered two ways to meet this threat. First, I contend in the first lecture that dreams do not contain real beliefs, and hence do not threaten the safety of our ordinary perceptual beliefs. Second, I propose in this second lecture a move beyond requiring that a belief must be safe in order to amount to knowledge, to a requirement of aptness rather than safety.

Consider indeed performances generally, not just intellectual performances such as judgments or beliefs. Your pertinent skill or competence, and your relevant situation for its exercise, can both be sufficiently fragile to render your performance unsafe, while it remains an apt performance nonetheless, one creditable to you as an attainment. Knowledge is simply such apt performance in the way of belief. Knowledge hence does not require the safety of the contained belief, since the belief can be unsafe owing to the fragility of the believer's competence or situation.[7]

When we sleep and dream, then, our situation is inappropriate for the manifestation of perceptual competence. Hence, even assuming that we do have perceptual beliefs in our dreams, these are not then apt beliefs, since even if and when they accidentally hit the mark of truth, they fail to do so in a way creditable to the believer's competence. But this does not affect the aptness of our perceptual beliefs in waking life.

In conclusion, animal knowledge is best viewed as apt belief, which enables a resolution of our skeptical paradox. As a bonus, it enables also a solution, at least in part, for the Gettier problem, the problem that beliefs can be true and justified without being knowledge. Our solution is that beliefs can be true and justified without being apt, whereas in order to constitute knowledge a belief must be apt, not just true and justified.

That solution is partial since so far it deals with animal knowledge only, but it can be extended to cover also the sort of knowledge that requires reflective and apt endorsement of one's animal knowledge. It may indeed be thought that dreams still pose a problem for our claims to *reflective* perceptual knowledge. But we have seen the resources available to us for meeting also this deeper skepticism.

The fifth lecture will aim to deepen our solution to the problem of dreams based on distinguishing apt belief, or animal knowledge, from apt belief aptly noted, or reflective knowledge. The ways in which our virtue-based solution goes beyond the imagination model will then emerge more fully. Meanwhile, the two intervening lectures will use our aptness-centered epistemology to illuminate, first, the nature and epistemic role of intuitions, and, second, epistemic normativity and the problem of how knowledge can be better than mere true belief.

SELECTION FROM "VIRTUE, LUCK, AND CREDIT"

Traditionally our knowledge is said to have "sources" such as perception, memory, and inference. Epistemic sources issue "deliverances" that we may or may not accept. Our senses may issue the deliverance about two adjacent lines that one is longer, for example, a deliverance rejected by those in the know about the Müller-Lyer illusion.

A deliverance of ⟨p⟩ to a subject S is a "saying" that p, one witnessed by S. Different sources involve different ways of saying that p. Someone may say it literally, of course, in person or in writing, and S may hear it or read it. If we can believe our eyes or ears, moreover, it's because they tell us things. We experience visually or aurally as if p. Normally we accept the deliverances of our senses, unless we detect something untoward.

Deliverances thus conceived make up a realm of the ostensible: ostensible perceptions, ostensible memories, ostensible conclusions, ostensible intuitions, and the like. We may or may not believe our eyes or ears, we may or may not trust our senses, or our memory, or our calculations or other reasonings.

Take any deliverance, by which I mean here *any particular delivering of a certain propositional content*. Any such deliverance is safe *outright* provided it would then so deliver its content only if true. A deliverance is safe *dependently* on some further fact if, and only if, though not safe outright, it would still so deliver its content, *in the presence of that further fact*, only if true.

Most often, when one accepts the deliverances of one's senses at face value, one does so in appropriate conditions for doing so, and such deliverances are then safe outright, because nothing threatens the appropriateness of the conditions. Given the jokester in the wings, however, the deliverance of the kaleidoscope perceiver's color vision is no longer safe outright. In order to constitute animal knowledge that the surface is red, the perceiver's belief must then apparently be based not only on that color deliverance, but also on the quality of the light.[8]

Put yourself in the place of the kaleidoscope perceiver. Given the jokester, that you see a red surface is something you can know only if you base your belief on the reason that the light is good. However, a belief based essentially on a basis can amount to knowledge only if the believer knows the basis to be true.[9] But the jokester precludes your knowing the light to be good. How then can you know the seen surface to be red? We need a closer look at deliverances and at how accepting a deliverance can give us knowledge.

Examples of deliverances are test results, indicator readings, eyewitness reports, media reports, perceptual appearances, and even rational intuitions and ostensible conclusions.[10] Contents are delivered by each such source. Acceptance of a deliverance thereby constitutes knowledge only if the source is reliable, and operates in its appropriate conditions, so that the deliverance is safe, while the correctness of one's acceptance is attributable to one's epistemic competence.[11]

Deliverances are "indications" when safe. A deliverance/indication I(p) "indicates" outright that p if, and only if, I(p) would be delivered only if it were so that p; and it indicates that p "dependently on condition C" if, and only if, both C obtains and C would obtain while I(p) was delivered only if it were so that p (although it is false that I(p) would be delivered only if it were so that p).

What then is required for someone to attain animal knowledge based on an indication? Here is one idea:

(I) S has animal knowledge that p based on indication I(p) only if either (a) I(p) indicates the truth outright and S accepts that indication as such outright, or (b) for some condition C, I(p) indicates the truth dependently on C and S accepts that indication as such, not outright, but guided by C (so that S accepts the indication as such *on the basis* of C).

Unfortunately, condition (I) will give the bad result that the kaleidoscope perceiver lacks animal knowledge. This at least is what we must say if we accept the following condition:

(F) S knows that p guided essentially by the fact that q (or based on the reason that q, or based on the fact that q), only if S knows that q.

Given F, the kaleidoscope perceiver does not know the seen surface to be red, if he can know it only guided by the fact that the light is good. The jokester precludes his knowing the light to be good.

What is thus true of the kaleidoscope case, because too easily might the light be bad, would then seem true of perceptual beliefs in general, because too easily might one be dreaming. So, we would be deprived of our solution to the problem of dreams.

In order to retrieve that solution, we modify our indication condition:

(I′) S has animal knowledge that p based on indication I(p) only if either (a) I(p) indicates the truth outright and S accepts that indication as such outright, or (b) for some condition C, I(p) indicates the truth dependently on C and either (i) S accepts that indication as such not outright but guided by C (so that S accepts the indication as such on the basis of C), *or else (ii) C is constitutive of the appropriate normalcy of the conditions for the competence exercised by S in accepting I(p).*[12]

That the light is good is constitutive of the appropriate normalcy of the conditions for the competence exercised by the kaleidoscope perceiver. Accordingly, it is not required by (I′) that the perceiver know that the light is good. Nor is it required by (I′) that the ordinary perceiver know that he is awake. Both the kaleidoscope perceiver and the ordinary perceiver can retain their animal perceptual knowledge even without knowing that the conditions are appropriately normal for the exercise of their perceptual competences. Nevertheless, the kaleidoscope perceiver and the ordinary perceiver are still dramatically different epistemically. They differ in whether they can know their respective conditions to be appropriately normal for the exercise of their perceptual competence. The jokester precludes the kaleidoscope perceiver from knowing this; but, despite how easily he might be dreaming, the ordinary perceiver is not similarly affected. Or so I will argue.

Some epistemic competences are dispositions to host a distinctive range of deliverances in certain coordinated circumstances. These deliverances are intellectual seemings, whereby the subject is attracted to assent to the content delivered. Other epistemic competences are dispositions to accept such deliverances at face value, absent any sign to the contrary.

The first of our two sorts of epistemic dispositions are "epistemic sources." A source is thus a disposition to receive a certain range of deliverances in certain conditions. Our second sort of epistemic competence is a disposition implicitly to trust a source. Think of the deliverances of the senses, or testimony, or memory, or reasoning, and so on. Some epistemic competences are dispositions to trust such a source absent any special sign to the contrary. Of course, sources are trustworthy only in conditions appropriate for their operation.

Such a disposition can be a "competence" only if its contained source is sufficiently reliable, at least in its distinctively appropriate conditions. So our color vision, as an epistemic competence, would involve a disposition to accept that a seen surface has a certain color if it appears to have that color, absent any sign to the contrary.[13]

Someone with good color vision has a distinctive cluster of dispositions to accept propositional contents, among them the following: to take it that one sees a red surface when one seems to see a red surface. A perceptual epistemic competence is thus constituted by a disposition implicitly to accept a range of material conditionals of the following form: if it appears F, then it is F. Each competence will have a distinctive range of such conditionals, and distinctive appropriate conditions. Thus, color vision will concern color properties, and the appropriate conditions will concern quality of light, distance, occlusion, size, and so on. These would be conditions to which we humans implicitly relativize in our wish to know of one's own and one's peers' abilities to tell what's what in the relevant range; and conditions to which we implicitly relativize in trusting such abilities.

What the kaleidoscope perceiver presupposes is not the strong conditional that the surface would not appear red were it not red (a falsehood), or that the surface would appear red only if really red (also false), but only the material conditional that if the surface appears red then it is red (a truth). That is what we must say in order to defend his animal knowledge, and by extension the animal knowledge of the ordinary perceiver. For if what one must presuppose in trusting the deliverances of our senses is the stronger conditional, then neither the kaleidoscope perceiver nor the ordinary perceiver will attain so much as animal knowledge. Neither the strong conditionals of the kaleidoscope perceiver nor the strong conditionals of the ordinary perceiver will be true. Too easily in each case might the deliverance have been delivered while false, in one case because the light might so easily have been bad, in the other case because the subject might so easily have been dreaming.

More is of course required for animal knowledge than simply that the implicit material conditional be true. When such a conditional functions as a rational basis for a perceiver's belief, this belief can amount to knowledge only if the basis belief (or presupposition) is knowledge as well. The basis belief must therefore be apt, which means that its correctness must be due to the exercise of a competence. What competence might it exercise? Answer: just the default competence that is manifest through one's implicit, dispositional acceptance of that range of material conditionals as one approaches any new situation ready to perceive. When that competence is exercised in its normal conditions it yields truth, at least predominantly. And, in any particular instance, the exercise of that competence *in its normal conditions* would yield truth. *This remains so even when there is a jokester in the wings.*

We have defended the kaleidoscope perceiver's animal knowledge because that is crucial to our defense of our ordinary perceptual knowledge from dream skepticism, given their relevant parity. However, we must also find some difference between the two, since it is intuitively so plausible that in some more demanding way the kaleidoscope perceiver would not know, whereas ordinary perceivers routinely do still know in that way.

Reflective knowledge goes beyond animal knowledge, and requires also an apt apprehension that the object-level perceptual belief is apt. What competence might a believer exercise in gaining such meta-apprehension? It would have to be a competence enabling him to size up the appropriateness of the conditions. Absent special reason for caution, the kaleidoscope perceiver exercises a default competence, by presuming the conditions to be appropriate, in taking his visual appearance at face value. Moreover, it is by hypothesis *true* that the conditions are appropriate. So, the kaleidoscope perceiver is right about the conditions, and he is even right that he believes aptly that the seen surface is red. But that is not enough. His meta-apprehension will be apt and thus knowledge only if its *correctness* is attributable to a meta-competence. Is this further requirement met?

Recall our principle C:

C. For any correct belief (or presupposition) that p, its correctness is attributable to a competence only if it derives from the exercise of that competence in conditions appropriate for its exercise, where that exercise in those conditions would not too easily have issued a false belief (or presupposition).

If the kaleidoscope perceiver's meta-competence is to yield knowledge, therefore, it must *not* be excessively liable to yield a falsehood when exercised in its appropriate conditions. Given the jokester, however, this requirement is not met, since too easily then might the perceiver have been misled in trusting the conditions to be appropriate in that default way.

The kaleidoscope perceiver has animal knowledge but lacks reflective knowledge. He has apt belief *simpliciter*, but lacks apt belief aptly presumed apt. This is in line with our intuition that somehow he falls short. The knowledge that he lacks, given the jokester, is reflective knowledge.

What of our ordinary perceptual knowledge, given the dream scenario? Can our perceptual beliefs reach the reflective level? They do reach the animal level, for they remain true attributably to our perceptual competences exercised in appropriate conditions, despite the proximate dream scenario. However, does not the ordinary perceiver join the kaleidoscope perceiver in failing aptly to apprehend the aptness of his object-level beliefs? If so, the skeptic wins: ordinary perceptual knowledge then falls short of the reflective level. In our most ordinary perceptual beliefs we would be in the position of the kaleidoscope perceiver. So we would fall short epistemically, massively so, just as the skeptic has always alleged.

Fortunately, the cases are disanalogous. Even on the orthodox conception, dreams may differ substantially in content from the normal content of wakeful perception. In addition, when asleep and dreaming we could hardly use the same epistemic competences as in wakeful perception, in their appropriate conditions. The very fact that we are asleep and dreaming destroys the appropriate normalcy of such conditions. Moreover, when asleep and dreaming we are unlikely to retain our normal competence for sizing up our object-level beliefs and competences.

Compare the kaleidoscope perceiver, threatened by the jokester, with the ordinary perceiver, threatened by the dream scenario. The object-level competence of the kaleidoscope perceiver is exercised in its appropriately normal conditions, despite the fact that both the competence and the conditions are endangered by the jokester. The object-level competence of the ordinary perceiver, too, is exercised in its appropriate conditions, even if the dream scenario endangers both his competence and its required conditions. Both the kaleidoscope perceiver and the ordinary perceiver therefore enjoy perceptual apt belief and animal knowledge. However, the bad-light possibility deprives the kaleidoscope perceiver of reflective knowledge, while the dream possibility does not analogously deprive the ordinary perceiver of reflective knowledge. Why so?

First, the kaleidoscope perceiver does not *aptly* presume his object-level perceptual belief to be apt. Any meta-competence in view through which he might get it right in so presuming, seems one that either: (a) is exercised in its normal, minimal conditions ("no apparent sign to the contrary"), but might too easily have been exercised to the effect of a false presumption, given the jokester; or else (b) is not exercised in its normal conditions, since the very presence of the jokester already spoils the conditions.

By contrast, the ordinary believer can aptly apprehend the aptness of his object-level perceptual belief. For, he can get it right in so presuming through a meta-competence exercised in its appropriate normal conditions. The relevant meta-competence is a default competence of taking it for granted that conditions are appropriately normal, absent some specific sign to the contrary. When asleep and dreaming we exercise no such competence, since:

(i) in a dream there *would* be signs to the contrary (recall Austin and Descartes), unlike how it is for the misled kaleidoscope perceiver;

and since:

(ii) when asleep we would not be using unimpaired the same relevant faculties that we use when we perceive our environment while awake.

The position of the ordinary perceiver vis-à-vis the dream scenario is thus different from that of the kaleidoscope perceiver vis-à-vis the jokester scenario. We can hence insist, against the dream skeptic, that in ordinary perception we acquire both perceptual apt belief, or animal knowledge, and perceptual apt belief aptly presumed apt, or reflective knowledge.

We now have a way to defend our ordinary perceptual knowledge as reflective and not only animal. Our virtue-based way is applicable both against the dream scenario and against the more radical "hallucination" scenarios. We thus go beyond our earlier defense based on the imagination model. That defense protects our perceptual knowledge at the animal level, and underwrites perceptual knowledge as reflective, but does this only against the dream scenario. We wish of course to protect our ordinary knowledge as reflective not only from the dream scenarios but also from the more radical scenarios. And it is this more ambitious defense that requires us to go beyond the imagination model, to our later virtue-theoretic reflections.

However, it may still be thought that any such more ambitious defense must fall into vicious circularity. The sixth, concluding, lecture will take up this hoary objection. Its topic is the traditional Pyrrhonian Problematic, "The Problem of the Criterion," that of how we could possibly attain reflective knowledge, apt belief that we aptly believe, through any of the traditional sources of knowledge, either singly or in combination.

Notes

1. Aptness is a matter of degree even beyond the degrees imported by its constitutive adroitness and accuracy, for a performance is apt only if its success is *sufficiently* attributable to the performer's competence.

2. Compare: "We have reached the view that knowledge is true belief out of intellectual virtue, belief that turns out right by reason of the virtue and not just by coincidence." (Sosa, *Knowledge in Perspective* (Cambridge: Cambridge University Press, 1991), p. 277). Also: "What in sum is required for knowledge and what are the roles of intellectual virtue and perspective? . . . [One] must grasp that one's belief non-accidentally reflects the truth [of the proposition known] through the exercise of such a virtue" (Sosa, 1991, p. 292). Also: "We need a clearer and more comprehensive view of the respects in which one's belief must *be non-accidentally true* if it is to

constitute knowledge. Unaided, the tracking or causal requirements proposed . . . permit too narrow a focus on the particular target belief and its causal or counterfactual relation to the *truth* of its content. Just widening our focus will not do, however, if we widen it only far enough to include the process that yields the belief involved. We need an even broader view" (Sosa, "Reflective Knowledge in the Best Circles," *The Journal of Philosophy* (1997): 410–30), from the sections entitled "Circular Externalism" and "Virtue Epistemology"; emphasis added). That broader view, as explained soon thereafter, puts the emphasis on the subject and on the subject's virtues or competences. And it is made clear that the belief must be non-accidentally true, and not just non-accidentally present. The view developed in the present paper is essentially that same view, now better formulated, based on an improved conception of aptness, and explicitly amplified to cover performances generally.

3. In *Sense and Sensibilia* (Oxford: Oxford University Press, 1962).

4. In Meditation Six.

5. Some competences are fundamental and minimally dependent on the episodic states of the subject. Others are more superficial, and dependent on the shape that the subject is in at the time. Intemperate drinking, for example, can reduce or remove one's competence to drive a car.

6. Compare J. L. Austin's *Sense and Sensibilia* (Oxford: Oxford University Press, 1962), pp. 48–9: "I may have the experience (dubbed 'delusive' presumably) of dreaming that I am being presented to the Pope. Could it be seriously suggested that having this dream is 'qualitatively indistinguishable' from *actually being* presented to the Pope? Quite obviously not. After all, we have the phrase 'a dream-like quality'; some waking experiences are said to have this dream-like quality, and some artists and writers occasionally try to impart it, usually with scant success, to their works. But of course, if the fact here alleged *were* a fact, the phrase would be perfectly meaningless, because applicable to everything. If dreams were not 'qualitatively' different from waking experiences, then *every* waking experience would be like a dream; the dream-like quality would be, not difficult to capture, but impossible to avoid. It is true . . . that dreams are *narrated* in the same terms as waking experiences: these terms, after all, are the best terms we have; but it would be wildly wrong to conclude from this that what is narrated in the two cases is *exactly alike*. When we are hit on the head we sometimes say that we 'see stars'; but for all that, seeing stars when you are hit on the head is *not* 'qualitatively' indistinguishable from seeing stars when you look at the sky."

Compare also the last paragraph of Descartes' *Meditations*: "I know that in matters regarding the well-being of the body, all my senses report the truth much more frequently than not. Also, I can almost always make use of more than one sense to investigate the same thing; and in addition, I can use both my memory, which connects present experiences with preceding ones, and my intellect, which has by now examined all the causes of error. Accordingly, I should not have any further fears about the falsity of what my senses tell me every day; on the contrary, the exaggerated doubts of the last few days should be dismissed as laughable. This applies especially to the principal reason for doubt, namely my inability to distinguish between being asleep and being awake. For I now notice that there is a vast difference between the two, in that dreams are never linked by memory with all the other actions of life as waking experiences are. If, while I am awake, anyone were suddenly to appear to me and then disappear immediately, as happens in sleep, so that I could not see where he had come from or where he had gone to, it would not be unreasonable for me to judge that he was a ghost, or a vision created in my brain [. . . like those that are formed in the brain when I sleep; (added in the French version)], rather than a real man. But when I distinctly see where things come from and where and when they come to me, and when I can connect my perceptions of them with the whole of the rest of my life without a break, then I am quite certain that when I encounter these things I am not asleep but awake. And I ought not to have even the slightest doubt of their reality if, after calling upon all the senses as well as my memory and my intellect in order to check them, I receive no conflicting reports from any of these sources. For from the fact that God is not a deceiver it follows that in cases like these I am completely free from error. But since the pressure of things to be done does not always allow us to stop and make such a meticulous check, it must be admitted that in this human life we are often liable to make mistakes about particular things, and we must acknowledge the weakness of our nature."

7. Consider the kind of simulation that a fighter pilot may have to go through. The pilot may well find himself in a situation that to him, strapped in as he is, turns out to be indistinguishable from real life flying and shooting, even though it is only simulation. Given the nearness of such possibilities for a pilot as he nears the end of his period of training, how do we assess his real life flying and his good shots in those stages of his training, where simulation alternates with real flight. How good the pilot is will be assessed in part by reference to how easily he could now miss. And what is to be taken into account in determining this? Should we take into account that when the pilot now takes a real shot as he flies a real plane, he might too easily be in an indistinguishable simulation wherein he would go through what would seem to him to be real shots, though obviously no real target would be hit? How plausible can that be? Surely what matters is how remote the possibilities are wherein he takes a real shot in relevantly similar circumstances and still misses. There is a nearby possibility wherein he acts in a way that to him is indistinguishable from that of taking a real shot although he "misses" in the sense that no real target is hit. But this possibility seems irrelevant to evaluating how good a shot that pilot is now, and how good his real shots are. And an analogous point must now be considered concerning the thinker who shoots his answers at a certain range of questions. What affects how good an intellectual, epistemic shot that thinker is, and the epistemic quality of his actual beliefs? It is now in doubt that any possible situation wherein the thinker takes his shot and misses is automatically relevant to his pertinent evalu-

ation and to the risk of error in his actual shot, if it is a situation that he cannot distinguish from the actual situation wherein he takes that shot.

8. *Outright* safety is not a requirement for knowledge, in any case, since a belief might amount to knowledge if guided by a condition dependency on which it is safe, even though one might easily enough have so believed based only on some other condition, dependency on which one's belief would not have been safe. Thus, one may have a good look and trust one's eyes in believing that p, and thus come to know that p, even if one might then too easily have trusted a lying bystander instead. So, one's belief is not safe outright, since it might too easily have been false. The more plausible requirement is *dependent* safety, safety dependent on a fact that also guides one's belief. That the bells toll might be something one knows by trusting the deliverances of one's good eyesight in its appropriate conditions, even if one might easily have trusted instead one's unreliable hearing, despite too much noise, misleading loudspeakers, etc. So, one's belief that the bells toll is not then safe outright, but it is safe as a belief based on the deliverance of one's sense of sight.

9. Here I am relying on two senses of "basing." Someone might base a belief that p on a "factual" reason, say the fact that q, by virtue of basing that belief on his awareness that q, where this awareness might take the form of a belief or perhaps the form of a propositional experience. If we are thus liberal on the ways a factual reason can form a basis, then we need to be similarly liberal about the form of knowledge required, which can now be highly implicit, and need not be linguistically expressible by the subject.

10. Here and in what follows I no longer distinguish explicitly in every case between deliverances as deliverings and deliverances as items delivered. I will rely on context to disambiguate.

11. One might of course know something through accepting a deliverance that is safe only dependently on a certain condition, so long as one accepts the deliverance based not only on its being a deliverance of its sort, but also on the holding of the condition. Thus, the deliverances of a speedometer that works sporadically might still be safe relative to the needle's being unstuck. Someone can know by accepting those deliverances guided by this condition, even if one who accepts them without such guidance would not share that knowledge. The difference is that the speedometer is then safe concerning the speed *dependently* on its needle's being unstuck.

Knowledge that a bird is flying by can be accidental by deriving from a casual glance in the right direction at the right time. The correct belief about the bird's flight is accidental, then, but in a way that contrasts with the belief of a driver who reads a speedometer that happens to be stuck on the right speed. In both cases the subject accepts a deliverance as such, but only the bird watcher accepts a safe deliverance. Not so the driver, whose readings are safe only dependently on a condition, the needle's not being stuck, by which she then fails to be guided.

It would not be enough to require that source X's deliverances merely guide S to believe the contents thus delivered. It must be required rather that X's deliverances guide S to accept those deliverances *as such*. S must accept the contents thus delivered as such, and this accepting must be guided by the deliverances, i.e., by the deliverings (and guided also by the factors dependently on which those deliverances are safe). Reason: what the absence of the deliverance would properly take away is its content's being accepted for the reason that it is thus delivered, on the basis of the deliverance; after all, that content might *also* be a deliverance of some other source, in which case it would not and should not be renounced merely because the first deliverance is rejected.

As for the notion of "guiding," let us understand this as nothing more than the converse of "basing": Factor F "guides" belief B if and only if belief B is "based" on F (perhaps in combination with other factors).

12. Again, condition b(ii) might better require that C be constitutive of conditions that are appropriately normal or *better* for the operation of that source. Note that even when the conditions are better, what matters is that they be conditions *for the operation of that source*. Such conditions would not be ones that would deliver the good deliverance on their own, without the source being operative.

13. Consider one's sources, one's dispositions to receive deliverances in certain distinctive ranges, i.e., one's dispositions to have corresponding intellectual seemings. Such a source, if reliable, will itself constitute a kind of "epistemic competence," in a broader sense.

4 The Nature of Knowledge

John Greco

Part I introduced an account of epistemic normativity and defended it by arguing against some alternatives. Parts II and III continue to defend the account, now by showing how it allows progress on a variety of problems in epistemology. Part II considers "problems for everyone"—perennial problems that any theory of knowledge must say something about. Part III turns to "problems for reliabilism" in particular.

Two perennial problems in epistemology concern the nature and value of knowledge. We want to know both what knowledge is and why knowledge is valuable. As Jonathan Kvanvig has recently argued, the two questions are not independent: a good account of what knowledge is ought also to explain why knowledge is valuable.[1] The present chapter focuses on the nature question. The next chapter turns to the value question.

1 Knowledge as Achievement

I have been arguing that knowledge is a kind of success from ability, intending this as a thesis about the nature of epistemic normativity. I now want to suggest that this same idea gives us a framework for understanding what knowledge is. In short,

KSA. *S* knows that *p if and only if S* believes the truth (with respect to *p*) because *S*'s belief that *p* is produced by intellectual ability.

The term "because" is here intended to mark a causal explanation. The idea is that, in cases of knowledge, the fact that *S* has a true belief is explained by the fact that *S* believes from ability. A number of philosophers, including myself, have recently defended the **KSA** account.

Reprinted from John Greco, "The Nature of Knowledge," in *Achieving Knowledge: A Virtue-Theoretic Account of Epistemic Normativity*, (Cambridge: Cambridge University Press, 2010), 71–90.

Here are some characteristic statements of the position:

We have reached the view that knowledge is true belief out of intellectual virtue, belief that turns out right by reason of the virtue and not just by coincidence.[2]

[In cases of knowledge] the person derives epistemic credit . . . that she would not be due had she only accidentally happened upon a true belief . . . The difference . . . here is the variation in the degree to which a person's abilities, powers, and skills are causally responsible for the outcome, believing truly that p.[3]

When we say that S knows p, we imply that it is not just an accident that S believes the truth with respect to p. On the contrary, we mean to say that S gets things right with respect to p because S has reasoned in an appropriate way, or perceived things accurately, or remembered things well, etc. We mean to say that getting it right can be put down to S's own abilities, rather than to dumb luck, or blind chance, or something else.[4]

In the present chapter I continue to defend the **KSA** account of knowledge, but in the context of three ideas that have been prominent in the recent literature. The first is that knowledge attributions are somehow "context sensitive." For example, we are more likely to attribute knowledge in low-stakes situations, where the cost of being wrong is minimal, than in high-stakes situations, where the cost of being wrong is considerable. How we should understand this phenomenon is a controversial issue. Thus some philosophers have argued that it is merely pragmatic, while others have argued that it is semantic. And there are variations on both positions. I take it, however, that the phenomenon itself is not controversial: our dispositions for making and accepting knowledge attributions are, as a matter of fact, influenced by features of practical context.[5]

A second idea in the recent literature, related to the first, is that knowledge is intimately related to practical reasoning. Again, the details concerning how we should understand this are controversial. Thus some philosophers have argued that knowledge is "the norm of practical reasoning," while others have argued against this. And again, there are variations on the theme. But also again, the idea itself is not controversial. Somehow and someway, knowledge and action are closely related. Perhaps we can say that knowledge is "something like" or "something close to" a norm of practical reasoning.[6]

Finally, I want to take seriously an idea from Edward Craig that is not uncontroversial, but I think very plausible. Specifically, that one purpose of the concept of knowledge is to flag good sources of information. Craig's idea is that we are highly dependent, information-sharing beings, and as such we have significant needs for identifying reliable informants. We gain insight into the concept of knowledge, Craig argues, if we understand it as serving such needs.[7]

These three ideas will inform the discussion that follows. Section 2 shows how **KSA** nicely explains a wide range of standard Gettier problems. Section 3 looks at barn facade cases, which require a different kind of treatment. Sections 4 and 5 discuss testimonial knowledge and innate knowledge, and defend **KSA** against the charge that it poorly explains at least some cases of such. Finally, Sections 6 and 7 discuss some further problem cases for the account.

2   Gettier Problems

Elsewhere I have argued that **KSA** explains a wide range of standard Gettier cases.[8] Here are two such cases.

Lehrer's Nogot Case.   On the basis of excellent reasons, S believes that her co-worker Mr. Nogot owns a Ford: Nogot testifies that he owns a Ford, and this is confirmed by S's own relevant observations. From this S infers that someone in her office owns a Ford. As it turns out, S's evidence is misleading and Nogot does not in fact own a Ford. However, another person in S's office, Mr. Havit, does own a Ford, although S has no reason for believing this.[9]

Chisholm's Sheep Case.   A man *takes* there to be a sheep in the field and does so under conditions which are such that, when a man *does* thus take there to be a sheep in the field, then it is *evident* to him that there is a sheep in the field. The man, however, has mistaken a dog for a sheep and so what he sees is not a sheep at all. Nevertheless, unsuspected by the man, there *is* a sheep in another part of the field.[10]

The proposal is this: In case of knowledge, S believes the truth because S believes from an intellectual ability or power. In Gettier cases, S believes the truth, and S believes from an ability, but S does not believe the truth *because* S believes from an ability. As I said above, the "because" is here intended to mark a causal explanation. We may therefore rephrase the proposal as follows: In cases of knowledge, the fact that S believes from an intellectual ability *explains why* S has a true belief. In Gettier cases, S believes from an ability and S has a true belief, but the fact that S believes from an ability does not explain why S has a true belief.

Next we need a principled rationale for dividing the cases this way. The rationale I have provided before exploits the pragmatics of causal explanation language.[11] First, consider that our causal explanations typically cite only one part of a broader causal condition. For example, when we say that poor lending practices caused the current crisis in the housing market, our explanation cites only one part of a complicated causal story. More specifically, our causal explanations intend to pick out an *important* or *salient* part of the causal story. But what are the mechanisms governing explanatory salience? What factors make it appropriate or correct to cite one partial cause rather than another in a causal explanation? This is a complicated matter that is poorly understood. However, the present proposal for treating Gettier problems exploits two fairly uncontroversial points.

The first is that explanatory salience is partially a function of our interests and purposes. For example, we will often cite partial causes that can be manipulated to good or bad effect, as when we cite a botched defensive play as the reason for losing the game. Clearly, a single play is only one of many factors in losing a game. But the thought is that defensive play is something that we can partially control. For example, we can work to improve it in future games. Another example is when we cite drunk driving as the cause of a car crash. Again, any crash will be the result of numerous contributing factors, but our interests and purposes will often make it appropriate to focus on the intoxicated driver.

The second point we want is that explanatory salience is partially a function of what is normal or usual. For example, we will not cite sparks as the cause of a fire in a welding shop, where sparks are flying all the time. Rather, we will want to find something unusual in the case, such as the presence of flammable material in a restricted area. An important category of this phenomenon—important, that is, for present purposes—is the abnormality manifested in deviant causal chains. Suppose you fire an arrow, which results in hitting your target. But suppose also that this results from countervailing winds, the first of which blows your arrow badly off course, the second of which blows it back to the target. We will not cite your skill as the cause of the bull's eye, although clearly a manifestation of skill was involved. In the case of a deviant causal chain, salience goes to what is deviant, and away from what is normal or usual.

Putting these two points together, we have the resources for explaining a wide range of Gettier cases. Given our interests and purposes as information-sharing beings, our intellectual abilities have a default salience in explanations of true belief. In Gettier cases, this default salience is trumped by something abnormal in the way that S gets a true belief. In effect, Gettier cases involve something akin to a deviant causal chain.

To summarize: In cases of knowledge, S believes the truth because S believes from intellectual ability—S's believing the truth is explained by S's believing from ability. But the success of this explanation requires more than that ability is involved. It requires that S's ability has an appropriate level of explanatory salience. Such salience is there by default in normal cases, owing to our interests and purposes as information-sharing beings in need of reliable informants. But default salience is trumped by abnormality in Gettier cases. Specifically, it is trumped by the abnormality manifested in the way that S ends up with a true belief.

This is by no means intended to be a fully informative analysis of the cases. For one, I have stayed clear of any close detail regarding either the nature of causal explanations or the pragmatics of causal explanation language. What is more, I have admitted that these are poorly and only partially understood. The claim I am making is that the present resources, meager as they are, go a long way toward explaining a range of Gettier cases.[12]

3 Barn Facade Cases

Consider now a case by Carl Ginet, cited by Alvin Goldman.

Fake Barn Country. Henry is driving in the countryside and sees a barn ahead in clear view. On this basis he believes that the object he sees is a barn. Unknown to Henry, however, the area is dotted with barn facades that are indistinguishable from real barns from the road. However, Henry happens to be looking at the one real barn in the area.[13]

The approach to standard Gettier cases that we saw in Section 2 will not handle this case. Here we seem to have a different kind of problem—one that cannot be usefully understood as a "deviant causal chain" between ability and true belief. On the contrary, the process by which Henry comes to perceive a barn seems perfectly normal, even if the environment Henry is in is not. A different strategy for explaining the case is required.

Here is an alternative explanation. First, we note that abilities in general are always relative to environments. For example, Derek Jeter has the ability to hit fastballs relative to normal environments for playing baseball. He does not have that ability relative to an active war zone, where he would be too distracted to focus on the ball. In general, when we attribute an ability we have in mind some relevant environment, as well as relevant conditions, etc. Second, we may now claim that Henry does not have the ability to tell barns from non-barns relative to the environment he is in. Relative to normal environments, we may assume that Henry can perfectly well discriminate between barns and non-barns. Relative to Fake Barn Country, however, Henry does not have that ability.

This reply to the Ginet–Goldman case is not ad hoc, since we already think of abilities in general in just this way. However, the reply does raise a different problem. Specifically, the reply raises a generality problem. For what gives us the right to say that Henry does not have an ability to tell barns from non-barns, relative to the environment he is in? That reply seems plausible only because we are thinking of Henry's environment in a particular way—as specified by an area including the many troublesome barn facades. But suppose we specify his environment more narrowly, to include only the particular farm he is on, where no barn facades are placed. Or suppose we specify his environment very widely, to include the entire face of the earth, where all in all few barn facades are to be found. Depending on how narrowly or how widely we specify S's environment E, we get very different results regarding whether S has the relevant ability relative to E. Hence we have a generality problem. Which way to specify the environment is the right way, and how do we know that the right way will adjudicate cases as the account requires? In fact, the problem is a bit worse than this, since **KSA** makes knowledge depend on a number of different parameters. Accordingly, **KSA** faces a version of the generality problem that arises for any reliabilist theory.[14]

To see this more clearly, consider the following. First, abilities are tied to *conditions* as well as environments. For example, when we say that Jeter has the ability to hit fastballs, we imply that he is reliable in conditions appropriate for playing baseball. It does not count against Jeter's ability, for example, that he cannot hit baseballs in the dark, or with sand in his eyes. Notice that the ideas of "conditions" and "environment" overlap—some states of affairs might be included in the description of either. For present purposes, we can think of "environments" as sets of relatively stable circumstances and "conditions" as sets of shifting circumstances within an environment.

Second, to say that someone has an ability implies that he is reliable in some *range of success* relevant to the ability in question. So, for example, we can attribute to Jeter an ability to hit fastballs, to hit fastballs or curveballs, to hit most major league pitchers, etc. Likewise, we can attribute to Henry an ability to perceive barns, to discriminate barns from non-barns, to classify large buildings, etc.

Finally, to say that someone has an ability to achieve some result is to say both more and less than that they have a good track record with respect to achieving that result. This is because abilities are dispositional properties: to say that S has the ability to achieve result R is to say that S has a disposition or tendency to achieve R across some *range of relevantly close worlds*. Actual track records can be the result of good luck rather than ability. Likewise, actual track records can be the result of bad luck rather than lack of ability. Again, to say that S has an ability is to say that S has a high rate of success across relevantly close possible worlds.

Putting these points together, we may conclude that abilities have the following structure.

S has an ability A(R/C) relative to environment E = Across the set of relevantly close worlds W where S is in C and in E, S has a high rate of success in achieving R.

And now it becomes apparent why **KSA** faces the same kind of generality problem as do reliabilist theories in general. Depending on how we specify the relevant W, C, R and E, we will get variable success rates with respect to S's believing the relevant sort of truth. How are we to specify the relevant parameters so as to pick out the disposition that is relevant for evaluating S's belief?

I suggest that we can solve this problem by making use of an idea that we invoked above: that the concept of knowledge serves the purposes of practical reasoning. Specifically, that the concept of knowledge is used to flag good information and good sources of information for use in practical reasoning. If this is right, then we have an answer to the generality problem: relevant parameters should be specified according to the interests and purposes of relevant practical reasoning.

Once again, this idea is fully in line with the way we think of abilities in general. For example, when I say that S has the ability to hit baseballs, the practical reasoning context helps to determine what I am claiming here. If I am a baseball executive in a discussion about whether to trade for Jeter, I will be claiming something very different than if I am a Little League coach trying to decide where to put the new seven-year-old in the line-up. For example, what conditions are relevant and what counts as the relevant environment will change dramatically. In general, such considerations will be determined by both (a) the nature of the ability in question, and also (b) the nature of the practical reasoning environment in which the question is relevant.

The present solution to the generality problem is closely related to the one defended by Mark Heller.[15] According to Heller, reliabilists make a mistake when they accept the challenge posed by the generality problem: i.e. to articulate a principled rule for specifying relevant levels of generality. The reason this is a mistake, Heller argues, is that relevant levels of generality are determined by context.

"Reliable" is a perfectly ordinary word that in perfectly ordinary situations is applied to tokens which are instances of several types, where those types have different degrees of reliability. Yet we somehow manage to use this word without difficulty in ordinary discourse. Just as our use of the term in ordinary discourse is context relative, reflecting the different concerns of different speakers on different occasions of use, "reliable" is also context dependent in epistemological discourse. Once this unsurprising fact is recognized, we should see that the problem of generality only arises because of unreasonable demands placed upon the reliabilist. It is unreasonable to demand a fixed principle for selecting the correct level of generality if what counts as correct varies from context to context.[16]

Heller presents his view as a version of attributor contextualism: " 'Reliable' is richly sensitive to the evaluator's context."[17] It is worth noting, however, that this is not an essential aspect of Heller's solution to the generality problem. To see this, we need only make the familiar distinction between attributor (or evaluator) context and subject context. What is doing the work in Heller's solution to the generality problem is that specifications of generality are context-dependent. We get attributor contextualism if they are dependent on the context of the attributor, as in Heller's view. But "subject-sensitive invariantists" such as Hawthorne and Stanley can adopt a similar strategy, making specifications of generality depend on the interests and purposes of the subject context. So long as interests and purposes vary across different subject contexts, the relevant mechanics of Heller's solution are preserved.

The version of Heller's solution that I want to defend is technically a version of attributor contextualism, although it is neither the subject context nor the attributor context *as such* that is important for specifying relevant levels of generality. Rather, it is the relevant practical reasoning context, which may be that of the subject, the attributor, or some third party. Specifically, the relevant parameters are set by the interests and purposes that are operative in the relevant practical reasoning context. So, for example, if we are trying to decide what *we* should do, the parameters are set by our practical reasoning concerns. If we are trying to decide what *S* should do, the parameters are set by her practical reasoning concerns, etc. We will see in Chapter 7 that the resulting view nicely handles tough cases for both attributor contextualism and subject-sensitive invariantism. The present point, however, is that we now have a plausible solution to the generality problem.

If the present approach to the generality problem is correct, then the examples and counterexamples that are employed in contemporary epistemology are, in the typical case, badly underdescribed. This is because those examples typically fail to specify a relevant practical reasoning context, which is precisely what is needed to determine whether a knowledge attribution is appropriate. The present approach, then, should bring with it a requisite shift in methodology. When adjudicating cases to test a proposed account of knowledge, we should be careful to specify a relevant practical reasoning context. If we do not specify such a context explicitly, then we can hardly assume that we are considering a common case, or attending to all the features of the case that are relevant.

With these considerations in mind, we may return to the Ginet–Goldman barn facade case, but this time being careful to specify a practical reasoning context. To that end, suppose that we are government employees, charged with counting barns in the area for the purposes of determining property taxes. Suppose also that barn facades are not taxed in the same way that working barns are. However, Henry is a new employee who does not realize that the area is populated with fake barns, and who has not yet received the special training needed to distinguish barns from barn facades. In this context, Henry sees a barn from a hundred yards and pulls out his log to record this. Clearly, it would be wrong to say that Henry knows in this case. Put differently, if Henry were in this context to say, "I know there is a barn over there," we would not view his claim as true.

But now consider a different practical reasoning context. Still in Fake Barn Country, we are working on a farm where we know that there are no barn facades. In fact, we know that there is only one structure on the property—a working barn. We and Henry are charged with getting a cow back to the barn. In this context, Henry sees a barn from a hundred yards and starts walking the cow in that direction. Now it seems right to say that Henry knows. Put differently, if Henry were in this context to say, "I know there is a barn over there," we most likely *would* view his claim as true.

Finally, here is a plausible explanation of these cases. Relative to the purposes at play in the first practical reasoning context, Henry is not a good source of information about there being a barn yonder, and information from him to that effect would not be actionable. But relative to the purposes at play in the second practical reasoning context, Henry is a good source of information about there being a barn yonder, and information from him to that effect would be actionable.

4 Testimonial Knowledge

Next consider the following case from Jennifer Lackey.

Having just arrived at the train station in Chicago, Morris wishes to obtain directions to the Sears Tower. He looks around, randomly approaches the first passerby that he sees, and asks how to get to his desired destination. The passerby, who happens to be a Chicago resident who knows the city extraordinarily well, provides Morris with impeccable directions to the Sears Tower.[18]

Lackey writes,

What explains why Morris got things right has nearly nothing of epistemic interest to do with him and nearly everything of epistemic interest to do with the passerby. In particular, it is the passerby's experience with and knowledge of the city of Chicago that explains why Morris ended up with a true belief rather than a false belief . . . Thus, though it is plausible to say that Morris acquired knowledge from the passerby, there seems to be no substantive sense in which Morris deserves credit for holding the true belief that he does.[19]

Often theories of testimonial knowledge are divided into two camps. On the first kind of theory, what is important for testimonial knowledge is that the source of testimony is in fact reliable. On the second kind of theory, it is also important that the believer knows, or at least justifiably believes, that the source is reliable. From a virtue-theoretic perspective, however, a third kind of theory comes into view. Namely, testimonial knowledge requires that the *believer* is a reliable *receiver* of testimony. That is, what is important is not so much that the testifier is reliable, or that the believer knows that he is, but that the believer herself is reliable in the way that she receives and evaluates testimony. This will plausibly involve reliable capacities for discriminating reliable sources of testimony from unreliable sources.

Suppose that this approach to testimonial knowledge is correct. Then we have to divide Lackey's example into two cases: one where Morris is a reliable receiver of testimony and one where he is not. From the perspective of a virtue theory, it is only in the first sort of case that Morris knows the location of his destination. But in that sort of case, it is also to Morris's credit that he forms a true belief to that effect. That is, his success is grounded in his ability to discriminate good from bad testimony and is therefore attributable to him.

But more needs to be said here. For as Lackey puts her objection, the credit for success seems due to the testifier *rather* than to Morris. Lackey writes, "What explains why Morris got things right has nearly nothing of epistemic interest to do with him and nearly everything of epistemic interest to do with the passerby."[20] From the present perspective, what Lackey says here is not quite right. For in the first sort of case, what explains why Morris got things right *does* have something of epistemic interest to do with him: namely, his ability to discriminate good testimony from bad. This is the important difference between the first sort of case, where Morris knows, and the second sort of case, where Morris does not know. But perhaps Lackey's thinking is this: Morris has *relatively* little to do with his success. So little, this thinking goes, that the importance of the testifier's contribution swamps the importance of Morris's contribution.

This line of objection is strengthened if we consider cases of expert testimony. For example, recall the case of the brilliant mathematician. She proves a difficult theorem and then informs me of her result. Plausibly, I can know that the theorem is true on that basis. According to the present line of objection, however, I do not deserve any credit at all for my believing the truth in this case. The mathematician has done all the work. Or to put the objection more carefully, I do not deserve "enough" credit, since my own abilities are not "important enough" in the explanation why I believe the truth here.

One thing we could do here is dig in. That is, we could insist that my contribution *is* importantly enough involved here, just insofar as I am a reliable receiver of testimony. Consider: if I would believe just anyone about the truth of difficult mathematical theorems, then I would not know even in the case where I happen to receive testimony from a reliable source. This sort of standoff would be unsatisfying, however, and Lackey raises a legitimate worry about it. Namely, that we are now letting our intuitions about whether S's contribution is "important enough" be governed by our intuitions about whether S knows. That is, we are *first* deciding whether S knows, and *then* deciding (on that basis) whether S's contribution is "important enough" in the case in question. And if that is the case, then the account loses much of its explanatory power. Specifically, it loses the power to explain the difference between knowing and not knowing in a broad range of cases.

So what can we do to avoid a standoff and to allay this worry? One thing we can do is draw analogies to non-epistemic cases where our intuitions are both firm and uncontroversial. The second thing we can do is give a principled account of the analogies.

First, consider an uncontroversial case of credit for success: Playing in a soccer game, Ted receives a brilliant, almost impossible pass, and then scores an easy goal as a result. In the case we are imagining, it is the athletic abilities of the passer that stand out. The pass was brilliant, its reception easy. Nevertheless, Ted deserves credit for the goal. Whatever help Ted got, he is the one who put the ball in the net. Now that is not to say that the passer does not deserve credit for the goal, or even that he does not deserve more credit than Ted. It is to say, however, that Ted was involved in the right sort of way so as to get credit. Compare this case with another: Ted is playing in a soccer game, but not paying attention. Never seeing the ball, a brilliant pass bounces off his head and into the goal. Here Ted does not deserve credit for the goal. He was involved in a way, but not in the right sort of way.

My claim here, of course, is that the first case is relevantly analogous to knowledge by expert testimony. The principled explanation is this: credit for success, gained in cooperation with others, is not swamped by the able performance of others. It is not even swamped by the outstanding performance of others. So long as one's own efforts and abilities are appropriately involved, one deserves credit for the success in question.

This explanation of the cases can be deepened by returning to an idea we have already invoked above: that our concept of knowledge serves the purposes of practical reasoning. In effect, we can use this idea to give an explanation why credit is not swamped in cases of knowledge from expert testimony, or in cases of knowledge from testimony in general. Put briefly: the purposes of practical reasoning are well served by the reliable reception of testimony and expert testimony. That is, in cases of testimonial knowledge, S has the right sort of ability, and employs it in the right sort of way, so as to serve the purposes of practical reasoning, i.e. those of S and those of the group that needs to depend on S as a source of good information. We can say something analogous to explain why Ted gets credit for scoring an easy goal: the purposes of soccer playing are well served by the reliable execution of easy goals. That is, in the soccer case Ted has the right sort of ability, and employs it in the right sort of way, so as to serve the purposes of soccer playing, i.e. those of Ted himself and those of the team that needs to depend on Ted to receive passes (easy or not) and score goals.

Nevertheless, a concession is in order. Namely, in these cases and others we must rely on our intuitions about when S's abilities are "importantly enough" involved in an explanation of success. In other words, we have no precise or systematic understanding of the rules governing explanatory salience. And therefore the **KSA** account of knowledge is not maximally specific. Neither is the account maximally informative. In so far as the rules governing explanatory salience are poorly understood, this deficit is inherited by our understanding of what knowledge is. On the positive side, the present account does not adjudicate cases in a way that is clearly wrong. There are no clear counterexamples. Second, intuitions about whether S knows tend to sway with intuitions about explanatory salience. That is, in cases where it seems that S knows, it seems that it is the case that S's cognitive abilities are important in an explanation why S believes the truth. And in cases where it seems that S does not know, it seems that S's abilities are less important in such an explanation. This would indicate that the **KSA** account is *correct*, even if it is neither maximally specific nor maximally informative.

5 Innate Knowledge

Lackey has criticized **KSA** as failing to give an adequate account of testimonial knowledge. She has also criticized **KSA** for failing to give an adequate account of innate knowledge.[21] In short, the objection goes, it seems wrong to understand innate knowledge as an achievement. Alternatively, it seems wrong to think that innate knowledge is something for which the knower deserves credit.

First, the present problem does not seem to arise for all kinds of innate knowledge. Specifically, it is natural to think of some cases of innate knowledge as arising from the exercise of innate ability. For example, one comes to believe, and thereby know, that the shortest distance between two points is a straight line. Call this "weakly innate knowledge."

More problematically, however, some innate knowledge seems poorly understood in terms of *exercising* an ability. For example, suppose that one knows that the shortest distance between two points is a straight line, but one never comes to believe this for the first time. Rather, one believes it from the start. Call this "strongly innate knowledge," understood as knowledge that is originally stative. It is not implausible that some human knowledge is like this. But putting aside the question whether strongly innate knowledge is actual, it seems plausible that such knowledge is possible. For example, consider the case of Swampman, a molecule for molecule duplicate of Donald Davidson who comes into the world whole cloth as the result of a fortuitous strike of lightning. Lore has it that Swampman comes into the world knowing everything that Davidson knows, although Swampman does not *come to believe* anything. If Swampman knows, then all his knowledge is strongly innate knowledge.[22]

Here is a proposal for dealing with this sort of case. Knowledge is a kind of success from ability, we continue to say, but this can be taken in two ways. In the standard case, knowledge is true belief resulting from the exercise of one's intellectual abilities. In the limit case, knowledge is true belief that (partly) *constitutes* one's intellectual abilities. The idea is that human beings might very well have some of their cognitive faculties structured by information that is hard-wired. Taking an idea from Kant, our spatial reasoning might be structured by innate knowledge of certain spatial relations.[23] Taking an idea from Reid, our sensory perception might be structured by innate knowledge of certain cause and effect relations.[24] Swampman would be an extreme case of the same thing: in his case, he comes into the world with cognitive abilities (for example, memory, reasoning) that are largely constituted by hard-wired information, in the same way that our cognitive abilities are (plausibly) constituted by less of the same. Such information would be stative in the relevant sense, but still "from ability" in a relevant sense as well.

6   More Objections to the KSA Account

In this section I consider two further objections to the **KSA** account of knowledge. The two objections have a similar structure. Specifically, they compare (a) clear cases of non-intellectual achievement with (b) clear cases where a believer fails to have knowledge. It is then argued that the cases are analogous in all relevant respects. Therefore, the objections conclude, knowledge cannot be fruitfully understood as intellectual or cognitive achievement. In effect, the claim is that **KSA** fails to specify a sense of "intellectual achievement" that explains how knowledge is analogous to other kinds of achievement.

A   Whitcomb's Hoodlums Case
Dennis Whitcomb asks us to consider the following example.

Hoodlums at the shooting range put weights in most of the arrows' tips. Champion archers shoot, and due to the weights they miss. I too go to shoot, and by luck I get the one quiver of unweighted arrows. Through skills that almost always bring target-hits, I make those hits. My shots are successful and, moreover, they are successful *through* virtue.[25]

Now consider a second example.

Hoodlums also work at the newspaper, and just before the presses start they replace one of the paper's truths *p* with the falsehood not-*p*. When the printing is almost done the editors catch the mistake, and they print a few corrected copies. By luck I read a corrected copy. In reading it I come to believe that *p*, but I don't come to know that *p*.

The two cases show, Whitcomb argues, that knowledge is not fruitfully understood in terms of success through virtue. He writes,

> The two cases are exactly analogous, so whatever sense in which virtue is at work in the first of them is a sense in which it is also at work in the second. Since in the second case I do not know, then, true belief is not through virtue turned into knowledge, at least not in the sense of virtue in which success in other domains is turned into success-through-virtue in those domains.

In order to meet this objection, we should challenge the first claim of this last passage: that the two cases are exactly analogous. Specifically, a closer look at the nature of abilities shows why the first case is an instance of success through ability (or virtue) whereas the second case is not. That is the important difference between the two cases, and what explains our failure to attribute knowledge in the second.

Recall the claim, defended above, that abilities in general have the following structure:

S has an ability A(R/C) relative to environment E = Across the set of relevantly close worlds W where *S* is in C and in E, *S* has a high rate of success in achieving R.

The way this structure is to be filled in, we noted, depends on the ability in question. So, for example, different abilities will specify a different R as the relevant kind of success attaching to the ability in question. Likewise, different abilities will specify different conditions relevant for exercising the ability in question. The conditions under which a good hitter is expected to hit baseballs, for example, differ from the conditions under which a good singer is expected to hit notes. Specifying the relevant values for R, C and E further depend on context, we noted: when I say that Jeter is a good hitter, I do not mean quite the same thing as when I say that my nine-year-old son is a good hitter (which he is, by the way).

We may now apply these considerations to Whitcomb's two examples as follows: The ability to hit a target, like any ability, is defined relative to conditions that are appropriate for that sort of ability. In particular, we do not require that an archer is reliable (relative to an environment) in conditions involving arrow-weighting hoodlums. Accordingly, worlds where meddling hoodlums affect performance are not deemed relevant for determining whether *S* has the ability in question, even if meddling hoodlums are in S's actual environment and even if worlds where they affect S's performance are "close" on some other ordering. This is similar to Jeter's ability to hit baseballs in Yankee Stadium—it does not matter whether there is some trickster in the stadium who could easily shut off the lights.

The situation is different in Whitcomb's second case, however. Here it does matter that S's performance would be affected by information-tampering hoodlums in the environment. Given the nature and purpose of our knowledge-related abilities, it is centrally relevant whether S can reliably negotiate such aspects of her environment. That is why in the newspaper case we can say that S does not believe the truth from an ability. *Relative to the environment she is in*, S does not *have* an ability to form true beliefs of the relevant sort in the relevant way. Or putting things more carefully: Relative to the environment she is in, *as specified by the practical reasoning contexts that most easily come to mind*, S does not have an ability to form true beliefs of the relevant sort in the relevant way.

The difference between the two cases, then, amounts to this: S's ability to hit the target is not defined in terms of performance with defective equipment. But the ability to form true beliefs *is* defined in terms of performance with misleading sources in the environment. That is, our concern with intellectual abilities is precisely a concern about good sources of information: we are interested in who among us is a reliable informant in a relevant domain, relative to the environment that our informants are actually in. And being a good source of information entails abilities to filter misinformation and the like. We may conclude, therefore, that S does not believe from an ability in the newspaper case. Or, more carefully, S does not believe from an ability, relative to the environments specified by likely practical reasoning contexts.

B   Pritchard's Force-Fields Case

Duncan Pritchard has also objected to the **KSA** thesis, arguing that there can be cognitive achievement without knowledge.[26] His argument employs the case of an archer, who "selects a target at random, skillfully fires at this target and successfully hits it because of his skill." But suppose that, unknown to Archie, there are force-fields around each of the other targets such that, if he had selected any of them, the force-fields would have caused him to miss. Pritchard argues that we still have an example of genuine achievement in the case. But then we must also consider the Ginet–Goldman barn facade case to involve genuine achievement, since that case is structurally analogous to the Archie case.

Pritchard's argument can be reconstructed as follows.

1. The Archie case (involving force-fields around archery targets) is analogous to the Ginet–Goldman barn facade case in all relevant respects.
2. The Archie case is a case of success from ability.

Therefore,

3. The barn facade case is a case of success from ability.
4. There is no knowledge in the barn facade case.

Therefore,

5. The barn facade case is a case of success from ability (i.e. cognitive achievement) without knowledge.

The proper response is to deny premise 1: The cases are not analogous because S lacks the relevant ability in the barn facade case, and therefore it is not a case of success from ability. Keeping in mind that abilities must be relativized to environments, it becomes evident that S lacks the ability to discriminate barns from barn facades when in barn facade country. Accordingly, the barn facade case is not a case of success from ability.

Notice that we would not say the same about Pritchard's Archie, who aims at and hits the one target that is not protected by a force-field. Again, this is because abilities are defined in accordance with the interests and purposes that are served by the ability in question. Accordingly, we may say that Archie manifests archery-relevant abilities when he hits this target, even if S does not manifest knowledge-relevant abilities when he forms his true belief about the barn.

Consider now the two cases and a third.

HENRY: If Henry cannot discriminate between barns and barn facades in the area, then he does not have the sort of ability (or the sort of reliability) that we are interested in when we are evaluating for knowledge. Suppose Henry were to say "I can tell a barn when I see one." We might properly say, "Not around here you can't." The "can" here is the can of ability. Suppose Henry were to say, "I know a barn when I see one." We might properly say, "Not around here you don't."

ARCHIE: Even if one cannot discriminate between good targets and bad targets (targets with force-fields around them) in the area, one still might have the sort of ability (and the sort of reliability) we are interested in when we are evaluating for archery skills and archery success. Compare Jeter's ability to hit baseballs during a night game, even when there is a trickster who could easily have killed the lights before his swing. This danger does not take away from his ability to hit baseballs, or his credit for the line drive hit.

MODIFIED ARCHER CASE: Imagine a sport called Archery*, where the goal of the contest is to first identify a good target and then shoot it. Suppose Archie lacks the first ability but picks out a good target by luck and shoots it with skill. In this case we might *not* credit him with an achievement, and precisely because he lacks the sort of ability we are interested in when evaluating for Archery* success. Or suppose he is properly skilled but running out of time. He randomly picks out a target, which lucky for him is a good one, and shoots it. Again, in this case we might properly withhold credit for an achievement, and precisely because he has not manifested the right sort of ability.

7 Kvanvig's Grabbit Case

I will end by considering one more kind of case. Consider a Tom Grabbit case where S sees Tom steal a book from the library.[27] In this version of the case, Tom has no twin brother but has a crazy mother who claims that he does. The mother's story is well known to police, who also know she is crazy and that Tom has no twin. This is analogous to a newspaper case where there are only a few misleading papers out there and everyone else knows about them and knows the real story that p. S reads a good newspaper and believes truly that p on that basis. The literature suggests that there is a tendency to grant knowledge in this type of case. In other words, we more easily grant knowledge in cases where the potentially misleading evidence is well known to others.

Here is an explanation for this, once again exploiting the idea that knowledge attributions are used to (a) flag good information and (b) flag good sources of information. Insofar as our focus is on purpose (b), we tend to be strict and to pay attention to how S would perform in the relevant environment. Insofar as our focus is on (a), we tend to loosen up when p is already "in the flow" of good information. In other words, we more easily attribute knowledge to S when the item of information in question is already well known.

The same considerations explain why in some cases we easily attribute knowledge to people replying to questions with known answers (for example, in a test situation). When a child answers that Providence is the capital of Rhode Island, we are often happy to say that he knows. But suppose that our focus is on the child's abilities rather than on whether he gives the correct answer. Now we are less likely to say he knows—now we want to know whether he was guessing.

Notes

1. Kvanvig, *The Value of Knowledge and the Pursuit of Understanding* (Cambridge, UK: Cambridge University Press, 2003).

2. Sosa, *Knowledge in Perspective* (New York, NY: Cambridge University Press, 1991) p. 277.

3. Wayne Riggs, "Reliability and the Value of Knowledge," *Philosophy and Phenomenological Research* 64 (2002), pp. 93–4.

4. John Greco, "Knowledge as Credit for True Belief," in Michael DePaul and Linda Zagzebski, eds., *Intellectual Virtue: Perspectives from Ethics and Epistemology* (Oxford: Oxford University Press, 2003) p. 116.

5. For example, see Stewart Cohen, "How to Be a Fallibilist," *Philosophical Perspectives* 2 (1988): 91–123; Keith DeRose, "Solving the Skeptical Problem," *Philosophical Review* 104 (1995): 1–52; and David Lewis, "Elusive Knowledge," *Australasian Journal of Philosophy* 74 (1996): 549–67.

6. For example, see Jeremy Fantl and Matthew McGrath, "Evidence, Pragmatics, and Justification," *Philosophical Review* 111 (2002): 6–94; John Hawthorne, *Knowledge and Lotteries* (Oxford: Oxford University Press, 2004); and Jason Stanley, *Knowledge and Practical Interests* (Oxford: Oxford University Press, 2005).

7. Edward Craig, *Knowledge and the State of Nature* (Oxford: Oxford University Press, 1990).

8. See Greco, "Knowledge as Credit for True Belief," and "Virtues in Epistemology," in Paul Moser ed., *The Oxford Handbook of Epistemology* (Oxford: Oxford University Press, 2002).

9. The example is taken from Keith Lehrer, "Knowledge, Truth and Evidence," *Analysis* 25 (1965): 168–75.

10. Quoted from Chisholm, *Theory of Knowledge*, second edition (Englewood Cliffs, NJ: Prentice-Hall, Inc.) p. 105.

11. See especially Greco, "Knowledge as Credit for True Belief."

12. Hence I concede a point made recently by Robert Shope, that aspects of **KSA** leave it unclear how the account adjudicates certain kinds of case. Shope is especially concerned here with problems regarding how to distribute explanatory salience. See Robert Shope, "Abnormality, Cognitive Virtues and Knowledge," *Synthese* 163, 1 (2008): 99–118.

13. The example is from Alvin Goldman, "Discrimination and Perceptual Knowledge," *Journal of Philosophy* 73 (1976): 771–91.

14. Shope points out that several cases can be interpreted as raising generality problems for the account. See Shope, "Abnormality, Cognitive Virtues and Knowledge."

15. Mark Heller, "The Simple Solution to the Generality Problem," *Noûs* 29, 4 (1995): 501–15.

16. Ibid., pp. 502–3.

17. Ibid., p. 503.

18. Jennifer Lackey, Review of Michael DePaul and Linda Zagzebski, eds., *Intellectual Virtue: Perspectives from Ethics and Epistemology*, Notre Dame Philosophical Review (2004), available at: http://ndpr.nd.edu/review.cfm?id=1462.

19. Ibid.

20. Ibid.

21. John Hawthorne has raised a similar objection in conversation.

22. This is Hawthorne's suggestion.

23. See Immanuel Kant, *Critique of Pure Reason*, trans. Norman Kemp (London: Macmillan, 1963), especially the "Transcendental Aesthetic."

24. "Now, there are three ways in which the mind passes from appearance of a natural sign to the conception and belief of the thing signified—by *original principles of our constitution*, by *custom*, and by *reasoning*." Thomas Reid, *Inquiry into the Human Mind*, in *Philosophical Works*, Chapter VI, section XXI.

25. Dennis Whitcomb, "Knowledge, Virtue and Truth," unpublished typescript.

26. See Duncan Pritchard, "The Value of Knowledge," in Edward N. Zalta, ed., *The Stanford Encyclopedia of Philosophy* (Fall 2008 edn), available at: http://plato.stanford.edu/archives/fall2008/entries/knowledge-value/; and *The Nature and Value of Knowledge: Three Investigations* (with Adrian Haddock and Alan Miller), (Oxford: Oxford University Press, 2010).

27. This case is raised by Kvanvig, *The Value of Knowledge*, as a counterexample to a virtue-theoretic account.

5 Apt Performance and Epistemic Value

Duncan Pritchard

1

Ernie Sosa is without doubt one of the towering intellectual figures of contemporary epistemology. Indeed, it is difficult to think of an area of epistemology where he has not made a distinctive and highly influential contribution. Moreover, I think it is fair to say—and this is the real mark of one of the greats—that the way younger epistemologists like myself instinctively approach epistemological topics is largely informed by his contribution to the subject. Sosa's new book, *A Virtue Epistemology: Apt Belief and Reflective Knowledge*, the first of two volumes, covers many of the issues in epistemology that his work is associated with, and I am delighted to be able to comment on this book here.[1] Given the breadth of topics covered in this work—from the nature of dreams, to intuitions and the problem of the criterion—I will not try to offer a critique of the book as a whole. Instead, I want to focus on one key thread, which is the important contribution that Sosa makes to the debate regarding epistemic value by appeal to a central notion in his work, that of apt performance.

2

Sosa's central idea is that the value of knowledge is not to be understood solely in terms of the value of cognitive success (i.e., true belief), but also in terms of the right relationship obtaining between the agent's relevant cognitive ability and the target cognitive success. In this way, argues Sosa, we can avoid a central problem in epistemology concerning the value of knowledge. For if that value is to be understood purely in terms of instrumental

Reprinted from Duncan Pritchard, "Apt Performance and Epistemic Value," *Philosophical Studies* 143 (2009): 407–416.

epistemic value relative to the good of cognitive success, then it seems that the epistemic value of knowledge is (somehow) composed of the epistemic value of cognitive success and the instrumental epistemic value contributed by the way that the cognitive success was produced in a truth-conducive fashion.[2] If that is right, however, then it is hard to see why knowledge should be of more epistemic value than mere true belief. After all, that a certain good is produced in a fashion that would normally produce that good does not usually contribute additional value. To illustrate this point, just consider the fact that a cup of coffee that was produced by a reliable coffee-making machine (i.e., one which regularly produces good coffee) is no more valuable than a second cup of coffee which is identical to the first in all the relevant respects (taste, smell, quantity, appearance, etc.,) but which was produced by an unreliable machine.[3]

But suppose now that the specific value of knowledge is a non-instrumental value that arises out of the relationship between the cognitive ability and the cognitive success as Sosa supposes (we will consider what this relationship is in a moment)? There is nothing mysterious about this, since there are clear precedents for non-instrumental—i.e., *final*—value arising out of the relational (rather than the intrinsic) properties of the relevant object. The first book published on the first ever printing press is valuable in this way, for example, not because of its intrinsic properties—an exact replica which shares all the relevant intrinsic properties will clearly be of less value, including less non-instrumental value—but precisely because of its relational properties; specifically, because of how it was produced. Cups of coffee are not valuable in this fashion, since the way they are produced does not seem to contribute final value, but perhaps the value of a cognitive success when it is knowledge is valuable in this manner—perhaps the way that the cognitive success is produced when it is knowledge accrues it a distinctive value. This is the possibility that Sosa explores. If he is right, then the specific value problem for knowledge just described evaporates, since the distinctive value of a cognitive success that qualifies as knowledge when compared with a mere cognitive success is captured in terms of the final value of that cognitive success due to its relational properties, and is not simply a function of the instrumental epistemic value of cognitive success.[4]

3

But how is cognitive success to be related to cognitive ability to confer this special kind of value? In short, Sosa's idea is that the cognitive success must be *because of* the cognitive ability. When this is satisfied—to put it in Sosa's terminology, when the belief is "accurate *because* adroit" (p. 79)—then the belief is "apt" and so qualifies as knowledge.[5] This is a compelling idea, since it does seem right that a special value enters the scene when, and only when, a success is because of ability. In particular, as Sosa points out, we value a mere success (such as a lucky hit with an arrow) or a skilful failure (such as a unfortunate miss with an arrow) very differently to a success that is the product of skill. Indeed, although this matter is a little complex as we will see in a moment, we also evaluate a success where skill is involved very differently if it can be shown that, nonetheless, the success is because of luck rather than due to the relevant skill (as in a Gettier-style case in which one's skilful attempt at hitting the target is successful, but ultimately because of luck rather than due to the skill in question). Moreover, Sosa is surely right that the difference in value that enters the scene when a success is because of ability includes final, non-intrinsic, value. That is, we value successes that are apt for their own sake on account of the way that the successes were produced.

Although Sosa does not put the point in quite this way, I think a useful way of characterising this thesis regarding apt performance and its distinctive value is in terms of the notion of an *achievement*. After all, a prerequisite of a success qualifying as an achievement is surely that the success be because of ability in the relevant way. Moreover, I think it is clear that achievements have the special kind of value that Sosa is interested in (at least with one or two qualifications). In particular, we value an achievement more than a mere success—and, specifically, a cognitive achievement (knowledge) more than a mere cognitive success—precisely because the success at issue in an achievement exhibits relational properties lacking in the mere success which suffice to confer final value on that success. In short, an achievement, but not a mere success, is valuable in its own right, and valuable in its own right precisely because of how it was produced.

I am very sympathetic to Sosa's proposal in this regard. Indeed, I wish it were true that a proposal of this sort could account for the distinctive value of knowledge, since it would provide an elegant and compelling response to the problem of epistemic value described above. I am not convinced that it does work, however.

In particular, while I grant that apt performance more generally, and apt belief in particular, is indeed of final value in roughly the way just described, I don't agree that knowledge should be equated with apt belief. There are two fundamental problems with the idea that knowledge is apt belief. The first is that there seem to be clear-cut cases in which agents have apt beliefs and yet lack knowledge; the second is that there seem to be clear-cut cases in which agents have knowledge and yet lack apt beliefs. Accordingly, unless Sosa is to ally his view to a rather radical form of epistemic revisionism—thereby depriving the view of much of its attraction—he will need to abandon the thesis that knowledge is apt belief. In the next two sections I will explain the problems facing the view, and in the final section I will offer a diagnosis of where I think Sosa has gone wrong.

4

I noted above that aptness can be undermined by luck, even when the agent is successful and the relevant skill is present. To illustrate this point, consider an archer skilfully firing at a target and hitting that target, but where the success in question is not because of the relevant skill but rather due to luck. Perhaps, for example, a freak gust of wind blows the arrow off-course, but that a second freak gust of wind happens to blow the arrow back on course again. Clearly, a success of this sort is not deserving of the special value we are interested in, and the right explanation of why seems to straightforwardly be that the success is not because of the relevant ability but simply down to luck. In short, the success in question does not constitute an achievement.

The same is also true in the epistemic case of course, in that the special epistemic value that we are interested in is absent when it comes to Gettier-ized true beliefs—i.e., skilfully formed true beliefs where the cognitive success in question is not because of cognitive ability but rather because of luck. As before, we can summarise this point by saying that the cognitive success in question does not constitute a cognitive achievement. So far, then, so good.

Notice, however, that there are two types of luck that are relevant for our purposes. The first is the Gettier-style luck just considered, where luck—to paraphrase Peter Unger (1968, 159)—'intervenes betwixt ability and success' and thereby ensures that the success is not because of the ability. It is not in question that luck of this sort is contrary to aptness, of either cognitive successes or successes more generally. The second type of luck is not of this intervening sort, however, but is rather what we might call 'environmental' luck. That is, like Gettier-style luck, it does ensure that the agent could very easily have not been successful, but, unlike Gettier-style luck, it does not ensure this by intervening between the ability and the success.

Consider again the archer case just described but where the two freak gusts of wind did not occur and so nothing intervened between the success and the ability. I think we would clearly say that this was in the relevant sense an apt success which accrues the distinctive kind of value that Sosa is interested in. Such a success is clearly an achievement, for example. But notice now what happens if we factor-in environmental luck of the relevant sort. Suppose, for example, that the archer chose her target at random from a range of targets on the range but that, unbeknownst to her, all of the targets bar the one that she actually chose contain a forcefield that repels anything that goes near it. As with the Gettier-style case described above, then, in which two freak gusts of wind interfere with the shot, the agent could very easily have missed. Crucially, however, environmental luck of this sort seems to in no way undermine the aptness of the shot. Indeed, the agent's success in this case is no less of an achievement because of this environmental luck, even though the luck at issue in the Gettier-style case does prevent the success from being an achievement.

Apt successes—and thus achievements—are hence perfectly compatible with a certain kind of luck. More specifically, apt successes—and thus achievements—can obtain even though the agent could very easily have been unsuccessful (i.e., even though the achievement is *unsafe*). Interestingly, it seems clear that Sosa would be quite happy to endorse this conclusion, for he explicitly argues (pp. 81ff.) that achievements can be unsafe in this way. He writes:

If the act is due to a competence exercised in its appropriate conditions, its success may be due to luck in various ways. It may be just an accident that the agent retains his relevant competence, for example, or that the conditions remain appropriate. Either way, the act fails to be *safely* successful, since it might too easily have failed, through lack of the required competence or conditions. It might still be apt, nevertheless, indeed attributably, creditably apt. (p. 81)

The problem, however, is that while it seems plausible to hold that achievements can be unsafe in this way, it does not seem plausible to hold that knowledge—i.e., on this view, specifically cognitive achievement—is compatible with the target belief being unsafe.

In order to see this point, consider a parallel case involving cognitive success. Suppose that we have an agent skilfully and successfully forming a belief that there is a barn in front of her. Suppose furthermore that luck does not intervene betwixt cognitive ability and cognitive success in this case (e.g., it is not that she isn't looking at a barn but rather a hologram of a barn, but that her belief is true nonetheless because there is real barn somehow obscured from view by the hologram barn). The belief so formed would surely then be an achievement and so would count as apt. But now add the following detail: suppose that our agent is, unbeknownst to her, in barn façade county where all the other barns in the vicinity are fakes, and that she could very easily have formed her belief that there is a barn in front of her by looking at one of these fake barns. Is the cognitive success still a cognitive achievement? Well, if the 'archer' case is anything to go by, environmental luck of this sort is entirely compatible with achievements, and so this case ought to qualify as a cognitive achievement, and hence as a case of apt belief. But is it a case of knowledge? Alas, it isn't, and the reason it isn't is that knowledge is of its nature *safe*—one cannot have knowledge and yet one's cognitive success be lucky in the sense that one could very easily have been wrong.[6] Knowledge, then, is resistant to luck in a way that mere apt belief isn't, and hence we should be wary about identifying knowledge with apt belief.

There are, of course, moves that Sosa can make in response to this objection. One option could be to concede that knowledge and apt belief can sometimes come apart. Given that Sosa wishes to account for the special value of knowledge by appeal to the thesis that knowledge is apt belief, however, then this line of response is not going to work. Alternatively, a second option might be to claim that the belief in this case isn't apt, perhaps because the luck involved prevents it from being because of cognitive ability in the relevant way. But then the problem is to explain why the successful shot in the corresponding archery case seems so clearly to be apt. That is, the apt performance account of achievements more generally now starts to sit uneasily with the apt belief account of cognitive achievements in particular. Given that the latter account is meant to be motivated by appeal to the former account, this is not a happy position to be in.

Sosa takes neither option, and instead embraces the conclusion that achievements, even cognitive achievements, can be unsafe. Thus, it is open to him to argue that the agent in the barn façade case can have knowledge, even though his belief is unsafe. More generally, he writes that an apt "belief can be unsafe because the subject might too easily become disabled, or because the conditions might too easily become inappropriate" (p. 82). Presumably, the barn façade case falls under the second of these descriptions, in that it is a case in which, as it happens, the conditions are good for seeing barns on the basis of a quick glance, though they could very easily have been very poor indeed.

I do not think that this line of response is completely unsound. After all, it is not as if Sosa doesn't motivate this counterintuitive thesis, for he tells a compelling story about apt performance that supports this very line. Indeed, although I will not be discussing this here, Sosa further motivates this thesis by arguing that the knowledge that results in such cases is necessarily merely animal knowledge, rather than being full, reflective knowledge (see, e.g., pp. 108–109). That is, it is merely apt belief, and not also apt belief aptly formed. That said, I do think that holding that the agent in the barn façade case and cases like it have knowledge is an uncomfortable thesis to defend, given the strength of our intuition that knowledge is incompatible with environmental epistemic luck. Furthermore, I claim that there is a way of approaching these issues that avoids making awkward claims like this. We can bring this point into sharper relief if we consider a second fundamental problem facing Sosa's claim that knowledge is apt belief, a difficulty that is brought out most cleanly by certain cases of testimonial knowledge.

5

Consider the following case, adapted from one offered by Jennifer Lackey (2007). Suppose that our hero gets off the train at an unfamiliar destination and walks up to the first adult she meets and asks for directions. Suppose further that this person has first-hand knowledge about the area and passes accurate directions on to our hero, who subsequently gets to where she wants to go on the basis of these directions. If circumstances are normal, then our agent can gain testimony-based knowledge in this straightforward fashion. But would we also say that her cognitive success was because of *her* cognitive abilities, and thus that her belief was apt? I think not. Cases like this illustrate the extent to which one's knowledge can be social, in the sense that it depends, in substantial part, on the cognitive abilities of others. For while our hero has clearly exercised some relevant cognitive abilities in gaining this knowledge—she wouldn't have asked *anyone*, after all, or believed *anything* she was told—to a large extent she is gaining this knowledge by simply trusting the word of a knowledgeable informant. This is why if anyone is to get any credit for our hero's cognitive success, then it is either the informant, who has first-hand knowledge of the area, or else the cognitive 'whole' of our hero-guided-by-the-informant. But it is not the hero alone who is deserving of credit, since it is not because of her cognitive ability that she was cognitively successful. So if we are to allow such cases, it follows that there is sometimes a lot less to knowledge than apt belief.

It's not clear what Sosa wants to say about this case. He argues at one point that an agent's cognitive success might only be partially creditable to the agent and yet could suffice for aptness nonetheless (p. 97). On this basis, he concludes that:

Testimonial knowledge can therefore take the form of a belief whose correctness is attributable to a complex social competence only practically seated in the individual believer. (p. 97)

If that's right, then perhaps the right thing to say about the Lackey case is that her cognitive success is only partially creditable to her (and partially creditable to her informant), and yet is sufficiently creditable for her belief to count as aptly formed and hence knowledge.

While I'm happy to grant that in genuine cases of knowledge the cognitive success in question might be properly creditable, in part, to factors outwith the powers of the agent, I don't think this sort of line really captures what is going on in Lackey-style cases. After all, the point of such cases is not merely that the cognitive success is partially creditable to others, but rather that the extent of the trust involved means that the cognitive success is *more* creditable to factors outwith the agent than it is to the agent. Compare an analogous case in which an agent, possessing very little by way of archery-relevant abilities, is assisted by an expert archer in taking a shot and accordingly hits the target (imagine, for example, that the archer stands behind our novice and steadies her arms, helps her take aim, guides her firing arm back to the appropriate point, and so on). In such a case, we would not regard the success in question as being an apt performance on the part of the novice for the simple reason that the success is more creditable to the expert archer assisting her. So it is with the Lackey-style cases. Thus, appealing to the thought that we can allow the cognitive success to be in part creditable to factors outwith the agent does not enable us to deal with such cases.

Of course, Sosa might insist that he is happy to allow apt performance even in these cases. There is some reason to think that he might want to take this line, for he notes elsewhere that the account he offers explains "how testimony-derived knowledge might count as apt, creditable belief, despite how little of the credit for the belief's correctness many belong to the believer individually" (p. 97). It is hard to see how such a view could be sustainable, however, for what now makes this an apt performance specifically on the part of agent at all? Furthermore, is the novice archer's analogous success to count as an apt performance on her part as well? This is clearly in conflict with intuition.

I don't doubt that there are lines of response available to Sosa on this score. However, when this objection is combined with the objection outlined above, I think the proper response is to think again about the under-lying nature of the proposal. This is what I now propose to do.

6

One could regard much of contemporary theorising about knowledge as falling into two general camps which each take their lead from two 'master' intuitions. On the one hand, there are those who take their lead from the master intuition that knowledge is true belief that is due to cognitive abil-ity in some way. Those attracted to reliabilist theories, virtue epistemology, not to mention standard forms of epistemic internalism tend to fall into this camp. On the other hand, there are those who take their lead from the master intuition that knowledge excludes luck in some substantive sense. Modal epistemologists of various stripes fall into this camp, for example.

On the face of it, any account of knowledge needs to respect both intu-itions, and—crucially—respect them *independently*. After all, one would an-tecedently think it unlikely that any purely modal anti-luck condition on knowledge could capture the idea that knowledge is due to ability any more than one would expect an ability condition on knowledge to capture the modal condition needed to exclude malignant epistemic luck. On the one hand, it certainly seems entirely possible that one's true belief could exhibit the relevant modal properties and yet fail to be such that it is the product of genuine cognitive ability. For example, just imagine a case in which the relevant modal properties are exhibited but where the reason why they are exhibited has nothing to do with the cognitive labours of the agent but reflects instead a quirk of the environment (e.g., that the relevant facts are such that they change to fit with what the agent believes). On the other hand, and we have seen one illustration of this above by considering how cognitive achievements are entirely compatible with environmental epistemic luck, we can certainly imagine cases where an agent's belief is due to *bona fide* ability and yet is subject to knowledge-undermining epis-temic luck nonetheless.

Nevertheless, we epistemologists are theorists, and as theorists we aspire to simplicity. Hence the attraction of either formulating a modal anti-luck condition which can capture the ability intuition or formulating an ability condition which can capture the anti-luck condition. I think Sosa falls into the latter camp, in that he wants the sense in which knowledge is non-lucky to fall out of his account of apt belief. But this gets him into a tangle. On the one hand, he is forced to allow knowledge in cases like the barn façade case where, intuitively, there is knowledge-undermining epistemic luck present. On the other hand, he struggles to account for the genuine knowledge present in certain testimonial cases where the agent doesn't appear to be exhibiting the requisite apt belief.

I think that the moral to be drawn from the problems facing a view like Sosa's is to recognise that our theory of knowledge must incorporate *both* an ability condition and an anti-luck condition. The view that results is what I call *anti-luck virtue epistemology*, and it holds, roughly, that knowledge is safe (i.e., non-lucky) true belief that is the product of the agent's reliable cognitive ability. Notice that such a position does not incorporate a 'because of' relation in the way that Sosa's view does. This is because the kinds of cases that seem to motivate the addition of such a clause—in particular, Gettier-style cases—are dealt with by the anti-luck condition (i.e., the safety condition). Moreover, since this relation is not added we do not face the problem of accounting for the agent's knowledge in Lackey-style cases. After all, it is not in question that the agent in this case is exercising her cognitive abilities to some substantive degree; what is at issue is just the extent to which she is properly creditable for her cognitive success.[7] Finally, notice that by incorporating an anti-luck condition one does not need to worry about how to deal with cases of environmental epistemic luck of the sort present in the barn façade case, since this is dealt with in just the same way that normal Gettier-style epistemic luck is dealt with by introducing the anti-luck (safety) condition.[8]

Of course, such a theory of knowledge is messy when compared with the wonderfully elegant view that Sosa describes. Moreover, my position does not have available to it the straightforward response to the problem of epistemic value that Sosa's view can offer.[9] Nevertheless, we are required to follow the truth wherever it may lead us, and I suggest that where the truth is leading us is towards this more complicated account of knowledge and not towards Sosa's aesthetically pleasing and subtly defended view.[10]

Notes

1. Sosa (2007). All page references given in the text are to this book.

2. I say 'somehow' because it is an open question how the component values are combined in knowledge to create the overall value of knowledge. Ordinarily at least, one cannot simply add values together to find their sum.

3. In essence, this is the 'swamping' problem much discussed in the contemporary literature. For discussion, see especially Kvanvig (2003), who attributes the problem

to Swinburne (1999; 2000). See also Zagzebski (2003). For scepticism about the 'coffee cup' case, see Goldman and Olsson (2009). I critically discuss the swamping problem at length in Pritchard (*forthcoming*).

4. Note that, as far as I am aware, Sosa never himself describes this value as final non-intrinsic value, though I take it from what he does say about this type of value that it is uncontroversial to describe his view in these terms. For more discussion of final non-intrinsic value, see Rabinowicz and Roennow-Rasmussen (1999; 2003). The general line of objection to the swamping argument just described can be found in an embryonic form in Percival (2003), and in a more explicit form in Brogaard (2007) and Pritchard (2008b). The first explicit statement of this line of objection that I'm aware of was in a talk that Sosa gave at the *Virtue Epistemology* conference I ran with Michael Brady at the University of Stirling in 2004. For an overview of the recent literature on epistemic value, see Pritchard (2007c; 2007d).

5. How is this 'because of' relation to be understood? Sosa does not say. The natural way to read it is in causal explanatory terms, such that the agent's adroitness is the best explanation of the agent's cognitive success, his accuracy. This is the type of reading that Greco (2007; 2009; 2008) opts for in his virtue-theoretic account of the value of knowledge, which he derives from earlier work by Sosa, and in places Sosa seems to take this line himself (see, for example, p. 96, where Sosa diagnoses why knowledge is lacking in the Nogot case by explicitly appealing to the fact that the agent's adroitness does not explain the correctness of the target belief). It is clear from other things that Sosa says on this matter, however—and this has been confirmed to me in conversation—that his actual view is very different, and makes appeal to the idea of a *power*. It would take us too far afield to get into the subtleties of this issue here. For more discussion of the explanatory account of the 'because of' relation in this context, see Greco (2007; 2009; 2008) and Pritchard (2008b; 2008c).

6. The *locus classicus* for discussions of safety is, of course, Sosa (1999). For further discussion of the safety principle, see Pritchard (Pritchard 2002; 2005, ch. 6; 2007a; 2007b).

7. It should be clear from the foregoing that, unlike Lackey (2007), I do not think that innate knowledge is even possible, at least where that is construed in such a way that it involves a true belief that is not even in part the product of the agent's reliable cognitive ability.

8. Indeed, the attractions of the view do not end there, since it can account for a lot of our other intuitions about knowledge as well. For more discussion of anti-luck virtue epistemology, see Pritchard (2008a; 2008b).

9. That said, I think that this view can adequately account for epistemic value, albeit in a way that does not take our intuitions about the value of knowledge at face value. For more on this point, see Pritchard (2008b; 2009).

10. An earlier version of this paper formed part of a symposium on Sosa's work that featured in the 2nd Annual On-Line Philosophy Conference (OPC2). I am grateful to Adam J. Carter and Ram Neta for comments on a previous version. Special thanks go to Ernie Sosa for extensive discussion on issues relating to this paper.

References

Brogaard, B. (2007). Can virtue reliabilism explain the value of knowledge? *Canadian Journal of Philosophy*, *36*, 335–354.

Goldman, A., & Olsson, E. (2009). Reliabilism and the value of knowledge. In A. Haddock, A. Millar, & D. H. Pritchard (Eds.), *Epistemic Value*. Oxford: Oxford University Press, 19–41.

Greco, J. (2007). The nature of ability and the purpose of knowledge. *typescript*.

Greco, J. (2009). The value problem. In A. Haddock, A. Millar, & D. H. Pritchard (Eds.), *Epistemic Value*. Oxford: Oxford University Press, 313–321.

Greco, J. (2008). What's wrong with contextualism? *The Philosophical Quarterly*, *58*, 232, 416–436.

Kvanvig, J. (2003). *The value of knowledge and the pursuit of understanding*. Cambridge: Cambridge University Press.

Lackey, J. (2007). Why we don't deserve credit for everything we know. *Synthese*, *158*, 345–362.

Percival, P. (2003). The pursuit of epistemic good. *Metaphilosophy*, *34*, 29–47; and reprinted In M. S. Brady & D. H. Pritchard (Eds.), *Moral and epistemic virtues* (pp. 29–46). Oxford: Blackwell.

Pritchard, D. H. (2002). Resurrecting the moorean response to the sceptic. *International Journal of Philosophical Studies*, *10*, 283–307.

Pritchard, D. H. (2005). *Epistemic luck*. Oxford: Oxford University Press.

Pritchard, D. H. (2007a). Anti-luck epistemology. *Synthese*, *158*, 277–297.

Pritchard, D. H. (2007b). Knowledge, luck, and lotteries. In V. F. Hendricks & D. H. Pritchard (Eds.), *New waves in epistemology*. London: Palgrave Macmillan.

Pritchard, D. H. (2007c). "The value of knowledge." In E. Zalta (Ed.), *Stanford Encyclopædia of Philosophy*. http://plato.stanford.edu/entries/knowledge-value/.

Pritchard, D. H. (2007d). Recent work on epistemic value. *American Philosophical Quarterly*, *44*, 85–110.

Pritchard, D. H. (2008a). Anti-luck virtue epistemology. *typescript*.

Pritchard, D. H. (2008b). The value of knowledge. *typescript.*

Pritchard, D. H. (2008c). Greco on knowledge: Virtues, contexts, achievements. *The Philosophical Quarterly, 58,* 437–447.

Pritchard, D. H. (2009). Knowledge, understanding, and epistemic value. In A. O'Hear (Ed.), *Epistemology (Royal Institute of Philosophy Lectures).* Cambridge: Cambridge University Press, 19–43.

Pritchard, D. H. (Forthcoming). What is the swamping problem? In A. Reisner & A. Steglich-Petersen (Eds.), *Reasons for belief.* Springer: Dordrecht Holland.

Rabinowicz, W., & Roennow-Rasmussen, T. (1999). A distinction in value: Intrinsic and for its own sake. *Proceedings of the Aristotelian Society, 100,* 33–49.

Rabinowicz, W., & Roennow-Rasmussen, T. (2003). Tropic of value. *Philosophy and Phenomenological Research, 66,* 389–403.

Sosa, E. (1999). How to defeat opposition to moore. *Philosophical Perspectives, 13,* 141–154.

Sosa, E. (2007). *A virtue epistemology: Apr belief and reflective knowledge.* Oxford: Oxford University Press.

Swinburne, R. (1999). *Providence and the problem of evil.* Oxford: Oxford University Press.

Swinburne, R. (2000). *Epistemic justification.* Oxford: Oxford University Press.

Unger, P. (1968). An analysis of factual knowledge. *Journal of Philosophy, 65,* 157–170.

Zagzebski, L. (2003). The search for the source of the epistemic good. *Metaphilosophy 34,* 12–28; and reprinted In M. S. Brady & D. H. Pritchard (Eds.), *Moral and epistemic virtues* (pp. 13–28). Oxford: Blackwell.

6   Manifest Failure: The Gettier Problem Solved

John Turri

Lore has it that before 1963, many philosophers thought knowledge was justified true belief, which view met its doom in Edmund Gettier's 1963 paper "Is Justified True Belief Knowledge?" Gettier produced two cases wherein, intuitively, the subject gains a justified true belief but fails thereby to know, demonstrating that knowledge differs from justified true belief, the latter not sufficing for the former. Examples in this mold we call Gettier cases.

Gettier cases follow a recipe. Start with a belief sufficiently justified (or warranted) to meet the justification requirement for knowledge. Then add an element of bad luck that would normally prevent the justified belief from being true. Lastly add a dose of good luck that "cancels out the bad," so the belief ends up true anyhow. It has proven difficult to explain why this "double luck" prevents knowledge.[1]

Here are two Gettier cases to focus our discussion.

(FORD)   Sarah observes her trusted colleague, Mr. Nogot, arrive at work driving a new Ford. Nogot reports to Sarah that he is ecstatic with his new Ford. Sarah has no reason to mistrust him, so she believes Nogot owns a Ford. From this she infers that someone in her office owns a Ford. But Nogot uncharacteristically is playing a practical joke on Sarah: he doesn't really own a Ford. Nevertheless, unbeknownst to Sarah, Mr. Havit, the newly hired clerk on his first day in the office, does own a Ford.[2]

(HUSBAND)   Mary enters the house and looks into the living room. A familiar appearance greets her from her husband's chair. She thinks, "My husband is sitting in the living room," and then walks into the den. But Mary misidentified the man in the chair. It's not her husband, but his brother,

Reprinted from John Turri, "Manifest Failure: The Gettier Problem Solved," *Philosophers' Imprint* 11 (2011): 1–11.

whom she had no reason to think was even in the country. However, her husband was seated along the opposite wall of the living room, out of Mary's sight, dozing in a different chair.[3]

Gettier cases generate the Gettier problem. The Gettier problem challenges us to diagnose why Gettier subjects don't know. Many assume that surmounting the challenge will lead to the correct theory of knowledge. Some denounce or reject the challenge.[4] But few are fully immune to its allure, and none denies its profound impact on contemporary epistemology.[5]

Harman's Solution

Gilbert Harman's solution to the Gettier problem is that reasoning from a false belief precludes knowledge, but Gettier subjects do reason from false beliefs, and so do not know.[6] If we distinguish implicit assumptions from beliefs, then we might extend Harman's proposal to cover false implicit assumptions too.

Harman's proposal handles both Gettier cases described above. Each subject reasons from a false belief: Sarah from *Nogot owns a Ford* and Mary from *My husband is in that chair*.

Some object that the proposal fails to rule out enough because Gettier cases needn't involve reasoning from false belief.[7] This objection is not fatal, however, because any Gettier subject arguably bases her belief on a false implicit assumption,[8] which, as I already noted, Harman's proposal naturally extends to exclude.

Harman's view faces a more pressing problem: it rules out too much. You can gain knowledge by reasoning from false beliefs. Consider:

(COUNT) Hans brings 100 copies of his handout to the talk. He wonders whether he brought enough for every attendee. He does a careful head-count, concludes there are 53 attendees, and infers that his 100 copies suffice. But Hans's head-count was wrong: there are only 52 attendees. One person, Franz, unobtrusively switched seats and got counted twice.[9]

Hans knows that his handouts suffice even though he infers this from a false belief. Harman's view gives the wrong result in such cases.[10]

Later I propose a solution to the Gettier problem that not only is consistent with knowledge from falsehood, but helps us understand why it is possible.

Zagzebski's Solution

Linda Zagzebski's solution to the Gettier problem is that knowledge requires you to believe the truth "because of" your intellectual virtues, but Gettier subjects do not believe the truth because of their virtues, and so do not know.[11] For present purposes we may rely on our intuitive understanding of intellectual virtue, so I won't elaborate Zagzebski's theory of it.[12]

Consider her diagnosis of why Mary doesn't know in HUSBAND. Mary exhibits

all the relevant intellectual virtues and no intellectual vices in the process of forming the belief, but she is not led to the truth through those virtuous processes or motives. So even though Mary has the belief she has because of her virtues and the belief is true, she does not have the truth because of her virtues.[13]

Crucial here is the distinction, as we might put it, between *having a belief, which is true, because of virtue* and *having a true belief because of virtue.* Some find the distinction "obscure."[14] Others object that Zagzebski's view is uninformative absent an account of the distinction.[15] Others argue that there is no notion of *because of* suited to her purpose.[16] Relatedly, some commentators object that Mary does believe the truth because of virtue.[17]

Zagzebski admits it is a shortcoming that she lacks an account of the pertinent *because of* relation.[18] Later I will make a suggestion helpful to her.

Greco's Solution

John Greco's solution is that knowledge is intellectually creditable true belief, but Gettier subjects are not creditable for true belief, so they don't know.[19]

Intellectual credit ("credit" for short) accrues just in case you believe the truth "because" of your reliable cognitive abilities ("abilities" for short). Greco provides a detailed and principled account of the relevant *because* relation, derived from a general theory of the pragmatics of causal discourse. You believe the truth because of your abilities just in case (i) those abilities form "an important and necessary part of the total set of causal factors that give rise" to your true belief, and (ii) no other factor "trumps" your abilities' explanatory salience.[20]

Gettier cases centrally feature "abnormalities" that trump your abilities' "default salience." As a result, you fail to believe the truth because of your abilities.[21] In FORD Sarah believes the truth because Havit happens to own a Ford, not because of her good eyesight or cautious consumption of testimony.[22] In HUSBAND Mary believes the truth because of the strange confluence of the unexpected brother and the hidden dozing husband, not because of her good eyesight and attentiveness. "In none of these cases," Greco says, "does the person believe the truth because of" her abilities.[23]

Many find this last judgment implausible.[24] They think the subject clearly does believe the truth because of her abilities. Indeed they think it is importantly because of them. This is hard to deny. Perhaps sensing this difficulty, Greco suggests that credit requires the subject's abilities to be the most salient part of the explanation, not just an important part.[25] If correct, this modification arguably handles our sample Gettier cases, because the Gettier subjects' abilities are not most salient.

But the modification rules out too much. In particular it rules out much testimonial knowledge. Consider this case:

(TOWER)   Morris just arrived at the Chicago train station and wants directions to the Sears Tower. He approaches the first adult passerby he sees ("Passerby") and asks for directions. Passerby knows the city extraordinarily well and offers impeccable directions: the tower is two blocks east of the station. Morris unhesitatingly forms the corresponding true belief.[26]

Morris gains knowledge of the tower's location. But Passerby's contribution is most salient in explaining why Morris learned the truth.[27] Greco's theory gives the wrong verdict in this case, as it will in many cases of testimonial knowledge.

Greco responds that Morris still deserves credit for learning the truth.[28] Credit for cooperative success can accrue to multiple individuals, even ones who contribute less than others. It generally requires only that your "efforts and abilities" be "appropriately involved."[29] Suppose we're playing ice hockey and you make an extraordinarily brilliant play to set me up for a goal. With the goalie prostrate outside his crease, and the defensernen dizzy and confused behind the net, I simply tap the puck in. Your contribution dwarfs mine, but I still deserve credit for the goal. Likewise in TOWER, Passerby does most of the work, yet Morris still gets credit because his intellectual abilities were appropriately involved.

I find this response plausible. But Greco's solution to the Gettier problem does not survive the exchange. If you are to gain knowledge, your abilities need only be "appropriately involved." But what is appropriate involvement? It requires more than believing the truth because of your abilities. For Gettier subjects believe as they do because of their abilities, yet their abilities are not appropriately involved.[30]

Lacking a better understanding of appropriate involvement, many will judge Greco's proposal incomplete. Later I will make a suggestion helpful to Greco.

Sosa's Solution

Ernest Sosa's solution to the Gettier problem is that knowledge is apt belief, but Gettier subjects do not believe aptly, so they do not know.[31]

What is apt belief? Beliefs share the "AAA structure" common to all evaluable performances. We can assess performances for accuracy, adroitness, and aptness. Accurate performances achieve their aim, adroit performances manifest competence, and apt performances are accurate because adroit. For beliefs, Sosa identifies accuracy with truth, adroitness with manifesting intellectual competence, and aptness with being "true *because* competent."[32] (Often I substitute 'competence' for 'intellectual competence.') Apt belief, then, is belief that is true because it is competent.

Regarding FORD, Sosa concedes that Sarah's competence helps explain her true belief's existence but denies that this entails that her competence helps explain, even "in the slightest," why her belief is true.[33] Sosa is right about the lack of entailment. Generally speaking, A might explain why B exists despite being irrelevant to B's having a certain property. A carpenter's skill might explain the existence of an abandoned house despite being utterly irrelevant to its state of abandon. A printing press's efficient operation might explain the existence of a stolen book despite being irrelevant to its theft.

Correct as far as it goes, the point does not take us far enough. It may not necessarily follow that the Gettier subject's belief is, even ever so slightly, true because it is competent, but it might nevertheless seem plausible. As noted earlier, some think it's plausible in HUSBAND. It seems especially so in this case:

(HOBBLED)   A competent, though not materful, inspection of the crime scene would yield the conclusion that a man with a limp murdered Miss Woodbury. Holmes saw through it and had already deduced that Dr. Hubble poisoned the victim under pretense of treating her.

Holmes also recognized that the scene would fool Watson, whose own inspection of the scene was proceeding admirably competently, though not masterfully. Watson had, after years of tutelage, achieved competence in applying Holmes's methods, and while Holmes was no sentimentalist, he didn't want Watson to be discouraged. "Look at him," Holmes thought, "measuring the distance between footprints, noting their comparative depth, and a half dozen other things, just as he ought to. There's no doubt where this will lead him—think how discouraged he will be." Holmes then resolved, "Because he's proceeding so competently, I'll see to it he gets it right!"

Holmes sprang into action. Leaving Watson, he hastily disguised himself as a porter, strode across the street to where Hubble was, and kicked him so hard that Hubble was thereafter permanently hobbled with a limp. Holmes then quickly returned to find Watson wrapping up his investigation.

"I say, Holmes," Watson concluded triumphantly, "whoever committed this brutal crime has a limp."

"Capital, Watson!" Holmes grinned. "I'm sure he does."

Watson's belief that the criminal has a limp is true, competent, and true because competent. But it doesn't amount to knowledge.[34]

Sosa could plausibly respond that Watson's belief is true because competent, but not in the right way. Knowledge requires more than merely being veridical because competent, more than mere aptness.[35] Knowledge is belief *properly* apt. But what more does proper aptness require?

Watson exercises his competence in an environment normal for its exercise, so requiring normalcy isn't the answer. Elsewhere Sosa speaks of a performance succeeding *"through* the exercise of a competence."[36] (Zagzebski also speaks of succeeding "through" virtue.)[37] Presumably it is this relation, lacking in Watson's case, that makes for proper aptness and thereby knowledge. But what is it for a performance to succeed through the exercise of a competence?

My Solution

Consider these two cases.

(OJ)   I sat at the table feeding baby Mario his breakfast. I took a sip of orange juice and unwisely set the glass down within Mario's reach. His little hand darted out to retrieve the glass and its colorful contents. Spoon in one hand, baby in the other, I helplessly watched the glass tumble down, down, down. It broke.

(CARAFE)   We just finished a delicious dinner. Maria turned to say something but in the process carelessly knocked a glass carafe, sending it careening from the table in my direction. Glass is fragile, so I reached out and caught it before it hit the ceramic tile floor. It remained intact.

In each case the outcome obtains because the glass is fragile. Yet we all recognize an important difference: the outcomes are not due in the same way to fragility. In OJ the glass breaks because it is fragile, and its breaking manifests its fragility. In CARAFE the glass remains intact because it is fragile, but its remaining intact does not manifest its fragility. Neither outcome obtains only because of fragility—in OJ Mario and the floor help out, in CARAFE my dexterity—but that doesn't spoil the point.

The examples highlight a general distinction between (a) an outcome manifesting a disposition and (b) an outcome happening merely because of a disposition. A glass may remain intact because it is fragile, or it may break because it is fragile, but only the latter outcome manifests its fragility. Outcomes include conditions, events, and processes. Dispositions include powers and susceptibilities. No metaphysical theory teaches us this distinction.

We excel at applying this distinction in a wide range of cases. Albert Pujols crushes home runs regularly because of his power; he also receives intentional walks regularly because of his power; his power manifests itself in the former case, but not the latter. Roger Federer regularly smashes wicked forehands because of his skill; he is also lauded regularly because of his skill; his skill manifests itself in the former case, but not the latter. Compare also these examples.

(BOIL) You place a cup of water in the microwave and press start. The magnetron generates microwaves that travel into the central compartment, penetrate the water, and excite its molecules. Soon the water boils.

(FIRE) You place a cup of water in the microwave and press start. The magnetron generates microwaves that cause an insufficiently insulated wire in the control circuit to catch fire, which fire deactivates the magnetron and spreads to the central compartment. Soon the water boils.

The outcome in BOIL manifests the microwave's boiling power. The outcome in FIRE does not. We have a plain way to mark the distinction: in BOIL, but not FIRE, the microwave boils the water.

I'll now deploy this intuitive metaphysical distinction to solve the Gettier problem.

Sosa identified a triple-A structure for performances. I suggest they have a quadruple-A structure.[38] To Sosa's three I add *adeptness*. A performance is adept just in case its succeeding manifests the agent's competence. For beliefs, adeptness is truth manifesting competence.

I further propose that knowledge is adept belief. More fully spelled out, you know Q just in case your truly believing Q manifests your cognitive competence. ('Truly believing' means "having a true belief that" not "strongly believing that.") I use 'cognitive competence' inclusively to cover any reliable cognitive disposition, ability, power, skill, or virtue.[39] I treat 'manifests' as primitive, relying on our robust pretheoretical understanding of it.

My solution to the Gettier problem is that knowledge is adept belief, but Gettier subjects don't believe adeptly, so they don't know. Gettier subjects believe the truth, so they succeed in a sense, but this success (*i.e.*, their believing the truth) does not manifest their competence. In a word, the Gettier subject is a manifest failure.

The manifest failure in Gettier cases resembles the manifest failure in FIRE. Recall the "double luck" recipe for generating Gettier cases (see Section 1). FIRE exemplifies that same pattern. The microwave initiates a process that would normally result in the water's boiling. Bad luck strikes: the magnetron is disabled, which would normally result in the water's not boiling. But then "good" luck strikes: the damaged circuit starts afire, resulting in the water's boiling anyhow. This all prevents the outcome (*i.e.*, the water's boiling) from manifesting the microwave's boiling power. Exactly the same thing happens in Gettier cases.

My proposal has several virtues. First, it places Gettier cases in a familiar pattern. We recognize in them the same thing we recognize in CARAFE, FIRE, and others: the outcome fails to manifest the relevant disposition.[40] Second, it deepens our understanding of knowledge by illuminating its relationship to other concepts fundamental to our way of thinking about the world, particularly manifestation. Third, it packages an elegant theory of knowledge. Fourth, it illuminates what some attractive proposals got right, and can explain phenomena that confounded others. Let me elaborate this fourth point.

Commentators criticized Zagzebski's special *because* relation as obscure, unworkable, and uninformative. But it avoids all those charges when supplemented by our principal distinction between (a) and (b). We desired Greco to provide an account of our ability's appropriate involvement in success. He could answer that our ability is appropriately involved just in case the success manifests it. We desired Sosa to provide an account of proper aptness. He could answer that we have proper aptness just in case the successful outcome manifests our competence. My solution directly builds upon and enhances the insights embodied in these three proposals. Indeed one might view my solution as a charitable way of interpreting and consistently developing the basic idea behind them.[41]

My proposal also can help explain why knowledge from falsehood is possible. You can proceed competently despite relying on false premises. Falsehood in the form of idealization pervades scientific theorizing and reasoning, much of which is competent and confers knowledge. (Some even consider falsification through idealization to be theoretically ideal in some ways.)[42] And for some purposes it doesn't matter if we believe that the gravitational constant is exactly, as opposed to approximately, 6.7 × 10 – 11 m^3/ks^2 or that *pi* equals exactly 3.14.[43] We might nevertheless reason from these false premises to reach a true conclusion, which outcome would manifest competence. For instance, by relying on that value for the gravitational constant, we could come to know that within the next thousand years the Moon will not crash into Earth due to Earth's gravity. Or by relying on that value for *pi*, we could come to know that a ten-meter-diameter circle has an area greater than fifty square meters.[44]

A Fake Objection

Objection: "Your view can't handle the fake-barn case. Ordinarily when Henry sees a barn, he knows it's a barn. So on your view, in the ordinary case Henry's belief is adept—his truly believing manifests his perceptual competence. Now change the case—Henry still sees the barn, but we recently secretly populated the surrounding countryside with fake barns. Totally unaware of our machinations, Henry happens to perceive the one real barn in the whole county. On that basis he believes it's a barn, and his belief is true. But had he instead set eyes on any of the numerous nearby fakes, he would have falsely believed it was a barn. Intuitively, in the modified case Henry doesn't know it's a barn. But nothing about his perceptual relationship to this barn differs from the ordinary case. So if his belief is adept in the ordinary case, it's adept in the modified case too. So your view gives the wrong verdict."

I lack the intuition that Good Henry (as I shall call him) does not know in the modified case, and my preferred response is simply to deny that my view gives the wrong verdict. But I recognize that some others will intuit otherwise, so I will try to say more. I begin with an argument that Good Henry does know that it's a barn.

Meet Bad Henry.

(HOOLIGAN)   Bad Henry is a hooligan who does bad things. He wants to destroy a barn. He will destroy a barn. He drives out into the country to find one. He pulls over after an hour, retrieves his bazooka, and takes aim with unerring accuracy at the roadside barn he sees. Calm, cool, and collected as he pulls the trigger, he thinks, "That sure is a nice barn . . . now *was* a nice barn—ha!" He destroyed the barn. He feels no remorse. He is forever after known as "Bad Henry, bane of barns." He is bad—*very* bad.

Bad Henry knowingly destroyed a barn. He knew he was destroying a barn as he pulled the trigger. To know that, he had to know it was a barn as he took aim. So he did know it was a barn.

Now we add the twist: Bad Henry was in Fake Barn Country and just happened to shoot at the only barn around. Indeed, Bad Henry destroyed the very barn that Good Henry gazed upon earlier that same day, from the very spot that Good Henry stood gazing. All the other "barns" were holograms. Nevertheless, the intuition remains: Bad Henry knew he was destroying a barn. So he did know it was a barn as he took aim.

I submit that Bad Henry knows it's a barn only if Good Henry knows it's a barn.[45] Bad Henry does know it's a barn. So Good Henry knows too.

But suppose I'm wrong about that. In that case, I offer three further responses to the original objection. One response is that while in Fake Barn Country, Henry lacks the perceptual competence to discriminate barns. And if he lacks the relevant competence, then his truly believing cannot manifest the competence, in which case he does not know, and the view gives the desired verdict.[46]

Another response is that adept performance requires the manifestation of competence in normal conditions.[47] Henry occupies an abnormal environment for the perceptual discrimination of barns, so he fails to believe adeptly, so he does not know. But this response probably rules out too much. If someone temporarily operates under conditions that make success unusually difficult, he might nonetheless perform adeptly. Tiger Woods won the U.S. Open playing on a damaged knee and multiply fractured leg. His victory manifested skill despite the inhospitable abnormal conditions. (You might think this victory manifests skill more than a victory under normal conditions does.) We should want to allow the same for more purely intellectual competences.

A third response involves a natural but more radical change to my theory of knowledge. We begin with a natural extension to our theory of performance-assessment. Performances have a quintuple-A structure. To the four previously mentioned I add *amplitude*. A performance is ample just in case its *safety* manifests the agent's competence. A performance is safe just in case it (i) succeeds and (ii) would not easily have failed. We then propose that knowledge is ample belief. Henry's belief is adept but not ample, so he doesn't know. And since ample belief requires adept belief, the modified proposal handles our Gettier cases the same way my earlier proposal did.

Does knowledge alone require amplitude? If so, it would not mark a fatal objection to the amended proposal because knowledge is bound to be unique in some respect. But locating something else with a similar modal profile would add credibility to this third response. I submit that *to overwhelm* also requires amplitude. To overwhelm an opponent in competition, you must not only succeed, but do so with a margin of safety manifesting your skill. So knowledge, understood as ample belief, shares its modal profile with another relation. Those attracted to this third response thus might liken knowledge to *overwhelming a fact*.[48]

Notes

1. My characterization is modeled on Zagzebski's (1994: 66; 1996: 288–9; 1999: 100–1). (Compare Sosa 1991: 238.) My interpretation of Zagzebski's analysis of Gettier cases is fairly standard (compare Pritchard 2005: 149), and Zagzebski informs me (personal communication) that the double-luck structure is common to all Gettier cases she's familiar with. But it's worth noting, as an anonymous referee pointed out, that at one point (1999: 115 n. 32) Zagzebski says, "Not all counterexamples in the Gettier literature have the double luck feature, although, of course, I have argued that cases with this feature can always be produced whenever there is a gap between truth and the other components of knowledge." It's not entirely clear what this qualification amounts to, but it at least suggests that Zagzebski doesn't think the double-luck structure is essential to Gettier cases. In any event, I'm claiming that the double-luck structure is essential to Gettier cases.

2. I adapted the case from Lehrer (1965: 169–70).

3. I adapted the case from Zagzebski (1996: 285–6). It resembles Chisholm's sheep-in-the-field case (1989: 93).

4. Pollock calls the Gettier problem a mere "intriguing side issue" that "warped the course of epistemology" (1999: 386). Foley laments its "corrupting consequences" (2004: 69–70). Some contend that Gettier subjects do know; see Matilal 1986: 137–40, Hetherington 1999, and Weatherson 2003. See also Sartwell 1992.

5. Matilal teaches us (1986: 135–7) that Gettier cases appeared long before Edmund Gettier. The classical Indian philosopher Śrīharṣa constructed similar examples in the 1100s to confound his opponents.

6. Harman 1973: 195. See also Clark 1963: 47.

7. *E.g.*, Feldman 1974. See also Saunders and Champawat 1964.

8. See Sosa 1991: Chapter 4. See also Lycan 2006: 153–8.

9. I adapted the case from Warfield 2005: 407–8. Saunders and Champawat 1964 also provide a nice example.

10. Harman specifies that knowledge precludes only reasoning essentially involving falsehood. This accommodates cases where your belief is based on multiple independent lines of cogent reasoning, each sufficing to fixate belief. You could know your conclusion provided at least one relevant line of reasoning was sound, even if others involved falsehood. In such a case, your reasoning does not essentially involve falsehood. But COUNT is not like this.

11. Zagzebski offers a different definition of knowledge, which she says "roughly coincides" with the definition I discuss in the main text (2009: 127). For our purposes, the important point is that both definitions feature the crucial "because of" relation.

12. Virtue epistemologists disagree over what constitutes an intellectual virtue, the two main camps being "virtue responsibilists" and "virtue reliabilists." This disagreement needn't concern us here. See Greco and Turri 2009 for more details.

13. Zagzebski 1996: 297.

14. Pritchard 2005: 197. See also Murphy 1998: 212. Pritchard interprets Zagzebski as requiring *sensitivity* for knowledge. "Zagzebski seems to have a modal claim in mind here. Not only should the agent form her true belief via her stable and reliable epistemic virtues, but she should also believe what she does *because* it is true where, intuitively, this means that were what is believed not true, then she would not form the belief that she did via her stable and reliable epistemic virtues. So construed, Zagzebski seems to be wanting to add a sensitivity condition to her virtue theory . . ." (Pritchard 2005: 197). But Zagzebski rejects defining *because of* counterfactually (1999: 111).

15. Murphy 1998: 212; Roberts and Wood 2007: 14–15.

16. Levin 2004.

17. Greco 2002: 309; Pritchard 2005: 196; Baehr 2006: 487–8; Battaly 2008: 16.

18. Zagzebski 1999: 108, 111, 112.

19. Greco 2003. He advertises a "solution" to the Gettier problem, but later restricts his remarks to "at least many" Gettier cases (2003: 131), and suspects his account will need refinement to handle some Gettier cases (2003: 132 n. 33). I restrict my discussion to Gettier cases that Greco says his view handles.

20. Greco 2003: 123, 127–132. See also Greco 2002: 308–11.

21. Greco 2003: 131.

22. Greco 2003: 131.

23. Greco 2003: 130. Greco 2003 doesn't explicitly address HUSBAND, but his account is clearly intended to apply to it.

24. See, *e.g.*, Pritchard 2005: 193; 2006: 38–9, and Lackey 2007: 347–8, 354.

25. Greco 2003: 130. Of cases like FORD and HUSBAND he says, "[the subject] does use reliable abilities or powers to arrive at her belief, but . . . this is not the most salient aspect of the case." See also Greco 2002: 309.

26. I adapted the case from Lackey 2007: 352.

27. Lackey 2007: 352.

28. Greco 2007.

29. Greco 2007: 65.

30. Greco's latest work on these issues (2009) remains faithful to the same basic line of thought advanced in his earlier work canvassed here. Lately Greco says, "S knows p if and only if S believes the truth (with respect to p) because S's belief that p is produced by intellectual ability," where 'because' is "intended to mark a causal explanation" (2009: 18). I detect no development of additional resources that would help resolve the question raised here.

31. Sosa 2007: Lectures 2 and 5. On Sosa's view, *animal knowledge* is apt belief. *Reflective knowledge* is "apt belief aptly noted," which is effectively knowing that you know. Here we set aside reflective knowledge.

32. Sosa 2007: 22–3.

33. Sosa 2007: 95–97. See also Sosa 2003: 171–2, and compare Zagzebski 1996: 297.

34. Notice that Watson's relevant belief is in the simple present tense: the criminal *has* a limp. On the most natural reading of the story, he also believes that the criminal *had* a limp at the time of the crime. But the latter belief isn't relevant for present purposes. (Thanks to an anonymous referee for pointing out the potential for a misreading here.)

35. Alternatively Sosa could retain the thesis that knowledge is apt belief, and claim that aptness requires something more than being true because competent.

36. Sosa 2007: 36, 31. He also speaks of performances succeeding "out of" competence (1991: 288), and "deriving from the proper exercise" of a competence (1991: 292), and "deriving sufficiently from a competence" (2003: 172; cf. 1991: 144–5).

37. Zagzebski 1996: 297; 1999: 107.

38. They actually have more than just a quadruple-A structure, but I set aside the presently irrelevant details. See Section 7 for more details.

39. Zagzebski, Sosa, and Greco (and others in the virtue epistemology camp) disagree over just which features of the subject's cognitive character are relevant to knowledge. I aim to avoid this dispute at present, since it can't be settled here, which is why I use 'competence' broadly. Elsewhere I question whether the relevant disposition, ability, etc., must be reliable. Here I assume it must be, since I cannot responsibly treat the issue here.

40. CARAFE and FIRE differ in why the outcome fails to manifest the disposition. I distinguish between *atypical* failure and *interventional* failure. A disposition associates with paradigmatic outcome types. *Breaking* and *cracking*, etc., are associated with fragility; *being carefully packed* and *remaining intact* are not, even if an item's being fragile frequently causes it to remain intact by being carefully packed or otherwise specially treated, CARAFE's outcome fails to manifest fragility because it is atypical for fragility. By contrast FIRE's outcome (*i.e.*, the water's boiling) is paradigmatic of the microwave's boiling power, but it still fails to manifest the power because something intervenes in the production of the outcome. Gettier cases appear to be interventional failures. The fake-barn case (considered below) involves neither atypical nor interventional failure; at worst, it involves *environmental* failure.

The inclusion of 'relevant' doesn't render the suggestion objectionably vague. It's included because there's no informative way of specifying in advance what the relevant disposition(s) will be. Sometimes it will be a power of perception, other times of intuition, other times of reasoning, other times of introspection, etc. Absent details, it's impossible to say whether Smith believes the Pythagorean theorem through, say, intuition, reasoning, or testimony. The same is true generally of the relation between outcomes and dispositions. The boulder resides at the top of the hill. Absent details, it's impossible to say whether this outcome manifests my herculean physical strength (I carried it up the hill), or my engineering skill (I devised a lever to easily convey it).

41. Greco and Sosa both mention "alternative" proposals that strongly suggest my way of putting things. Greco speaks of true beliefs "revealing reliable cognitive character" (2003: 123; but compare: "what does it mean to say that an action reveals character, other than that the action results from character?" 120); Greco understands "subjective justification" in terms of dispositions you "manifest" when believing conscientiously (2003: 127); Sosa speaks of success that "manifests competence," though he chooses to not "tarry over this promising alternative" (2007: 80). More recently Sosa has tarried over it, much to our benefit (2009). See also Shope 2004: 306.

42. See Strevens 2008.

43. Compare Warfield 2005: 414. The latest experiments suggest the gravitational constant equals $6.693 \times 10 - 11$ m^3/ks^2 (Fixler et al. 2007).

44. I don't pretend that my discussion here settles all questions related to knowledge from falsehood. I claim only that we have located a principled explanation for why it is possible, which is a virtue of the view.

A related issue is whether you can know a proposition that is approximately true but nevertheless, strictly speaking, false. I think this is a possibility worth considering; indeed, it may even be correct. Fortunately my proposed definition of knowledge can be adjusted to accommodate it without sacrificing the ability to solve the Gettier problem. Call a performance that fails but nearly succeeds *an approximation*. Now we can simply append a disjunct to my proposal in the main text: You know Q just in case either your truly believing Q manifests your cognitive competence, or your approximating Q manifests your cognitive competence. Call this the *approximation (or better)* account of knowledge. (Thanks to Pavel Davydov for convincing me that it was worth mentioning this view in this context.)

45. I imagine that those attracted to the view that your "practical environment" can affect what you know might have principled grounds for disagreeing. See *e.g.* Fantl and McGrath 2002, 2007, Hawthorne 2004: Chapter 4, and Stanley 2005: Chapter 5.

46. Greco suggests something similar (2007: section 5).

47. Sosa requires such for apt performance (2007).

48. For help with this paper, I thank Pavel Davydov, John Greco, Glen Koehn, Sharifa Mohamed, Duncan Pritchard, Bruce Russell, Ernest Sosa, Olivia Tang, Angelo Turri, Linda Zagzebski, and especially Christopher Kane. Thanks also to gracious audiences at Wayne State University and the University of Western Ontario, and two anonymous referees for *Philosophers' Imprint*.

References

Baehr, Jason S. 2006. "Character in Epistemology." *Philosophical Studies* 128 (2006), 479–514.

Battaly, Heather. 2008. "Virtue Epistemology." *Philosophy Compass* 3.4: 639–663.

Chisholm, Roderick M. 1989. *Theory of Knowledge*, 3rd ed. Englewood Cliffs, NJ: Prentice Hall.

Clark, Michael. 1963. "Knowledge and Grounds: A Comment on Mr. Gettier's Paper." *Analysis* 24.2: 46–48.

DePaul, Michael, and Linda Zagzebski, eds., 2003. *Intellectual Virtue: Perspectives from Ethics and Epistemology*. Oxford: Oxford University Press.

Fantl, Jeremy, and Matthew McGrath. 2002. "Evidence, Pragmatics, and Justification." *Philosophical Review* 111.1: 67–94.

Fantl, Jeremy, and Matthew McGrath. 2007. "On Pragmatic Encroachment in Epistemology." *Philosophy and Phenomenological Research*, 75.3: 558–589.

Fixler, J.B., et al. 2007. "Atom Interferometer Measurement of the Newtonian Constant of Gravity." *Science*, 5 January 2007, 74–77.

Foley, Richard. 2004. "A Trial Separation between the Theory of Knowledge and the Theory of Justified Belief." In Greco, ed.

Gettier, Edmund. 1963. "Is Justified True Belief Knowledge?" *Analysis* 23.6: 121–123.

Goldman, Alvin. 1976. "Discrimination and Perceptual Knowledge." *The Journal of Philosophy* 73.20: 771–791.

Greco, John. 2002. "Virtues in Epistemology." In Moser, ed.

Greco, John. 2003. "Knowledge as Credit for True Belief." In DePaul and Zagzebski, eds.

Greco, John, ed. 2004. *Ernest Sosa and His Critics*. Blackwell: 2004.

Greco, John. 2007. "The Nature of Ability and the Purpose of Knowledge." *Philosophical Issues* 17.1: 57–69.

Greco, John. 2009. "Knowledge and Success from Ability." *Philosophical Studies* 142.1: 17–26.

Greco, John, and Ernest Sosa, eds. 1999. *The Blackwell Guide to Epistemology*. Malden, MA: Blackwell.

Greco, John, and John Turri. 2009. "Virtue Epistemology." *Stanford Encyclopedia of Philosophy*. Ed. Edward Zalta. ⟨http://plato.stanford.edu/entries/epistemology-virtue/⟩

Harman, Gilbert. 1973. *Thought*. Princeton: Princeton University Press.

Hawthorne, John. 2004. *Knowledge and Lotteries*. Oxford: Oxford University Press.

Hetherington, Stephen. 1999. "Knowing Failably." *The Journal of Philosophy* 96.11: 565–587.

Hetherington, Stephen, ed. 2006. *Epistemology Futures*. Oxford: Oxford University Press.

Lackey, Jennifer. 2007. "Why We Don't Deserve Credit for Everything We Know." *Synthese* 158.3: 345–361.

Lehrer, Keith. 1965. "Knowledge, Truth and Evidence." *Analysis* 25.5: 168–175.

Levin, Michael. 2004. "Virtue Epistemology: No New Cures." *Philosophy and Phenomenological Research* 69.2: 397–410.

Lycan, William G. 2006. "On the Gettier Problem problem." In Hetherington, ed.

Matilal, Bimal Krishna. 1986. *Perception: An Essay on Classical Indian Theories of Knowledge*. Oxford: Oxford University Press.

Moser, Paul K., ed. 2002. *The Oxford Handbook of Epistemology*. Oxford: Oxford University Press.

Murphy, Mark C. 1998. Review of *Virtues of the Mind. Philosophical Books* 39.3: 210–212.

Pritchard, Duncan. 2005. *Epistemic Luck*. Oxford: Oxford University Press.

Pritchard, Duncan. 2006. "Greco on Reliabilism and Epistemic Luck." *Philosophical Studies* 130.1: 35–45.

Roberts, Robert C., and W. Jay Wood. 2007. *Intellectual Virtues: An Essay in Regulative Epistemology*. Oxford: Clarendon Press.

Sartwell, Crispin. 1992. "Why Knowledge Is Merely True Belief." *The Journal of Philosophy* 89.4: 167–180.

Saunder, John, and Narayan Champawat. 1964. *Analysis* 25.1: 8–9.

Shope, Robert. 2004. "The Analysis of Knowing." In *Handbook of Epistemology*. Ed. Ilkka Niiniluoto, Matti Sintonen, Jan Woleński. Dordrecht: Kluwer.

Sosa, Ernest. 1991. *Knowledge in Perspective: Selected Essays in Epistemology*. Cambridge: Cambridge University Press.

Sosa, Ernest. 2003. "The Place of Truth in Epistemology." In DePaul and Zagzebski, eds.

Sosa, Ernest. 2007. *A Virtue Epistemology: Apt Belief and Reflective Knowledge*, v. 1. Oxford: Oxford University Press.

Sosa, Ernest. 2009. "Knowing Full Well." *Philosophical Studies* 142.1: 5–15.

Stanley, Jason. 2005. *Knowledge and Practical Interests*. Oxford: Oxford University Press.

Strevens, Michael. 2008. *Depth: An Account of Scientific Explanation*. Cambridge, MA: Harvard University Press.

Unger, Peter. 1968. "An Analysis of Factual Knowledge." *Journal of Philosophy* 65.6: 157–70.

Warfield, Ted. A. 2005. "Knowledge from Falsehood." *Philosophical Perspectives* 19: 405–416.

Weatherson, Brian. 2003. "What Good Are Counterexamples?" *Philosophical Studies* 115.1: 1–31.

Zagzebski, Linda. 1994. "The Inescapability of Gettier Problems." *The Philosophical Quarterly* 44.174: 65–73.

Zagzebski, Linda. 1996. *Virtues of the Mind: An Inquiry into the Nature of Virtue and the Ethical Foundations of Knowledge*. Cambridge: Cambridge University Press.

Zagzebski, Linda. 1999. "What Is Knowledge?" In Greco and Sosa, eds.

Zagzebski, Linda. 2009. *On Epistemology*. Belmont, Calif.: Wadsworth.

C   Epistemic Value

7   The Search for the Source of Epistemic Good

Linda Zagzebski

Abstract

Knowledge has almost always been treated as good, better than mere true belief, but it is remarkably difficult to explain what it is about knowledge that makes it better. I call this "the value problem." I have previously argued that most forms of reliabilism cannot handle the value problem. In this article I argue that the value problem is more general than a problem for reliabilism, infecting a host of different theories, including some that are internalist. An additional problem is that not all instances of true belief seem to be good on balance, so even if a given instance of knowing p is better than merely truly believing p, not all instances of knowing will be good enough to explain why knowledge has received so much attention in the history of philosophy. The article aims to answer two questions: (1) What makes knowing p better than merely truly believing p? The answer involves an exploration of the connection between believing and the agency of the knower. Knowing is an act in which the knower gets credit for achieving truth. (2) What makes some instances of knowing good enough to make the investigation of knowledge worthy of so much attention? The answer involves the connection between the good of believing truths of certain kinds and a good life. In the best kinds of knowing, the knower not only gets credit for getting the truth but also gets credit for getting a desirable truth. The kind of value that makes knowledge a fitting object of extensive philosophical inquiry is not independent of moral value and the wider values of a good life.

Philosophers have traditionally regarded knowledge as a highly valuable epistemic state, perhaps even one of the great goods of life. At a minimum, it is thought to be more valuable than true belief. Contemporary proposals on the nature of knowledge, however, make it difficult to understand why

Reprinted from Linda Zagzebski, "The Search for the Source of Epistemic Good," *Metaphilosophy* 34 (2003): 12–28.

knowledge is good enough to have received so much attention in the history of philosophy. Some of the most common theories cannot even explain why knowledge is better than true belief. I propose that the search for the source of epistemic value reveals some constraints on the way knowledge can be defined. I believe it will also show that the common view that epistemic good is independent of moral good is largely an illusion.

1   What Makes Knowledge Better Than True Belief?

It is almost always taken for granted that knowledge is good, better than true belief *simpliciter*, but it is remarkably difficult to explain what it is about knowledge that makes it better. I call this "the value problem."[1] I have previously argued that most forms of reliabilism have a particularly hard time handling the value problem.[2] According to standard reliabilist models, knowledge is true belief that is the output of reliable belief-forming processes or faculties. But the reliability of the source of a belief cannot explain the difference in value between knowledge and true belief. One reason it cannot do so is that reliability per se has no value or disvalue. A reliable espresso maker is good because espresso is good. A reliable water-dripping faucet is not good because dripping water is not good. The good of the product makes the reliability of the source that produces it good, but the reliability of the source does not then give the product an additional boost of value. The liquid in this cup is not improved by the fact that it comes from a reliable espresso maker. If the espresso tastes good, it makes no difference if it comes from an unreliable machine. If the flower garden is beautiful, it makes no difference if it was planted by an unreliable gardener. If the book is fascinating, it makes no difference if it was written by an unreliable author. If the belief is true, it makes no difference if it comes from an unreliable belief-producing source.

This point applies to any source of a belief, whether it be a process, faculty, virtue, skill—any cause of belief whose value is thought to confer value on the true belief that is its product, and which is thought to confer value because of its reliability. If knowledge is true belief arising out of the exercise of good traits and skills, it cannot be the reliability of the agent's traits and skills that adds the value. Those traits or skills must be good for some reason that does not wholly derive from the good of the product they produce: true belief. As reliabilism has matured, the location of reliability has shifted from processes to faculties to agents.[3] There are advantages in this progression, but if the good-making feature of a belief-forming process or faculty or agent is only its reliability, then these versions of reliabilism all share the same problem; being the product of a reliable faculty or agent does not add value to the product.[4] Hence, if knowledge arises from something like intellectual virtue or intellectually virtuous acts, what makes an intellectual trait good, and hence a virtue, cannot be simply that it reliably leads to true belief. This, then, is the first moral of the value problem: *Truth plus a reliable source of truth cannot explain the value of knowledge.*

It follows that there must be a value in the cause of a true belief that is independent of reliability or truth conduciveness, whether we call it virtue or something else. Suppose we succeed in identifying such a value. Is that sufficient to solve the value problem? Unfortunately, it is not, so long as we think of knowledge as the external product of a good cause. A cup of espresso is not made better by the fact that the machine that produces it is valuable, even when that value is independent of the value of good-tasting espresso. What the espresso analogy shows is not only that a reliable cause does not confer value on its effect but also that there is a general problem in attributing value to an effect because of its causes, even if the value of the cause is independent of the value of the effect. I am not suggesting that a cause can never confer value on its effect. Sometimes cause and effect have an internal connection, such as that between motive and act, which I shall discuss in a moment. My point is just that the value of a cause does not transfer to its effect automatically, and certainly not on the model of an effect as the output of the cause. So even if the cause of true belief has an independent value, that still does not tell us what makes knowledge better than true belief if knowledge is true belief that is good in some way other than its truth. The second moral of the value problem, then, is this: *Truth plus an independently valuable source cannot explain the value of knowledge.*

It follows from the second moral that to solve the value problem it is not enough to find another value in the course of analysing knowledge; one needs to find another value in the right place. Consider Alvin Plantinga's theory of warrant as proper function. A properly functioning machine does not confer value on its product any more than a reliable one does. The problem is not that proper function is not a good thing but that it is not a value in the knowing state itself. The first two morals of the value problem, then, reveal a deeper problem. We cannot explain what makes knowledge more valuable than true belief if we persist in using the machine-product model of belief that is so common in epistemological discourse.[5] Knowledge cannot be identified with the state of true belief that is the output of a valuable cause, whether or not the cause has a value independent of the value of true belief.[6]

In other work I have proposed that in a state of knowledge the agent gets to the truth because of the virtuous features of her belief-forming activity.[7] Wayne Riggs and John Greco's response to the value problem is that the extra value of knowing in addition to true belief is the state of affairs of the epistemic agent's getting credit for the truth that is acquired.[8] Ernest Sosa's response to the value problem is similar. He says that in a state of knowing, the truth is attributable to the agent as his or her own doing.[9] These approaches clearly are similar, but they solve the value problem only if we reject the machine-product model of knowledge.[10] For the same reason that the espresso in a cup is not made better by the fact that it is produced by a reliable espresso maker or a properly functioning espresso maker, it does not get any better if the machine gets credit for producing the espresso. That is to say, the coffee in the cup does not taste any better.

The conclusion is that true belief arising from cognitive activity cannot be like espresso coming out of an espresso maker. Not only is the reliability of the machine insufficient to make the coffee in the cup any better; nothing about the machine makes the product any better. So if knowledge is true belief that is made better by something, knowledge cannot be the external product of the believer in the way the cup of espresso is the external product of the machine.

Let us look at the idea that knowing has something to do with the agent getting credit for the truth, that she gets to the truth because of something about her as a knowing agent—her virtues or virtuous acts. There are theoretical motives for this idea that have nothing to do with the value problem, such as the proposal that it avoids Gettier problems,[11] so it is supported by other constraints on the account of knowledge. But my concern in this article is the way this move can solve the value problem. If I am right that knowing is not an output of the agent, it must be a state of the agent. I am not suggesting that this is the only alternative to the machine-product model,[12] but if we think of a belief as part of the agent, the belief can get evaluative properties from features of the agent in the same way that acts get evaluative properties from the agent. In fact, the idea that in a state of knowing the agent gets credit for getting the truth suggests that her epistemic state is attached to her in the same way her acts are attached to her. An act is not a product of an agent but is a part of the agent, and the agent gets credit or discredit for an act because of features of the agent. In particular, an agent gets credit for certain good features of an act, for example, its good consequences or the fact that it follows a moral principle—because of features of the act that derive directly from the agent—for example, its intention or its motive. If believing is like acting, we have a model for the way the agent can get credit for the truth of a belief because of features of the belief that derive from the agent. I propose, then, that this is the third moral of the value problem: *Knowing is related to the knower not as product to machine but as act to agent.*[13]

The value problem arises for a group of theories wider than those that are reliabilist or even externalist. Internalists generally do not think of a true belief as the product of what justifies it, and so they accept the first part of the third moral. Nonetheless, some of them are vulnerable to the first moral of the value problem because they analyse justification in such a way that its value is explained by its truth conduciveness. Laurence BonJour does this explicitly in the following passage:

The basic role of justification is that of a *means* to truth, a more directly attainable mediating link between our subjective starting point and our objective goal. . . . If epistemic justification were not conducive to truth in this way, if finding epistemically justified beliefs did not substantially increase the likelihood of finding true ones, then epistemic justification would be irrelevant to our main cognitive goal and of dubious worth. It is only if we have some reason for thinking that epistemic justification constitutes a path to truth that we as cognitive beings have any motive for preferring epistemically justified beliefs to epistemically unjustified ones. Epistemic justification is therefore in the final analysis only an instrumental value, not an intrinsic one. (BonJour 1985, 7–8)[14]

Notice that in this passage BonJour understands the value of justification the same way the reliabilist does, as something that is good because it is truth conducive. The internality of justification has nothing to do with its value on BonJour's account. But as we have seen, if the feature that converts true belief into knowledge is good just because of its conduciveness to truth, we are left without an explanation of why knowing p is better than merely truly believing p. And this is the case whether or not that feature is accessible to the consciousness of the believer. BonJour does not appeal to the machine-product model, and so the problem in his case is more subtle than it is for the reliabilist. Nonetheless, the problem is there, because a true belief does not gain any additional good property from justification. In contrast, the traditional account of knowledge as justified true belief does not have the value problem, because the justifying beliefs do not or do not simply produce the belief that is a candidate for knowledge. Instead, they give it a property, justifiedness. They make *it* justified. The conclusion is that if knowing p is better than truly believing p, there must be something other than the truth of p that *makes believing p better*. My proposal is that if believing is like acting, it can be made better by certain properties of the agent.

Consider a few of the ways an act acquires properties because of features of the agent. The class of acts subject to moral evaluation has traditionally been called the voluntary. A voluntary act is an act for which the agent gets credit or blame. The voluntary includes some acts that are intentional and some that are non-intentional. Acts that are voluntary but non-intentional can be motivated, and perhaps always are. My position is that acts of believing are generally in the category of acts that are voluntary but non-intentional, although for the purposes of this article it is not necessary that this position be accepted. What is important is just the idea that beliefs can be and perhaps typically are motivated, and that the motive can affect the evaluation of the belief in a way that is analogous to the way the motive can affect the evaluation of an overt act.

What I mean by a motive is an affective state that initiates and directs action. In my theory of emotion, a motive is an emotion that is operating to produce action. The appreciation for a value is an emotion that can initiate and direct action. When it does, it is a motive in the sense I mean. Acts motivated by appreciation of a value may not be intentional even when they are voluntary. My thesis is that, other things being equal, acts motivated by love of some value are highly valuable.[15]

As I analyse virtue, a motive disposition is a component of a virtue. A virtuous act is an act motivated by the motive of some virtue V and is characteristic of acts motivated by V in the circumstances in question.[16] An act can be compassionate, courageous, or generous, or unfair, cruel, and so on. The name of the virtue or vice out of which an act is done is typically given by the name of the motive out of which it is done, and the motive is a feature of the agent who performs the act. If believing is like acting, it can be virtuous or vicious. The properties of true believing that make it better than mere true believing are properties that it obtains from the agent in the same way good acts obtain evaluative properties from the agent. In particular, a belief can acquire value from its motive, in addition to the value it may have in being true.

The idea that to know is to act is not very common these days, although it has a lot of precedent in philosophical history.[17] Sometimes the word *judge* is used to distinguish that which can be converted into knowledge from belief, which is commonly understood as a disposition or a passive state rather than as an act. I shall continue to use the word *believe* to refer to an act since I think it is an acceptable use of the term, but some readers might find the substitution of the word *judge* in what follows clearer.

What motives of the agent could make believing better? I have previously argued that it is motives that are forms of the basic motive of love of truth.[18] The motivational components of the individual intellectual virtues such as open-mindedness or intellectual fairness or intellectual thoroughness or caution differ, but they are all based on a general love or valuing of truth or a disvaluing of falsehood.[19] The motivational components of the intellectual virtues are probably more complex than this since, for example, intellectual fairness may consist in part in respect for others as well as in respect or love of truth.[20] But love of truth is plausibly the primary motive underlying a wide range of intellectual virtues.[21] If love of truth is a good motive, it would add value to the intellectual acts it motivates.

What sort of value does love of truth have? Assuming that if something is valuable it is also valuable to appreciate or love it, then love of true belief has value because true belief has value. But the motive of love of truth also derives value from distinctively moral motives. That is because moral permissibility, praise, and blame rest on epistemic permissibility, praise, and blame.[22]

Let me propose a condition for impermissibility. When something of moral importance is at stake when someone performs an act S, then if S is a case of acting on a belief B, it is morally important that B be true. It is, therefore, impermissible for the agent to believe in a way that fails to respect the importance of the truth of B. That implies that the agent must believe out of certain motives. In particular, I suggest that the agent's motives must be such that they include a valuing of truth or, at a minimum, that they do not involve a disvaluing or neglect of truth.[23]

If moral blameworthiness rests on epistemic blameworthiness, then the same reasoning leads to the conclusion that moral praiseworthiness or credit rests on epistemic praiseworthiness or credit.[24] Suppose now that an act S is a case of acting on a belief B and that act S is an instance of an act type that is morally praiseworthy in the right conditions. I propose that act S is credited to the agent only if the truth of belief B is credited to the agent. So if knowing B is something like truly believing when the truth of B is credited to the agent, it follows that the agent gets moral credit for an act S based on belief B only if S knows B.[25]

Suppose also that I am right that there is a motivational requirement for getting credit for the truth that involves love of truth. It follows that the motive of love of truth is a requirement for love of moral goods, or at least is a requirement for love of those moral goods for which one gets praise or blame in one's acts. The praiseworthiness of love of truth is a condition for moral praiseworthiness. There is, therefore, a moral motive to have knowledge. The value that converts true believing into knowing is a condition for the moral value of acts that depend upon the belief.

In spite of the moral importance of having true beliefs, we usually think that true belief is good in itself. The value of true belief is a distinctively epistemic value that allegedly permits epistemologists to treat the domain of belief and knowledge as something independent of acts subject to moral evaluation. This brings us to the deeper value problem of knowledge: In what sense, if any, is true belief good? If true believing is not good, we have a much more serious problem than that of finding the value that makes knowing better than true believing.

2   The Value of True Belief

I have been treating knowledge as something the knower earns. It is a state in which the prize of truth is credited to her; perhaps she is even deserving of praise for it. But why should we think that? I have already mentioned that this idea was developed because it avoids Gettier problems, but that objective is surely only a small part of the task of defining knowledge. Knowledge is worth discussing because it is worth having. But the fact that knowledge is valuable does not force us to think of it as something we earn or get credit for or are responsible for or praised for, although that way of looking at it follows from the sports analogies used in discussions of the value problem by Sosa, Greco, and Riggs, and from the analogy of winning a battle used by Michael DePaul.[26] They all treat knowledge as an achievement or points earned in a game rather than the blessings of good fortune. I think they are right about that, but it is worth mentioning that the fact that knowing is a valuable state does not force us to think of it in that way. Some goods are just as good if we do not have to work for them—for example, good health and a safe environment—and some may even be better if we do not have to work for them—for example, love and friendship. Good health, safety, love, and friendship are all good in the sense of the desirable. The sense of good that we earn or get credit for is the sense of good as the admirable. I have argued that if we think of knowing as being like acting, it is the sort of thing that can be virtuous or vicious, which is to say, admirable or reprehensible. Knowledge is admirable. But surely knowledge is also desirable because its primary component, true belief, is thought to be desirable. That is to say, we think that true belief is good *for* us.

True belief may be desirable, but it is certainly not admirable. It is not something for which we get credit or praise. That is, true belief by itself does not carry credit with it, although I have said that in cases of knowing we get credit for the truth because of other features of the belief. The kind of value that makes knowing better than true believing is the admirable, whereas the kind of value true believing has is the desirable. But now we encounter a problem, because surely not all true beliefs are desirable. For one thing, many people have pointed out that some truths are trivial. This is a problem for the value of knowledge, because even if knowing a trivial truth is better than merely truly believing it, how much better can it be? There is only so much good that knowing a trivial truth can have. If it is fundamentally valueless to have a true belief about the number of times the word *the* is used in a McDonald's commercial, it is also valueless to know it. So even if trivial truths are believed in the most highly virtuous, skilful, rational, or justified way, the triviality of the truth makes the knowing of such truths trivial as well. The unavoidable conclusion is that some knowledge is not good for us. Some might even be bad for us. It can be bad for the agent and it can be bad for others—for example, knowing exactly what the surgeon is doing to my leg when he is removing a skin cancer; knowing the neighbour's private life. It follows that either not all knowledge is desirable or some true beliefs cannot be converted into knowledge.

A common response to this problem is to say that truth is conditionally valuable. It is not true belief per se that is valuable but having the answer to our questions. Our interests determine the difference between valuable true beliefs and nonvaluable or disvaluable ones. Sosa gives the example of counting grains of sand on the beach. He says that we do not think that believing the outcome of such a count has value, because it does not serve any of our interests.[27] But, of course, somebody *might* be interested in the number of grains of sand on the beach, yet it seems to me that knowing the count does not get any better if he is. If a truth is trivial, believing it is not improved by the fact that the epistemic agent has peculiar or perverse interests. In fact, the interests may even make it worse, because we add the perversity of the interests to the triviality of the truth.[28]

Perhaps we can appeal to the idea of importance to save the intuition that our interests and goals have something to do with the truths that are valuable to us, by making the value more significant.[29] Maybe some things are just important *simpliciter*, where that means there are truths whose importance is not reducible to what is important to so-and-so. Perhaps there are degrees of distance from the individual in the concept of importance, where some things are important to people in a certain role or in a certain society, and some are important to everybody. But I don't think this move will help us. There are no important 'truths' if a truth is a true proposition, since propositions are not important in themselves, and if truth is a property of propositions, truth is not what is important. Instead, it is the state of truly believing the proposition that is important. So when we say that some truths are important and others are not, what we really mean is that some true *beliefs* are important and others are not. And then to say this means no more than that the value of true beliefs varies. But we already knew that. What we want to know is what makes them vary. The idea of important true beliefs is just another way of posing the problem. It is not a solution to the problem.

Another form of conditional value is instrumental value. It has been argued that satisfaction of our desires or reaching our goals is what reason aims at. True belief is surely a means to reaching our ends, most of which are non-epistemic. A good example of this position is that of Richard Foley, who argues that the epistemic goal of truth is instrumentally valuable as a means to other goals, whose value is left undetermined.[30] Clearly, many true beliefs have instrumental value, but instrumental value is a form of conditional value, since the condition for the value of the means is the value of the end. If the end is disvaluable, so is the means.[31] Conditional value is like a suspected terrorist: someone who is a suspected terrorist may not be a terrorist, and a belief that has conditional value may not have value. No form of conditional value possessed by true belief has the consequence that all true beliefs are valuable.

There is still the possibility that true belief has intrinsic value. Perhaps every true belief has some intrinsic value simply in virtue of being true, whether or not it is good for us. That may well be the case, but I do not see that it will have the consequence that every true belief is valuable on balance, because intrinsicality is unrelated to degree. Intrinsicality pertains to the source of a belief, not to its amount. So even if every true belief has some intrinsic value, it is unlikely that the intrinsic value of every true belief is great enough to outweigh the undesirability or other negative value some true beliefs have from other sources.

The inescapable conclusion is that not every true belief is good, all things considered. Whether we are considering admirability or desirability, or an intrinsic or extrinsic source of value, on balance it is likely that there are some true beliefs that have no value and probably some that have negative value.

Now consider what follows for the value of knowing. In the first section I concluded that knowing is better than true believing only if it is true believing in which the agent gets credit for getting the truth. But if a given true belief is not valuable, how can the agent get credit for it if the truth in that case is not such that it is something someone should be given credit for? So long as some true beliefs are disvaluable, it makes just as much sense to say she is blamed for the truth as that she is praised for it. Assuming that every true belief is intrinsically good, it is good that the agent gets credited with the truth because of what is admirable about the agent's epistemic behaviour—her intellectually virtuous motives and acts. But the truth credited to her may not be much of a prize.

Consider also what happens to my proposal that knowledge is better than true belief because it is a case in which the truth is reached by intellectually virtuous motives and acts, the value of which can be traced back to the value of the motive of valuing truth. But if the truth in some cases is not valuable on balance, why should we be motivated to value it? Of course, we are assuming that true belief has some intrinsic value, and we can also assume that true belief is usually good for us, in which case it is reasonable to think that it is good to value it *as* something with some intrinsic value, however slight, as well as something that is usually good for us. But if we are looking for a value that has the potential to be a significant good, we still have not found it.

What is more, so long as some true beliefs are not desirable, the agent's getting the truth can be credited to her even though the agent's getting a *desirable* truth is not credited to her. And even when the truth *is* desirable, it may be a matter of luck that she got a desirable truth rather than an undesirable one. I think this leads us into a problem parallel to the Gettier problem. Gettier cases arise when there is an accidental connection between the admirability of a belief and its truth. Similarly, it is possible that there is an accidental connection between the admirability of a belief and its desirability. I think it is too strong to deny such cases the label of knowledge; nonetheless, they are not as good as they can be. They are not the best instances of knowledge, not the ones that are great goods. The solution to Gettier cases is to close the gap between the admirability of a belief and its truth. The solution to the new value problem is to close the gap between the admirability of a true belief and its desirability. To get a truly interesting value in knowledge, therefore, it should turn out that in some cases of knowing, not only is the truth of the belief credited to the agent but the desirability of the true belief is also credited to the agent. This is a general formula that can be filled out in different ways, just as the formula for the definition of knowledge can be filled out in different ways, depending upon the theorist's conception of credit, and that in turn depends upon a general theory of agent evaluation. In the next section I shall outline the contours of a virtue-theoretic account of knowledge that satisfies the constraints identified in the first two sections of the article.

3 Knowledge, Motives, and *Eudaimonia*

I have claimed that good motives add value to the acts they motivate, and this includes epistemic acts. Motives are complex, and I have not investigated them very far in this article, but a feature of motives that is relevant to our present concern is that they themselves are often motivated by higher-order motives. Higher-order motives are important because they keep our motivational structure compact and aid us in making first-order motives consistent. If good motives can confer value on the acts they motivate, it follows that higher-order motives can confer value on the lower-order motives they motivate the agent to acquire. As we are looking for an additional source of value in some cases of knowledge, it is reasonable to look at the source of the value of the motive of true believing in the particular cases of knowing that are more valuable than ordinary knowing.

We have already seen at least two ways in which the valuing of truth in particular cases is required by other things we value. That is, we have a motive to have the motive for truth because of other good motives. First, if something of moral importance is at stake when we perform an act and that act depends upon the truth of a certain belief, then it is morally important that the belief be true. The motive for true belief in such cases is motivated by the higher-order motive to be moral or to live a good life. Second, since true belief is a means to most practical ends, the motive to value truth in some domain is motivated by the motive of valuing those ends, which is in turn motivated by the desire to have a good life. I propose that the higher-order motive to have a good life includes the motive to have certain other motives, including the motive to value truth in certain domains. The higher-order motive motivates the agent to have the motives that are constituents of the moral and intellectual virtues, and in this way it connects the moral and intellectual virtues together. If knowledge is true belief credited to the agent because of its place in her motivational structure, it gets value not only from the truth motive but also from the higher-order motive that motivates the agent to value truth in some domain or on some occasion. And that motive has nothing to do with epistemic value in particular; it is a component of the motive to live a good life.

My proposal, then, is this. An epistemic agent gets credit for getting a true belief when she arrives at a true belief because of her virtuous intellectual acts motivated by a love of truth. She gets credit for getting a desirable true belief when she arrives at a desirable true belief because of acts motivated by love of true beliefs that are components of a good life. The motive for desirable true beliefs is not the full explanation for the agent's getting credit for acquiring a desirable true belief, for the same reason that the motive for true belief is not the full explanation for the agent's getting credit for acquiring a true belief, but my position is that motives are primary causes of the other valuable features of cognitive activity. When the agent succeeds in getting a desirable true belief because of her admirable intellectual motives, there is a non-accidental connection between the admirability of a belief and its desirability. That connection avoids the parallel to Gettier problems that I mentioned above, and it results in some instances of knowledge being a great good.

Let me review the various ways a belief can be good.

(1) All true beliefs probably have some intrinsic value simply in virtue of being true whether or not they are good for us. When the truth is credited to the agent, the belief is also admirable. That is knowledge.

(2) Some true beliefs are good for us; they are desirable. They can be desirable whether or not they are admirable. But some true beliefs are undesirable. It is also possible that some false beliefs are desirable, but I have not discussed those cases in this article.

(3) Admirable beliefs are those that are virtuous. Admirable beliefs can be false.

(4) Some true beliefs are both desirable and admirable. The most interesting cases are those in which there is a connection between their admirability and their desirability. A belief is admirable, and given its admirability, it is no accident that the agent has a desirable true belief. These are the most highly valuable instances of knowledge.

The problems we have encountered with the value of true belief indicate, I think, that the standard approach to identifying the value of knowledge is the wrong way round. The issue should be not what is added to true belief to make it valuable enough to be knowledge but what is added to virtuous believing to make it knowledge. And, of course, the answer to that question is obvious: It must be true. When we approach the value problem in this way, the harder question is answered first and the easier one second. That is not the usual order, but I think it is the right one. If we begin in the usual way, by starting with true belief, we are starting with something that may have no value of any kind, neither admirability nor desirability. Furthermore, by starting with the value of virtuous believing we can explain why even false virtuously motivated belief is admirable.

Let me conclude by briefly considering what makes virtue in general a good thing. Suppose that Aristotle is right in thinking of virtuous acts as components of *eudaimonia*, a life of flourishing. If I am also right that believing is a form of acting, it follows that virtuous believings are components of eudaimonia. Eudaimonia is a challenging concept to elucidate for many reasons, but one aspect that contemporary commentators find particularly troublesome is Aristotle's apparent idea that eudaimonia fuses the admirable with the desirable. Nobody disputes the conception of eudaimonia as a desirable life; in fact, eudaimonia is generally defined as a desirable life. It then has to be argued that virtuous—that is, admirable-activity is a component of the desirable life. And that, of course, is hotly disputed. The same problem arises over the value of knowing. Nobody is likely to dispute the claim that some true beliefs are desirable. What can be disputed is whether beliefs that are intellectually virtuous, either in the way I have described or in some other, are also components of a desirable life. The question Why should we want to have admirable beliefs? is really no different from the question Why should we want to do admirable acts? If virtuous acts are desirable, it is because it is more desirable to act in an admirable way. Similarly, if knowing a proposition is more desirable than truly believing it, it is because it is more desirable to believe in an admirable way. But I can see no way to defend that without a general account of eudaimonia, or a good life. That means that the debates currently going on in virtue ethics on the relation between virtuous activity and the good life are relevant to an understanding of an intellectually good life as well as to an understanding of a life that is good *simpliciter*.

4   Conclusion

The question What is knowledge? is not independent of the question Why do we value knowledge? For those who consider the former question prior, compare the pair of questions What is knowledge? and Can we get it? It is common for anti-sceptic naturalistic epistemologists to say that whatever knowledge is, it has to be defined as something we have. We are not interested in a non-existent phenomenon. I say that knowledge has to be defined as something we value. We are not interested in a phenomenon with little or no value. It is possible that no phenomenon roughly coinciding with what has traditionally been called knowledge has the value I have been looking for in this article. If so, we would have to move to an Error theory like that of J. L. Mackie in ethics. But I do not yet see that this will be necessary, since it is possible to give an account of knowledge that both satisfies the usual contemporary constraints and identifies a phenomenon with interesting value. I also think we should conclude that if knowledge is a state worthy of the sustained attention it has received throughout the history of philosophy, it is because its value goes well beyond the epistemic value of truth and what conduces to true belief. Knowledge is important because it is intimately connected to moral value and the wider values of a good life. It is very unlikely that epistemic value in any interesting sense is autonomous.

Acknowledgements

I thank Philip Percival, my commentator at the conference at the University of Stirling, for his interesting and helpful comments. Earlier versions of this article were presented at the University of California, Riverside, Tulane University, the University of Oklahoma, and the Eastern Division Meetings of the American Philosophical Association, December 2001. I thank the audiences at those presentations. Particular thanks go to my commentator at the APA session, Michael DePaul, for his help in improving the article.

Notes

1. For an exception to the almost universal view that knowledge is a better state than true belief, see Sartwell 1992. This move displaces the problem to that of identifying the value of true belief, which will be addressed in the second section.

2. I mention the value problem briefly in Zagzebski 1996 and discuss it in some detail in Zagzebski 2000. Another version of the value problem is proposed in DePaul 2001.

3. Sosa's earlier theory is what I call faculty reliabilism. Greco has a theory he calls agent reliabilism. In Greco 1999, he uses the term *agent reliabilism* for a class of theories beyond his own, including Sosa's, Plantinga's, and my early theory.

4. On the other hand, reliabilists usually have particular faculties and properties of agents in mind, properties they call virtues, e.g., a good memory, keen eyesight, and well-developed powers of reasoning. The goodness of these virtues is not limited to their reliability, and so long as that is recognised, the theory has a way out of the value problem. But for the same reason, it is misleading to call these theories forms of reliabilism.

5. The machine-product model has been used by Alston, Plantinga, Sosa, Goldman, and others. The word *output* is frequently used, and some of them illustrate their discussion with analogies of machines and their products.

6. My colleague Wayne Riggs has thought of the location issue as a way out of the value problem. See Riggs 2002.

7. Zagzebski 1996, part 3.

8. See Riggs (1998) and Greco (2003).

9. See Sosa (2003).

10. So far as I can tell, Greco and Riggs reject the machine-product model, but Sosa uses it repeatedly, including in Sosa forthcoming, the article in which he proposes his way out of the value problem.

11. I argued this in Zagzebski 1996. See also Riggs (1998) and Greco (2003). DePaul 2001, note 7, argues that Gettier cases produce another form of the value problem, because we think that the value of the agent's epistemic state in Gettier cases is not as valuable as the state of knowledge.

12. Another alternative is that knowledge is identified with the entire process culminating in the belief, and it gets value from the value in the process as well as the truth of the end product of the process. I have proposed that it would serve the purposes of Sosa's account of epistemic value to think of knowledge as an organic unity in the sense used by Franz Brentano and G. E. Moore. That would permit the value of the whole to exceed the value of the sum of the parts. See Zagzebski (2004). DePaul (2001, section 6) also discusses the possibility that knowledge is an organic unity.

13. I explore the requirement of agency in knowledge in Zagzebski 2001.

14. DePaul (1993, chap. 2) insightfully discusses the problem of BonJour and others in explaining the value of knowledge. I thank DePaul for bringing this passage to my attention.

15. I also think that acts motivated by love of some value are more valuable than those that *aim* at the same value but without the motive of love or appreciation for the value. So some nonintentional acts have moral value because they arise from a good motive. In contrast, some intentional acts may aim at a good end but have less value because they do not arise from a good motive. I discuss this in more detail in Zagzebski 2003.

16. In Zagzebski 1996 I distinguish a virtuous act from an act of virtue. Unlike the latter, a virtuous act need not be successful in its aim. I use *act of virtue* as a term of art to identify an act good in every respect. It is an act that arises out of a virtuous motive, is an act a virtuous person would characteristically do in the circumstances, is successful in reaching the aim of the virtuous motive, and does so because of the other virtuous features of the act.

17. Aquinas and other medieval philosophers seem to have thought of knowing as involving an act of intellect. There may be passages in Plato that suggest this also. See Benson 2000, chap. 9.

18. I argue this in Zagzebski 1996, part 2, and in more detail in Zagzebski 2003.

19. I have argued in Zagzebski 2003 that loving truth is not the same as hating false-hood, but I do not think the difference makes a difference to the point of this article.

20. Respect, love, and appreciation in most contexts are quite different, but I do not think the differences make much of a difference in the context of an emotional at-titude towards truth. Since most epistemologists do not think *any* emotional attitude towards truth makes any difference to epistemic status, it is quite enough to try to show that one of these attitudes makes a difference.

21. Some intellectual virtues may aim at understanding rather than truth. I argue that epistemologists have generally neglected the value of understanding in Zagzeb-ski 2001b§. See also Riggs 2003.

22. The *locus classicus* for discussion of the connection between the moral permis-sibility of acts and the permissibility of beliefs is Clifford's article, "The Ethics of Belief." W. K. Clifford concludes that an unjustified belief is morally impermissible. See also Montmarquet 1993 for a good discussion of the relation between the per-missibility of acts and beliefs.

23. The issue of what is involved in epistemic permissibility is a difficult one, be-cause of the 'ought implies can' rule. But unless we are willing to say that no belief is impermissible, there must be some things we ought and ought not to believe, so the 'ought implies can' rule does not prohibit us from speaking of epistemic permissibility. I am not going to discuss the extent to which we can control each of our beliefs. My point is just that so long as we do think there are acts of belief that are impermissible, it follows that either we have whatever power over believing is intended in the 'ought implies can' rule or else the 'ought implies can' rule does not apply to these beliefs. In other words, I think the intuition that impermissibility applies in the realm of belief is stronger than the 'ought implies can' rule.

24. Praiseworthiness differs somewhat from credit in most people's vocabulary, in that deserving praise is a stronger commendation than deserving credit. I think the difference is only one of degree and do not believe that much hangs on the difference.

25. There is no doubt a variety of qualifications to be made here. For example, the agent generally gets credit of some kind for *S* even when *B* is false so long as her intel-lectual motive sufficiently respects the importance of the truth of *B*, she does what intellectually virtuous persons characteristically do in her circumstances, and her belief is only false because of her bad luck.

26. DePaul 2001, 179. DePaul also uses the example of a commercial for a financial institution in which a pompous gentleman announces, "We make money the old-

fashioned way: we earn it." The implication is that it is better to get money by working for it rather than by luck or inheritance. As DePaul points out, that implies that there is something valuable in addition to the money itself.

27. See Sosa 2001.

28. In addition to Sosa, Christopher Stephens uses our interests as a way to resolve the problem of the two values—getting truth and avoiding falsehood. Goldman 2001 identifies interest as a value that unities the epistemic virtues.

29. This idea is briefly discussed by Riggs (2003).

30. See Foley 2001. Foley seems to be content with allowing the value of the goal to be set by the agent.

31. A given means could serve more than one end. I would think that the value of a means in a particular case is determined by its end in that case. This is compatible with a means of that type having value when it serves some other end that is good.

References

Benson, Hugh. 2000. *Socratic Wisdom*. Oxford: Oxford University Press.

BonJour, Laurence. 1985. *The Structure of Empirical Knowledge*. Cambridge, Mass.: Harvard University Press.

DePaul, Michael. 1993. *Balance and Refinement*. New York: Routledge.

———. 2001. "Value Monism in Epistemology." In *Knowledge, Truth, and Duty*, edited by Matthias Steup. Oxford: Oxford University Press.

Foley, Richard. 2001. "The Foundational Role of Epistemology in a General Theory of Rationality." In *Virtue Epistemology: Essays on Epistemic Virtue and Responsibility*, edited by Abrol Fairweather and Linda Zagzebski. Oxford: Oxford University Press.

Goldman, Alvin. 2001. "The Unity of the Epistemic Virtues." In *Virtue Epistemology: Essays on Epistemic Virtue and Responsibility*, edited by Abrol Fairweather and Linda Zagzebski. Oxford: Oxford University Press.

Greco, John. 1999. "Agent Reliabilism." *Philosophical Perspectives* 13: 273–96.

———. 2003. "Knowledge as Credit for True Belief." In *Intellectual Virtue: Perspectives from Ethics and Epistemology*, edited by Michael DePaul and Linda Zagzebski. Oxford: Oxford University Press, 111–134.

Montmarquet, James. 1993. *Epistemic Virtue and Doxastic Responsibility*. Lanham, Md.: Rowman and Littlefield.

Riggs, Wayne. 1998. "What Are the 'Chances' of Being Justified?" *Monist* 81: 452–72.

———. 2002. "Reliability and the Value of Knowledge." *Philosophy and Phenomenological Research* 64, no. 1 (January): 79–96.

———. 2003. "Understanding Virtue and the Virtue of Understanding." In *Intellectual Virtue: Perspectives from Ethics and Epistemology*, edited by Michael DePaul and Linda Zagzebski. Oxford: Oxford University Press, 203–226.

Sartwell, Crispin. 1992. "Knowledge is Merely True Belief." *American Philosophical Quarterly* 28: 157–65.

Sosa, Ernest. 2001. "For the Love of Truth?" In *Virtue Epistemology: Essays on Epistemic Virtue and Responsibility*, edited by Abrol Fairweather and Linda Zagzebski. Oxford: Oxford University Press.

———. 2003. "The Place of Truth in Epistemology." In *Intellectual Virtue: Perspectives from Ethics and Epistemology*, edited by Michael DePaul and Linda Zagzebski. Oxford: Oxford University Press, 155–179.

Zagzebski, Linda. 1996. *Virtues of the Mind: An Inquiry into the Nature of Virtue and the Ethical Foundations of Knowledge*. Cambridge, U.K.: Cambridge University Press.

Zagzebski, Linda. 2000. "From Reliabilism to Virtue Epistemology." In *Knowledge, Belief, and Character*, edited by Guy Axtell. Lanham, Md.: Rowman and Littlefield.

———. 2001a. "Must Knowers Be Agents?" In *Virtue Epistemology: Essays on Epistemic Virtue and Responsibility*, edited by Abrol Fairweather and Linda Zagzebski. Oxford: Oxford University Press.

———. 2001b. "Recovering Understanding." In *Knowledge, Truth, and Obligation*, edited by Matthias Steup. Oxford: Oxford University Press.

———. 2003. "Intellectual Motivation and the Good of Truth." In *Intellectual Virtue: Perspectives from Ethics and Epistemology*, edited by Michael DePaul and Linda Zagzebski. Oxford: Oxford University Press, 135–154.

———. 2004. "Epistemic Value Monism." In *Sosa and His Critics*, edited by John Greco. Oxford: Basil Blackwell, 190–198.

8   Knowing Full Well: The Normativity of Beliefs as Performances

Ernest Sosa

Abstract

Belief is considered a kind of performance, which attains one level of success if it is true (or accurate), a second level if competent (or adroit), and a third if true because competent (or apt). Knowledge on one level (the animal level) is apt belief. The epistemic normativity constitutive of such knowledge is thus a kind of performance normativity. A problem is posed for this account by the fact that suspension of belief seems to fall under the same sort of epistemic normativity as does belief itself, yet to suspend is of course precisely *not* to perform, certainly not with the aim of truth. The paper takes up this problem, and proposes a solution that distinguishes levels of performance norrmativity, including a first order where execution competence is in play, and a second order where the performer must assess the risks attendant on issuing a first-order performance. This imports a level of reflective knowledge that ascends above the animal level.

Two of Plato's best-known dialogues are inquiries about knowledge. The *Theaetetus* inquires into its nature, the *Meno* also into its value. Each dialogue, I will suggest, involves the same more basic question: What sort of normativity is constitutive of our knowledge? A belief that falls short of knowledge is thereby inferior. It is better to know than to get it wrong, of course, and also better than to get it right just by luck. What is involved in such evaluation? An answer to this more basic question enables a solution for both Platonic problems.

We shall assume that knowledge requires at a minimum a belief that is true. Our inquiry into the nature of knowledge thus takes a more specific form. Our question is this: What condition must a belief satisfy, in addition to being true, in order to constitute knowledge? The question of the nature

Reprinted from Ernest Sosa, "Knowing Full Well: The Normativity of Beliefs as Performances," *Philosophical Studies* 142 (2009): 5–15.

of knowledge has been central to epistemology in recent decades, as it was for Plato.

The Gettier problem derives from the fact that the further condition that a belief must satisfy cannot be just its being competently held, competently acquired or sustained.[1] This is clear once we realize that a belief can be false despite being competent. If the believer then competently deduces something true from his false belief, this true conclusion cannot thereby amount to knowledge. Yet, if we competently deduce a conclusion from a premise that we competently believe (even after drawing the conclusion), we thereby competently believe that conclusion as well.

Post-Gettier, the Platonic problem takes this form: What further condition, added to, or in place of, *being competently held*, must a true belief satisfy in order to constitute knowledge?

On the contemporary scene, the second Platonic problem, that of the *value* of knowledge, has more recently moved to center stage. For Plato this was the problem of how knowledge can be quite generally more valuable than its corresponding true belief, if a merely true belief would be no less useful. Thus, a true belief as to the location of Larissa will guide you there no less efficiently than would the corresponding knowledge. In line with this, we ask: How if at all can knowledge be *as such* always better than the corresponding merely true belief?

In connection with both problems, we will assume that there is some further condition (however simple or complex) that a belief must satisfy in order to constitute knowledge, beyond being a belief and being true. This condition must add normatively positive content, moreover, sufficient to explain how it is that *knowledge*, which must satisfy this further condition, *is as such always better than would be the corresponding merely true belief.* When one ponders a question, for example, there is some respect in which it would always be better to answer knowledgeably than to answer correctly but just by luck.

Let's begin with the *Meno* problem.

1   The Value of Knowledge

The aim of belief is said to be truth. When you sincerely pose a question to yourself, for example, you want a correct answer. When you reach an answer to your question through adopting a certain belief, the aim of your belief is the truth of the matter. If the aim of a belief is thus truth, then once true that belief would seem to have what really matters epistemically, irrespective of its aetiology.

How then can a truth-reliably produced true belief be better than one that is no less true, regardless of how reliably it may have been produced? Conclusion: knowledge is really no better as such than merely true belief.

"Any argument leading to that conclusion," it may well be replied, "must have its premises examined: perhaps the aim of belief, and of inquiry, is not just truth, but also knowledge. This would explain how and why it is that knowledge (with its required aetiology) is after all better than merely true belief."

What follows will defend this reply by placing it in context, by explaining its content, and by drawing some implications.

2   A Step Back

How indeed *is* truth our aim? How should we understand the value we place on it? More explicitly, our aim is presumably to *have* the truth. So, it is the *attained* truth that has corresponding value. How then should we more fully describe our true objective? Is it just the accumulation of believed truths? Compare how we assess accurate shots, those that hit their targets. What is it that people value under this rubric? Is it the accumulation of accurate shots?

Someone casually draws a large circle on the beach right by his feet, aims his gun, and hits the target. Does he thereby attain, at least in some small part, a previously standing objective: namely, that of securing accurate shots? Is that an objective we all share, given how we all share the concept of a *good* shot? Don't we all want good things (other things equal)?

That, I trust we agree, is quite absurd.

Yet, the shot at the beach could be an accurate, good shot nonetheless, as the marksman hits his target in the sand. Although, from one point of view, given the low or even negative value of the target, this accurate shot has little value of its own, yet from another, performance-internal perspective it is graded as quite accurate, a good shot, maybe even an excellent shot if the marksman steps back far enough from the target. Even when the shot is difficult, however, its status does not derive from any standing preference of people for an accumulation of accurate, difficult shots. There is no normative pressure on us to bring about good shots, not even if we grasp perfectly well what it takes to be a good shot, and have this uppermost in our consciousness at the time. There is no normative pressure to bring about even excellent shots, none whatever that I can discern. (N.B.: What we are not normatively pressured to accumulate is *shots, nor even excellent shots, regardless of how excellent they may be.*)

Compare now our intellectual shots, our beliefs. A belief may answer a question correctly, but may have very little value nonetheless, if the question is not worth asking. The value of a target will surely bear on the worth of any shot aimed at that target. Arbitrary selection of an area by your feet at the beach yields a silly target. Similarly, suppose you scoop up some sand and proceed laboriously to count the grains. You then take up the question of how many grains are contained in that quantity of sand. If you reach your objective of answering that question correctly, what is your performance worth? Do you thereby fulfill, at least in some small part, a previously standing objective, that of securing more and more true beliefs? This seems about as implausible as is the corresponding view about the shot at the beach.

In what way, then, *does* the truth of our beliefs have value? One thing that does plausibly have prima facie value is the satisfaction of our curiosity. So, even if the question as to the number of grains is of little worth, if someone gets interested in that question anyhow, then the satisfaction of his curiosity will in an obvious way have value *to him* (and perhaps even, to some small extent, *for him*). This is of course a way for the truth to have value to someone and for someone. After all, if one is curious as to whether p, this is just to be curious as to whether it is true that p. There are not two instances of curiosity here: (a) as to whether p, and (b) as to whether it is true that p. So, what we want when we value the truth *in that way* is to have our questions answered, and of course answered correctly.

Sheer curiosity, whatever its basis, thus invests the right answer to a question with some value, though the value might be small and easy to outweigh, as with the question about the grains of sand. Having the answer to that particular question may add so little to the life of the believer, while cluttering his mind, that it is in fact a detriment all things considered, if only through the opportunity cost of misdirected attention.

Similar considerations apply to the shot aimed from a foot away at the sand on the beach. The sheer desire to hit that target, whatever its basis, gives value to the agent's hitting the mark. But it might well be that hitting that mark imports little value for anyone. Spending his time that way may even be a detriment to the agent's life. Nor is it plausible that we humans have generally a standing desire for accurate shots, nor that we place antecedent value on securing such shots. Accuracy will give value to that shot at the sand only dependently on the gunman's whim to hit that target.

Even if that shot at the beach fulfils no human interest antecedent to the gunman's whim, it may still be a better shot, better as a shot, than many with higher overall value. Take a shot at close quarters in self-defense that misses the targeted head of the attacker but hits him in the shoulder and stops the attack. A bad, inaccurate shot, this one, but more valuable than the accurate shot at the beach. (Had it been better as a shot, moreover, a more accurate shot, it might have constituted a terrible murder, since the attack did not justify shooting to kill.)

Are beliefs like shots in that respect? Is a belief a performance that can attain its internal aim while leaving it open whether it has any intrinsic value, and whether it serves or disserves any external aim? Let us explore this view of belief.

3 Knowledge as a Special Case

All sorts of things can "perform" well or ill when put to the test. Rational agents can do so, but so can biological organs, designed instruments, and even structures with a function, such as a bridge. A bridge can perform well its function as part of a traffic artery. When a thermostat activates a furnace, it may perform well in keeping the ambient temperature comfortable. When a heart beats, it may perform well in helping the blood circulate. And so on.

A puppet performs well under the control of a puppeteer if its hinges are smooth, not rusty, and well oiled, so that its limbs are smoothly responsive. A bridge might perform well by withstanding a storm. We credit the puppet, as we do the bridge, if its good performance flows appropriately from its state and constitution.

The puppet "performs" (well or ill), as does the bridge, and thus produces performances. But it would be quite a stretch to consider it an "agent." Human beings are different, in any case, if only because we are *rational* agents. Not only are there reasons why we perform as we do. There are also reasons that we *have* for so performing, and *for* which, *motivated* by which, we perform as we do. This is not just a matter of having aims in so performing. After all, the thermostat and the heart do have their aims. But they are motivated by no such aim; no such aim gives them reasons motivated by which they perform as they do.[2]

Human motivation is on another level, even when the performance is physical, as in athletic or artistic performance.

The archer's shot is a good example. The shot aims to hit the target, and its success can be judged by whether it does so or not, by its accuracy. However accurate it may be, there is a further dimension of evaluation: namely, how skillful a shot it is, how much skill it manifests, how adroit it is. A shot might hit the bull's-eye, however, and might even manifest great skill, while failing utterly, *as a shot*, on a further dimension. Consider a shot diverted by a gust of wind initially, so that it would miss the target altogether but for a second gust that compensates and puts it back on track to hit the bull's-eye. This shot is both accurate and adroit, yet it is not accurate *because* adroit, so as to manifest the archer's skill and competence. It thus fails on a third dimension of evaluation, besides those of accuracy and adroitness: it fails to be *apt*.

Performances generally admit this threefold distinction: accuracy, adroitness, aptness. At least so do performances with an aim (assuming any performance could ever be wholly aimless).

A performance is better than otherwise for not having *failed*, i.e., for not having fallen short of its objective. In line with that, it is *good* if it succeeds, if it reaches its objective. A performance is at least good *as such* for succeeding, even if it is a murderer's shot. The shot itself may still be an excellent shot, despite how deplorable is the broader performance in which it is embedded.

A performance that attains its first-order aim without thereby manifesting any competence of the performer's is a lesser performance. The wind-aided shot scores by luck, without thereby manifesting appropriate competence. It is hence a lesser shot by comparison with one that in hitting the mark manifests the archer's competence.[3] A blazing tennis ace is a lesser shot if it is a wild exception from the racket of a hacker, by comparison with one that manifests superb competence by a champion in control. And so on. Take any performance with a first-order aim, such as the archery shot and the tennis serve. That performance then has the induced aim of *attaining* its first-order aim. A performance X attains its aim ⟨p⟩, finally, not just through the fact that p, but through the fact that it *brings it about* that p.[4]

The case of knowledge is just the special case where the performance is cognitive or doxastic. Belief aims at truth, and is accurate or correct if true. Belief has accordingly the induced aim of *attaining* that objective. Belief aims therefore not just at accuracy (truth), but also at aptness (knowledge). A belief that attains both aims, that of truth and that of knowledge, is for that reason better than one that attains merely the first. That then is a way in which knowledge is as such better than merely true belief.[5]

The account of epistemic normativity as a sort of performance normativity has thus two virtues. It provides an explanation of the nature of knowledge, which amounts to belief that is apt, belief that is an apt epistemic performance, one that manifests the relevant competence of the believer in attaining the truth. And, secondly, it explains also the extra value of knowledge beyond that of merely true belief.

Unfortunately, the account encounters a troubling objection, which we next consider.

4   The Problem of Withholding

What's the problem?

The normative judgment that knowledge is as such better than merely true belief is of a piece with the normative judgment that withholding is better than believing when the evidence is insufficient. Since both judgments are epistemically normative, one would expect them to be closely akin. But that is not what one finds on first inspection.

If truth is the first-order aim of our cognitive endeavors, it is not obvious how to assess suspension of judgment with respect to that objective, so it is correspondingly hard to see how we could apply our AAA normative structure of performances to such withholdings. These are after all precisely *non*-performances. How then can they be brought within the sphere of our performance normativity? And if they are not thus assimilable, serious doubt is cast on our claim to have uncovered the most relevant epistemic normativity involved in our intuition that knowledge is as such better than merely true belief.

Let our archer now be a hunter rather than a competitor athlete. Once it is his turn, the competitor must shoot, with no relevant choice. True, he might have avoided the competition altogether, but once in it, no relevant shot selection is allowed. The hunter by contrast needs to pick his shots, with whatever skill and care he can muster. Selecting targets of appropriate value is integral to hunting, and he must also pick his shots so as to secure a reasonable chance of success. The shot of a hunter can therefore be assessed in more respects than that of a competitor/athlete. The hunter's shot can be assessed twice over for what is manifest in it: not only in respect of its execution competence, but also in respect of the competence manifest in the target's selection and in the pick of the shot.

Not taking a shot at a particular target may or may not involve a performance. You might *fail to take that shot* because at the time you are asleep, for example. Alternatively, you might intentionally and even deliberately forbear. If your deliberate forbearing has an aim, moreover, and if the aim is attained, then your forbearing succeeds, and may even be a performance, indeed one that is apt.

Suppose a domain in which an agent puts in performances with an aim, whether athletic, artistic, academic, etc. This yields a derivative aim: *to avoid failure.* You can aim to avoid failure, moreover, without aiming to attain success, at least not ground-level success. When a hunter decides not to take a shot at a certain high-value target, for example, his performance, his forbearing, has its own aim of avoiding failure. To forbear is precisely *not* to aim at first-order success. Nevertheless, forbearing has an aim of its own: namely, avoiding failure.

Take then a hunter's performance of forbearing, which succeeds in avoiding ground-level failure. It does attain *that* aim. Is it thereby apt? Yes, so it is by our account; that is what we have to say. The forbearing *is*, after all, a performance with an aim of its own, and it does attain that aim, in doing which it does manifest a sort of competence.

What if it is a shot that the hunter very obviously *should* have taken? What if he makes a big mistake forbearing?

How do we avoid the unwelcome result that the forbearing is apt despite being one that obviously should not even have occurred? One option is to grant that it is a *narrowly* apt performance, while defining a broader aptness that it lacks. Let us explore this option.

Consider Diana's forced choice between taking a shot and forbearing from doing so. If she opts to take the shot, then her archery skills come into play. If they produce a hit, then her performance, her shot, manifests her narrow competence, and is hence narrowly apt. Compatibly with this, nonetheless, her shot selection might have been incompetent.

That is one way for a narrowly apt shot to be broadly objectionable. The huntress who forbears taking a shot that she obviously *should* take fails in her performance of forbearing. Her forbearing avoids ground-level failure, but is deplorable nonetheless.

5   Varieties of Aptness

A performance is apt if its success manifests a competence seated in the agent (in relevantly appropriate conditions). It does not matter how fragile was the continued presence of the competence, or its appropriate conditions, when the agent issued the performance. A performance can thus easily fail to be "meta-apt," because the agent handles risk poorly, either by taking too much or by taking too little. The agent may fail to perceive the risk, when he should be more perceptive; or he may respond to the perceived risk with either foolhardiness or cowardice. He might perform on the ground level although the risk of failure is too high; or he might forbear although it is pusillanimous of him not to plunge ahead.

The aptness of a performance is thus to be distinguished from its meta-aptness. Either one can be present without the other.

An archer/hunter's shot selection and risk taking may be excellent, for example, and in taking a certain shot he may manifest his competence at assessing risk, while the shot itself nevertheless fails, being unsuccessful (inaccurate) and hence inapt. The shot is hence meta-apt without being apt.

Conversely, the hunter may take excessive risk in shooting at a certain target, given his perceived level of competence (he has been drinking) and the assessed potential for wind (it is stormy). When he shoots, he may still fall just below the level of competence-denying inebriation, however, and the wind may happen to fall calm, so that his shot is (through *that* stroke of luck) quite apt. Here the shot is apt without being meta-apt.

Our shift from the competitor archer to the hunter archer, with his much wider latitude for target or shot selection, imports therefore the following distinction.

A shot is *apt* iff the success it attains, its hitting the target, manifests the agent's first-order competence, his skillful marksmanship.

A shot is *meta-apt* iff it is well-selected: i.e., iff it takes appropriate risk, and its doing so manifests the agent's competence for target and shot selection.

Neither aptness nor meta-aptness is sufficient for the other. They vary independently.

If Diana shoots, her shot might itself be both apt and meta-apt. If she forbears, her forbearing might be meta-apt, though of course it will not be apt on the ground level, since it does not even aim for success on that level. The forbearing might be meta-apt, nevertheless, in being a proper response to the perceived level of risk, a response that manifests her meta-competence.

Sometimes an agent responds properly by performing on the ground level, in which case that *positive performance* is meta-apt; sometimes the proper response is to forbear, so that the *forbearing* is meta-apt.

Arguably, a shot could be both apt and meta-apt while still falling short in that it is not *in virtue of being meta-apt* that it is apt. Thus, a shot might manifest a hunter's risk-assessment competence, and it might issue from his competence as an archer, in conditions appropriate for such shots, while yet the shot might be apt, not through the meta-competence of the archer, but only through a kind of luck.

6 Full Aptness and Reflective Knowledge

A performance attains thus a special status when it is apt at the ground level and also its aptness is explained through competent risk assessment. Suppose this risk-assessment issues in the performer's knowing that his situation (constitutional and circumstantial) is favorable (where the risk of failure is low enough) for issuing such a performance. If these conditions all obtain, then the performance's aptness might stem from its meta-aptness; that is to say, its aptness might be relevantly explicable through the performer's meta-knowledge that his first-order performance is likely enough to succeed and be apt.

This applies to performances such as a shot that hits its prey. That shot is superior, more admirable and creditable, if it is not only apt, but also meta-apt, and, further, *fully* apt: that is, apt because meta-apt. This happens, for example, when the aptness of Diana's shot stems from her meta-competence in assessing risk properly, so that the shot attains its first-order success in important part because she runs appropriate risk.

Aptness comes in degrees. One shot is more apt than another, for example, if it manifests a more reliable competence. On one dimension, a shot by a tennis champion may be no better than a similarly paced and placed shot by a hacker. On another dimension, however, the champion's shot manifests his prowess on the court, while the hacker's nearly identical shot is just lucky, and skillful only minimally or not at all. The champion's shot manifests competence, moreover, on two levels. It manifests his sheer athletic ability to hit with good pace and placement, and with impressively good percentage. But it can and normally does manifest also her good shot selection, her ability to attempt shots with a favorable percentage of success. The hacker's shot falls short on both dimensions.

The champion's shots are apt, meta-apt, and *fully* apt: i.e., apt because meta-apt. For a shot to have the property of being apt is for its success to manifest a competence seated in the agent. This whole arrangement is itself something that the agent might be able to arrange (or not), and not simply by exercising the first-order competence seated in him. The agent might be able to choose when and where to exercise that competence, for one thing, and might manifest more or less competence in such a choice.

The same is true of the archer/hunter's shot. It can be apt in that its success, its accuracy, manifests the agent's competence in relevantly appropriate conditions (no wind, enough light, distance within proper bounds, and so on). But it can also manifest the agent's meta-competence for target and shot selection. If so, then it is no accident that the shot is made in specific conditions where the archer's competence is up to the task of producing success with a high enough percentage. In other words, the agent's risk perception is then competent enough, and this competence is manifest in his knowledge that the level of risk is appropriate. On one level, how apt the shot is depends on the degree of competence manifest by its success. But, on another level, the full aptness of the shot depends also on the meta-competence manifest by its success. What is required for this fuller aptness is that the agent's first-order aptness derive sufficiently from his assessment, albeit implicit, of the chances of such success (and, correlatively, of the risk of failure).

Here the agent is on a meta-level. He must take into account the likelihood that his competence is (and will remain) intact and that the relevant conditions are (and will remain) appropriate, and he must assess how likely it is that his action from such a competence in such conditions will succeed. Suppose he takes his chances of such success to be high enough (and the risk of failure low enough), and he is right, knowledgeably so, the chances being as he takes them to be, and his competence and conditions being relevantly as envisaged. Suppose further that he exercises his competence accordingly, so that the (first-order) aptness of his shot is owed to his meta-competence, is owed sufficiently to his getting it right about the chances of success, and to his getting *this* right as a manifestation of that meta-competence. The agent's shot is then more fully apt and more fully creditable in proportion to how fully all of that falls into place.

We have thus found a further level of *performance-based* normativity. *Epistemic* normativity is, once again, a special case also in this more complex and subtle way. Animal knowledge is first-order apt belief. Reflective knowledge is animal belief aptly meta-endorsed by the subject. We can now see that knowing something full well requires that one have animal and reflective knowledge of it, but also that one know it with full aptness. It requires, that is to say, that the correctness of one's first-order belief manifest not only the animal, first-order competences that reliably enough yield the correctness of the beliefs that they produce. One's first-order belief falls short if it is not appropriately *guided* by one's relevant meta-competence. This meta-competence governs whether or not one should form a belief at all on the question at issue, or should rather withhold. It is only if this meta-competence is operative in one's forming a belief at all on that subject matter that one's belief can reach the epistemic heights. One's first-order belief is apt in proportion to how reliable is the first-order competence manifest in its success. What is more, it is more fully apt in proportion to how reliable is the meta-competence that its success also manifests. This meta-competence is manifest at a remove, however, because the meta-knowledge *that it is a belief likely enough to be apt on the ground level* is constituted by the fact that the correctness of the corresponding meta-belief itself manifests the subject's relevant meta-competence).

Fully apt performances are in general better as performances than those that succeed without being apt at all, and also than those that are apt without being fully apt. Diana's apt shot that kills its prey is a better shot if apt than if successful only by luck and not through competence. Moreover, it is also a better, more admirable, more creditable shot, if its success flows also from her target-selecting, shot-picking competences. Her shot is more creditable in that case than it is when the right competence *is* manifest in conditions required for a successful first-order performance, *but* only by luck *external* to any such selection meta-competence on her part.

Epistemic normativity is again just a special case of all that. Apt belief, *animal knowledge*, is better than belief that succeeds in its aim, being true, without being apt. Apt belief aptly noted, *reflective knowledge*, is better than mere apt belief or animal knowledge, especially when the reflective knowledge helps to guide the first-order belief so that it is apt.[6] In such a case the belief is fully apt, and the subject *knows full well*.

Notes

1. This is the celebrated Gettier problem, with a vast literature.

2. True, we could perhaps, just barely, make sense of an extended sort of "motivation" even in those cases, as when a nearby torch fools the thermostat into activating the air conditioner even when the room is already cool. It still in some broad sense has a reason for performing as it does, a "motivating reason." Despite the non-trivial resemblance, nonetheless, this is clearly a metaphorical extension, if only because of the vastly greater complexity involved in human motivation.

3. A shot might manifest an archer's competence without its accuracy doing so. The shot with the two intervening gusts is a case in point. How does that shot manifest the archer's competence? By having at the moment of release an angle, direction, and speed that would take it to the bull's-eye, in relevantly normal conditions.

4. Just as its being true that p entails its being true that it is true that p, so one's bringing it about that p may entail that one brings it about that one brings it about that p, assuming such iteration always makes sense.

5. Even if performances do not have the automatically induced aims just suggested, we still retain an account of why knowledge is better than merely true belief, since apt performances, in general, are as such better than those that attain success only by luck. So, beliefs provide just a special case of that general truth. This account still depends of course on our view of knowledge as apt belief, belief that manifests the relevant competence of the believer in reaching its aim of truth.

6. In fact proper reflective knowledge will *always* guide or help to guide its corresponding animal belief. Proper reflective knowledge will after all satisfy requirements of coherence, which means not just logical or probabilistic coherence of the respective belief contents, but also the mutual basing relations that can properly reflect such coherence among the contents. Cross-level coherence, from the object to the meta, and conversely, is a special case of such coherence, and it imports "guidance" of the animal belief by the relevant meta-beliefs (or, in other words, basing of the former on the latter). It bears emphasis that the meta-aptness of a belief, which we have found to be an important factor in its *epistemic* evaluation, requires ascent to a good enough perspective concerning the first level potential attitudes among which the subject must opt (whether he opts with full conscious deliberation or through a less explicit procedure). Coherence among first-level attitudes is not enough. The subject must ascend to a level wherein he assesses relevant risk, whether in full consciousness or less explicitly, and opts on that basis. Included in that analysis is perforce some assessment of one's relevant competence(s) and situation, and this must itself be performed adequately, if it is to yield a fully creditable first-level performance. Its assessment as thus fully creditable is moreover fully epistemic. For it is an assessment as to whether belief is the proper response to one's situation rather than suspension of belief.

9 Can Virtue Reliabilism Explain the Value of Knowledge?

Berit Brogaard

I Introduction

A fundamental intuition about knowledge is that it is more valuable than mere true belief. This intuition is pervasive. We have an almost universal desire to know and nearly no desire to believe the truth accidentally. However, it turns out to be extremely difficult to explain why knowledge is more valuable. Linda Zagzebski and others have called this the "value problem."[1] They argue that the value problem is particularly difficult to unravel for generic reliabilism. According to generic reliabilism, knowledge is true belief produced by reliable belief-forming processes or faculties. But, the critics argue, "the reliability of the source of a belief cannot explain the [value difference] between knowledge and true belief."[2] For reliably formed beliefs allegedly are valuable only insofar as they tend to be true. So if a belief is already true, then the fact that it is also reliably formed adds no further value to the belief. In general, the good of the product makes the reliability of its source good but the reliability of the source does not add value to the product. The critics, furthermore, believe that even if generic reliabilism could find a reason that a reliable source is independently valuable, this would not solve the value problem, because the value of a cause does not transfer to its effect. If we want to guarantee that a belief-producing source confers value on its outcome, we must shift our focus from the belief alone to the overall state of knowing p. For a source can confer value on its effect only if cause and product are internally connected.

Virtue reliabilism is a common response to these difficulties.[3] Virtue reliabilism says that knowledge is true belief produced by one of the agent's intellectual virtues, i.e., one of her enduring and reliable cognitive abilities.

Reprinted from Berit Brogaard, "Can Virtue Reliabilism Explain the Value of Knowledge?," *Canadian Journal of Philosophy* 36 (2006): 335–354.

The focus shifts from evaluating the belief itself to the state the agent is in when she is responsible for believing something true. Virtue reliabilism, it is said, thus has more resources for addressing the value problem. When a true belief is virtuously produced, the truth of the belief is attributable to the agent as his or her own doing. When it is produced accidentally, its truth is attributable to lucky circumstances. Forming a true belief in a virtuous way is thus more valuable than doing so accidentally, because the agent deserves more credit in the former case. While the extra credit the knower is due does not make the known belief more valuable, it supposedly adds value to the overall state of knowing that p. A similar response is apparently unavailable to the generic reliabilist, because (1) she fails to remove focus from the true belief to the overall state of knowing that p, and (2) she makes no distinction between the true beliefs that derive from stable and reliable dispositions and those that derive from "strange and fleeting" mechanisms.

In this paper I argue that the appearance that virtue reliabilism is better equipped to handle the value problem is illusory. More specifically, I argue (1) that to solve the value problem the generic reliabilist need not make a shift from a focus on evaluating the belief itself to a focus on the overall state of knowing that p, and (2) that it is far from clear that a principled distinction can be drawn between the reliable belief-forming methods that are grounded in the knower's intellectual virtues, and those that are not. Without a principled distinction of this sort it cannot be established that the extra value of knowledge derives from the extra credit the knower is due. At the end of the paper, I argue that virtue reliabilism fails to address another side of the value problem, which is that of explaining why knowing p is sometimes more valuable than being justified in believing truly that p. I conclude by considering what it would take for a theory to explain this value difference.

II The Machine-Product Model of Belief

Zagzebski compares the reliability of the source of a belief to the reliability of an espresso maker.[4] This tasty cup of espresso is not made any better by the fact that it comes from a reliable espresso maker. The lesson of Zagzebski's espresso analogy is that a reliable belief-forming mechanism does not automatically confer value on true belief. One reason Zagzebski gives in support of this claim is that a reliable belief-forming mechanism purportedly is valuable only insofar as it is truth-conducive. If truth is all that matters—if we want reliably formed belief only because such beliefs tend to be true—then mere true belief ought be treasured to the same extent as reliably formed true belief.

It may be objected that the overall value of a reliable source derives from the value of all the true beliefs it produces and so will be greater than the value of any true belief it produces on some single occasion.[5] It would follow that a reliable source of truth could explain a difference in value between knowledge and true belief. The objection is amiss, however. To say that a mechanism is truth-conducive is not to say that it actually produces true beliefs but only that it is likely to do so. But if a reliable source is valuable only insofar as it is likely to produce true beliefs, then a reliably produced belief is valuable only insofar as it is likely to be true, and an entity that already has *F* cannot acquire additional value by acquiring the property of *being likely to be F*.

Thus it might be suggested that we look for a value in the source of true belief that is independent of reliability or truth-conduciveness. According to Zagzebski, however, identifying a value in the cause of true belief that is independent of truth-conduciveness is not sufficient to solve the value problem.[6] This is because, she says, a source may be valuable even if its effect is not. In other words, the value of a source never transfers to its product automatically. So even if we were to show that a reliable belief-forming mechanism had, say, intrinsic value (suppose, for example, that the mechanism is an intrinsically valuable intellectual virtue) this would be insufficient to explain the extra value of knowledge. The problem is not, of course, that an intrinsically valuable mechanism is not a good thing but that the value of the mechanism does not accrue to the known belief itself.

Zagzebski thinks the problem facing generic reliabilism is that it adheres to what she calls the "machine-product model of belief."[7] On this model, a known belief is the external product of a good source. But if the product is external to the source, Zagzebski says, then the value of the source does not transfer to the product. So if knowledge is true belief that is the output of a valuable source, then it has no more value than true belief. Zagzebski believes that if knowledge is to have more value than true belief, its source must have an internal connection of the same sort as that between an act and its motive. The state consisting of a virtuous motive and right action has more value than right action alone. Zagzebski therefore suggests that we understand knowledge, not as a state consisting of a known belief, but as a whole consisting of the true belief and its source. If knowledge is such a whole, and the source of the belief has independent value, then knowledge is more valuable than true belief. Virtue reliabilism identifies knowledge with a broader state that comprises not only the known belief but also the intellectual virtues of the agent. So, according to Zagzebski, the extra value of knowledge derives in part from the independent (i.e., intrinsic) value of intellectual virtue.

A similar suggestion has been made by Wayne Riggs.[8] According to Riggs, a person who is causally efficacious in bringing about some valuable product is due some amount of credit for having done so. So, it is natural to think that at least part of the extra value of knowledge derives from the knower's achievement in acquiring it. But, Riggs argues, the value of the knower's achievement contributes to the value of knowledge only if knowledge is regarded as the *state* the agent is in when she is causally responsible for her belief. Since virtue reliabilism shifts our focus from the belief itself to the state the agent is in when she is causally responsible for believing something true, virtue reliabilism can explain (at least some of) the value of knowledge.

III   Value and External Sources

According to the virtue reliabilists, there are thus two reasons that virtue reliabilism is better equipped than generic reliabilism to address the value problem. One is that generic reliabilism, unlike virtue reliabilism, adheres to the machine-product model of belief. But, the virtue reliabilists reason, we cannot explain what makes knowledge more valuable than true belief if we use the machine-product model of belief, because a valuable source does not automatically confer value on its product. The other is that generic reliabilism, in contrast to virtue reliabilism, takes the source of knowledge to be valuable only because it is reliable. But, the virtue reliabilists insist, truth plus a reliable source of truth cannot explain the value of knowledge.

I will now argue that these two arguments in favor of virtue reliabilism are less than fully convincing. First, while it might be true that a valuable source does not automatically confer value on its product, it is not true that an external source cannot ever confer value on its product. Second, while it might be true that generic reliabilism cannot explain the value of knowledge because it holds that the source of knowledge is valuable only insofar as it is reliable, it is unclear how virtue reliabilism differs from generic reliabilism in this respect. I will discuss the first problem in this section, and the second in the three subsequent sections.

Riggs and Zagzebski both hold that we cannot explain the value of knowledge if we adhere to what Zagzebski calls the "machine-product model of belief." So they suggest that we remove focus from the belief alone to the overall state of knowing that p. Riggs adds further reason for making such a shift in focus. He doubts that there is any such thing as an item of knowledge, because he cannot think of any intrinsic property of a known belief that is not also a property of an accidentally true belief.[9]

I think the latter reason is amiss. Whatever can be said in favor of making a shift in focus from known belief to the overall state of knowing that p, the shift is not needed in order to be able to distinguish true belief from knowledge. If Riggs were right, then by analogy there would be no such thing as a true belief, because there is no intrinsic property of a true belief that is not also a property of a false belief. But on the standard conception of identity, two entities can be intrinsically alike and yet numerically distinct. Moreover, plenty of things exist partly in virtue of their extrinsic properties. A bachelor would not be what he is without being single. Or consider a paperweight, an insurance policy, or a door lock. Neither would be what it is without its extrinsic properties.

I presume the real reason that both Riggs and Zagzebski want us to remove focus from the belief alone to the overall state of knowing that p is that they adhere to a Moorean conception of value. On a Moorean conception of value, if two things have the same intrinsic properties, then they are equally valuable. Evidently, if two things have the same intrinsic properties, then they have the same amount of instrumental value.[10] Moreover, they have the same amount of intrinsic value. So, if non-instrumental (or final) value is intrinsic, then intrinsically indistinguishable things are equally valuable. Known belief is intrinsically indistinguishable from accidentally true belief. So, given a Moorean conception of value, known belief is no better than true belief.

Presumably the Moorean account of value is what Riggs and Zagzebski have in mind when they think we must shift our focus from the belief itself to the overall state of knowing that p. Unfortunately, the Moorean conception of value is questionable. As Wlodek Rabinowitcz and Toni Roennow-Rasmussen have argued, we often attribute extra value to things that are extrinsically related to something else that we value.[11] They argue that when the extra value of a thing derives from something else we value, the thing is valued for its own sake in spite of the fact that the extra value is not intrinsic or unconditional. For example, we may value Princess Diana's dress more than an exact copy simply because the former but not the latter belonged to Diana. The dress's extra value depends on its relation to Diana. Likewise, we tend to value a tropical wilderness more if it has never been visited by humans. The extra value of the tropical wilderness thus depends on its relation to humans. Since we sometimes assign different quantities of non-instrumental or final value to intrinsically indistinguishable things, final value need not supervene on the intrinsic properties of the thing in question.

If Rabinowitcz and Roennow-Rasmussen are right, then the final value of an object can derive partly from an external source. But then, pace Riggs and Zagzebski, it is not clear that the generic reliabilists' adherence to the machine-product model of belief prevents them from explaining the extra value of knowledge. For the value of a source may transfer to the product, even if the source and the product are not internally connected.

A related idea is suggested by Philip Percival:[12] it is quite obvious, he says, that there is no difference between the value of a tasty cup of espresso produced by a reliable espresso machine and a tasty cup produced by an unreliable machine if the value of an espresso is "determined by its taste." Likewise, I will add, there is no difference between the value of Princess Diana's dress and an exact copy of her dress if the value of a dress is determined by its appearance. But, Percival reasons, making a claim about belief parallel to the claim about espresso "begs the question." Zagzebski says that if the belief is true, then it makes no difference if it is produced by a reliable or unreliable mechanism. But Percival argues, even if it "makes no difference" to the value of the belief "in the point of truth," it does not follow that it makes no difference to the value of the belief in some other respect.

IV   Strange and Fleeting Processes

Thus, Zagzebski and her allies have failed to show that reliabilism is unable to account for the value we typically ascribe to knowledge. What they have shown is that the reliabilists cannot conceive of reliability as being valuable only in virtue of being truth-conducive. However, if the reliabilists can give some reason why reliability is independently valuable, then their work is done. The virtue reliabilists may respond that even if it is true that we do not have to regard knowledge as a state of the agent in order for knowledge to have extra value over mere true belief, the only reason the generic reliabilists have in fact given for the claim that reliability is valuable is that it is truth-conducive. The virtue reliabilists, on the other hand, have apparently shown that reliability (of the right sort) is independently valuable because, on their view, reliably produced true belief of the sort that counts as knowledge is to the agent's credit. Being the product of something independently valuable can add value to the product. For example, being a Picasso painting can add value to a painting. Likewise, the virtue reliabilists might say, being the outcome of an intellectual virtue can add value to true belief.

Virtue reliabilism thus fares better than generic reliabilism, even if the above criticism holds up. Or so the virtue reliabilists will most likely have us think. Whether the remainder of their criticism can be sustained, however, depends on whether there is some other significant difference between virtue reliabilism and generic reliabilism. According to the virtue reliabilists, not all reliable belief-forming mechanisms give rise to knowledge. Namely, "strange and fleeting" ones do not.[13] If the virtue reliabilists are right, i.e., if there is a principled distinction to be made between the reliable mechanisms that are strange and fleeting and those that are stable dispositions, then the remainder of their criticism can be sustained. If no such distinction can be drawn, then virtue reliabilism collapses into a form of generic reliabilism.

John Greco has provided the following example to show how virtue reliabilism and generic reliabilism come apart:

René thinks he can beat the roulette tables with a system he has devised. Reasoning according to the Gambler's Fallacy, he believes that numbers which have not come up for long strings are more likely to come up next. However, unlike Descartes' demon victim, our René has a demon helper. Acting as a kind of epistemic guardian angel, every time Rene forms a belief that a number will come up next, the demon arranges reality so as to make the belief come out as true. Given the ever present interventions of the helpful demon, René's belief forming process is highly reliable. But this is because the world is made to conform to René's beliefs, rather than because René's beliefs conform to the world.[14]

Though René reasons fallaciously, his beliefs about which numbers will come up next are reliably produced, owing to the demon's intervention. Forming beliefs via the gambler's fallacy is not in general a reliable way of forming beliefs, but forming beliefs via the gambler's fallacy and a demon helper who arranges reality in the right way is. So, the source of René's beliefs is reliable in general. And it is reliable in the particular instances as well. For it is a widely acknowledged that a belief is reliable in the particular instance if it could not easily have been wrong,[15] and in the nearby possible worlds in which René forms his belief via the gambler's fallacy and a demon helper, his belief is true. Thus, if the generic reliabilist requires for knowledge true belief produced by a mechanism that is reliable in general and in the particular instance as well, then the generic reliabilist must admit that René knows which numbers will come up next. Virtue reliabilism is apparently not committed to this consequence. For according to the virtue reliabilist, all instances of knowledge result from a stable and reliable disposition that makes up the agent's character. But the source of René's belief is supposedly not sufficiently grounded in "a stable and reliable disposition that makes up his character." So, René does not know which numbers will come up next.

The examples are easily multiplied. Consider a variation of Alvin Goldman's barn facsimile case. In the original rendering, S is driving in the country and stops in front of a barn. Unbeknownst to S, S is looking at one of the few real barns in an area spawned with facsimiles. The facsimiles are so realistic that if S had stopped in front of any of them, S would have been tricked into thinking she was looking at a real barn. The standard intuition is that S does not know that she is looking at a real barn, because she could easily have had the same belief while looking at a facsimile. In the variation a guardian angel would blur S's vision if she were to look at a fake barn. Again, it is only natural to think that S does not have the knowledge that she is looking at a barn. However, since the relevant belief-forming mechanism is the faculty of vision extended by a protective device (viz., the guardian angel), S's belief is produced by a mechanism that is reliable in general and in the specific instance as well. The mechanism is reliable in general because most beliefs formed by the same mechanism would be true. In fact, we may suppose that if a person is looking at a barn façade, then the angel will blur her vision, and she will not form the belief that she is looking at a barn. The mechanism is reliable in the particular instance as well because S's belief could not easily have been wrong. Had she looked at a barn façade, then the angel would have blurred her vision, and she would not have formed the belief that she is looking at a barn. So, the generic reliabilist is apparently committed to the somewhat counterintuitive consequence that S knows she is looking at a barn. The virtue reliabilist is not so committed. Of course, in the actual world the agent's belief is produced by her cognitive abilities. But her cognitive abilities do not protect her against false beliefs. Without the epistemic helper her belief that she is looking at a barn could easily have been wrong. So her true belief, it seems, is not sufficiently determined by her own cognitive abilities and powers.

Virtue reliabilism thus appears to be significantly different from generic reliabilism. Since the generic reliabilist admits that any reliable mechanism can be a source of knowledge, a mechanism can be a source of knowledge even when its success owes to an external manipulator rather than to the agent's own abilities. So, she must grant our two agents knowledge. The virtue reliabilist, in contrast, need not grant our two agents knowledge, for the source of their beliefs is not sufficiently grounded in their own cognitive abilities, and for that reason it is ruled out by virtue reliabilism as being a source of knowledge. With this distinction in place, the virtue-theoretical response to the value problem is straightforward. More value accrues to true belief that derives from the agent's own cognitive abilities, because achieving true belief of this sort is to the agent's credit.

V   Virtue Reliabilism on the Cheap

Unfortunately, the examples just considered do not favor virtue reliabilism over generic reliabilism. In Greco's case of the gambler, René has very un-reliable faculties when unprotected by a helpful demon, but a demon inter-venes and systematically adjusts his beliefs to the facts. The virtue reliabilists claim to be able to explain the alleged fact that René does not know which numbers will come up next. But their explanation is at best incomplete. For they are already committed to the claim that a device that systematically adjusts the agent's belief to the facts can be a source of knowledge. Con-sider David Lewis's example of the prosthetic eye. According to Lewis:

A prosthetic eye consists of a miniature television camera mounted in, or on, the front of the head; a computer; and an array of electrodes in the brain. The computer receives input from the camera and sends signals to the electrodes in such a way as to produce visual experience that matches the scene before the eyes. When pros-thetic eyes are perfected, the blind will see.[16]

In the case of a prosthetic eye, the scene before the eyes causes matching visual experience by peculiar, non-standard causal processes yet a pros-thetic eye can be a means for genuine seeing. Lewis adds:

some prosthetic eyes are more convincing than others as means for genuine seeing . . . it seems better if the computer is surgically implanted rather than carried in a knapsack, but better if it is carried in a knapsack rather than stationary and linked by radio to the camera and electrodes.[17]

Some prosthetic eyes are more believable than others "as means for genu-ine seeing." But once we accept that a prosthetic eye that is incorporated into the subject can help her see, why rule out that prosthetic eyes that are external to the subject can be means for genuine seeing? Lewis agrees:

Why should that matter, once we grant that the standard process is not required? I see no real limits on how a prosthetic eye might work. Even the least convincing cases of prosthetic vision are quite convincing enough.[18]

Whether the means for seeing is natural or artificial, internal or external, incorporated into your head or located safely at home has no bearing on whether you can see. Prosthetic eyes are means for genuine seeing. Given the naturalistic tendencies of virtue reliabilism, it is not clear what could prompt an eschewal of this contention. The virtue reliabilists admit that virtues can be acquired. What's more, they tend to hold that the acquisition and use of the skills need not be under our control.[19] Acquired skills of perception, including those that make use of advanced technology, can yield knowledge. As Greco puts it,

innate vision can give rise to knowledge if it is reliably accurate. But so can acquired skills of perception and acquired methods of inquiry, including those involving highly specialized training or even advanced technology. So long as such habits are both stable and successful, they make up the kind of character that gives rise to knowledge.[20]

Thus, the virtue reliabilists hold that a belief is sufficiently causally determined by the agent's abilities and powers when the belief is produced by innate abilities or acquired methods of inquiry that are both stable and successful. A prosthetic eye is just another example of such an acquired skill or ability, and so should not be dismissed as a method that can give rise to knowledge.

But supernatural devices of the above sort are close kin to prosthetic eyes. Both sorts of device assist the agents in achieving correct beliefs about their surroundings. In both cases the innate cognitive faculties are unreliable when they are not coupled with the device in question. But they are stable and successful when they are indeed coupled with the device in question. The fact that the belief-forming mechanism is external to the agent does (and should not) matter. What matters is that her belief is right in a neighborhood of worlds not too distant from the actual world. It would be otherwise if all she had were a perfectly veridical belief system. Having the latter is consistent with her beliefs not being the products of reliable belief-forming processes. But in this case the agent does not merely have true beliefs. In close counterfactual situations, she has a perfectly veridical belief system as well.

It is even more evident that the belief-forming device used in the modified barn case can be a source of knowledge. Once it is admitted that acquired methods of inquiry, including those involving advanced technology, can give rise to knowledge, it must be admitted that a belief-forming device coupled to another device that can detect the first's limitations can give rise to knowledge. Suppose, for example, that a device, M1, is reliable within the values 4–7 of a given parameter. Suppose M1 is coupled to M2, which reliably detects the values of the parameter in question, and allows M1 to operate only if they fall within the range for which M1 produces the right output. The coupled mechanism, M1 + M2, is reliable even for values outside the success range for M1, for if a value outside the range had been detected, there would have been no output.[21] Given that the virtue reliabilists admit that acquired methods of inquiry, including those involving advanced technology, can be sources of knowledge, it would be difficult for them to deny that the coupled mechanism, M1 + M2, can be a source of knowledge. But if the virtue reliabilists admit M1 + M2 can give rise to knowledge, then they must also admit that the coupled device consisting of the agent's cognitive faculties and the epistemic helper can give rise to knowledge. For the latter device is not significantly different from the coupled device consisting of M1 and M2. The agent's cognitive faculties are coupled with a supernatural device, which reliably detects the range for which the faculties produce the right output and allows them to operate only if they are successful. The cognitive faculties coupled with the supernatural device are thus reliable for values that fall outside the range for which the faculties produce the right output. So, the allegedly strange mechanism is not all that strange after all. Since it is both stable and successful in the same way that the coupled mechanism, M1 + M2, is stable and successful, it makes up the kind of mechanism that gives rise to knowledge.

In short, the virtue reliabilists do not succeed in drawing a principled distinction between the sources of belief that are grounded in the agent's virtuous abilities and those that are not, because the sources that allegedly are ruled out by virtue reliabilism as being sources of knowledge because they are insufficiently grounded in the agent's abilities are not very different from a wide range of "acquired methods of inquiry" that are not ruled out by virtue reliabilism as being sources of knowledge.

VI Achieving to Some Degree

It may be true that in most cases of knowledge the truth of the belief is attributable to the agent as her own doing, but the boundary of the class of known beliefs does not run precisely along the boundary of the class of true belief attributable to the agent. We might say that the distinction between the reliable methods that are strange and fleeting and those that are stable dispositions is one of degree, not kind. To the extent that it is one of degree and not kind, there will be a whole range of cases which varies when it comes to how causally responsible the agent is for her true belief. There might be cases in which the truth of the belief is definitely attributable to the agent's own abilities and powers, and cases in which it is definitely attributable to something other than the agent's own abilities and powers.

But the virtue reliabilist cannot say that only those cases in which the truth of the belief in question is definitely attributable to the agent's own abilities count as knowledge. The virtue reliabilist must count a range of borderline cases as knowledge as well. And any attempt to draw a distinction between the cases in which the agent is sufficiently causally responsible and the cases in which the agent is not will be ad hoc. Without a clear distinction between the reliable methods that are strange and fleeting and those that are not, there is no clear distinction between generic reliabilism and virtue reliabilism. Thus, virtue reliabilism does not have the advantage over generic reliabilism that it alone can explain (some of) the extra value of knowledge. Either they both can, or neither can. If they can both explain (some of) the extra value of knowledge, then it may be in the following way: in some cases, knowledge is very valuable because the agent deserves a lot of credit. In other cases, knowledge is scarcely more valuable than true belief because the agent does not deserve much credit at all. Maybe this suggestion does have something to recommend it. It apparently accommodates the intuition that in the case of Greco's René, the knowledge he has (if any) is not very valuable and not really something we strongly desire to have. However, my point still stands: the virtue reliabilist is not so radically different from generic reliabilism that this explanation is reserved for virtue reliabilism alone.

VII   The Other Side of the Value Problem

The value problem is usually taken to be the problem of explaining why knowledge is more valuable than mere true belief. But there is another side to the value problem, which has received less attention, namely, the problem of explaining why knowledge is more valuable than mere justified true belief. This may not seem to be a problem for an externalist theory, like virtue reliabilism, because externalist theories have traditionally avoided all talk of justification. However, virtue reliabilists have recently drawn our attention once again to the importance of justification. Consider the following well-known case. S lives in an evil demon world. Internally speaking, S's cognitive faculties are in as good working order as ours. Furthermore, some of her beliefs are also true. Still, she fails to know, since she is the victim of a massive deception. Though S fails to know, it is natural to think that she is justified nonetheless.[22] Virtue reliabilists tend to explain the intuition in the following way: the victim is justified because her cognitive faculties count as intellectual virtues relative to our environment.[23] They count as virtues relative to our environment because they are generally reliable relative to our environment. But S fails to have knowledge even when her beliefs are true and justified, because her cognitive faculties fail to work properly in the particular instances.

The example just considered suggests that the virtue reliabilist is faced with the problem of explaining not only the extra value of knowledge over mere true belief but also the extra value of knowledge over mere justified true belief. For the virtue reliabilist, the problem is that of explaining why knowledge is more valuable than true belief produced by a mechanism which is reliable in our normal situation for forming belief but which fails in the particular instance.

Even if there were an obvious way to make out the knowledge-as-credit thesis, the thesis will not help the virtue reliabilist explain why knowledge is more valuable than mere justified true belief. When a true belief derives from a source that fails to be reliable in the particular instance, the belief could easily have been wrong. But whether or not a true belief possesses this property has no bearing on whether the belief is to the agent's credit. For, as the above example suggests, it is never solely in virtue of the agent's cognitive abilities that her true belief possesses this property. Unless the agent is placed in a suitable environment, her cognitive abilities will not produce any true beliefs.[24] We think the person who lives in the evil demon world is justified in believing what she does, because her cognitive abilities would have been in as good working order as ours, had she only been in the right environment. But then her cognitive abilities are as decent as ours, and any of her cognitive achievements are as admirable as any of ours. The fact that she didn't get to the truth on her own is not her own fault and does not prove her cognitive abilities defective. Equally, the fact that we *do* get to the truth on our own is attributable just as much to our environment as to our cognitive abilities. So if the truth of our beliefs is attributable to us, then the truth of the victim's beliefs is attributable to her as well. For she does not differ from us in terms of her cognitive abilities, but only in terms of her emplacement.

The virtue reliabilist may attempt to salvage her position by stipulating that only beliefs produced by mechanisms that work properly in general and in the specific instances are virtuously produced. Since beliefs produced by mechanisms that fail in the specific instances are not virtuously produced, the agent deserves less credit for forming them. But this stipulation is squarely at odds with widely received views about virtue. Consider two variations of Keith Lehrer and Tom Paxson's well-known Grabit case.[25] S sees her acquaintance, Tom Grabit, steal a book from the library. But unsuspected by S, Tom's mother has said that Tom has a doppelganger who is indistinguishable from Tom and who was in the library at the time. In the first case, Tom's mother is lying: Tom has no doppelganger (or at least not one who was in the library at the time). Since Tom's mother is lying, let's suppose S's true belief that Tom stole the book could not easily have been wrong. In the second case, Tom's mother is telling the truth: Tom's doppelganger was in the library at the time. Since S could easily have been looking at Tom's doppelganger without being able to tell the difference, her belief that Tom stole the book could easily have been false. However, it would certainly be odd to say that S is more virtuous when Tom's mother is lying than when she is telling the truth. A person's belief that she is seeing her acquaintance can be virtuous even if she is unable to rule out the possibility that she is looking at her acquaintance's doppelganger. Otherwise, very few of us would ever be virtuous. It seems that the virtue reliabilists must admit that S can believe out of intellectual virtue—that S's believing the truth can be to her credit—even if she is to some extent lucky that her belief is true. On this proposal, the truth of the belief in question cannot be to the agent's credit if the agent does not form her belief via a mechanism that is reliable in our normal situation for forming beliefs, but it can be to her credit if the mechanism fails in the particular instance. But if an agent may deserve credit for her true belief when the belief is justified but fails to be adequately grounded, then virtue reliabilism does not have the resources to explain why knowledge is more valuable than mere justified true belief.

VIII   The Extra Value of Knowledge over Mere Justified True Belief

I suggested above that the knowledge-as-credit thesis might be able to explain why we value some instances of knowledge more than some instances of true belief, even if the explanation would not be reserved for virtue reliabilism alone. On this proposal, some instances of knowledge would be more valuable than some instances of true belief because the agent's achievement is more admirable in virtue of her greater responsibility for it. Still, we have been given no reason to believe that reliabilism under any name can respond to the other side of the value problem. What is it about knowledge compared to justified true belief that causes us to hold it in such high regard? It is not that the agent who has knowledge is due a certain amount of credit than the agent whose belief is merely true and justified is not. For without a suitable environment none of our cognitive abilities are truth-conducive. So, even if it is solely in virtue of our cognitive abilities that we arrive at justified true belief, it is never entirely in virtue of our cognitive abilities that we arrive at knowledge.

Jonathan Kvanvig has argued that we tend to hold knowledge in such high regard because of the kind of cognitive handle one allegedly has on reality when one knows something.[26] We want to avoid accidentally true beliefs because they show that we lack an accurate picture of the interrelationship between things. Having only accidentally justified true beliefs bars such understanding of the explanatory connections in nature. However, Kvanvig concludes that we legitimately desire or value something that is confused with knowledge. Knowledge, he argues, does not require explanatory understanding, and explanatory understanding does not require knowledge. So what we really ought to desire or value is not knowledge but understanding. Kvanvig draws the lesson that since it is not really knowledge we want but something else, knowledge is really not all that important.

Kvanvig's proposal is appealing. But, I will now argue, the claim that knowledge does not require explanatory understanding is true only if internal justification is not required for knowledge. As we will see, if internal justification *is* required for knowledge, then knowledge does indeed require explanatory understanding. My lesson will be as follows: generic reliabilism and virtue reliabilism both fall short of explaining all of the value of knowledge, but this should not lead us to think that knowledge does not have the value usually attributed to it. Before drawing the unduly pessimistic conclusion that knowledge is not really all that important, we must consider other explanations of what it is about knowledge compared to justified true belief that causes us to hold it in such high regard. As I will argue, we tend to hold knowledge in such high regard because when we are justified in believing truly that p, but we fail to know that p, we lack an adequate understanding of the explanatory connections in the world.

Let me begin my defense of this thesis with an argument for the following claim: anyone who is (internally) justified in believing that p will believe (at least dispositionally) that her evidence is a reliable indicator of p. For example, if you believe it is raining because water is pouring down outside your window, you believe (at least dispositionally) that the water pouring down outside your window is a reliable indicator of rain. The argument is straightforward. If you are justified in believing p, then you believe p on the basis of the evidence you have for p. If, for example, you have evidence for p, and believe that p, but believe that the evidence indicates that q, then we would not say that you are justified in believing that p. But you believe p *on the basis of* evidence for p only if you believe (at least dispositionally) that the evidence is a reliable indicator of p, i.e. only if you believe that the evidence would not be present unless p were the case.

I say 'dispositionally' because many of our beliefs are dispositional in nature. For example, until you read this sentence you were most likely not consciously entertaining the thought that elephants are bigger than spiders. But it wouldn't be unreasonable to say that you had the belief nonetheless. Likewise, we do not typically have conscious thoughts about our evidence. If water were pouring down outside your window, you would most likely form the belief that it is raining without any conscious thought about what explains what. However, you would most likely insist, if asked, that water would not be pouring down outside your window if it were not raining. But the latter is virtually the same as believing that the water outside your window is a reliable indicator of rain. The picture about to unfold is thus quite plausible psychologically speaking. While we do not typically have conscious thoughts about our evidence, we do quite often have dispositional beliefs about it.

Now, your evidence for p is a reliable indicator of p only if you could not easily have had the same evidence and a false belief that p.[27] Suppose, for example, that you believe Tom Grabit stole a book from the library, because you saw someone who looks like Tom Grabit steal a book from the library. If Tom's kleptomaniac twin brother was in the library at the time in question, then you could easily have had the same evidence but a false belief. So, your evidence is not a reliable indicator of "Tom Grabit stole the book." But if you could easily have had the same evidence and a false belief that p, then your second-order belief that your evidence is a reliable indicator of p is false.

It follows that if you fail to know in the Grabit case, then you fail to have a true belief about the nature of your justification. For even an internalist about justification must require that known beliefs be well grounded. Your belief that p is well grounded and so counts as knowledge only if you could not easily have had the same evidence and a false belief that p. Hence, if your second-order belief that your evidence is a reliable indicator of p is false, you fail to know that p. If you know that p, on the other hand, you truly believe that your evidence is a reliable indicator of p, that is, you have a true second-order belief which you would not have had, had you been justified in believing truly that p, but had failed to know that p.

How does this explain the extra value of knowledge? Well, if you are justified in believing truly that p, but you fail to know that p, then you implicitly believe that your reasons for believing p are good reasons—i.e., reasons that make p warranted. But the second-order belief about your reasons for believing p is false. On the other hand, if you know that p, then your second-order belief about your reasons for believing p is true. So, if you know that p, then you truly believe, not only that p is true, but also that you believe p because the evidence in your possession is a reliable indicator of p. Hence, if you know that p, then you truly believe your belief that p is warranted, and you understand why this is so. As Kvanvig points out, our worst cognitive fears include the fear of being duped and the fear of missing something important.[28] When we justifiably believe but fail to know, our worst cognitive fears are realized. We are missing something important when we have evidence for our beliefs but fail to understand how the evidence makes our beliefs warranted. We are being duped when we have a false belief that our evidence for p is a reliable indicator of p. Thus, a theory of knowledge that requires that the knower be internally justified appears to be able to explain why knowing that p is more valuable than being merely justified in believing truly that p. We aspire to knowledge, on this account, because of the cognitive grasp we have of the explanatory connections among reason, belief and truth when we know something. The extra value of knowledge derives from the significance of believing truly that our beliefs are warranted, and understanding why this is so.

Since an internalist can explain why knowing p is more valuable than being merely justified in believing truly that p, she can explain why knowledge is more valuable than mere true belief. Knowledge is more valuable than mere true belief for much the same reason that knowing p is more valuable than being merely justified in believing truly that p; it is more valuable because of the understanding we have of the explanatory connections among reason, truth, and belief when we know something. Having only true beliefs entails a grasp of the facts your beliefs are about, but if you have only feeble reasons for believing as you do, but you believe your reasons make your belief warranted, you have a false second-order belief about the nature of your justification. If you have no reasons at all for believing as you do, you are clearly missing something important. What you are missing is an ability to explain why you believe as you do.

The lesson of the above is this: none of the existing versions of reliabilism has given us any reason why we should care about *knowledge* as opposed to accidentally true belief. A theory of knowledge that requires internal justification, in contrast, can explain what it is about knowledge compared to accidentally true belief that causes us to hold it in such high regard. A theory of this sort thus appears to have more explanatory power than does reliabilism. The question that remains is whether the claim that knowledge is more valuable than accidentally true belief should serve as an adequacy condition on a theory of knowledge. An affirmative answer to this question may help us settle the debate between internalism and externalism once and for all.[29]

Notes

1. See e.g. M.R. Depaul, "Is Truth Our Epistemic End?" (Pacific Division APA, 1989); L. Zagzebski, *Virtues of the Mind* (Cambridge: Cambridge University Press 1996), 300–2; "The Search for the Source of Epistemic Good," *Metaphilosophy* **34** (2003): 12–28; W. Jones, "Why Do We Value Knowledge?" *American Philosophical Quarterly* **34** (1997): 423–40; J. Kvanvig, "Why Should Inquiring Minds Want to Know?" *The Monist* **81** (1998): 426–51; *The Value of Knowledge and the Pursuit of Understanding* (Cambridge: Cambridge University Press 2003); and W.D. Riggs, "Reliability and the Value of Knowledge," *Philosophy and Phenomenological Research* **65** (2002): 79–96.

2. Zagzebski, "The Search for the Source of Epistemic Good," 12–13.

3. See e.g. John Greco, "Virtues in Epistemology," in *The Oxford Handbook of Epistemology*, P.K. Moser, ed. (Oxford/New York: Oxford University Press 2002), 311; W.D. Riggs, "Reliability and the Value of Knowledge," L. Zagzebski, "The Search for the Source of Epistemic Good"; and J. Kvanvig, *The Value of Knowledge.*

4. "The Search for the Source of Epistemic Good," 13.

5. See Philip Percival, "The Pursuit of Epistemic Good," *Metaphilosophy* **34** (2003): 38.

6. "The Search for the Source of the Epistemic Good," 14–15.

7. *Ibid.*

8. W.D. Riggs, "Reliability and the Value of Knowledge," 95.

9. W.D. Riggs, "Reliability and the Value of Knowledge," 95.

10. More cautiously: two things that have the same intrinsic properties have the same amount of instrumental value in the same sort of environment.

11. Wlodek Rabinowicz and Toni Roennow-Rasmussen, "A Distinction in Value: Intrinsic and for its own sake," *Proceedings of the Aristotelian Society* 100, part 1 (1999): 33–49; and "Tropic of Value," *Philosophy and Phenomenological Research* **66** (2003): 389–403.

12. P. Percival, "The Pursuit of Epistemic Good," 33.

13. J. Greco, "Agent Reliabilism," *Philosophical Perspectives* **13** (1999): 273.

14. J. Greco, "Agent Reliabilism," 286.

15. See e.g. S. Luper, "The Epistemic Predicament: Knowledge, Nozickian Tracking, and Skepticism," *Australasian Journal of Philosophy* **62** (1984): 26–60; S. Luper, "The Causal Indicator Analysis of Knowledge," *Philosophy and Phenomenological Research* **47** (1987): 563–87; R.M. Sainsbury, "Easy Possibilities," *Philosophy and Phenomenological Research* **57** (1997): 907, and E. Sosa, "How to Defeat Opposition to Moore," *Philosophical Perspectives* **13** (1999): 141–52.

16. D. Lewis, "Veridical Hallucinations and Prosthetic Vision," in *Perceptual Knowledge*, J. Dancy, ed. (Oxford: Oxford University Press 1988), 85.

17. *Ibid.*

18. *Ibid.*

19. Zagzebski is an exception. She argues that the acquisition and use of our intellectual virtues are always under our voluntary control.

20. J. Greco, "Agent Reliabilism," 287.

21. This example is due, near enough, to Mark Sainsbury. See R.M. Sainsbury, "Easy Possibilities," *Philosophy and Phenomenological Research* **57** (1997): 911. Sainsbury uses this example to show that features of our situation (so-called hidden snags) that may defeat knowledge by shrinking the range of our reliability need to be actual and not merely possible. I am using the example here in my own way.

22. This problem is due to Keith Lehrer and Stewart Cohen. See their "Justification, Truth and Coherence," *Synthase* **55** (1983): 191–208.

23. See Ernest Sosa, "Intellectual Virtue in Perspective," in *Knowledge in Perspective: Collected Essays in Epistemology* (Cambridge: Cambridge University Press 1991), 288ff.

24. A point urged vigorously by Jonathan Kvanvig. See *The Value of Knowledge*, 180ff.

25. K. Lehrer and T. Paxson, "Knowledge: Undefeated Justified True Belief," *Journal of Philosophy* **66** (1969), 228.

26. See J. Kvanvig, "Why Should Inquiring Minds Want to Know?" and *The Value of Knowledge*, ch. 8.

27. See e.g. S. Luper, "The Causal Indicator Analysis of Knowledge."

28. *The Value of Knowledge*, 202–3.

29. I would like to thank an anonymous referee, Matt Bell, Phillip Dennis, John Gabriel, Tom Paxson, Duncan Pritchard, Joe Salerno, Barry Smith, Jim Stone, and the participants in a seminar at the University of Missouri, St. Louis, for their helpful comments and/or discussion.

10 Epistemic Normativity

Stephen R. Grimm

How should we make sense of our epistemic evaluations? To judge a belief to be *justified* or *rational*, for example, is obviously to think something positive about it, and similarly to judge a belief to be *unjustified* or *irrational* is to think something negative. But what is the source or basis of these judgments?

Among contemporary epistemologists, perhaps the most prominent way to make sense of our epistemic evaluations is in teleological terms.[1] On this way of looking at things, a belief earns positive marks, from an epistemic point of view, just to the extent that it seems to promote or in some way bring about the things with intrinsic epistemic value. And similarly, a belief earns negative marks just to the extent that it seems to *fail* to promote or bring about the things with intrinsic epistemic value. I will say more about the motivation for this view in Section 1, but one of my basic goals in this paper will be to show that the teleological view—at least, as it is popularly understood—is mistaken.[2] In short, the problem for the view is that our practice of epistemic evaluation is broader and more wide-ranging than the view can capture. After considering a recent proposal by Ernest Sosa that seems to improve on the teleological account, I then suggest that Sosa's proposal too faces significant difficulties. I close by recommending a way of thinking about the nature of our epistemic evaluations that seems to avoid the problems canvassed earlier.

1 The Teleological Account

Although the teleological account is widely popular, in the first part of this paper I will focus on the way in which three philosophers in

Reprinted from Stephen R. Grimm, "Epistemic Normativity," in *Epistemic Value*, ed. Adrian Haddock, Alan Millar, and Duncan Pritchard (Oxford: Oxford University Press, 2009), 243–264.

particular—Alvin Goldman, William Alston, and Michael Lynch—develop the view. Goldman, Alston, and Lynch are worth considering as a group, because although they eventually differ on the question of the value of true belief, they all begin at least by stressing the following two points. First, that as human beings we often value possessing certain epistemic goods *for their own sake*, and not merely for the sake of whatever further goals—especially, further practical goals—we might happen to have. And second, that the reason *why* we value these goods for their own sake is because of, or due to, our natural curiosity.

In the following passages Goldman, Alston, and Lynch not only endorse both claims, but help to show the way in which they seem to be naturally related:

[Goldman:] Our interest in information has two sources: *curiosity* and practical concerns. The dinosaur extinction fascinates us, although knowing its cause would have no material impact on our lives. We also seek knowledge for practical reasons, as when we solicit a physician's diagnosis or compare prices at automobile dealerships. (Goldman 1999: 3; emphasis added)[3]

[Alston:] [Although having true beliefs furthers our practical goals] the attainment of knowledge and understanding are *also of intrinsic value.* "All men by nature desire to know," said Aristotle, and this dictum has been reaffirmed by many of his successors. Members of our species seem to have a built-in drive to get to *the truth about things that pique their curiosity* and to understand how and why things are as they are and happen as they do. So it is as close to truistic as we can get in philosophy to take truth as a good-making characteristic, and falsity as a bad-making characteristic, of beliefs and other outputs of cognition. (Alston 2005: 31; emphasis added)[4]

[Lynch:] We care about the truth for more than just the benefits it brings us.... There are times in our lives when we simply want to know for no other reason than the knowing itself. *Curiosity* is not always motivated by practical concerns. Consider extremely abstract mathematical conjectures. With regard to at least some such conjectures, knowing their truth would get us no closer to anything else we want. (Lynch 2004: 15–16; emphasis added)

What I am calling the 'first' point therefore seems to be the more fundamental one: namely, that certain epistemic goods seem to possess a kind of intrinsic value. That is, they seem to be goods worth acquiring for their own sake, and not merely for the sake of whatever further practical goods they might help to produce.[5] What I am calling the 'second' point, concerning the role of *curiosity*, in turn seems to be offered as a kind of explanation or defense of the first. After all, it might be thought, although little needs to be said on behalf of the idea that certain practical goods (such as pleasure, perhaps) are worth realizing for their own sake, it might be less obvious that epistemic goods have the same kind of status. Indeed, it might be thought that in comparison with other goods we obviously value for their own sake, the notion of a purely *epistemic* good seems like little more than a fiction.[6] The appeal to curiosity, it seems clear, is meant to cut off just these concerns. Just as there are a range of practical goods we naturally desire, so too, the above passages suggest, there are also purely *epistemic* goods—goods the wanting of which can be explained in terms of our natural curiosity—that we naturally want to possess.[7]

But what are these 'purely epistemic' goods, exactly? In the passages quoted above there is not as much consistency as one might expect. Goldman first speaks vaguely of acquiring information and then of gaining knowledge, Alston first of acquiring knowledge or understanding and then more vaguely of something like possessing the truth, and Lynch first of caring for the truth and then of knowing the truth.

Despite this initial diversity, as we will see in a moment the considered view of all three seems to be that *believing the truth* is the thing that possesses intrinsic epistemic value, at least for creatures like us. When we are uncertain about how things stand with respect to certain subjects (Why *did* the dinosaurs die so suddenly, anyway?) our curiosity is naturally piqued by those subjects. Finding out the truth with respect to such subjects—in other words, believing the truth with respect to such subjects—accordingly possesses an intrinsic worth or value all its own.

Once we take believing the truth to be intrinsically valuable from an epistemic point of view, at any rate, for many philosophers the following teleological account of epistemic appraisal has come to seem very natural and compelling:

The teleological account of epistemic appraisal: A belief earns positive marks (counts as justified, rational, virtuous, etc.), from an epistemic point of view, just in case it does well with respect to the things with intrinsic epistemic value (i.e. helps to promote them or bring them about). Likewise, a belief earns negative marks just in case it does poorly with respect to the things with intrinsic epistemic value.[8]

As the following passages suggest, Goldman, Alston, and Lynch all endorse this view in very similar terms, and make it clear (or, at least, clearer) that by their lights true belief is the thing with intrinsic epistemic value.[9]

[Goldman:] I shall attempt to make a case for the unity of epistemic virtues in which the cardinal value, or underlying motif, is something like true, or accurate, belief. . . . The principal relation that epistemic virtues bear to the core epistemic value will be a teleological or consequentialist one. A process, trait, or action is an epistemic virtue to the extent that it tends to produce, generate, or promote (roughly) true belief. (2002: 52)

[Alston:] We evaluate something epistemically (I will be mostly concerned with the evaluation of beliefs) when we judge it to be more or less good from the epistemic point of view, that is, for the attainment of epistemic purposes. . . . The evaluative aspect of epistemology involves an attempt to identify ways in which the conduct and the products of our cognitive activities can be better or worse vis-à-vis the goals of cognition. And what are those goals? Along with many other epistemologists I suggest that the primary function of cognition in human life is to acquire true beliefs rather than false beliefs about matters that are of interest to us. (2005: 28)[10]

[Lynch:] Once again, the key point is that the value of believing what is justified is parasitic on the value of believing what is true. Having justified beliefs is good because justified beliefs ate likely to be true. (2004: 50)

Although more would need to be said here about many aspects of the view,[11] I hope that by now the basic idea is clear enough: again, that the reason why we think of an individual belief as good or bad is because of some sort of 'doing well' relationship that the belief bears towards the things with intrinsic epistemic value, where the things with intrinsic epistemic value are taken to be true beliefs.

2   Two Views of Value

We just saw that Goldman, Alston, and Lynch all motivate their views by pointing out that, when we are uncertain about how things stand with respect to certain subjects, our curiosity is naturally piqued by those subjects. Suppose for the moment we grant that some subjects *do* in fact naturally elicit our curiosity: perhaps something like the dinosaur extinction falls into this category. Finding out the truth with respect to these subjects will then seem to be intrinsically worthwhile, from a purely epistemic point of view.

The question we now need to ask, however, and the one that reveals an instability in the teleological view, is whether it is really plausible to think that just *any* subject falls into this category. Suppose I am uncertain about how many motes of dust there are on my desk now, for example, or about the now-defunct phone number of some random person in Bangladesh. Is my curiosity really naturally elicited by *these* subjects? Are these really the kinds of subjects that Aristotle had in mind when (as Alston notes in his earlier passage) he claimed at the outset of the *Metaphysics* that "All men by nature desire to know"?

Significantly, this is where opinions begin to divide. According to Lynch,[12] for example, finding out the truth with respect to just *any* subject—even apparently trivial subjects like the number of motes of dust on my desk—possesses genuine, intrinsic epistemic value: it possesses a value worth pursuing for its own sake, from a purely epistemic point of view. Of course, Lynch is quick to acknowledge that the value to be found in trivial subjects of this sort is usually trumped by our other concerns—the value is therefore only prima facie, by his lights. But on his view, and had we world enough and time, finding out the truth with respect to any of these topics would indeed be intrinsically worthwhile, from a purely epistemic point of view.[13]

Let's call this the *unrestricted* view of the value of true belief, according to which believing the truth with respect to just *any* subject possesses a kind of intrinsic epistemic value.[14] The reason why opinions begin to divide here is that many philosophers have found the unrestricted view of the value of true belief incredible, including (most notably) fellow advocates of the teleological account such as Goldman and Alston.

Goldman offers his own counterexamples that tell against the unrestricted view (1999: 88; 2002: 61). What is the 323rd entry in the Wichita, Kansas, phone directory? Who was placed sixth in the women's breast stroke in the 1976 Summer Olympics? What was the full name of Domenico Scarlatti's maternal grandmother? According to Goldman, since finding out the answer to questions of this sort seems wholly lacking in value—even, it seems, from a 'purely' epistemic point of view—"We can no longer suggest that higher degrees of truth possession are all that count in matters of inquiry" (2002: 61). Instead, on his view, we need to shift to what we might now call a *restricted* or *qualified* view of intrinsic epistemic value, where what matters is not possessing the truth on any topic but rather only on "topics of interest" (2002: 61; cf. Goldman 1999: 89).

In his (2005) book Alston too argues that an unrestricted view of the value of true belief cannot be maintained.[15] Since the true beliefs that we could gain from activities like memorizing phone books apparently lack intrinsic value, Alston suggests, along with Goldman he concludes that we need to restrict the realm of those things with intrinsic epistemic value to truths concerning "matters that are of interest or importance to us" (2005: 32).[16]

Despite their initial agreement, the advocates of the teleological account we have been considering so far therefore part ways conspicuously when it comes to identifying the thing (or things) with intrinsic epistemic value. Although all begin with the claim that true beliefs are the things with intrinsic epistemic value, in the face of certain obvious objections—especially, what we might think of as the 'trivial truths' objection—Goldman and Alston immediately back off their claim and relativize the intrinsically valuable things to true beliefs on, roughly, 'matters of interest or importance to us.'

But how dramatic is this difference, and what does it have to teach us about the viability of the teleological view? If Goldman is to be believed, the qualification represents only a 'slight' revision to the teleological view. As he writes:

But can't we incorporate the element of interest by a slight revision in our theory? Let us just say that the core epistemic value is a high degree of truth possession *on topics of interest.* Admittedly, this makes the core underlying value a somewhat 'compound' or 'complex' state of affairs. But, arguably, this is enough to preserve the idea of thematic unity, and thereby preserve Unitarianism. (2002: 61)[17]

Alston too seems to think that the revision is quite slight; at any rate, he seems to even lack Goldman's misgiving that such a qualification immediately "makes the core underlying value a somewhat 'compound' or 'complex' state of affairs."[18]

What I want to argue in the following section, however, is that this difference concerning the nature of the intrinsic epistemic value is dramatic indeed, and that it exposes a fundamental problem at the heart of the teleological view.

3   A Dilemma

To see why, suppose we take it, along with Goldman and Alston, that not all true beliefs are intrinsically valuable but only true beliefs with respect to subjects of interest or importance to us. This then leads us to the crucial question: How should we make sense of our epistemic appraisals with respect to those beliefs (or, better, those topics) that apparently *lack* intrinsic epistemic value—that is, that are not interesting or important, from a purely epistemic point of view?

If we take the teleological account at its word, such a belief would deserve a positive or negative appraisal only to the extent that it did well with respect to the things with intrinsic epistemic value. But by hypothesis a true belief on such a topic would *lack* any such value.[19] And from this it would seem to follow that a positive or negative appraisal of the belief would simply be out of place.

But now the problem should be clear, for positive and negative appraisals of such beliefs clearly do *not* seem out of place. Suppose that on a lazy whim you decide to scan your desktop for motes of dust. After a bit of distracted counting, you then conclude that the desktop is harboring eighteen motes. Given the sloppiness of your method, however, we can suppose that this answer really amounted to little more than a guess: you might very easily have concluded, for example, that there were rather more motes or rather fewer.

What now should we say about your belief? Even if it turns out to be true, is it justified? Well-formed? Rationally held? I take it that on all counts the answer is No. Given your lack of responsiveness to the truth about the motes, your belief would presumably earn low marks with respect to virtually any type of epistemic appraisal on offer.

The problem for the restricted teleological account[20] offered by Goldman and Alston, however, is to explain why this should be so. Recall that according to the teleological account a belief inherits its epistemic status from its 'doing well' relationship to the things with intrinsic epistemic value. But if there is nothing with intrinsic epistemic value to do well with respect to, then it is hard to see where this inherited value or status might come from. From nothing, nothing comes, it would seem.

This then leads us, by way of summary, to the following dilemma for the teleological account of epistemic appraisal. For suppose that, with Goldman and Alston, it is *not* the case that believing the truth with respect to just any subject is intrinsically worthwhile, from an epistemic point of view. If so, then the teleological account seems unable to explain why our beliefs with respect to subjects that lack this kind of value—for short, 'trivial' beliefs—are appropriate candidates for epistemic appraisal. Suppose instead that along with Lynch, we accept an unrestricted view of intrinsic epistemic value. Combined with the teleological account, we can then make sense of the fact that 'trivial' as well as 'non-trivial' beliefs are appropriate candidates for epistemic appraisal, for such beliefs would be derivatively either good or bad to the extent that they promote or respect the things with intrinsic value. But, again, the problem with this account is that an unrestricted view of intrinsic epistemic value is deeply implausible. It hardly seems to be the case that finding out how things stand with respect to just any subject is intrinsically worthwhile, even from a purely epistemic point of view.[21]

In the following section I will consider a recent proposal by Ernest Sosa that seems to allow us to keep the spirit of the teleological account while avoiding the sorts of problems that arise when we try to take a stand on a particular account of intrinsic epistemic value. Before moving on, however, I want to consider one way that Goldman and Alston might try to blunt their particular horn of the dilemma just described.

Recall that Goldman and Alston both qualified their initial views by restricting the scope of intrinsic epistemic value to (roughly) 'matters of interest or importance.' But now it might be thought that the sort of problem cases imagined above—as when we negatively appraise my sloppy counting of motes of dust—are not *really* problems because they are not fairly described. As I described the mote-counting case, for example, I gave the impression that I could care less about how things stood with respect to this subject; instead, I was just looking to pass the time. But it is implausible to suppose that anything like a genuine *belief* could issue from such a process, for the very process of forming a belief seems to require that I care about how things stand with respect to the subject in question.[22] Thus when a topic *interests* me enough to trigger a belief—in other words, when I care about it enough—it might be thought that this implies the presence of something *worth* caring about, hence the presence of a value that could be used to ground further epistemic appraisals.

The basic problem with this response, however, is that it loses track of the fact that not just any sort of good was supposed to ground the teleological account, but rather a good that was distinctively 'epistemic'; in other words, a good that we took to be intrinsically worth realizing from a 'purely' epistemic point of view, or (apparently) simply insofar as we were *curious* beings. Assuming the sort of interest described in the desktop case was serious enough to issue in a belief, however, it was nonetheless still at bottom a practical interest—it was an interest that stemmed from my desire to put off my work for a little while longer, or to give my mind a little rest, and so on. It was, presumably, not an interest that derived from a purely (or even partly) curiosity-driven inclination of mine.

The teleological view, at least as developed by philosophers such as Goldman and Alston, therefore has significant problems trying to make sense of how our concepts of epistemic appraisal apply to apparently 'trivial' topics. But perhaps the teleological view is better understood in a different way—one that retains the appealing structural features of the view while bypassing the difficulties that surround the question of epistemic value. As we will see in the following section, Sosa's recent work offers just such an alternative.

4 Sosa's View

Sosa begins his account by noting that as human beings we are "zest-fully judgmental" across a wide range of areas, including art, literature, science, politics, sports, food, wine, and even coffee (2007: 70). In Sosa's terms, each of these areas of evaluation therefore represents a kind of *domain*—more exactly, each area represents a *critical* domain. Why 'critical'? Because, Sosa suggests, once we identify the values that are *fundamental* within each domain we can then appraise or assess (hence criticize) the *derivative* value of other items in the domain in terms of how well they promote, bring about, or perhaps in some way duly respect the domain's fundamental values. The fundamental values within a given domain therefore serve as the goal around which the critical domain is structured.

Consider, for example, the domain of assassinship. Because for an assassin killing one's target is the goal around which the practice of assassinship is structured (or so it seems), we can therefore evaluate various elements of the assassin's conduct in terms of how effectively the conduct realizes this goal. Or consider the critical domain associated with the card game whist. Since the goal of whist is to take the majority of tricks, particular moves in whist can therefore be evaluated in terms of how well they realize *this* fundamental goal.

Moreover, what focusing on these more unusual sorts of domains helps to bring out, Sosa suggests,[23] is that our ability to evaluate particular items within a domain does not turn on our judgments about the worth of the fundamental values that structure the domain. Thus with respect to some domains, such as whist playing, we might think that the fundamental values involved are too trivial to possess any intrinsic worth. And with respect to others, such as assassinship, we might even think that the fundamental values that structure the domain possess positive *dis*value. Nonetheless, as Sosa notes, this hardly seems to get in the way of our ability to appraise particular elements within the domain:

Paradoxically, one can be an adept critic within such a domain even while discerning no domain-transcendent value in it. Thus, someone knowledgeable about guns and their use for hunting, for military ends, etc., may undergo a conversion that makes the use of guns abhorrent. The good shot is thus drained of any real value that he can discern. Nevertheless, his critical judgment within that domain may outstrip anyone else's, whether gun lover or not. Critical domains can be viewed as thus *insulated*, in ways suggested by our example. (2007: 73–4)

The basic insight Sosa wants to build on, then, is that we can evaluate items within a domain in terms of how effectively they promote or bring about the fundamental values of the domain, while all the while remaining agnostic about whether the domain's fundamental values are valuable or worth pursuing intrinsically.

So, how does this basic insight help to shed light on our concepts of epistemic appraisal? According to Sosa, epistemic appraisals too take place within an insulated critical domain, a domain in which the fundamental value is true belief. Unlike Goldman, Alston, and Lynch, however, Sosa argues that in order to make sense of our concepts of epistemic appraisal there is no need to take a stand on whether true belief is something that possesses intrinsic value or is worth pursuing for its own sake. In Sosa's words: "Truth may or may not be intrinsically valuable absolutely, who knows? Our worry requires only that we consider truth the epistemically fundamental value, the ultimate explainer of other distinctively epistemic value" (2007: 72).

5 A Closer Look

What should we make of Sosa's proposal? On the positive side, the view naturally accommodates our ability to appraise beliefs on *any* topic, even apparently 'trivial' topics. Since the fundamental epistemic value for Sosa is simply true belief, it follows that 'trivial' beliefs can be appraised and evaluated just as readily as more 'important' beliefs. In this way the account captures the full scope of our epistemic appraisals; unlike the Goldman–Alston view, it doesn't leave the trivial out. The view can also make good sense of our appraisals concerning how *effectively* a particular believer reaches the truth goal. Although the terms he uses are a bit Sosa-specific, there clearly seems to be a sense in which we can evaluate a belief as 'adroit' or as 'maladroit' (i.e. as deriving, or not, from a reliable competence on the part of the believer to realize the truth), or as 'apt' or 'inapt' (i.e. as realizing, or not realizing, the truth *because of* such a competence).[24] Sosa's view therefore interestingly unites our appraisal of beliefs to our appraisal of performances more generally. Thus, just as we can judge an archer's shot to be adroit or maladroit (relative to the goal of striking the bullseye) or we can judge a tennis player's serve as apt or inapt (relative to the goal of hitting the ball in the appropriate box), so too we can judge the truth-oriented merits of someone's believing: as a performance that manifests various degrees of skill and efficiency relative to the truth goal.

Despite these virtues, what I want to suggest now is that by remaining agnostic about the domain-transcendent value of true belief, Sosa seems to introduce a new problem—seems to, indeed, lose sight of one of the most important aspects of our epistemic appraisals. For notice: when we judge a belief to be unjustified or irrational, we seem to be doing more than just evaluating (in this case, in a negative way) the skill or virtuosity of the believer's performance. In addition, we seem to be in some sense *criticizing*, perhaps even *reproaching*, them for believing in this way.[25] To judge someone's belief to be unjustified or irrational is thus to judge that the person's attitude towards the content of the belief *should* be reconsidered, in some apparently binding sense of 'should.'[26] As Hilary Kornblith puts the point:

> If you tell me that a belief of mine is unjustified, this gives me reason to give up that belief. The epistemic claim is something about which I should care, and an account of the source of epistemic norms must explain why it is that I should care about such things. (2002: 145)

What's more, even what we referred to earlier as the Sosa-specific appraisals such as 'apt' and 'inapt' seem to carry with them this normative force. Thus, and to extend Kornblith's point, if I accept that a certain belief of mine is 'inapt' I seem now to have a reason to do something about my attitude toward the content of the belief: perhaps to change my attitude altogether, or perhaps to try to get into a better epistemic position with respect to the subject at issue, and so on. Simply sticking with the original attitude in the face of the 'inapt' judgment does not seem to be acceptable. If at all possible, it seems that I *should* try to do something about my position.[27]

Can Sosa make sense of the way in which this binding sense of 'should' attaches to our epistemic evaluations (especially, it seems, our negative evaluations)? In one sense it might be thought that he can, for there does seem to be a natural place for a 'should' even within Sosa's insulated domains of critical appraisal. Thus, we might say that, given that such-and-such is the goal, one *should* proceed in this way—and not in that way—in order to realize the goal. So, for example, given the goal of acquiring a true belief with respect to a given subject, one *should* base one's belief on good evidence, rather than hazard a random guess, because basing one's belief on good evidence is a more effective way of realizing the goal at issue.

The problem of course is that this sense of 'should' is quite weak; in roughly Kantian terms, it is the 'should' of calculation rather than the stronger, binding 'should' associated with duty or obligation. In this weaker sense of 'should,' after all, the assassin *should* use a high-powered rifle, rather than a flimsy slingshot, in order best to realize his goal of killing the target. The sense of 'should' associated with our judgment that a particular belief is unjustified, however, seems deontologically more substantial than that.

To make better sense of the binding sense of 'should' that seems to attach to our epistemic appraisals, it is worth recalling that we can appraise or evaluate beliefs relative to several different goals.[28] Suppose, for example, I am wondering whether God exists. It might be the case that if I were to believe that God did *not* exist then I would experience tremendous psychological distress: I would find it very hard to go on in a world that suddenly seemed devoid of meaning. We can therefore appraise how well my belief about God does not just with respect to the goal of realizing the truth but also with respect to this other goal—roughly, what we might think of as the goal of 'psychological comfort.'

Imagine now that after soberly weighing the evidence I decide that God does not exist, thus (as expected) bringing with it significant psychological distress. Relative to the goal of psychological comfort ('comfort,' for short), we can therefore appraise my belief in a variety of different ways: we can say that it was 'comfort unjustified,' 'comfort irrational,' 'comfort inapt,' 'comfort maladroit,' and so on. Suppose we settle on one of these judgments: that the belief was 'comfort unjustified'—that is, unjustified from the point of view of psychological comfort. If I accept this judgment, does it now follow that I have *reason* to give up my belief, or that I *should* give up my belief? I take it that in some weak, calculative sense of a 'reason' or of 'should' this might be right. Thus, relative to the goal of psychological comfort, I have a reason to give up my belief; alternatively: relative to this end, I should give it up. But it seems clear that neither the 'reason' nor the 'should' at issue here is binding in the way considered above—in neither case does it seem that we can be justly blamed or criticized for failing to orient our belief towards the goal of psychological comfort, for example.

Once we consider things from the truth perspective, however, we can see the normative force of our evaluations has a dramatically different character. Suppose, for example, that instead of soberly weighing up the evidence I formed my belief about God by hazarding a random guess. Relative to the goal of believing the truth, naturally, this belief will earn a variety of negative appraisals: thus we might say (extending our artificial evaluations for the moment) that the belief was 'truth unjustified,' 'truth irrational,' 'truth inapt,' 'truth maladroit,' and so on. Notice now, however, that if I were to agree that my belief was truth-unjustified, for example, I would now have more than a calculative reason to give up my belief, a reason that would be potentially dispensable, if for some reason I no longer cared about the truth. Instead, I would seem to have a *binding* reason. In accepting this judgment, I would agree that I should not be holding this belief, in some non-optional sense of 'should.'

It seems clear enough, then, that even though we can evaluate beliefs relative to countless different 'fundamental values' and hence countless different domains, the end of realizing the truth enjoys a special sort of status when it comes to the evaluation of belief. What's more, the fact that realizing the truth enjoys this special status seems to account for the particular normative force that our epistemic appraisals possess. Given Sosa's agnosticism about the domain-transcendent value of true belief, however, it is not clear that he can make sense of the fact that the truth perspective is in some sense the privileged perspective—as we might say, the binding perspective—when it comes to the evaluation of belief.

Before moving on, I should note that, towards the end of his most recent discussion of epistemic normativity, Sosa offers a distinction that might seem to accommodate the sort of bindingness we've just been emphasizing. Thus Sosa suggests that we need to distinguish between two sorts of epistemic normativity: on the one hand, the sort of normativity that is *constitutive* of knowledge, and on the other hand, the sort of normativity that is relevant to the study of 'intellectual ethics' (2007: 89–91). On this way of looking at things, the normativity associated with 'intellectual ethics' has to do with appreciating and pursuing the sorts of intellectual topics that are in some sense 'finer' (2007: 89) and hence more *worthy* of our attention. But according to Sosa this sort of normativity—which would seem to bring with it a kind of binding character—has little if anything to do with the sort of normativity that is *constitutive* of knowledge. Thus while we might blame or criticize someone for spending their life counting blades of grass (say), these judgments are separable from our normative judgments about whether a particular belief counts as apt or inapt, adroit or maladroit, and so on.

Although Sosa seems right that there is an important distinction to be made here, the question we still need to ask is whether it helps to explain the distinctive normative force of our epistemic appraisals. And it seems to me that it does not. As I noted at the outset, in trying to offer an account of epistemic normativity we are presumably looking for an explanation of why our epistemic appraisals have the particular force that they evidently have. I have argued, moreover, that our epistemic appraisals have a particular binding or reason-giving force that other sorts of appraisals lack (say, appraisals concerning comfort-aptness or inaptness). But Sosa's distinction seems to offer no explanation of this last fact. Even if we grant him (as I think we should) that a judgment that S should not be counting blades of grass seems categorical rather than merely hypothetical, we still have no explanation for why a judgment that S's grass belief was maladroit (say) goes hand in hand with a judgment that S should try to improve his cognitive position with respect to the grass, if possible—where the 'should' here again seems to be a categorical one, rather than a merely hypothetical one.[29] It seems that we need to look further, then, in search of the source of the special sort of normativity that attaches to our epistemic appraisals.

6   Our Position

Let's take stock. Recall that Section 3 closed with a dilemma for the teleological account of epistemic appraisal. If we suppose that only truths of interest or importance are intrinsically valuable (from a 'purely' epistemic point of view—whatever exactly that comes to), then it looks like we lose our ability to explain how our epistemic appraisals apply to unimportant, 'trivial' beliefs. If we suppose instead that *any* truth is intrinsically valuable, then it looks like we've reached an absurdity; only someone really desperate, apparently, would think *that*. Our discussion of Sosa's view, in turn, suggested that attempts to make sense of our epistemic appraisals should not lose sight of the distinctive normative force of these appraisals. Thus to judge a belief to be justified (for example) is not simply to judge that it is skillfully oriented to the truth but rather that it *should* be so oriented, in some binding sense of 'should'—just as to deem a belief to be unjustified is to judge that it should *not* be so oriented, in some binding sense of 'should not.' To suppose that it is only, or even primarily, the skillfulness of the belief that we are appraising when we make positive appraisals of this kind seems to lose sight of the fact that a belief can be skillfully aimed at almost any goal. There thus seems to be something special about the truth goal that Sosa's truth agnosticism apparently leaves out.

Overall, this leaves us with two main points in need of reconciliation. First, the fact that our epistemic appraisals not only can be, but patently are, applied to the full range of our beliefs. Second, that our epistemic appraisals seem to have a distinctive normative (binding) force, suggesting that the truth goal is not simply one goal among others when it comes to the evaluation of belief, but rather a goal with a special status.

What I want to propose in this section is that the best way to make sense of these two claims is to accept a *modified* version of the thesis that any true belief has a special value or worth—a version that attempts to explain the unrestricted value of true belief in a slightly different way, or (better) from a slightly different perspective. More exactly, I want to argue that the best way to make sense of the two claims is by shifting away from the standard first-person question about the value of true belief—wherein we ask (as Goldman, Alston, and Lynch asked) about the value of true belief in terms of our own intellectual goals or well-being—and by moving instead towards a more communal or social view of the value of truth.[30]

To appreciate how the switch from a first-person perspective to a social perspective might help, consider first the following passage from Thomas Kelly. Here Kelly makes a point that will by now be familiar: namely, that it hardly seems to be the case that believing the truth with respect to just any subject is worthwhile or valuable, even from a 'purely epistemic' point of view. More radically, Kelly also insists that even believing something *false* about many subjects does not bring with it any obvious disvalue. As he writes:

In addition to those many truths such that my believing them would contribute to the achievement of some goal that I have, there are also (countless) truths such that my believing them would not contribute to any goal that I actually have. Whether Bertrand Russell was right- or left-handed, whether Hubert Humphrey was an only child—these are matters of complete indifference to me. That is, I have no preference for having true beliefs to having no beliefs about these subjects; nor, for that matter, do I have any preference for having true beliefs to false beliefs. There is simply no goal—cognitive or otherwise—which I actually have, which would be better achieved in virtue of my believing true propositions about such subjects, or which would be worse achieved in virtue of my believing false propositions about them. (2003: 624–5)

Let's grant for the moment that Kelly is right about this: that believing the truth with respect to such topics would not contribute to any personal goals he might happen to have. What's it to him, then, if he forms a belief about whether (say) Humphrey was an only child by means of a random guess? And yet, as we saw before, such a random guess would not only earn low marks from an epistemic point of view (count as unjustified, irrational, etc.), but also earn our criticism and perhaps even reproach. Why so?

Considered from a social point of view, it would seem that the answer to this question can be found by noting that even though we might not care less about some belief (or better, some topic), it is nonetheless the case that other people might care about the topic a great deal. For example, while finding out the truth with respect to whether Humphrey was an only child may not hold any value for us, or may not elicit our curiosity in any way, presumably for Humphrey's biographer (say) getting this right will be quite important—if not in itself, or for its own sake, then at least for the sake of producing an accurate account of Humphrey's life. And given that someone in the biographer's shoes might depend on us as potential sources of information about this topic, it seems that we have an obligation not to be cavalier when we form beliefs about the question—in other words, an obligation to try to position ourselves well with respect to this question, even though, given our own cognitive goals, we might very well be thoroughly uninterested.[31]

In short, what turning away from one's personal goals and concerns and towards our broader role in the information economy (as it were) helps to remind us is that the concerns of others—especially the practical concerns of others—are remarkably plastic and unpredictable. As such, it reminds us that, even though a topic may hold no interest or value from our first-person point of view, it may well hold interest or value for someone else. And as a potential source of information for others, we have an obligation to treat *any* topic or any question with due respect.[32]

Suppose this approach works with respect to the Humphrey question. But what about the *really* trivial topics, like the 323rd entry in the Wichita, Kansas, phone directory? Or the number of motes of dust on my desk at this very moment? Although it is harder to imagine how someone might have an interest in these questions, once again we need only bear in mind how odd and varied people's practical concerns can be. For the Wichita phonebook fact-checker, for example, it might well be important—not epistemically important, but practically, presumably—to know the name of the 323rd person in the directory. Less realistically, but still possibly, we can imagine that someone with a particular antipathy towards dust might well wonder whether his new 'anti-dust' strategies have really succeeded in cutting down the number of motes of dust on his desk, as he fondly hopes.

It therefore seems that the basic idea we need to make sense both (*a*) of the apparently unlimited range of our epistemic appraisals as well as (*b*) of their normative force is that, given our nature as information-dependent and information-sharing creatures, we have an obligation not just to be sources of information for others but to be *good* sources of information. This obligation stems, moreover, not from the fact that believing the truth with respect to just any subject is intrinsically valuable, but rather because any subject might *come* to have value—if only value of a practical sort—in light of the varied and unpredictable concerns others might have.[33]

Plausibly, then, the best way to make sense of the value of true belief is to think of it along the lines of a *common good*. Consider, for example, the value we associate with other classic examples of common goods such as *clean water.*[34] Given the central place of clean water in all of our lives, there is strong temptation to regard the value of clean water as intrinsic, as inherently worth possessing or acquiring, or at least as inherently worthy of our respect. From a first-person point of view, however, this does not always seem to be the case. Suppose, for example, I have my own guaranteed lifetime supply of water (perhaps a valet carries it around in jugs behind me, wherever I happen to go), more than enough to satisfy whatever thirst I might happen to have. Would any particular parcel of clean water still seem intrinsically valuable in this case—worth acquiring or possessing? It doesn't seem so, at least from my first-person point of view. And yet it looks like the nature of an intrinsic good that its goodness is a necessary feature of the thing, not the kind of property that can come and go.

That said, to appreciate the sense in which any particular parcel of water would nonetheless be worthy of our respect, suppose my imaginary valet and I are crossing a bridge over a wide expanse of clean water. What should my attitude towards this water be? By hypothesis, I am not interested in taking a drink from it; I have my jugs, after all. But while drinking this water is no goal of mine—while it is something I can find no personal value in—it seems clear enough that this stretch of water possesses a value that is worthy of my respect. Were I to dump a barrelful of sludge in the water, for example, this would clearly be something for which I would deserve blame or censure. But why's that, exactly?

Some might appeal at this point to the intrinsic value of preserving natural systems, which I would here be damaging.[35] But another, more straightforward answer should again strike us as plausible: namely, that other people might well need this water to satisfy their needs. Indeed, even if I have some reason to think that no one would really be harmed by the loss of this particular parcel of water, that would not seem to justify the dumping. For, given the unpredictable nature of the needs of others, and given how contamination of this sort can spread in unpredictable ways, others very well might turn out to depend on this water. And since clean water plays such an indispensable role in human well-being, we plausibly have an obligation not to pollute in this way, but rather to treat the water with due respect.

The comparison between the value of true belief and clean water is not perfect, but I think it nonetheless focuses our attention in the right way. It is not perfect, because while we could potentially flourish without clean water of any kind (perhaps we could flourish on Twin Earth, for example, with twater, not water), it hardly seems to be the case that we could flourish without truth of any kind. The comparison focuses our attention in the right way, however, because it helps us to see the way in which both belong to the category of common goods, goods that are, at least contingently, crucial to human well-being. Even though particular instances of these goods might thus not intrinsically contribute to my well-being, they should nonetheless be duly respected because of the central role that they might play in the lives of others, and perhaps even (who's to say?) in our own.

7 Conclusion

We can now offer a few tentative conclusions.

The first conclusion, and one that we can draw from our discussion of Goldman and Alston in particular, is that any attempt to relativize the teleological account of epistemic appraisal to 'questions of interest and importance' (or the like) faces multiple problems. For one thing, there is the problem of offering an account of what it is that makes some questions important and others unimportant, from a purely epistemic (as opposed to practical) point of view. For another thing there is the problem of how to make sense of our epistemic appraisals with respect to those questions that lie on the 'unimportant' side of the ledger (assuming such a side exists). Although in this paper I focused on the second sort of criticism, to my mind the significance of the first problem has yet to be fully appreciated, and will almost certainly prove to be the more important (and difficult) issue going forward. For example: supposing that it is true, *why* exactly is it true that counting motes of dust counts as trivial and lacking in value, from a 'purely epistemic' point of view, while finding out (say) whether one has a hand does not? Or if the hand question too counts as trivial then when, exactly, *does* one come to a question that counts as epistemically important or significant? It is hard to know how even to begin to answer these questions. And yet one often hears appeals to the epistemically 'significant' or 'important' as if these notions were well understood, or could be put to good theoretical use.

The second conclusion is that, if we follow Sosa in adopting a kind of agnosticism about the value of true belief, then we seem at a loss to explain the distinctively normative—that is, binding or action-guiding—character of our epistemic appraisals. Thus, given certain arbitrarily specified ends, we can evaluate how well someone does with respect to those ends—just in the way that Sosa describes. But it doesn't follow that a judgment that someone has failed to do well with respect to those ends is binding or action guiding in the way that a judgment that someone's belief has done poorly with respect to the truth is binding or action guiding. In order to get at the distinctively normative (as opposed to merely evaluative) character of our epistemic appraisals, we need to dig deeper.

We were then left with the following question: how *can* we make sense of the distinctively normative force of our epistemic appraisals? And according to the proposal I sketched in the final part of the paper the best way to do this is to appreciate true belief's status as a common good (rather than, for example, as an intrinsic good, one the having of which always adds value to the life of the possessor). The way I developed this idea, moreover, was by emphasizing the fact that, as information-dependent and information-sharing creatures, we naturally—and, it seems, rightfully—depend on others as sources of information.

I will close by suggesting that if this final proposal is on the right track, moreover, then it is a mistake to suppose that the sort of normativity that characterizes our epistemic appraisals is basic or irreducible. Instead, epistemic normativity would seem to be explicable in terms of a deeper, and more obviously moral, sort of normativity: namely, the sort of normativity that derives from our obligation to help others carry out their projects and concerns (broadly understood). Although in one way this suggestion does not make the normative force of our epistemic appraisals any less mysterious—for what is the source of our non-hypothetical obligation to assist others, after all?—it does suggest that it is a mistake to try to offer an account of epistemic normativity in isolation, and without attending to what, if anything, we owe to one another from a moral point of view.[36]

Notes

1. In addition to the figures to be discussed below, see e.g. BonJour (1985: 7–8), Foley (1987: ch. 1), and Lehrer (1990: 112). For a more extensive list, see David (2001: 152).

2. The qualification "as it is popularly understood" will prove to be important later. There I will suggest that if one thinks about the goals that are being promoted (respected, etc.) in a different way, then it could be more plausible to think that we appraise our beliefs in terms of how well they promote these other goals and concerns.

3. This passage highlights the role of curiosity, but it is not as clear as it might be that Goldman associates this with a true-belief-for-its-own-sake claim. It is thus helpful to read this passage in conjunction with a passage from his earlier *Epistemology and Cognition* (1986). There he writes: "Even if the desire for truth-acquisition is ultimately traceable to biological fitness (curiosity about one's environment can promote survival), it still appears in the organism as an 'autonomous' desire. People do

not desire true belief merely as a means to survival, or the achievement of practical ends. Truth acquisition is often desired for its own sake, not for ulterior ends. It would hardly be surprising, then, that intellectual norms should incorporate true belief as an autonomous value, quite apart from its possible contribution to biological or practical end" (Goldman 1986: 98).

4. Notice that, although Alston begins this passage by suggesting (along with Aristotle) that it is knowledge and understanding that is desired for its own sake, by the end of the passage (and in keeping with the rest of the argument in the book) he claims that it is truth that is the "good-making characteristic"—in other words, the intrinsically valuable thing.

5. Perhaps, as Goldman suggests, the nature of the dinosaur extinction is like this—though one would have thought the practical relevance of this topic (sudden and catastrophic extinction!) was fairly clear.

6. According to Stephen Stich (1990: 131), for example, although we do value many things intrinsically—health, happiness, the welfare of our children, etc.—the truth (Stich's main candidate for a putatively epistemic good) is not one of them. Similarly, although Hilary Kornblith (2003: ch. 5) is critical of many aspects of Stich's view, he seems to agree that there are no epistemic goods that are worth pursuing for their own sake.

7. In addition to the authors cited above, Ram Neta is another who makes this connection explicit. As he writes. "Knowledge and other positive epistemic statuses are worthy of pursuit by inquisitive creatures not (or not just) because they are instrumentally valuable. They may, of course, be instrumentally valuable—we need not disagree with Kornblith on that point. But that's not the only thing that makes them worthy of pursuit for inquisitive creatures. What makes them worthy of pursuit for inquisitive creatures like ourselves is that, like health, friendship, and love, their attainment is partly constitutive of our well-being. Knowledge, and epistemic excellence more generally, it part of what constitutes the natural and valuable phenomenon of an inquisitive creature's well-being" (2007: 352).

8. This account is doubtless incomplete as it stands (though complete enough for our purposes), because presumably *withholdings* too can be appraised epistemically. For more on this see DePaul (2004).

9. I use the notion of 'intrinsic value' in what I take to be the standard way here, to mean a value that is worth pursuing and realizing for its own sake. When Goldman speaks of truth as a 'cardinal value' we pursue for its own sake, I therefore assume by this he means what we standardly mean by an 'intrinsic value.' (It is possible that by the talk of 'cardinal' instead of 'intrinsic' value, however, Goldman has something more like the Sosa view, which we will consider shortly, in mind.) Similarly, Lynch (elsewhere) prefers to speak of the for-its-own-sake value that believing the truth possesses as a 'constitutive value' (see e.g. Lynch 2004: 127)—'constitutive' in the

sense that it is an essential constitutive part of a flourishing life, which is an end we all desire. As Lynch notes, the notion of a constitutive value is theoretically quite similar to the notion of an intrinsic value: "Being constitutively good, like being an intrinsic good, makes something worth caring about for its own sake, as opposed to caring about it for what it leads to" (2004: 128).

10. Notice that, unlike Goldman (and Lynch, looking ahead), Alston claims not simply that true belief is the intrinsically valuable thing, but "true beliefs rather than false beliefs about matters that are of interest to us." This is not a trivial difference, as I will argue at length in Section 3, but for the moment we can put the distinction to one side.

11. For example, what sort of reliability matters? 'Actual world' likelihood (where 'actual' is a name, rather than an indexical)? 'Normal world' likelihood? Something else? This is none too clear, as Goldman's various stances over the years suggest.

12. Among others: Kvanvig (2003: 41) and Horwich (2006: 347) also defend this view.

13. As Lynch, responding to the sort of natural objection we will next consider, writes: "Come on, what about really trivial truths? Surely there are all sorts of true beliefs I could have that are not even *prima facie* good? Without a doubt, there are all sorts of true beliefs that are not worth having, all things considered. But the fact that I should not bother with those sorts of beliefs doesn't mean that it isn't still *prima facie* good to believe even the most trivial truth" (2004: 55).

14. Lynch puts his point more formally as follows: "It is *prima facie* good, for all p (to believe that p if and only if it is true that p)" (2005: 331).

15. It is worth noting that his 2005 book represents something of a change in his thinking about the nature of epistemic value. In his earlier "Concepts of Epistemic Justification," for example, he there characterized the epistemic goal as that of "maximizing truth and minimizing falsity in a large body of beliefs," although he explicitly called that a "tough characterization" (1989a: 83–4).

16. And, indeed, many epistemologists writing on the topic of our 'epistemic goal' quite naturally relativize the goal to something like 'topics of interest and importance.' See e.g. Haack (1993: 199) and David (2005: 299). The temptation to make this move is obviously very powerful.

17. "Unitarianism" is Goldman's term for the view that the only intrinsic epistemic value—in his words, the "cardinal" epistemic value—is true belief.

18. See e.g. Alston's discussion in 2005: 30–3.

19. Some philosophers even insist (on a slightly different note) that a *false* belief on this topic holds no intrinsic disvalue. See e.g. Kelly (2003: 624–5).

20. That is, the problem arises for an account that combines the teleological view of appraisal with a restricted view of intrinsic epistemic value.

21. For more on the selectiveness of our sense of curiosity, see Harman (1999: 100) and Grimm (2008).

22. See Nishi Shah (2003), and Shah and David Velleman (2005). It is also true that a typical person will have what we might think of as 'standing concerns': thus if I hear a loud noise nearby, or see a flash in the distance, I will (as it were) automatically form a belief about these subjects. Thanks to Robert Audi for helping to clarify this point.

23. I should add that the examples just mentioned are meant to *illustrate* Sosa's view, they are not Sosa's own.

24. Sosa has been working with this distinction for some time; see e.g. Sosa 1991. For his most recent version, see his 2007: ch. 2.

25. As Nicholas Wolterstorff notes: "We say to each other such things as, 'You should have known better than to think that Borges was an English writer,' 'You should be more trusting of what our State Department says,' and 'You should never have believed him when he told you that the auditors had approved that way of keeping books.' Not only do we *regret* the knowledge and ignorance of other human beings, their beliefs, disbeliefs, and non-beliefs; we reproach them, blame them, chastise them, using the deontological concepts of ought and ought not, should and should not. Of course we also praise them for believing and not believing, knowing and not knowing, as they do" (2005: 326).

26. Notice that in suggesting that beliefs are subject to criticism in this way we do not have to accept that belief is subject to our direct voluntary control. I think (along with Alston 1989*b*, Plantinga 1993, and virtually everyone else) it is obvious that it is not. Instead it seems that all we need suppose is that belief is under *enough* control to make critical judgments appropriate. At any rate, these types of judgments are central enough to our epistemic appraisals that any theory of epistemic normativity should seek to accommodate them (see e.g. Audi 2001, as well as the previous footnote). Notice as well that while I have argued that a judgment that a belief is (say) truth-unjustified carries with it the judgment that the subject of the belief should try to improve her cognitive position with respect to the belief, I do not mean to say that it is always psychologically possible to give up the belief. Sometimes, as a result of brainwashing, perhaps, or possible psychological trauma, it might not be. But it does not follow that the 'unjustified' judgment does not have this binding sense of 'should' attached to it. Consider a comparison with the judgment *cruel*. I take it that when we judge a particular action to be cruel, this brings with it the idea that the agent should not act in this way, even that the agent has a binding reason not to act in this way. But it seems equally clear that we might apply this judgment to the actions of a particular agent even if, for some peculiar psychological reasons, the agent

felt compelled to act this way, perhaps to the point where he could not have acted otherwise. Indeed, in a loose, analogical way, we sometimes even apply the judgment 'cruel' to the behavior of animals, even though it seems unlikely that they have the sort of voluntary control over their actions that would make judgments of blame and censure strictly appropriate.

27. Alan Millar (2004: 92–9) and Terence Cuneo (2007: 67–70) likewise tie the notion of normativity to the notion *of having a reason.*

28. I do not want to suggest that this point is unfamiliar to Sosa (indeed, he begins many of his papers with the very distinction)—just that its force needs to be appreciated properly here.

29. It is worth noting that Sosa's position, as far as I can see, does not exclude the possibility of identifying a further source for the bindingness that characterizes our epistemic appraisals. The problem is only that the view as it stands leaves this further sort of normativity unexplained.

30. It might sound odd to accuse Goldman, at least, of being insensitive to the social value of true belief, for perhaps more than any current epistemologist he has emphasized the importance of the social dimension of knowing! To my mind, however, his teleological framework of epistemic appraisal does not sufficiently reflect this fact. Thus, for example, his basic framework is essentially indistinguishable from Alston's, who does *not* stress the social in the same way.

31. There is a difficult question here about whether we have positive obligations to (say) seek out information concerning subjects about which we are currently ignorant. It seems to me that the answer is sometimes yes, sometimes no, though I will not take a stand on that question here.

32. My colleague Allan Hazlett reminds me that this sort of view, right down to the concern with apparently 'trivial' truths, can be found in W. C. K. Clifford's classic essay "The Ethics of Belief." For these reasons I am tempted to call the view of normativity developed here Cliffordian, at least in the sense that it suggests that epistemic normativity is ultimately grounded in moral normativity.

33. Cf. Craig (1990), Greco (2010), Weinberg (2006), Kusch (2009).

34. Goods such as *clean air* also come to mind, but focusing on water should be enough to make the point. Kusch (2009) also interestingly compares the value of true belief to the value of clean water.

35. E.g. Aldo Leopold (1966: 240–2).

36. Thanks to Robert Audi, Heather Battaly, Jason Baehr, Michael DePaul, John Greco, Adrian Haddock, Allan Hazlett, Martin Kusch, Alan Millar, Duncan Pritchard, Wayne Riggs, Ernest Sosa, and Fritz Warfield for helpful comments on earlier versions of this paper.

References

Alston, W. (1989*a*). "Concepts of Epistemic Justification," in his *Epistemic Justification*. Ithaca, NY: Cornell University Press.

―――― (1989*b*). "The Deontological Concept of Epistemic Justification," in his *Epistemic Justification*. Ithaca, NY: Cornell University Press.

―――― (2005). *Beyond Justification: Dimensions of Epistemic Evaluation*. Ithaca, NY: Cornell University Press.

Audi, R. (2001). "Doxastic Voluntarism and the Ethics of Belief," in M. Steup (ed.), *Knowledge, Truth, and Duty*. New York: Oxford University Press.

BonJour, L. (1985). *The Structure of Empirical Knowledge*. Cambridge, MA: Harvard University Press.

Clifford, W. C. K. (1877 [1999]). *The Ethics of Belief and Other Essays*. Prometheus Books, Amherst, NY: Harvard University Press.

Craig, E. (1990). *Knowledge and the State of Nature*. Oxford: Clarendon Press.

Cuneo, T. (2007). *The Normative Web: An Argument for Moral Realism*. New York: Oxford University Press.

David, M. (2001). "Truth as an Epistemic Goal," in M. Steup (ed.), *Knowledge, Truth, and Duty*. New York: Oxford University Press.

―――― (2005). "Truth as the Primary Epistemic Goal," in E. Sosa and M. Steup (eds.), *Contemporary Debates in Epistemology*. Oxford: Blackwell Publishing.

DePaul, M. (2004). "Truth Consequentialism, Withholding, and Proportioning Belief to the Evidence," *Philosophical Issues*, 14: 91–112.

Foley, R. (1987). *The Theory of Epistemic Rationality*. Cambridge, MA: Harvard University Press.

Goldman, A. (1986). *Epistemology and Cognition*. Cambridge, MA: Harvard University Press.

―――― (1999). *Knowledge in a Social World*. New York: Oxford University Press.

―――― (2002). "The Unity of the Epistemic Virtues," in his *Pathways to Knowledge*. New York: Oxford University Press.

Greco, J. (2010). *Achieving Knowledge*. New York: Cambridge University Press.

Grimm, S. (2008). "Epistemic Goals and Epistemic Values," *Philosophy and Phenomenological Research*, 77.

Haack, S. (1993). *Evidence and Inquiry*. Oxford: Blackwell Publishing.

Harman, G. (1999). "Pragmatism and Reasons for Belief," in his *Reasoning, Meaning, and Mind*. Oxford: Clarendon Press.

Horwich, P. (2006). "The Value of Truth," *Noûs*, 40: 347–60.

Kelly, T. (2003). "Epistemic Rationality as Instrumental Rationality: A Critique," *Philosophy and Phenomenological Research*, 66: 612–40.

Kornblith, H. (2002). *Knowledge and its Place in Nature*. New York: Oxford University Press.

Kusch, M. (2009). "Testimony and the Value of Knowledge." In Adrian Haddock, Alan Miller, and Duncan Pritchard, (eds.), *Epistemic Value*. Oxford: Oxford University Press, 248–257.

Kvanvig, J. (2003). *The Value of Knowledge and the Pursuit of Understanding*. Cambridge, MA: Cambridge University Press.

Lehrer, K. (1990). *Theory of Knowledge*. Boulder, CO: Westview Press.

Leopold, A. (1966). "The Land Ethic," in his *A Sand County Almanac*. New York: Oxford University Press.

Lynch, M. (2004). *True to Life: Why Truth Matters*. Cambridge, MA: MIT Press.

—— (2005). "Replies to Critics," *Philosophical Books*, 46: 331–42.

Millar, A. (2004). *Understanding People: Normativity and Rationalizing Explanation*. New York: Oxford University Press.

Neta, R. (2007). "How to Naturalize Epistemology," in D. Pritchard and V. Hendricks (eds.), *New Waves in Epistemology*. London: Palgrave Macmillan.

Plantinga, A. (1993). *Warrant: The Current Debate*. New York: Oxford University Press.

Quine, W. v. O. (1986). "Reply to Morton White," in *The Philosophy of W. V. Quine*, ed. L. Hahn and P. Schlipp. La Salle, IL: Open Court Publishing Company.

Shah, N. (2003). "How Truth Governs Belief," *Philosophical Review*, 112(4): 447–82.

—— and Velleman, J. D. (2005). "Doxastic Deliberation," *Philosophical Review*, 114(4): 497–534.

Sosa, E. (1991). "Intellectual Virtue in Perspective," in his *Knowledge in Perspective: Selected Essays in Epistemology*. New York: Cambridge University Press.

—— (2003). "The Place of Truth in Epistemology," in M. DePaul and L. Zagzebski (eds.), *Intellectual Virtue: Perspectives from Ethics and Epistemology*. New York: Oxford University Press.

Sosa, E. (2007). *A Virtue Epistemology: Apt Belief and Reflective Knowledge*. New York: Oxford University Press.

Stich, S. (1990). *The Fragmentation of Reason*. Cambridge, MA: MIT Press.

Weinberg, J. (2006). "What's Epistemology For? The Case for Neopragmatism in Normative Metaepistemology," in S. Hetherington (ed.), *Epistemology Futures*. New York: Oxford University Press.

Wolterstorff, Nicholas (2005). "Obligation, Entitlement, and Rationality," in M. Steup and E. Sosa (eds.), *Contemporary Debates in Epistemology*. Oxford: Blackwell Publishing.

11 Knowledge and Final Value

Duncan Pritchard

1 Introduction

We saw in the last chapter that in order to answer the value problem we need to explain why knowledge is more valuable, not only as a matter of degree but also as a matter of kind, than any epistemic standing that falls short of knowledge. We noted that offering such an explanation requires us to explain why knowledge, unlike that which falls short of knowledge, has *final* value. Moreover, we saw that if one could account for the final value of knowledge then one would thereby have a resolution to the swamping problem as well (in the form of either a monistic or pluralist response to this difficulty). The goal of this chapter is to examine the best—indeed, the *only*—response to the value problem in the contemporary literature which proceeds by arguing that knowledge has final value. As we will see, this response to the value problem is ultimately unsuccessful, though the failure of this account of epistemic value highlights some important epistemological morals, both as regards the problem of epistemic value and also regarding the very project of understanding knowledge.

2 Robust Virtue Epistemology

The account of knowledge which has the best shot at accounting for the final value of knowledge is a type of virtue epistemology, what I will refer to as a *robust* virtue epistemology. This is the sort of virtue-theoretic account of knowledge that is offered by, for example, Ernest Sosa (1988;

Reprinted from Duncan Pritchard, "Knowledge and Final Value," in Duncan Pritchard, Alan Millar, and Adrian Haddock, *The Nature and Value of Knowledge: Three Investigations* (Oxford: Oxford University Press, 2010), 25–47.

1991; 2007), Linda Zagzebski (1996; 1999) and John Greco (e.g. 2003; 2007a; 2007b; 2009). What makes such a virtue-theoretic proposal robust is the fact that it attempts to exclusively analyse knowledge in terms of a true belief that is the product of epistemically virtuous belief-forming process.

The big attraction of virtue-theoretic accounts of knowledge is that they capture our strong intuition that knowledge is the product of one's reliable cognitive abilities.[1] A true belief that is gained in a way that is completely unconnected with one's cognitive abilities, even if that belief is reliably formed or would count as justified by the lights of certain conceptions of justification, just would not count as knowledge. We will explore the motivation for virtue epistemology in greater detail in the next chapter (and also examine some specific cases that lend support for the view). For now, however, this rather schematic presentation of the view will suffice even though it glosses over the many important differences between different types of virtue epistemic proposal (for example, depending on what one builds into one's conception of an epistemic virtue, one will be led to adopt a very different kind of virtue epistemology). As we will see in a moment, we do not need to worry about the specifics of different robust virtue-theoretic accounts since what is salient for our purposes is simply the *structure* of these proposals.

On the face of it, robust virtue epistemology does not look particularly promising because of the difficulty of specifying the virtue-theoretic condition on knowledge in such a way as to deal with the problem of knowledge-undermining epistemic luck—e.g., of the sort found in Gettier-style cases. After all, no matter how reliable an epistemic virtue might be, it seems possible that it could generate a belief which is only true as a matter of luck.

Consider, for example, the case of 'Roddy.'[2] Using his highly reliable cognitive faculties, Roddy the shepherd forms a true belief that there is a sheep in the field that he is looking at. Unbeknownst to Roddy, however, the item that he is looking at in the field is not a sheep at all, but rather a sheep-shaped object—a rock, say—albeit one which is obscuring from view a genuine sheep that is hidden behind (and which ensures that his belief is true). Here, then, we appear to have a true belief that is the product of the agent's epistemic virtue and yet which does not qualify as knowledge because of the presence of knowledge-undermining epistemic luck.

With cases like this in mind, one might naturally be tempted to opt for a *modest* virtue epistemology, one that does not try to completely analyse knowledge in terms of a virtue-theoretic condition but which is instead willing to endorse in addition a further codicil that can deal with Gettier-style cases.[3]

In contrast, robust virtue epistemology attempts to get around this problem by, in effect, 'beefing-up' the virtue-theoretic demand on knowledge. Rather than allowing that knowledge is merely true belief that arises out of the agent's cognitive abilities—which, as we have just seen, is compatible with Gettier-style cases—the strengthened virtue-theoretic thesis is that knowledge only results when the agent's true belief is *because of* the operation of her cognitive abilities.

How are we to read the 'because of' relation here? There is as yet no consensus amongst robust virtue epistemologists on this score, but the most developed view in the literature in this regard—due to Greco (2007*a*; 2007*b*)—takes the causal explanatory line that a true belief is because of an agent's cognitive abilities when it is *primarily* creditable to the agent that her belief is true.[4] Although this way of reading the because of relation does generate some surprising results, we will set these potential problems to one side in order to give the account the best run for its money.[5]

So construed, this strengthened proposal certainly deals with the case of Roddy, since while his true belief is indeed produced by his cognitive abilities, it is not the case that his belief is true *because of* the operation of his cognitive abilities in the relevant sense, since we would not count his true belief as being primarily creditable to his cognitive abilities. Instead, his belief is true because of a helpful quirk of the environment—that there happened to be a sheep behind the sheep-shaped object that he was looking at. In contrast, had he actually been looking at a sheep (in normal circumstances), then his belief *would* have been true because of the operation of his cognitive abilities. Moreover, what goes for Roddy will intuitively also go for other Gettier-style cases, since they each share the same relevant properties (i.e., the cognitive success in question is not properly attributable to the agent's cognitive abilities, but rather to some other factor outwith our hero's cognitive agency).

It seems, then, that robust virtue epistemology may well have the resources to deal with the kind of knowledge-undermining epistemic luck in play in Gettier-style cases. If that's right, then there is no need to add a codicil to one's virtue-theoretic account of knowledge in order to make it Gettier-proof. From a theoretical point of view, this is very satisfying, since having such a codicil in one's account of knowledge looks *ad hoc*. Why should knowledge have this structure such that the virtue-theoretic component captures almost all the cases, but not quite? Robust virtue epistemology thus appears to have a lot going for it.

3   Knowledge and Achievement

As Greco (2009) points out, a further advantage of understanding knowledge along robust virtue-theoretic lines is that it seems to capture the idea of knowledge as being a kind of cognitive achievement. That is, we might broadly think of achievements as being successes that are because of one's ability (i.e., primarily creditable to the exercise of one's ability), and virtue epistemology seems to be offering the epistemic analogue of this claim—on this view, knowledge is cognitive success that is because of one's cognitive ability. As we will see, that knowledge turns out to be a type of achievement on this view is key to its defence of the final value of knowledge.

In order to see the plausibility of this general account of achievement, consider the following case. Suppose that our hero—let's call him 'Archie'—selects a target at random and uses his bow to fire an arrow at that target with the intention of hitting it. Suppose further that he does indeed hit the target. If, however, the success in question is purely a matter of luck—if, for example, Archie does not possess the relevant archery abilities—then we would say that this success is not an achievement on Archie's part. Similarly, even if Archie has the relevant archery abilities and is in addition successful in hitting the target, we still wouldn't count his success as an achievement if the success was not *because of* Archie's archery abilities (i.e., where his success is not primarily creditable to his archery abilities but rather to some further factor).

This is important because of the possibility that the success in question is 'Gettierized.' If, for example, a dog ran on to the range and grabbed the arrow (which was heading towards the target) in mid-flight and proceeded to deposit it on the target, then we would not regard this successful outcome as Archie's achievement, even if the original firing of the arrow had been highly skilful. Instead, what is required for an achievement is that Archie's hitting of the target is *because of* the exercise of his relevant archery abilities, where this means that his success is primarily creditable to his abilities rather than to some factor independent of his abilities. Call this the *achievement* thesis.

There are some *prima facie* problems with the achievement thesis. In particular, there are grounds for thinking that as it stands it is too permissive. After all, we tend to think of achievements in such a way that they involve the overcoming of an obstacle of some sort, and yet it seems consistent with the achievement thesis that the mere success-through-agency at issue in this thesis need involve nothing of the sort. Relatedly, it seems an essential part of achievements that they involve certain motivational states on the part of the subject with regard to the success in question—in particular, that the subject is actively seeking to bring this success about. But since the achievement thesis makes no mention of such motivational states it seems to allow that achievements could be entirely passive. More generally, the problem is that the achievement thesis seem to count as achievements successes which are just too easy to legitimately fall into this category.

We will come back to the problem of easy achievements in chapter four since it raises issues that are not directly relevant to our present concerns. For now, we will take it that the achievement thesis is on roughly the right lines in order to give the robust virtue epistemologist's argument for the final value of knowledge the best run for its money. What is important for our present purposes is that if this account of achievement is right then it follows that knowledge, by the lights of the robust virtue epistemologist at any rate, is just a specifically cognitive type of achievement. That is, achievements are successes that are because of ability and yet knowledge, according to the robust virtue epistemologist, is just cognitive success (i.e., true belief) that is because of cognitive ability (i.e., epistemic virtue, broadly conceived). The achievement thesis when combined with robust virtue epistemology thus entails the claim that knowledge is a type of achievement, what we will call the *knowledge-as-achievement* thesis, or [K = A] for short.

The reason why the [K = A] thesis is important for our purposes is because achievements are, plausibly, distinctively valuable. More specifically, it is plausible to hold that the kind of successes that count as achievements are valuable for their own sake because of how they are produced (i.e., they are finally valuable because of their relational properties). If this is right, and we can show that knowledge (unlike that which falls short of knowledge) is a type of achievement, then we may be in a position to thereby show that knowledge has a kind of value—final value—which that which falls short of knowledge lacks, and hence show that it is distinctively valuable.[6]

In order to see why achievements might be thought to be finally valuable, consider again the case of 'Archie.' This time, though, suppose that Archie—in the manner of Robin Hood—is trying to escape from an adversary and the target he is firing at is a mechanism which will drop the drawbridge in front him, thereby ensuring that he gets to safety. From a practical point of view, it may not matter whether the hitting of the target is because of Archie's archery abilities or through dumb luck (e.g., by a lucky deflection). Either way, it still results in the dropping of the drawbridge, thereby enabling Archie to escape. Nevertheless, we would value Archie's success very differently if it were the product of luck (even when the relevant ability is involved, but the success in question is 'Gettierized'), rather than it being because of his ability such that it is an achievement. In particular, we would regard Archie's achievement of hitting the target through ability as, in this respect, a good thing in its own right, regardless of what other instrumental value it may accrue.

Moreover, what goes here for Archie's achievement of hitting the target seems to be equally applicable to achievements more generally: achievements are finally valuable. Imagine, for example, that you are about to undertake a course of action designed to attain a certain outcome and that you are given the choice between merely being successful in what you set out to do, and being successful in such a way that you exhibit an achievement. Suppose further that it is stipulated in advance that there are no practical costs or benefits to choosing either way. Even so, wouldn't you prefer to exhibit an achievement? And wouldn't you be right to do so? If that's correct, then this is strong evidence for the final value of achievements.

Indeed, that achievements are valuable in this way is hardly surprising once one reflects that they constitute the exercise of one's agency on the world. A life lacking in such agential power, even if otherwise successful (e.g., one's goals are regularly attained), would clearly be severely impoverished as a result. A good life is thus, amongst other things, a life rich in achievement. Call the claim that achievements are finally valuable the *value of achievements* thesis.[7]

Now, if knowledge is simply a type of achievement, and achievements are finally valuable, then it immediately follows that knowledge has final value too. Robust virtue epistemology, when combined with a claim about the nature of achievements (the achievement thesis) and a claim about the final value of achievements (the value of achievements thesis), thus entails the thesis that knowledge has final value. More formally, we can express the reasoning in play here as follows:

From Robust Virtue Epistemology to the Final Value of Knowledge
- (P1)   Achievements are successes that are because of ability. (Achievement thesis)
- (P2)   Knowledge is a cognitive success that is because of cognitive ability. (Robust Virtue Epistemology)
- (C1)   So, knowledge = cognitive achievement. (K = A thesis)
- (P3)   Achievements are finally valuable. (Value of Achievements thesis)
- (C2)   So, knowledge has final value.

Since the inferences in play here are clearly valid, if one wishes to object to this argument then one will need to deny one of the premises in play.

Let's start with the two premises concerning achievements more generally, (P1) and (P3). We have already noted that there is a *prima facie* worry regarding (P1) which concerns 'easy' achievements. In order to give this argument the best run for its money, however, we will let this premise stand for now (we will consider the status of (P1) in more detail in chapter four).

That brings us to (P3), the value of achievements thesis. One worry that one might have about this thesis is that some achievements seem to have very little value—or are even *dis*valuable—because, for example, they are pointless or just plain wicked. Are even achievements of this sort of final value? Note, however, that the value of achievements thesis, properly construed, is only that achievements have final value *qua* achievements. This is entirely consistent with the undeniable truth that some achievements may have no practical value, and may even accrue *dis*value, perhaps because of the opportunity cost incurred by seeking the pointless achievement over a more substantive achievement or because of the wicked nature of the achievement in question. Indeed, there may well be situations in which the all things considered value of Archie's success of hitting the target when it is due to luck is much greater than the all things considered value of a corresponding success attained because of Archie's ability. It is important to recognise that the value of achievements thesis when properly understood is entirely consistent with this possibility.[8]

This point is also important when it comes to understanding the way in which this thesis that knowledge, *qua* cognitive achievement, accrues final value can help us answer the tertiary value problem. In particular, we need to note that the mere fact that knowledge (unlike that which falls short of knowledge) is, *qua* cognitive achievement, of final value will not necessarily be enough to resolve the tertiary value problem. This is because of the possibility that which falls short of knowledge is generally of greater non-final value than knowledge. If this were so, then it could still be true that knowledge is generally of less all things considered value than that which falls short of knowledge, even granting the fact that knowledge, in contrast to that which falls short of knowledge, is finally valuable. Nevertheless, it is plausible to suppose that knowledge is not generally of *less* instrumental value than that which falls short of knowledge. And with this assumption in play the final value of knowledge would ensure that the tertiary value problem is met and, with it, the primary and secondary value problems too. In what follows we will let this assumption stand.

In any case, while we will reconsider the status of (P3) in more detail in chapter four when we look again at (P1), we have sufficient grounds for taking this premise to be well-founded. This leaves only (P2), which is the robust virtue epistemological account of knowledge itself. As we will see in a moment, this thesis faces some fairly severe problems. Primarily, we will be arguing against this claim by showing that the K = A thesis (i.e., (C1)) that it (along with (P1)) generates is false. Ultimately, however, the way that we will be arguing against (C1) should leave no-one in any doubt that whatever other difficulties the other premises in this argument might face, it is (P2) that is the key weak link in the robust virtue epistemologist's argument for the final value of knowledge. As a result, this argument fails to demonstrate its conclusion, (C2).

4 Interlude: Is Robust Virtue Epistemology a Reductive Theory of Knowledge?

We noted in the last chapter in our discussion of the swamping problem that there are two *prima facie* plausible responses to that problem which are consistent with the final value of knowledge. What is key to both responses is that they reject the epistemic value T-monism that is essential to the setting-up of the swamping problem and argue instead that knowledge is a fundamental epistemic good. The first proposal (the monistic response) advances a form of epistemic value monism—epistemic value K-monism—which treats knowledge as the only fundamental epistemic good. The second proposal (the pluralist response) is a form of epistemic value pluralism which treats knowledge as a fundamental epistemic good in addition to true belief.

We noted in the last chapter that if knowledge is finally valuable then it thereby follows that it is a fundamental epistemic good. As a result, if the robust virtue epistemic defence of the final value of knowledge is successful, then it will on the face of it lend support to *both* of these responses to the swamping problem. (It will also constitute a decisive strike against the third response to the swamping problem that we considered—the practical response—since this was inconsistent with the final value of knowledge). This raises the question of whether the robust virtue epistemic account of knowledge is more naturally allied with one of these responses to the swamping problem over the other.

In order to answer this question, we need to decide whether robust virtue epistemology offers a reductive account of knowledge. That is, is the proposal meant to 'decompose' knowledge into constituent parts which can be understood independently of knowledge? The reason why this question is important in this regard is that we saw in the last chapter that epistemic value K-monism is naturally wedded to a 'knowledge-first' account of knowledge whereby knowledge is treated as a primitive relative to which other epistemic standings are defined (rather than *vice versa*, as is the case with reductive accounts of knowledge). This is not to suggest that it would be in principle incoherent to advance epistemic value K-monism while nevertheless endorsing a reductive account of knowledge. The point is rather that if one does not already accept knowledge-first epistemology then it is unclear where the motivation for this form of epistemic value monism comes from.

I take it that most, if not all, robust virtue epistemologists regard their account of knowledge as a reductive account, and this certainly seems the default reading to take of the view (i.e., the reading that we should take unless we have grounds for the contrary). If that is right, then this response to the value problem is naturally allied to the pluralist response to the swamping problem. Moreover, on the face of it it does seem right to conceive of robust virtue epistemology in this way. After all, *prima facie* at least, it does seem possible to define cognitive abilities independently of knowledge—e.g., as, roughly, the stable, reliable and cognitively integrated belief-forming traits of the agent.

Still, the devil is in the detail, and it certainly might well turn out on closer inspection that ultimately one is unable to define cognitive abilities without making appeal to knowledge. Indeed, in the extreme case, it may turn out that cognitive abilities need to be defined as those belief-forming traits which are knowledge-conducive, and if that's the case then clearly robust virtue epistemology cannot be a reductive theory of knowledge. The robust virtue-theoretic response to the value problem would then be more naturally allied to the monistic response to the swamping problem.

Notice, however, that we do not need to take a stand on this issue here, since either way so long as the robust virtue epistemological account can demonstrate the final value of knowledge, then it will be in a position to answer both the value problem and the swamping problem. The issue of whether the view constitutes a reductive account of knowledge merely influences what kind of conception of epistemic value is in play. That said, although this issue may not be important for our present purposes, one might still regard this issue as salient in light of broader epistemological concerns. For example, one might for various reasons be antecedently suspicious of reductive accounts of knowledge, and hence regard any view which was committed to such a reduction as being *prima facie* implausible.

It is because of these broader epistemological concerns that I have flagged this issue here.

5 Achievement without Knowledge

In any case, despite the surface appeal of the robust virtue epistemologist's argument for the final value of knowledge, it faces some critical problems. In particular, the key concern lies with the intermediate conclusion (C1), the K = A thesis. As we will see, this claim is highly problematic on closer inspection. In particular, there are instances of knowledge which don't involve the corresponding cognitive achievement, and there are cognitive achievements which aren't also instances of knowledge. Moreover, as we will see, the case against the K = A thesis in no way depends on the specific account of achievement in play, and thus although there are two premises involved in the argument for the K = A thesis—the achievement thesis, (P1), and the robust virtue epistemological account of knowledge, (P2)—it is the second premise that is the problem. Crucially, however, without the K = A thesis, the robust virtue epistemologist's argument for the final value of knowledge will fail to go through. In this section we will be focussing on the left-to-right entailment that makes up the K = A thesis—viz., the idea that it is sufficient for knowledge that one exhibit the corresponding cognitive achievement.

Consider again the case of Archie, who selects a target at random from a target range and then successfully fires an arrow at that target. We noted above that if Archie lacks any kind of archery skill, such that his success is entirely lucky, then we would not count his success as being an achievement. Similarly, even if Archie has plenty of skill at archery but his success is 'Gettierized'—such that it is not *because of* his skill—then we wouldn't count it as an achievement. So far so good.

But now consider a third case in which Archie again selects a target at random, skilfully fires at this target and successfully hits it because of his skill. On the account of achievement on the table, his hitting of the target is a genuine achievement. Suppose, however, that unbeknownst to Archie there is a forcefield around each of the other targets such that, had he aimed at one of these targets, he would have missed. It is thus a matter of luck that he is successful, in the sense that he could very easily have not been successful. Notice, however, that luck of this sort does not seem to undermine the thesis that Archie's success is a genuine achievement. Indeed, we would still ascribe an achievement to Archie in this case even despite the luck involved. It is, after all, *because of* his skill that he is successful, even though he could very easily have not been successful in this case. That is, his success in this case is still primarily creditable to his archery abilities, even despite the luck involved in that success.

The problem that cases like this pose for the robust virtue epistemologist is that if we allow Archie's success to count as an achievement, then we seem compelled to treat *cognitive* successes which are relevantly analogous as also being achievements. Given the K = A thesis, however, this would mean that we would thereby be compelled to regard the cognitive achievement in question as knowledge, even despite the luck involved.

In order to see why this is a problem for those virtue epistemologists who defend the K = A thesis, consider the case of 'Barney' which is structurally analogous to the 'Archie' case. Barney forms a true belief that there is a barn in front of him by using his cognitive abilities. That is, unlike a Gettier-style case—such as the case of 'Roddy' described above—Barney does not make any cognitive error in forming his belief in the way that he does. Accordingly, we would naturally say that Barney's cognitive success is because of his cognitive ability and so we would, therefore, attribute a cognitive achievement to Barney. That is, his cognitive success in this case is primarily creditable to his cognitive abilities. According to the K = A thesis, then, we should also treat Barney as knowing that what he is looking at is a barn. The twist in the tale, however, is that, unbeknownst to Barney, he is in fact in 'barn façade county' where all the other apparent barns are fakes. Intuitively, he does not have knowledge in this case because it is simply a matter of luck that his belief is true.[9]

Cases like that of 'Barney' illustrate that there is a type of knowledge-undermining epistemic luck—what we might call *environmental* epistemic luck—which is distinct from the sort of epistemic luck in play in standard Gettier-style cases like that of 'Roddy.'[10] In particular, the kind of epistemic luck in play in standard Gettier-style cases 'intervenes' between the agent and the fact, albeit in such a way that the agent's belief is true nonetheless (i.e., Roddy is not looking at a sheep at all, even though he reasonably believes that he is, but his belief that there is a sheep in the field is true nonetheless). In contrast, in cases of environmental epistemic luck like that involving Barney, luck of this intervening sort is absent—Barney really does get to see the barn and forms a true belief on this basis—although the epistemically inhospitable nature of the environment ensures that his belief is nevertheless only true as a matter of luck such that he lacks knowledge.

In short, then, robust virtue epistemology is only able to exclude Gettier-style epistemic luck and not also environmental luck. The moral to be drawn is thus that there is sometimes *more* to knowledge than merely a cognitive achievement, contrary to what the robust virtue epistemologist (who defends the K = A thesis) argues. That is, there can be cases in which (environmental) knowledge-undermining luck is involved where the luck does not in the process undermine the achievement in question. Merely exhibiting a cognitive achievement will not suffice to exclude all types of knowledge-undermining epistemic luck. Call this the problem of *environmental luck*.

How might the defender of the K = A thesis respond to this problem? One response might be to try to evade it by reformulating the achievement thesis, and thus (P1). On the face of it, this might seem like a viable way of dealing with this issue since there are, after all, two premises—the achievement thesis, (P1), and the robust virtue epistemic account of knowledge, (P2)—being used to generate the K = A thesis, (C1). In order to see why such a strategy would be hopeless, however, we only need to note that the 'Barney' case is a counterexample *both* to the K = A thesis and to the more specific robust virtue epistemological claim that knowledge is cognitive success that is because of cognitive ability (i.e., (P2)). After all, it is both true that (i) Barney exhibits a cognitive achievement but does not possess the corresponding knowledge, and that (ii) Barney's cognitive success is because of his cognitive ability and yet he lacks the corresponding knowledge. There may well be good reasons to reformulate the achievement thesis—indeed, we will consider some reasons on this score in chapter four—but this issue is by-the-by here given that however the achievement thesis is formulated a key premise in the robust virtue epistemologist's argument for the final value of knowledge is blocked.

A second response to the problem that is superficially appealing is to argue that abilities need to be understood relative to suitable environments in a far more fine-grained that we standardly suppose. One could thus argue that neither Archie nor Barney exhibit an achievement in cases where there is environmental luck in play since contrary to intuition they are not exercising the relevant abilities. Accordingly, the 'Barney' case can pose no problem for the K = A thesis.[11]

Now it is undeniable that abilities should be understood relative to suitable environments. In crediting you with the ability to play the piano, for example, we are not thereby supposing that you can play the piano underwater. Even so, I take it that we tend to understand what constitutes a suitable environment in a very coarse-grained fashion. Intuitively, for example, Archie is employing the very same archery ability in the case in which there is environmental luck present as he does in corresponding cases where such luck is absent, and the same point goes for Barney's exercise of his barn-spotting ability in barn façade and corresponding non-barn façade environments.

Still, the proponent of the K = A thesis might well extract from the problem of environmental luck the moral that a more fine-grained conception of the relativization of abilities to suitable environments is required in order to deal with this problem. I think this would be a very theory-driven way of responding to the problem of environmental luck, and I also think that it would ultimately generate a very counterintuitive conception of abilities, one that is in the final analysis extremely fine-grained indeed.[12] Still, if the proposal worked then this might be a price worth paying in order to have a response to the problem. The key difficulty facing this response to the problem of environmental luck, however, is that it completely fails to understand what the source of this difficulty is.

In order to see this, consider again the ability to play the piano. We noted above that we would not evaluate the possession of such an ability relative to an environment in which the agent is underwater. Whatever ability our agent is exhibiting, or trying to exhibit, in such a case, it is not her ordinary ability to play piano. Imagine, however, that, unbeknownst to our agent, she is in an environment in which she could very easily have been underwater right now but in fact is not. It is thus a matter of luck that she is not presently underwater. (Perhaps, say, she is standing in an empty chamber which in most near-by possible worlds is full of water right now.) While standing there, she sits down at her piano and begins to play. What ability is she exhibiting? Intuitively, the ability on display here is the very ability to play the piano that she exhibits in normal circumstances. After all, although she could very easily be underwater right now, in fact she is not.[13]

The point of this case is that no matter how fine-grained we might want to make the relativization of abilities to suitable environments, we surely do not want to hold that our piano player is not manifesting her ordinary piano-playing abilities in a case like this. What this demonstrates is that while it is undoubtedly true that abilities should be understood relative to suitable environments, however that point is to be understood it must be compatible with the fact that it can be a matter of luck that one is in a suitable environment to exercise one's ability in the first place. Critically, however, that is just to allow that the presence of environmental luck is compatible with one exercising one's normal abilities (i.e., the abilities one exercises in corresponding cases which don't involve environmental luck). After all, what is key to cases of environmental luck is that while circumstances were indeed as it happens propitious for the exercise of the relevant ability, they could so very easily have not been. Properly understood, then, the issue in hand is not the degree to which abilities should be understood relative to suitable environments, but only whether it is possible for it to be a matter of luck that one is in suitable conditions to exercise one's ability. As we have seen, it can be, and hence however one relativizes abilities to suitable conditions one must allow that environmental luck—and thus environmental *epistemic* luck—is compatible with the exercise of the target ability. Responding to the problem of environmental luck by appeal to the relativization of abilities to suitable environments is thus a theoretical dead-end.[14]

With these options rejected, the prospects for the defender of the K = A thesis look somewhat dim. One possibility might be to argue that there is something special about the cognitive achievement at issue in knowledge which ensures that it is resistant to even this type of luck, even though non-cognitive achievements are entirely compatible with this kind of luck. There may be a case that can be made for this, though it will obviously face the charge of being *ad hoc*. Alternatively, one might simply insist that achievements exclude luck, and thus that we should not, contrary to intuition, treat Archie's success as an achievement when his success is lucky in the relevant fashion. The problem facing this proposal, however, is to explain why our intuitions about achievements are so off-the-mark in this case.[15]

Perhaps the robust virtue epistemologist who wishes to retain the K = A thesis could make one of these strategies—or some third strategy, such as denying the intuition that knowledge is incompatible with environmental epistemic luck[16]—stick. I don't think the result would be a happy one, but it is often the case that our theories force us to make awkward theoretical moves in order to save the theory, so that such a move is not that compelling need not be a decisive count against the view. The more fundamental problem, however, is that there is a further difficulty on the horizon for a view of this sort. Once these two objections for the K = A thesis are taken together, however, they suggest not a mere 'patching-up' of the original proposal, but a radical rethink.

6 Knowledge without Achievement

Consider the following example, due to Jennifer Lackey (2007: §2). Our protagonist, who we'll call 'Jenny,' arrives at the train station in Chicago and, wishing to obtain directions to the Sears Tower, approaches the first adult passer-by that she sees. Suppose further that the person that she asks has first-hand knowledge of the area and gives her the directions that she requires. Intuitively, any true belief that Jenny forms on this basis would ordinarily be counted as knowledge. Relatedly, notice that insofar as we are willing to ascribe knowledge in this case then we will be understanding the details of the case such that the true belief so formed is non-lucky in all the relevant respects (i.e., it is not subject to either Gettier-style or environmental epistemic luck). For example, we are taking it as given that there is no conspiracy afoot among members of the public to deceive Jenny in this regard, albeit one which is unsuccessful in this case.

The moral that Lackey draws from this example is that sometimes one can have knowledge without the success in question being of credit to the agent. I think this conclusion is ambiguous. In particular, we need to make a distinction between a true belief being *of credit* to an agent, in the sense that the agent is deserving of some sort of praise for holding this true belief, and the true belief being *primarily creditable* to the agent, in the sense that it is to some substantive degree down to her agency that she holds a true belief. Lackey's focus when employing this example is on the former claim,[17] and this is not surprising since a number of commentators—see, for example, Greco (2003) in particular—have expressed their view in such a way that it seems to straightforwardly support this thesis. That said, strictly speaking the robust virtue-theoretic proposal is the latter claim.

Now this may initially seem to be an idle distinction, in that one might naturally suppose that in every case in which the former description holds the latter description holds, and *vice versa*—*viz.*, that when your belief is primarily creditable to your cognitive agency then it is of credit to you, and where it is of credit to you then it is primarily creditable to your cognitive agency. The problem, however, is that closer inspection of these two formulations reveals that they in fact make very different demands. Moreover, one kind of case in which they come apart is precisely scenarios like the 'Jenny' example where an agent gains knowledge by to a large degree trusting the word of another.

In order to see this, we just need to note that it is of *some* credit to Jenny that she has a true belief in this case. It is, after all, a *person* that she asks for directions, and not, say, a lamppost or a dog. Moreover, the person she asks is not a small child, or someone who one might reasonably expect to be unreliable on this score (e.g., someone who is clearly a tourist). In addition, if the testimony which Jenny received were obviously false, then we would expect her to be sensitive to this fact. If, for example, the informant told her that she should get back on the train and go home to New York, then we would expect her to treat these directions as entirely spurious. So the moral to be drawn from this case is not that sometimes knowledge can be possessed even though the cognitive success in question is of no credit to the agent concerned.[18]

Nevertheless, what is true is that it is not *primarily creditable* to Jenny that she has formed a true belief in this case, and this is where the true moral of these cases resides. More specifically, that Jenny has a true belief in this case does not seem to be *because of* her cognitive abilities, but rather because of the cognitive abilities of the informant who knows this proposition on a non-testimonial basis. One can thus have a true belief that is deserving of credit and yet that true belief not be primarily creditable to one's cognitive agency.[19]

Given that the true belief needs to be primarily creditable to the agent in order for it to count as a cognitive achievement, it follows that while Jenny has knowledge in this case she does not exhibit a cognitive achievement. Again, then, we have seen that there is a problem associated with the idea that knowledge is to be identified with cognitive achievement.

It is not obvious how the proponent of the K = A thesis can respond to cases of this sort. As before, notice that there is no mileage in trying to pin the blame here on the achievement thesis, (P1). This is because, as with the 'Barney' case, the 'Jenny' case is a counterexample *both* to the K = A thesis and to the more specific robust virtue epistemological claim that knowledge is cognitive success that is because of cognitive ability (i.e., (P2)). After all, it is both true that (i) Jenny has knowledge while failing to exhibit the corresponding cognitive ability, and that (ii) Jenny has knowledge even though her cognitive success is not because of her cognitive ability. As we noted above, there may well be good reasons to reformulate the achievement thesis but this issue is entirely by-the-by here given that however the achievement thesis is formulated a key premise in the robust virtue epistemologist's argument for the final value of knowledge is blocked.

But if this response to the 'Jenny' case doesn't work, then what other options are there? None that are particularly palatable, that's for sure. On the one hand, one might bite the bullet and concede that Jenny lacks knowledge after all. On the other hand, one might try to resist this counterintuitive commitment by maintaining that it is primarily creditable to her that her belief is true, and thus that she is exhibiting a *bona fide* achievement after all (and hence has knowledge too). Both strategies involve denying some pretty strong intuitions about this case and so anyone taking either line will face a tough up-hill struggle.

Indeed, notice that taking the latter line will almost certainly commit one to a very restrictive account of testimonial knowledge, a view that is usually known as global reductionism. Although this view does have some adherents—most notably Elizabeth Fricker (e.g. 1995)—it is very unpopular, and most in the literature on the epistemology of testimonial belief regard it as a position to be avoided at all costs.[20] It is perhaps for this reason that Greco (2007b) opts for the former line, although he does not make a very strong case for it.

By analogy, he argues that one might score a very easy goal as a result of that goal being set-up by a display of tremendous skill. He maintains that the skill involved in setting up this easy goal does not undermine the achievement of the agent who scores the goal. Given that we grant the account of achievement in question—such that achievements are nothing more than successes that are primarily creditable to one's agency—then I think that Greco's claim that this easy goal constitutes an achievement is correct (though remember that we will be questioning the adequacy of this account of achievement in the next chapter). The problem, however, is that this case is not relevantly analogous to the case of 'Jenny.' After all, what is crucial to that example is not that someone appropriately skilful helps Jenny, but rather more specifically that Jenny gains her true belief by (for the most part at least) *trusting* this other person. This is why, for example, other cases in which we depend on the skills of others—as when one takes an inner city road sign a face-value—do not generate the same epistemological moral. In such cases my knowledge depends on—i.e., is made easy by—the skills of others, but it is not that I am merely trusting what the sign tells me: I have all kinds of independent grounds for believing what inner city road signs tell me.

An example that would be relevantly analogous to the 'Jenny' case is someone who lacks archery abilities who is being assisted by a skilled archer in firing an arrow and is thereby successful. (For example, the skilled archer helps the novice to take aim, steadies his arm, corrects her posture, and so on.) While the unskilled archer's abilities might have played *some* role in the successful outcome—such that it is *to some degree* creditable to him that he is successful—we would surely say that this success is primarily creditable to the skilled archer (or, at least, creditable to the combined efforts of the unskilled archer and the skilled archer). We certainly wouldn't regard the success in question as being primarily creditable to the novice archer. On this basis, then, we would maintain that the unskilled archer's success does not constitute a *bona fide* achievement, and hence cases like this should give us no cause to reconsider our original assessment of the

'Jenny' example as one in which the agent likewise does not exhibit an achievement.

In any case, whatever the defender of the K = A thesis says in response to the 'Jenny' example, remember that she must also simultaneously deal with the other problem outlined above—concerning the apparent possibility of cognitive achievements which are not cases of knowledge. Indeed, notice that it is significant that these two problems pull robust virtue epistemologists who endorse the K = A thesis in two different directions. Whereas the 'Jenny' case puts pressure on them to *weaken* their robust virtue epistemology and thus allow cases of knowledge which this view would ordinarily exclude, the 'Barney' case, in contrast, puts pressure on them to *strengthen* their account in order to explain why merely exhibiting a cognitive achievement does not suffice for knowledge. This is why when these two problems are expressed in tandem they pose such a tricky difficulty for the robust virtue epistemologist.

It seems, then, that the K = A thesis is unsustainable. Moreover, the source of the problem with the K = A thesis that we have explored here is clearly the robust virtue epistemological account of knowledge, (P2). Without the K = A thesis, however, the robust virtue epistemologist loses the ingenious basis on which she argued for the final value of knowledge.[21]

7 Back to the Value Problem

Does that mean that the response to the value problem offered by robust virtue epistemology must be completely abandoned? Perhaps not. On the face of it, one might think that there is a fairly straightforward way of resurrecting the K = A account of the value of knowledge along these new lines. After all, while we have noted that there are cases of knowledge where the agent does not exhibit a cognitive achievement, and cases of cognitive achievement where the agent does not possess knowledge, one can nonetheless consistently argue that knowledge is the kind of epistemic standing that *tends* to go hand-in-hand with cognitive achievement. Since we have granted the *prima facie* plausibility of the thesis that achievements, and thus cognitive achievements, are finally valuable, the fact that knowledge at least tends to go hand-in-hand with cognitive achievement would suffice to show that knowledge at least tends to be finally valuable, even if it is sometimes not of final value. Would that be enough to answer the tertiary value problem?

In order to answer this question, we first need to form a view about just how extensive the cases of knowledge are which are not cognitive achievements. After all, although the testimonial case we have examined might initially seem quite peripheral, on reflection one might plausibly contend that quite a lot of our testimonial knowledge is gained in this fashion. Moreover, there is also good reason to hold that there may be non-testimonial cases that have the relevant features. For example, one might claim that just as there is a substantive degree of ungrounded trust of others involved in the 'Jenny' case offered above, so there is a substantive degree of ungrounded *self*-trust involved in much of our other knowledge, such as an ungrounded trust in the reliability of our faculties. If this is right, then it may turn out that very little of our knowledge, if any, involves a cognitive achievement. The prospects for meeting the value problem with a proposal of this sort would then be dim indeed.[22]

Even if we can block this worry by arguing for a close relationship between knowledge and cognitive achievement, however, a second, and more substantive, worry remains. Recall that to say that knowledge is distinctively valuable is to say that is it more valuable, not just as a matter of degree but of kind, than that which falls short of knowledge. On this view, however, there is an epistemic standing which falls short of knowledge and which is no less valuable (indeed, which is in its nature finally valuable): cognitive achievements that are not also cases of knowledge. If that's right, then even if knowledge is the kind of thing that tends to be finally valuable, it still won't follow that knowledge is in the relevant sense distinctively valuable.

So once one rejects the idea that knowledge is a kind of achievement, the final value of achievements is no longer able to offer us a way of responding to the tertiary value problem. But given that this approach to the value problem constituted the best—indeed, the *only*—response to the value problem that seemed able in principle to support the key claim that knowledge is finally valuable, this means that the prospects for answering the value problem now appear dim indeed.

That leaves the swamping problem. Here the more modest strategy of arguing that knowledge tends to be finally valuable may gain more purchase. For recall that we noted in chapter one that so long as knowledge is at least *sometimes* finally valuable then it will constitute a fundamental epistemic good. If that's right, however, then that would suffice to block the swamping argument, since that argument essentially trades on a commitment to epistemic value T-monism. Of course, as we noted earlier in this chapter, that one blocks the swamping argument by appeal to the fact that knowledge is a fundamental epistemic good leaves it open whether one is committed to a monistic or a pluralist response to that problem. But which way one jumps on this issue rests on further theoretical claims which are of secondary importance to us here.

So even though the robust virtue epistemic defence of the final value of knowledge is ultimately unsuccessful, so long as we accept the thesis that cognitive achievements are finally valuable (a claim that we will explore in more detail in chapter four) there may be scope to use the fact that knowledge at least tends to go hand-in-hand with cognitive achievements as a means of answering the swamping problem. Whether or not this is the best way to deal with the swamping problem is an issue that we will return to.

8   Concluding Remarks

Given what is at stake in answering the value problem—and thus the tertiary value problem—one might argue that we simply cannot leave matters at that, and that instead we must continue to seek a resolution to this problem. Indeed, it has been suggested by some that it is an adequacy condition on any theory of knowledge that it is able to account for the distinctive value of knowledge, in the sense that if one's theory is unable to do this then this is a definitive strike against one's view.[23]

This way of thinking about the value problem and its role in the theory of knowledge is, however, surely too strong. Instead, what is presumably required is *either* that one's theory of knowledge can answer the value problem *or* that one's theory is able to provide some plausible account of why knowledge isn't really distinctively valuable after all, even though it appears to be. That is, provided one's theory of knowledge can answer the second of the two desiderata just identified, then that should suffice.

In the next chapter we will be exploring a new theory of knowledge—what I call *anti-luck virtue epistemology*—which has many of the advantages of robust virtue epistemology and none of its failings. Although this account of knowledge is unable to account for the final value of knowledge, it does enable us to gain an understanding of why knowledge may initially appear to be finally valuable. This diagnostic story regarding our intuition about the distinctive value of knowledge is further reinforced in chapter four where we will explore an epistemic standing—understanding, or at least a core kind of understanding anyway—which is finally valuable, and which has a close relationship to knowledge. As we will see, this discussion will lead us to rethink some of the claims about the nature and value of achievements that we have looked at in this chapter. So although the main conclusion drawn in this chapter is a negative one, from the ashes of the failure of robust virtue epistemology to adequately respond to the value problem we will be extracting some important positive epistemological conclusions.

Notes

1. Note that henceforth I will take it as given that a genuine cognitive ability is reliable.

2. This example is adapted from one offered by Chisholm (1977: 105).

3. For example, in early work, Greco (1999; 2000) took just this line. As we will see in a moment, these days he advocates a robust form of virtue epistemology.

4. Those familiar with the literature in this respect will recognise that often virtue epistemologists like Greco (e.g. 2003) make a stronger claim in this regard. That is, they do not simply argue that the true belief in question is primarily creditable to the knowing agent but also that it is *of credit* to the knowing agent that she believes truly (i.e., that she is deserving of some sort of praise, at least when assessed from a purely epistemic point of view). I think this is a mistake, and I explain why in §4.

5. One surprising consequence—noted in Greco (2007*b*; 2008)—is that robust virtue epistemology becomes committed to a kind of attributer contextualism due to the context-sensitivity of causal explanations. As it happens, Greco welcomes this result, but as I have argued elsewhere—e.g., Pritchard (2008*c*)—he is unwise to do so. But if one does not analyse the because of relation in causal explanatory terms, then what are the alternatives? This is unclear. Zagzebski (e.g. 1999) ultimately treats this relation as a primitive, though she notes that a good approximation is the sensitivity principle (i.e., if the proposition believed had not been true then the agent would not have believed it). Perhaps the best alternative account on offer is that put forward by Sosa (2007) who argues that we should think of the relation in terms of the exercise of a power. For further discussion of Sosa's proposal, see note 1.

6. While epistemic virtue theorists are aware that they may be able to account for the distinctive value of knowledge by appeal to the value of an achievement, they unfortunately mischaracterise the kind of value in question, since they hold that it is *intrinsic value* rather than final value that is at issue. See, for example, Greco (2009, §4). Crucially, however, intrinsic value is not the same as final value. This is because intrinsic value concerns only the value generated by the intrinsic properties of the target item, and yet something can be finally—i.e., non-instrumentally— valuable because of its *relational* (and hence non-intrinsic) properties. Think, for example, of the first book produced on the first ever printing press. Moreover, it is important to our discussion that we focus on final value rather than intrinsic value because on the account of the value of knowledge under consideration it is clearly because of the *relational* properties of the true belief in question—i.e., that it is true belief that is skilfully attained—that it constitutes a cognitive achievement and

hence on this view accrues a distinctive kind of value. Thus, the additional value that is generated is final value, not intrinsic value. For more on this point see Pritchard (2008e, §2). Brogaard (2007) is one commentator who has recognised this point. See also Percival (2003). For two recent, and influential, discussions of the intrinsic value/final value distinction, see Rabinowicz & Roennow-Rasmussen (1999; 2003).

7. I discuss the relevance of achievements to the problem of the meaning of life in Pritchard (2008a).

8. An alternative way of dealing with this problem would be to argue that it can be in the nature of something to be finally valuable even though sometimes it isn't. For example, one might argue that pleasure is in its nature finally valuable even though some pleasures (i.e., the 'bad' ones) lack final value. According to this proposal, then, it would be in the nature of achievements to be finally valuable even though some of them (i.e., the wicked or trivial ones) lack final value. I am grateful to Mike Ridge for this suggestion.

9. This case was originally offered by Goldman (1976), although he credits the example to Carl Ginet.

10. In Pritchard (2005: ch, 5) I delineate the core kind of knowledge-undermining epistemic luck and label it 'veritic luck'. Both environmental epistemic luck and Gettier-style 'intervening' epistemic luck fall under the more general category of veritic luck.

11. This strategy forms a key part of the response to the problem of environmental luck offered by Greco (2007b: §5).

12. For more discussion of this point, see Pritchard (2008c; cf. Pritchard 2008b) and Kvanvig (2009).

13. Moreover, notice that since our agent is unaware of how modally close she is to disaster, it is not as if her awareness of this danger could have a bearing on whether this environment is suited for the exercise of this ability.

14. One can strengthen this point by noting that it is in fact incidental to both the 'Archie' and 'Barney' cases that the relevant deception is *actually* occurring in the subject's environment, albeit in such a way that it does not affect the exercise of the target ability. That is, one could redescribe both cases as involving no deception in the actual world but only in most near-by possible worlds and the cases would still demonstrate the same point. Interestingly, Sosa (2007) is one philosopher who has recognised that what is at issue here is the 'fragility' of the exercise of one's abilities (i.e., that it can be a matter of luck that one is in a position to exercise them). His response has been to argue that an agent like Barney *does* have knowledge—i.e., he claims that knowledge is entirely compatible with environmental epistemic luck of this sort. Given the strong intuitions which support the barn façade case, such an

approach will inevitably be highly contentious. For further discussion of Sosa's view in this regard, see Pritchard (2009). See also note 1.

15. Greco (2003: §3; cf. Greco 2009: §5) takes the line that achievements are by their nature luck-excluding (with the consequence, presumably, that Archie's success is not an achievement in the case in which the other targets have the arrow-excluding force fields around them). Elsewhere, in Greco (2007b: §5), he argues that there is something peculiar about knowledge which ensures that it is luck-excluding in a more exacting fashion than non-cognitive achievements. For further discussion of Greco's response(s) to the problem of environmental luck, see Pritchard (2008c; cf. Pritchard 2008b) and Kvanvig (2009).

16. This is the line taken by Sosa (2007).

17. The title of the paper in which this example appears is "Why We Don't Deserve Credit for Everything We Know."

18. A second type of case that Lackey (2007) offers—that of innate knowledge—might fare better in this regard. After all, if there is such a thing as innate knowledge then it would presumably be such that it involves a true belief which is *neither* of credit to the agent nor primarily creditable to the agent. For my own part, I do not hold that innate knowledge is even possible, but this is an issue that cannot be usefully engaged with here.

19. Moreover, the distinction between credit-worthy true belief and true belief that is primarily creditable to one also comes apart in the other direction. There could, after all, be true beliefs that are primarily creditable to one's cognitive agency and yet for which you are deserving of no credit at all (e.g., where the cognitive achievement in question is very easy).

20. This is not the place to explore this issue in more detail. For more on the epistemology of testimony, see Adler (2006).

21. One might think that the alternative robust virtue-theoretic account offered by Sosa (2007) could potentially offer a way out of this problem. Rather than understanding the 'because of' relation that is key to robust virtue epistemology in causal explanatory terms, Sosa instead understands it in terms of the manifestation of a power. To see how these two accounts can come apart, consider a glass that was broken as a result of someone deliberately smashing it against a wall. Ordinarily, the most salient part of the causal explanation of why the glass broke will be that someone smashed it against the wall, and in this sense it will be true to say that the glass broke because it was smashed against the wall. Note, however, that this is consistent with the claim that it was because of the glass's fragility that it broke, since here we are talking about the manifestation of a power and not offering a causal explanation. Sosa's idea is that when the robust virtue epistemology claims that knowledge is cognitive success that is because of cognitive ability, it is the 'manifestation of a

power' reading that we should adopt, and not the causal explanatory reading. Although Sosa is offering a genuine alternative to Greco's reading of the robust virtue-theoretic account of knowledge, I think it should be clear that his view is no less susceptible to the problem posed here. In the Barney case, for example, it is surely even clearer that Barney's cognitive success constitutes the manifestation of his cognitive powers than that it is primarily creditable to his cognitive abilities. Indeed, Sosa recognises this, which is why he argues that, contrary to intuition, environmental epistemic luck is compatible with knowledge possession. Moreover, Sosa's view will also struggle with the Jenny case, since again it is surely even clearer that Jenny's cognitive success is not the manifestation of *her* cognitive powers than that her cognitive success is not primarily creditable to her cognitive ability. This is not to say that Sosa's proposal is a complete non-starter as a type of robust virtue epistemology, since for one thing it at least avoids some of the counterintuitive consequences of Greco's view. The point is rather that adopting such a reading of robust virtue epistemology doesn't offer any easy resolution of the problem in hand.

22. This would constitute one way of recasting the sceptical problem in value-theoretic terms. That is, the primary target of the sceptical argument would not be knowledge *simpliciter*, but rather a distinctively valuable epistemic standing. The advantage of reading the sceptic in this way is that it would clearly be irrelevant to respond to the sceptic by offering an account of knowledge on which knowledge was not distinctively valuable (indeed, this would constitute a kind of capitulation). The relevance of the problem of epistemic value to radical scepticism is discussed more fully in chapter four. See also Pritchard (2008*d*).

23. One finds a claim of roughly this sort expressed in a number of works. See, for example, Zagzebski (1999), Williamson (2000: ch. 1) and Kvanvig (2003: ch. 1). For a critical discussion of this assumption, see DePaul (2009). It is important to note, however, that these authors almost certainly have a different view of what it would take for knowledge to be distinctively valuable to that which has been argued for here.

References

Adler, J. (2006). "Epistemological Problems of Testimony," in E. Zalta, ed., Stanford Encyclopedia of Philosophy. http://plato.stanford.edu/entries/testimony-episprob.

Brogaard, B. (2007). "Can Virtue Reliabilism Explain the Value of Knowledge?," *Canadian Journal of Philosophy* 36: 335–54.

Chisholm, R. (1977). *Theory of Knowledge* (2nd ed.). Englewood Cliffs, New Jersey: Prentice-Hall.

DePaul, M. (2009). "Ugly Analyses and Value," in A. Haddock, A. Millar, and D. H. Pritchard, eds., *Epistemic Value*, 112–38. Oxford: Oxford University Press.

Fricker, E. (1995). "Telling and Trusting: Reductionism and Anti-Reductionism in the Epistemology of Testimony," *Mind* 104: 393–411.

Goldman, A. (1976). "Discrimination and Perceptual Knowledge," *The Journal of Philosophy* 73: 771–91.

Greco, J. (1999). "Agent Reliabilism," *Philosophical Perspectives* 13: 273–96.

———. (2000). *Putting Skeptics in Their Place: The Nature of Skeptical Arguments and Their Role in Philosophical Inquiry.* Cambridge: Cambridge University Press.

———. (2003). "Knowledge as Credit for True Belief," in M. DePaul and L. Zagzebski, eds., *Intellectual Virtue: Perspectives from Ethics and Epistemology*, 111–34. Oxford: Oxford University Press.

———. (2007a). *Epistemic Evaluation: A Virtue-Theoretic Approach.* Manuscript.

———. (2007b). "The Nature of Ability and the Purpose of Knowledge," *Philosophical Issues* 17: 57–69.

———. (2008). "What's Wrong With Contextualism?," *The Philosophical Quarterly* 58: 416–36.

———. (2009). "The Value Problem," in A. Haddock, A. Millar, and D. H. Pritchard, eds., *Epistemic Value*, 313–21. Oxford: Oxford University Press.

Kvanvig, J. (2003). *The Value of Knowledge and the Pursuit of Understanding.* Cambridge: Cambridge University Press.

———. (2009). "Responses to Critics," in A. Haddock, A. Millar, and D. H. Pritchard, eds., *Epistemic Value*, 339–52. Oxford: Oxford University Press.

Lackey, J. (2007). "Why We Don't Deserve Credit for Everything We Know," *Synthese* 158: 345–61.

Percival, P. (2003). "The Pursuit of the Epistemic Good," *Metaphilosophy* 34: 29–47.

Pritchard, D. (2005). *Epistemic Luck.* Oxford: Oxford University Press.

———. (2008a). "Absurdity, *Angst*, and the Meaning of Life," *manuscript.*

———. (2008b). "A Defense of Quasi-Reductionism in the Epistemology of Testimony," *Philosophica* 78: 13–28.

———. (2008c). "Greco on Knowledge: Virtues, Contexts, Achievements," *Philosophical Quarterly* 58: 437–47.

———. (2008d). "Radical Skepticism, Epistemic Luck and Epistemic Value," *Proceedings of the Aristotelian Society*, Supplementary Volume, 82: 19–41.

———. (2008e). "The Value of Knowledge," *manuscript.*

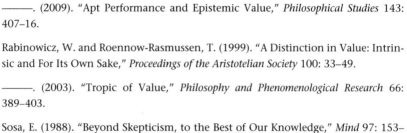

———. (2009). "Apt Performance and Epistemic Value," *Philosophical Studies* 143: 407–16.

Rabinowicz, W. and Roennow-Rasmussen, T. (1999). "A Distinction in Value: Intrinsic and For Its Own Sake," *Proceedings of the Aristotelian Society* 100: 33–49.

———. (2003). "Tropic of Value," *Philosophy and Phenomenological Research* 66: 389–403.

Sosa, E. (1988). "Beyond Skepticism, to the Best of Our Knowledge," *Mind* 97: 153–89.

———. (1991). *Knowledge in Perspective: Selected Essays in Epistemology*. Cambridge: Cambridge University Press.

———. (2007). *A Virtue Epistemology: Apt Belief and Reflective Knowledge*, vol. 1. Oxford: Oxford University Press.

Williamson, T. (2000). *Knowledge and Its Limits*. Oxford: Oxford University Press.

Zagzebski, L. (1996). *Virtues of the Mind: An Inquiry into the Nature of Virtue and the Ethical Foundations of Knowledge*. Cambridge: Cambridge University Press.

———. (1999). "What Is Knowledge?," in J. Greco and E. Sosa, eds., *The Blackwell Guide to Epistemology*, 92–116. Oxford: Blackwell.

D   Credit and Luck

12   Knowledge as Credit for True Belief

John Greco

I begin by reviewing two kinds of problem for fallibilism about knowledge. The first is the lottery problem, or the problem of explaining why fallible evidence, though otherwise excellent, is not enough to know that one will lose the lottery. The second kind of problem is Gettier problems. I will argue that both kinds of problem can be resolved if we note an important illocutionary force of knowledge attributions: namely, that when we attribute knowledge to someone we mean to give the person credit for getting things right. Put another way, we imply that the person is responsible for getting things right. The key idea here is not that knowledge requires responsibility *in* one's conduct, although that might also be the case, but that knowledge requires responsibility *for* true belief. Again, to say that someone knows is to say that his believing the truth can be credited to him. It is to say that the person got things right owing to his own abilities, efforts, and actions, rather than owing to dumb luck, or blind chance, or something else.[1]

I   The Lottery Problem

The lottery problem for fallibilism is stated nicely by Stewart Cohen.[2] On the one hand, fallibilists want to say that there can be knowledge by inductive reasoning. Thus fallibilists define themselves against rationalists, who hold that only deductive grounds can give rise to knowledge. On the other hand, it seems that a ticket holder does not know that she will lose the lottery, even if the odds are heavily in favour of her losing. So here is the problem for fallibilism: how is it that in general one can know through

Reprinted from John Greco, "Knowledge as Credit for True Belief," in *Intellectual Virtue: Perspectives from Ethics and Epistemology*, ed. Michael DePaul and Linda Zagzebski (Oxford: Oxford University Press, 2003), 111–134.

inductive grounds, but in the lottery case one fails to know, though one's inductive grounds are excellent?

To sharpen the problem, consider two cases of inductive reasoning.

Case 1   On the way to the elevator S drops a trash bag down the garbage chute of her apartment building. A few minutes later, reasoning on the basis of past experience and relevant background knowledge, S forms the true belief that the bag is in the basement garbage room. Of course her grounds for so believing are merely inductive: it is possible that the trash bag somehow gets hung up in the chute, although this is extremely unlikely.[3]

Case 2   S buys a ticket for a lottery in which the chances of winning are ten million to one. A few minutes later, reasoning on the basis of past experience and relevant background knowledge, S forms the true belief that she will lose the lottery. Of course her grounds for so believing are merely inductive: it is possible that she buys the winning ticket, although this is extremely unlikely.

Many will have the intuition that S knows in Case 1 but not in Case 2. But how so, given that her reasons are excellent in both cases? This is what the fallibilist needs to explain.

A   Nozick's Tracking Account

The difficulty of the problem is illustrated by some accounts that fail to solve it. According to Robert Nozick, S knows *p* just in case S's believing p tracks the truth.[4] Complications aside, this amounts to the following:

S knows *p* just in case
1. *p* is true.
2. If *p* were true then S would believe *p*.
3. If *p* were false then S would not believe *p*.

Nozick's account does a good job explaining why S does not know in the lottery case: if S were going to win the lottery, she would still believe that she is going to lose. However, the tracking account rules incorrectly in the garbage chute case. This is because it is possible, although an extremely unlikely occurrence, that the trash bag gets hung up in the chute. But if the bag did get hung up, S would still believe that the bag is in the basement, and so S fails to satisfy clause (3) of Nozick's account. In fact, the garbage chute case and ones like it were originally formulated as counterexamples to Nozick's account.[5]

B   Sosa's Safety Account

Let us say that one's belief is sensitive to the truth just in case it satisfies Nozick's clause (3). Ernest Sosa suggests that a belief is better safe
than sensitive, where a belief is safe just in case one would have it only
if it were true.[6] Complications aside, Sosa's suggestion amounts to the
following:

S knows p just in case

1. p is true.
2. S believes p.
3. S would believe p only if p were true. Alternatively, S would not believe
   p unless p were true.

Sosa's clause (3) is ambiguous between the following two interpretations:

Strong Safety: In close worlds, always if S believes p then p is true. Alternatively, in close worlds never does S believe p and p is false.

Weak Safety: In close worlds, usually if S believes p then p is true.
Alternatively, in close worlds, almost never does S believe p and p is
false.

But now there is a problem. If Sosa means to endorse strong safety as a
condition on knowledge, then his account does no better than Nozick's
with Case 1: S would believe that the bag is in the basement even if it were
hung up in the chute, and so S fails to satisfy a strong safety condition on
knowledge.[7] This suggests that Sosa means his safety condition to be interpreted as weak safety. But now his account rules incorrectly that there is
knowledge in Case 2: it is true that in close worlds, usually if S believes she
will lose the lottery then it is true that she will lose, and so in the lottery
case S satisfies a weak safety condition.

That is how Sosa's account rules on the lottery case when complications
are set aside. When complications are not set aside, Sosa adds that there are
other conditions required for knowledge, or at least for full-blooded, reflective knowledge. For example, in one place Sosa says that a belief's safety
"must be fundamentally through the exercise of an intellectual virtue,"
where an intellectual virtue is a reliable or trustworthy source of truth.[8] In
another place he says: "For reflective knowledge one not only must believe
out of virtue. One must also be aware of doing so."[9] But it seems clear that
these added requirements do not make a difference in the lottery case, for
there S *does* believe through reliable inductive reasoning, and might even
be aware that she does.

C   Cohen's Contextualism

Finally, consider Cohen's own solution to the lottery problem. According to Cohen, the problem is solved by recognizing that attributions of knowledge are sensitive to context, and, more specifically, that the standards for knowledge are sensitive to context. We have knowledge in cases of ordinary inductive reasoning, such as that employed in the garbage chute case, because the standards, that are operative in ordinary contexts are low enough to admit such cases as counting for knowledge. We do not have knowledge in the lottery case, however, because in that context the standards for knowledge are raised—the possibility of winning the lottery becomes salient, and our inductive evidence, as good as it is, does not rule out this possibility.[10]

I do not wish to deny Cohen's general point that the standards for knowledge are sensitive to context—it seems to me that they are. What is less clear is how this is supposed to solve the lottery problem for fallibilism. The problem is that Cohen gives us no explanation why the standards for knowledge should get raised so high in the lottery case. More specifically: he gives no explanation why the standards should be raised beyond S's capacities to meet them. Cohen is quite explicit that he means to remain within the framework of fallibilism. Moreover, in the lottery case it is stipulated that S has excellent (although fallible) reasons for believing that she will lose. So why, on a fallibilist account of knowledge, does S fail to know that she will lose? To be clear, I am not claiming that S *does* know in the lottery case—I agree that she does not. My complaint is that nothing in Cohen's account explains *why* S does not know.

The same problem can be viewed from a different angle. Cohen says that when S reasons about the odds, the very form of her reasoning makes the possibility that S wins salient. And once made salient, Cohen says, that possibility cannot be ruled out. But again, why can't it be? Why isn't S's reasoning about the odds good enough to rule out the possibility of winning, even once made salient? It has been stipulated that S has excellent reasons for thinking she will not win the lottery, so why doesn't she know that she will not win? In sum, Cohen's contextualism does not explain what it was supposed to explain: given that we are fallibilists about knowledge, and given that we think inductive grounds are good enough to know in other cases, why are S's grounds not good enough to know in the lottery case?[11]

II   Gettier Problems

It has long been understood that fallibilist accounts of justification give rise to Gettier problems. For example, consider the following.

Case 3   On the basis of excellent (although fallible) reasons, S believes that her co-worker Mr Nogot owns a Ford: Nogot testifies that he owns a Ford, and this is confirmed by S's own relevant observations. From this S infers that someone in her office owns a Ford. As it turns out, S's evidence is misleading, and Nogot does not in fact own a Ford. However, another person in S's office, Mr Havit, does own a Ford, although S has no reason for believing this.[12]

Clearly S does not know that someone in her office owns a Ford. The problem for the fallibilist is to explain why this is so, given that S has excellent evidence for this true proposition.

III   A Proposal for Resolving the Two Problems for Fallibilism

We may distinguish two questions one might try to answer when giving an account of knowledge. The first is the 'What is knowledge?' question. This question asks what conditions a person must satisfy to count as knowing. The second is the 'What are we doing?' question. This question asks what illocutionary act is being performed when we say that someone knows. I will have more to say about the 'What is knowledge?' question below. But I think that the key to solving our two problems for fallibilism lies in the 'What are we doing?' question.

So what are we doing when we attribute knowledge to someone? Clearly, we might be doing any number of things. But one of the central functions of knowledge attributions is to give credit for true belief. When we say that S knows *p*, we imply that it is not just an accident that S believes the truth with respect to *p*. On the contrary, we mean to say that S gets things right with respect to *p* because S has reasoned in an appropriate way, or perceived things accurately, or remembered things well, etc. We mean to say that getting it right can be put down to S's own abilities, rather than to dumb luck, or blind chance, or something else. But then this gives us a resource for solving the two problems for fallibilism reviewed above. For in the lottery case, it *does* seem to be just a matter of chance that S gets it right when S believes that she will lose the lottery. And in Case 3 (the Gettier case), it seems just a matter of luck that S gets it right that someone in her office owns a Ford. In the garbage chute case, however, we think that it is owing to S's good reasoning that she gets things right—we give S credit for arriving at the truth in this case, and we are therefore willing to say that she knows.

This is the main idea that I want to pursue.[13] The idea needs to be developed, however. For one, my treatment of the two problems has remained largely intuitive so far. More importantly, the main idea I am proposing is faced with the following problem. First, I have said that we are willing to give S credit for her true belief in cases of knowledge, but not in the lottery case or in Gettier cases. Second, I have said that this is because in the former, but not in the latter, S's arriving at the truth is owing to her own efforts and actions, or more exactly, to her own abilities. But it is not clear why the various cases can be distinguished in this way. Consider that in the lottery case, S uses excellent reasons to draw the conclusion that she will lose. And in the Gettier case, S reasons flawlessly to the conclusion that someone in her office owns a Ford. But then it seems that S arrives at the truth because of her abilities in all of the cases above, and not only in the cases where we judge that S has knowledge. Clearly, more needs to be said.

By way of saying more, I will draw on some important work in moral theory. Specifically, I want to look at Joel Feinberg's fascinating discussion of attributions of moral blame.[14] From this it will be easy enough to construct a general theory of credit attribution, and a theory of intellectual credit attribution in particular. With this groundwork in place, it will be possible to explain why it is appropriate to give S credit for her true belief in cases of knowledge, and appropriate to withhold such credit in the lottery case and Gettier cases. More specifically, it will be possible to explain why, in cases of knowledge, it is appropriate to say that S gets things right *because* of her own abilities, whereas in the lottery case and Gettier cases, it is appropriate to deny this.

A   Feinberg on Blaming

Feinberg's account of moral blaming takes off from the following central idea: when we attribute blame to a person for some occurrence, part of what we are doing is assigning causal responsibility to that person for the occurrence. Put another way, when we blame S for X's occurring, we imply that S figures importantly in a correct causal explanation of why X occurred. To get further insight into our practices of blaming, therefore, Feinberg makes some observations about the pragmatics of causal explanations in general. One important aspect of causal explanation language is this: in general, when we say that Y occurs because X occurs, or that Y's occurring is due to X's occurring, we mark out X's occurring as a particularly important or salient part of the causal story behind Y's occurring. For example, to say that the fire occurred because of the explosion is not to say that the explosion caused the fire all by itself. Rather, it is to say that the explosion is a particularly important part, perhaps the most important part, of the

whole story. Or to change the example: to say that the fire occurred because of S's negligence is not to say that S's negligence caused the fire all by
itself. Rather, it is to say that S's negligence is a particularly salient part,
perhaps the most salient part, of the set of relevant factors that caused the
fire.[15]

What determines salience? Any number of things might, but Feinberg
cites two kinds of consideration as particularly important. First, among the
various necessary parts of a complete causal process, an explanation will
often pick out what is abnormal in the case, or what is contrary to expecta-
tions. For example, we will say that sparks caused the fire if the presence of
sparks in the area is not normal. That explanation would misfire, however,
if we were trying to explain the cause of a fire in a welding shop, where
sparks are flying all the time. Or suppose that a white elephant walks into
a room and causes a panic. Of course the white elephant entering the room
is not sufficient all by itself to cause the panic—it would not if the room
were part of a zoo and the people inside were animal trainers. But if the
room is a place where white elephants are not expected to be, and if
the people inside *are* as we would expect them to be, we have no trouble
picking out the elephant as 'the' cause of the commotion.

Another major factor governing salience is our interests and purposes.
For example, often when we are looking for something's cause we are looking for something that we can manipulate to good effect. If the thing to be
explained is smoke coming from the engine, for example, we will look for
a part that needs to be replaced. Here it is perfectly appropriate to say that
the cause of the smoke is the malfunctioning carburettor, although clearly
a faulty carburettor cannot cause smoke all by itself. Or witness the various
explanations of New York City's plunging crime rate. The police attribute
it to good policing, the mayor attributes it to broader social policy, and opposing politicians attribute it to things over which the mayor has no control, such as an upturn in the national economy. Of course any honest
person would admit that the crime rate is influenced by all of these things.
But different people have different interests, and so highlight different
parts of the causal conditions that were together sufficient for the drop in
crime.

None of this need be insincere, nor is salience something that is merely
subjective. The argument over 'the' cause of the drop in crime is an argument over which of many causal factors should be deemed most important, given our collective interests and given what we know about human
behaviour, how we want to spend limited resources, what policies have
what costs, etc. Likewise, a correct explanation of what caused a panic

focuses on what is in fact abnormal about the situation. As was noted above, if the presence of elephants in the room were not in fact abnormal, then a correct explanation would have to focus elsewhere. In sum, correct causal explanations pick out some salient necessary part of a total set of causal factors, where salience is determined by a number of factors, including what is in fact normal and what are our actual interests.[16]

We may now revisit Feinberg's point that attributions of blame imply causal explanations. This is most obvious in cases where the thing for which the person is blamed is a consequence of the person's actions. For example, to blame someone for the fire is to imply that her actions caused it: she is the one who struck the match, or who did not pay attention, or who did pay the arsonist. Alternatively, we can blame a person for the action itself, implying that she herself was the action's cause, or perhaps that her choice was or her efforts were. As Feinberg notes, the distinction between blaming someone for her action and blaming someone for a consequence of her action is often merely verbal. For example, we can say either 'She caused the fire by striking the match,' or 'She started the fire.' Likewise, 'She caused his death by poisoning his food' substitutes for 'She killed him.'

Finally, Feinberg argues that when we blame someone for an action we imply that the action reveals something important about the person himself: "In general, I should think, a person's faulty act is registerable only if it reveals what sort of person he is in some respect about which others have a practical interest in being informed."[17] Feinberg's position is perhaps too strong on this point; it would seem that people can be rightfully blamed for actions that are out of character. Nevertheless, there does seem to be a *kind* of blame that Feinberg is right about. In other words, even if not all blaming implies that the person's action reveals a faulty character, there is a strong sort of blame, which is common enough, that does. Moreover, this strong sort of blame has a counterpart in a strong sort of credit. Often enough, credit for an action implies a judgement about the person as well, implying not only that the person is responsible for doing something good, but that this is a manifestation of virtuous character.

Putting all this together, Feinberg's account of blame for an action can be summed up as follows.

A person S is morally to blame for action A only if
a. A is a morally faulty action,
b. A can be ascribed to S, and
c. A reveals S's faulty moral character.

Feinberg concludes that attributions of blame share the same pragmatics as causal explanations. His argument for this emphasizes clause (b) of the above account: attributing blame involves ascribing action, and ascribing action involves causal citation. What I want to emphasize, however, is that clause (c) acts the same way. Clause (c) also ensures that attributions of blame involve causal citation, for what does it mean to say that an action reveals character, other than that the action results from character? In other words, clause (c) can be read:

c'. S did A *because* S has a faulty moral character.

This might seem too strong, and it is if we read (c') as saying that S's character was sufficient all by itself to cause S's action. Similarly, it is too strong if we read (c') as saying that, given S's character, S had to do A. But it is not too strong if we remember the pragmatics of causal explanation language reviewed above. For according to that account, to say that S's action is a result of her character is to say that S's character is an important part, perhaps the most important part, of the story. Taken this way, (c') is not too strong at all, but rather reflects our common-sense attitudes about the sources of human action. The fact is, we cite character in explanations of human behaviour all the time, as when we say that he made the remark because he is insensitive (as opposed to having a bad day), or that she failed to spend the money because she is cheap (as opposed to hard up for cash at the moment).[18] Feinberg's analysis reveals that such explanations are implied in attributions of blame, or at least in attributions of a certain sort of blame. And this implies that attributions of blame (of that special sort) will inherit the pragmatics of causal explanations. Clearly, any action will be the result of a number of factors, including a person's character. But sometimes we want to say that character is particularly salient—that it is an important part, perhaps the most important part, of the story behind why the person acted as he did.

B   A General Theory of Credit Attribution

Feinberg's account of moral blaming can easily be broadened in two ways. First, I have already noted that the counterpart of blame for an action is credit for an action. In fact, we can use credit as the general term, and talk about positive credit (i.e. praise) and negative credit (i.e. blame) for an action. Second, there are kinds of credit other than moral.[19] For example, we credit athletes for athletic feats and thinkers for intellectual ones. Accordingly, I propose the following as a general theory of credit.

A person S deserves credit of kind K for action A only if

a. A has value of kind K,
b. A can be ascribed to S, and
c. A reveals S's K-relevant character. Alternatively: S's K-relevant character is an important necessary part of the total set of causal factors that give rise to S's doing A.

Two examples will illustrate this account.

Case 4   Ken Griffey Jr. runs full speed toward the center field wall, leaps with outstretched glove, and catches the ball while diving to the ground. The home team crowd, just robbed of a game-winning double, shake their respective heads in admiration of Griffey's spectacular catch.

Case 5   Griffey Jr. runs full speed toward the center field wall, trips, and falls face down on the ground. The ball bounces off his head, goes straight in the air, and comes down in his glove. The home team crowd, just robbed of a game-winning double, shake their respective heads in disgust.

In both cases, the action in question has clear athletic value—catching the ball before it hits the ground is essential to winning baseball games. Moreover, in both cases the catch is ascribable to Griffey—we can be sure that a broadcaster announcing the game will be yelling, "Griffey caught the ball! Griffey caught the ball!" But only in Case 4 will Griffey be given credit for catching the ball, and that is because in Case 4 Griffey's catching the ball is the result of his relevant character, i.e. his great athletic abilities. In Case 5 Griffey's catching the ball was just dumb luck, and so the home team crowd is not just a bunch of sore losers. They are right to be disgusted.

A similar phenomenon occurs when a poor fielder makes a spectacular catch. In this case he will be given credit of a sort—he will get pats on the back from his teammates and applause from the crowd. But it won't be the same kind of credit that Griffey gets. *Griffey* makes spectacular catches all the time—*his* catches manifest his great skills. Not so when Albert Belle makes such a catch. If the catch is difficult, it is almost just good luck that he makes it. And opposing fans will treat it that way, withholding the credit they would readily give to Griffey. Or consider Bucky Dent's infamous home run to knock the Red Sox out of the play-offs. To this day Boston fans do not give Dent credit for the home run or the Yankees credit for the win. Dent was just a singles hitter, and his fly ball would have been a routine out in any park but Fenway. The home run was just bad luck, Boston fans think, having little to do with Dent's abilities as a hitter.

Finally, it is interesting that the case can be viewed in more than one way. Yankee fans *do* give Dent credit for the home run—to them, he will always be considered a great hero. This is because Yankee fans don't think that Dent's home run was just a matter of luck. Their thinking emphasizes the idea that *some* luck is always involved in sports, but Dent got his bat on the ball, he was strong enough to muscle it out there, and he was able to take advantage of Fenway's short left field. In other words, their account of the home run downplays luck and emphasizes Dent's abilities. This is a common enough phenomenon in sports: losers try to deny credit by emphasizing the role of luck, and winners try to take credit by putting the emphasis back on ability. Hence the attractive but dubious claims that 'Good teams make their own luck' and 'It all comes out even in the end.'

C A Theory of Intellectual Credit Attribution

When we attribute knowledge to someone we imply that it is to his credit that he got things right. It is not because the person is lucky that he believes the truth—it is because of his own cognitive abilities. He figured it out, or remembered it correctly, or perceived that it was so. Applying the account of credit attribution above, we have:

S deserves intellectual credit for believing the truth regarding p only if
a. believing the truth regarding p has intellectual value,
b. believing the truth regarding p can be ascribed to S, and
c. believing the truth regarding p reveals S's reliable cognitive character.
   Alternatively: S's reliable cognitive character is an important necessary part of the total set of causal factors that give rise to S's believing the truth regarding p.

And hence:

S knows p only if believing the truth regarding p reveals S's reliable cognitive character. Alternatively: only if S's reliable cognitive character is an important necessary part of the total set of causal factors that give rise to S's believing the truth regarding p.

We are now in a position to apply these results to the two problems for fallibilism.

IV The Lottery Problem Solved: Chance Undermines Credit

The application to the lottery problem is initially straightforward: knowledge attributions imply attributions of intellectual credit for true belief, and intellectual credit implies that the true belief is the result of S's own intellectual abilities. But here as in other cases, salient chance undermines credit. In the lottery case, but not in the garbage chute case, it seems just a matter of chance that S believes the truth. In the garbage chute case, but not in the lottery case, S's true belief is appropriately credited to her, i.e., to her intellectual abilities.

This was our initial treatment of the case. But this initial treatment gave rise to the following problem: S employs admirable inductive reasoning no less in the lottery case than in the garbage chute case. In both cases, therefore, S's abilities make up a necessary part, but only a part, of the whole story regarding S's believing the truth. The present account of credit solves this problem. For it is only in the garbage chute case that S's abilities are a *salient* part of the story. In the lottery case, what is most salient is the element of chance.

Why does the element of chance become salient in the lottery case? I would suggest that the very idea of a lottery has the idea of chance built right into it. Here is the way we think of the lottery case: first, S reasons on the basis of excellent grounds that she will lose the lottery. Second, the lottery is held and reality either does or does not match up with S's belief—it's just a matter of chance. Notice that things are different if S believes that she lost the lottery because she reads the results in the newspaper.[20] Here again her evidence is merely inductive, but now the role of chance does not play an important part in the story. Here is the most natural way to think of the newspaper case: first the lottery is held and the facts are fixed. Second, S infers from a reliable source that she has lost the lottery. Now it is not just a matter of chance that she believes the truth—she believes the truth because she has the good sense to believe what she reads about the results.

Two more cases help to explore the implications of the present account.

Case 6   On the basis of excellent evidence, S believes that her friend will meet her in New York City for lunch. However, S's friend has bought a ticket in the lottery, and if he were to win then he would be in New Jersey to collect his winnings. In fact, the friend loses the lottery and meets S for lunch.[21]

Intuitively, people can know things about their friends even when, unknown to them, their friends have bought tickets in the lottery and would behave differently if they won. On the other hand, there is some intuitive pull towards thinking that S does not know in Case 6, since if her friend were to win the lottery then he would not meet her for lunch. The present account explains these conflicting intuitions by distinguishing contexts of attribution. In contexts where considerations about the lottery are not important, the salience of chance is low and so attributions of knowledge can still be appropriate. However, in contexts where considerations about the lottery are important, the salience of chance rises, and therefore knowledge attributions are undermined. Handling Case 6 this way allows us to say that knowledge is closed under known entailment. Taking a page from the book of standards contextualists, we may note that there is no single context relative to which (a) S knows that her friend will meet her for lunch, (b) S knows that her friend will meet her for lunch only if he loses the lottery, and (c) S does not know that her friend will lose the lottery. If the context does not make chance salient, then relative to that context S can know that her friend will meet her for lunch. But if the context does make chance salient, then relative to that context S knows neither that her friend will meet her for lunch nor that he will lose the lottery.[22]

Now consider another case.

Case 7   S is visiting from another culture and knows nothing about lotteries. However, over a long period of time S observes many people exchanging dollar bills for small slips of paper, which they invariably discard after a brief examination. On the basis of excellent inductive reasoning, S concludes that the next person in line will soon discard his slip of paper. And in fact S's belief is true.[23]

This case threatens a counterintuitive result: that relative to S's context, S knows that the next person in line will discard his ticket. Put another way, if S were to express a knowledge claim, then, relative to S's own context of attribution, his claim would be true. This result threatens because S understands nothing about the workings of lotteries. And therefore, it seems, chance could not be a salient factor in S's context. However, this way of interpreting the case assumes that salience is a psychological phenomenon—that salience is a function of where someone's attention is, or how he is thinking about things. This is admittedly one meaning of the term, but it is not the one that we want here. On the contrary, I have argued that salience is a function of (a) what is in fact normal or abnormal in the case, and (b) what interests and purposes are in fact operative in the context of attribution. Therefore, whether something is salient relative to a context of attribution, in the sense intended here, is not a question about how anyone is thinking.

What we are looking for is not psychological salience but explanatory salience. The way to identify what is salient in this sense is to ask where a correct explanation would have to focus. As noted above, a correct explanation of a car fire might properly focus on sparks coming from the engine, whereas a correct explanation of a fire in a welding shop must focus somewhere else. But this has nothing to do with how people are thinking about the cases. Rather, it has to do with what is in fact normal and abnormal in cars and welding shops. Likewise, if a drunk driver runs a light and is involved in a collision, then almost always a correct explanation will focus on the driver's impaired condition. Given the interests and purposes that are usually in place, other explanations of the collision are almost always inappropriate.

These considerations explain why it is correct to say that S does not have knowledge in Case 7, even relative to S's own context of attribution. For although the role of chance has no psychological salience for S, it does have explanatory salience; that is, any correct explanation of why S believes the truth would have to refer to the lottery. This is because playing the lottery is pretty much the only thing going on here. Relative to almost any context we can imagine, including S's own, an explanation that did not refer to the lottery would leave the most important thing out. This is in contrast to Case 6. In that case any number of factors contribute to S's believing the truth regarding her friend meeting her for lunch. And relative to most contexts that we can imagine, the fact that her friend loses the lottery will play no important part in a correct explanation of why she believes the truth.

Finally, it will be helpful to compare the present account with standards contextualism. First, both accounts are contextualist; that is, they both make the truth conditions of knowledge claims relative to the context of attribution. But the way this works in the two accounts is different. According to standards contextualism, the context of attribution determines the standards for knowledge, so that standards are higher or lower relative to different contexts. On the present account, however, the context of attribution determines the salience of various contributing causal factors, thus determining responsibility for true belief. Standards are not raised or lowered according to context; rather, responsibility for a complex event (someone's believing the truth) is creditable or not creditable to the believer according to context.

Second, I argued above that familiar versions of standards contextualism do not explain why S's inductive reasoning does not allow her to know that she will lose the lottery. The standards contextualist says that in the lottery case the standards for knowing get raised because the possibility of winning becomes salient. But this does not tell us why S's reasoning fails to meet those standards, even if raised. The present account does better in this respect. The very idea of a lottery involves the idea of chance, and so we have an explanation why chance is salient in cases where the lottery is salient. We can then apply a familiar general principle of credit attribution: that salient chance undermines credit.

V Gettier Problems Solved: Abnormality Trumps Interest

Recently I have argued that the following conditions are necessary for knowledge.[24]

S knows p only if

1. S's believing p is *subjectively* justified in the following sense: S's believing p is the result of dispositions that S manifests when S is trying to believe the truth, and
2. S's believing p is *objectively* justified in the following sense: the dispositions that result in S's believing p make S reliable in believing p. Alternatively, the dispositions that result in S's believing p constitute intellectual abilities, or powers, or virtues.

The thinking behind the subjective justification condition is that knowledge requires that belief be appropriate from the knower's point of view. More specifically, the knower must have some awareness that a belief so formed has a good likelihood of being true. Some authors have required that the knower *believe* that this is so, but I have resisted this way of understanding the kind of awareness in question. It seems that people rarely have beliefs about the genesis of their beliefs, and so it would be too strong to require that they always have one in cases of knowledge. Accordingly, I have stated the subjective justification condition in terms of dispositions to believe rather than actual beliefs, or even dispositional beliefs. People manifest highly specific, finely tuned dispositions to form beliefs in some ways rather than others. And this fact, I take it, amounts to an implicit awareness of the reliability of those dispositions.

The objective justification condition can be interpreted along the lines of Sosa's weak safety condition above: to say that S is reliable in believing p is to say that, at least in relevantly close worlds, usually if S believes p then p is true. Notice that clause (2) makes the knower the seat of reliability: it says that S is reliable, not that some process is, or that S's method is, or that S's evidence is. The thinking here is that knowledge must be grounded in the knower. That is, it must be grounded in the knower's own abilities, rather than in a process or method that might be engaged in accidentally, or on evidence that might be trusted on a whim.

I now want to add a third condition on knowledge, understanding knowledge attributions to imply attributions of intellectual credit, and understanding intellectual credit along the lines above. I propose that adding this third condition makes the three sufficient as well as necessary for knowledge.

3. S believes the truth regarding p *because* S is reliable in believing p. Alternatively: the intellectual abilities (i.e., powers or virtues) that result in S's believing the truth regarding p are an important necessary part of the total set of causal factors that give rise to S's believing the truth regarding p.

I claimed above that clause (3) allows us to handle a range of Gettier cases. Intuitively, in cases of knowledge S's reliable character has salience in an explanation of how S comes to get things right. In Gettier cases, S's reliable character loses its salience in favour of something else. What we want now is an account of why this is so. Hence we have two questions before us: first, why is it that S's cognitive abilities have salience in cases of knowledge? Second, why is it that they do not have salience in Gettier cases?[25]

To answer the first question we may turn to a point that has been emphasized by Sosa. He writes:

All kinds of justification involve the cognitive or intellectual virtues, faculties, or aptitudes of the subject. We care about justification because it tends to indicate a state of the subject that is important and of interest to his community, a state of great interest and importance to an information-sharing social species. What sort of state? Presumably, the state of being a dependable source of information over a certain field in certain circumstances.[26]

For present purposes Sosa's point may be glossed this way: for beings like us, dependability (or reliability) of cognitive character is of fundamental social importance. But this implies that cognitive character will have a kind of default salience in the explanation of true belief. Unless something else is present that trumps the salience of S's cognitive abilities, those will be the most important part of the story, or at least a very important part of the story.

We may now turn to the second question: why is it that S's cognitive abilities are not salient in Gettier cases? Gettier cases seem to fall into three categories in this respect. First, there are cases where S's abilities are not salient in an explanation of true belief because S's abilities are not involved at all. Here is one such case.

Case 8 Charlie has excellent reasons to believe that he will make his connection in Chicago. However, Charlie does not recognize these reasons for what they are, nor does he base his belief on them. Rather, he believes that he will make his connection because he is overcome with wishful thinking at the prospects of seeing his fiancée. As it turns out, his belief is true.

Here it is straightforward that Charlie does not believe the truth because of his intellectual abilities, since his abilities are not involved at all in the production or maintenance of his belief. As I have described the case, he believes the truth entirely out of wishful thinking.

Second, there are cases where S's belief is produced by faculties that would normally be considered abilities, but where S is not reliable in the environment where those faculties are used. Here are two.

Case 9 Henry is driving in the countryside and sees a barn ahead in clear view. On this basis he believes that the object he sees is a barn. Unknown to Henry, however, the area is dotted with barn façades that are indistinguishable from real barns from the road. However, Henry happens to be looking at the one real barn in the area.[27]

Case 10 Rene is the victim of an evil demon, who causes him to be systematically deceived. Despite admirable intellectual care and responsibility, almost all of Rene's beliefs are false. However, his belief that he is sitting by the fire, which is based on appropriate sensations and background beliefs, happens to be true.[28]

In Case 9 S's belief is the result of perception, and normally S's perception would constitute a cognitive virtue, i.e., a reliable ability or power. However, reliability is relative to an environment, and S's perception is not reliable relative to the environment in the example. Similar things can be said about Case 10—Rene's beliefs are caused by his cognitive faculties, and in a normal environment these faculties would constitute abilities or powers. But in Rene's actual environment his faculties are unreliable.

Finally, there are Gettier cases where S does use reliable abilities or powers to arrive at her belief, but where this is not the most salient aspect of the case. Case 3 regarding the Ford is one. Here are two others.

Case 11 A man *takes* there to be a sheep in the field and does so under conditions which are such that, when a man *does* thus take there to be a sheep in the field, then it is *evident* to him that there is a sheep in the field. The man, however, has mistaken a dog for a sheep and so what he sees is not a sheep at all. Nevertheless, unsuspected by the man, there *is* a sheep in another part of the field.[29]

Case 12 Smith looks at his watch and forms the belief that it is 3 o'clock. In fact, Smith's watch is broken. But by a remarkable coincidence, it has stopped running exactly twelve hours earlier, and so shows the correct time when Smith looks at it.[30]

In all three of these cases, reliable cognitive character gives rise to the belief in question—Lehrer's office worker reasons from her evidence, Chisholm's sheep-watcher trusts his vision, and Russell's time-teller trusts his watch. But in none of these cases does the person believe the truth because of reliable character. On the contrary, an explanation of how the person comes to get things right would have to focus somewhere else. In Case 3, S believes the truth because someone else in her office owns a Ford. Chisholm's sheep-watcher believes the truth because there is a sheep in another part of the field. Russell's time-teller believes the truth because his watch has stopped running exactly twelve hours before he looked at it. In each of the cases, there is something else that is more salient than S's cognitive abilities in the explanation of how S came to get things right.

Why is that so in this third category of Gettier cases? I propose that, in at least many such cases, there is something odd or unexpected about the way that S comes to believe the truth, and that the salience of the abnormality trumps the default salience of S's cognitive abilities. We have already seen that the salience of abnormalities is a general phenomenon. When a white elephant enters the room, all bets are off for other explanations regarding why the room emptied out. The odd or the unexpected undermines the salience of other factors involved in the event. In fact, Gettier cases are often told so as to increase this effect. Typically, there is a first part of the case where an entirely normal scene is described. Then comes the 'big surprise' part of the case, where we get the odd twist: what S sees is actually a dog, but there happens to be a sheep in another part of the field; S's evidence is misleading, but someone else in the office owns a Ford.

Not all abnormalities undermine the salience of cognitive character, however. For example, an unlikely coincidence reminds the detective of evidence he has neglected, and this missing piece of the puzzle allows him to solve the crime. Less dramatically, an unusual noise causes someone to turn her head, and something else comes into plain view. We would like an account of which abnormalities undermine the salience of character in the explanation of true belief and which do not. Here is a suggestion that seems to handle the above cases well: abnormalities in the way one *gets* one's evidence do not undermine credit, whereas abnormalities regarding the way one gets a true belief, given that one has the evidence that one does, do undermine credit. Put another way, in cases where something unusual does take away the salience of character, it seems just a matter of good luck that S ends up with a true belief, *even given that she has the evidence that she does.*[31]

We may understand this point in a way that generalizes to other kinds of credit: we may say that, in general, situational luck does not undermine credit. In other words, luck in the way that one gets into one's situation does not undermine credit for what one does once in that situation. This, I take it, is one of the lessons of the literature on moral luck. A general prohibition on luck shrinks the sphere of moral responsibility to nothing, and hence an adequate theory of moral responsibility must allow for the influence of some kinds of luck but not others.[32]

In sum, the present account goes some way towards explicating the content and pragmatics of knowledge attributions, although we must recognize that it does not go all the way. It goes some way because it analyses knowledge in terms of credit attribution and credit attribution in terms of the content and pragmatics of causal explanations. It does not go all the way, however, because the pragmatics of causal explanations, and especially those concerning the salience of partial causes, are not fully understood. For example, the account given above in this regard is clearly only a partial account.[33] Nevertheless, our intuitions about knowledge seem to follow our intuitions about causal explanation: in cases of knowledge, we think that S believes the truth because she is reliable, whereas in Gettier cases we think that S's believing the truth must be explained in some other way.

VI Concluding Remarks

I would like to end with two considerations that lend further support to the account of knowledge that has been offered here. First, the account predicts certain phenomena that do in fact take place. Second, the account suggests a solution to the value problem for knowledge.

A Conflicting Knowledge Attributions

If the preceding account of knowledge is correct, then there should be arguments over knowledge attribution that mirror arguments over other kinds of credit attribution. More specifically, there should be cases where disagreements over whether someone has knowledge reflect different emphases on the relative importance of S's contribution to arriving at the truth.

This is in fact the case. For example, consider the following conversation between a gambler and his wife.

Gambler: I told you so, Honey! I knew that horse would win!
Wife: You knew no such thing, you idiot! That horse could have lost—you nearly threw away our rent money again!
Gambler: No—I knew she would win! I've been watching that horse for months now, and I knew that she would run great in these conditions.
Wife: You son-of-a-bitch.

The conversation lends itself to the following interpretation: the gambler is trying to take credit for his true belief that the horse would win, and his wife is trying to deny him credit. In doing so, he tries to emphasize his ability to pick winning horses, and she tries to emphasize the role of luck.

In the context set by the above example I would tend to agree with the wife. But perhaps there are other contexts relative to which the gambler's claim to know is correct. Consider a conversation that might take place among gambling buddies.

First Gambler: How did you know that horse was going to win?
Second Gambler: Are you kidding? I've seen her run in mud before, and the only horse in the race that could touch her was pulled just before post time. When I saw that, I ran to the betting window.
First Gambler: You son-of-a-bitch.

In this context the claim to know is accepted by all involved. Perhaps this is because gamblers are deluded about the relative importance of luck and ability in picking horses. Alternatively, in the present context the role of luck is taken for granted, and so all emphasis is rightly put on the relative abilities among the gamblers. If the 'amateur' in the next row also picked the winner, he *wouldn't* be given credit for his true belief.

B   The Value Problem

Recently, Linda Zagzebski has called attention to the value problem for knowledge.[34] An adequate account of knowledge, she points out, ought to explain why knowledge is more valuable than mere true belief. In closing, I will suggest how the present account solves that problem.

In Book II of the *Nicomachean Ethics*, Aristotle makes a distinction between (a) morally virtuous action and (b) action that is merely as if morally virtuous. One important difference, says Aristotle, is that morally virtuous actions "proceed from a firm and unchangeable character" (II. 4). Moreover, it is morally virtuous action, as opposed to action that is as if virtuous, that is both intrinsically valuable and constitutive of the good life: "human good turns out to be activity of soul exhibiting excellence" (I. 7). The same point holds for intellectually virtuous action, where the distinction between 'virtuous action' and 'action as if virtuous' translates to a distinction between knowledge and mere true belief. Following Aristotle, therefore, we get an answer to the value problem: as is the case regarding moral goods, getting the truth as a result of one's virtues is more valuable than getting it on the cheap.[35]

Notes

I would like to thank Robert Audi, Heather Battaly, Michael Bergmann, Stewart Cohen, Keith DeRose, Tamar Gendler, Stephen Grimm, Daniel Nolan, Philip Quinn, Wayne Riggs, Ted Sider, Eleonore Stump, Ernest Sosa, Fritz Warfield, and Linda Zagzebski for their helpful comments in discussion and on earlier versions of the chapter.

1. The idea that knowledge entails credit for true belief can be found in Sosa (1988) and (1991), and Zagzebski (1996) and (1999b). More explicitly, Wayne Riggs argues that in cases of knowledge "we deserve credit for arriving at true belief non-accidentally." See Riggs (2002: 95).

2. Cohen (1988) and (1998).

3. The example is from Sosa (2000). We can imagine that the bag's getting hung up is extremely unlikely because everything would have to go just right for that to occur, including the trajectory of the bag, its contents, the distribution of its weight, etc.

4. See Nozick (1981).

5. Here is another counterexample to Nozick's account, due to Jonathan Vogel (1987: 212): "Suppose two policemen confront a mugger, who is standing some distance away with a drawn gun. One of the officers, a rookie, attempts to disarm the mugger by shooting a bullet down the barrel of the mugger's gun. (I assume that the chances of doing this are virtually nil.) Imagine that the rookie's veteran partner knows what the rookie is trying to do. The veteran sees him fire, but is screened from seeing the result. Aware that his partner is trying something that is all but impossible, the veteran thinks (correctly as it turns out) [that the] rookie missed."

6. See Sosa (2000), (1999a) and (1999b).

7. Here I am assuming that there is a close world in which the bag gets hung up in the chute. If that seems wrong, we can invoke Vogel's rookie cop example from n. 5.

There it seems uncontroversial that there is a close world where the rookie's bullet enters the mugger's barrel.

8. Sosa (1999*a*: 383, n. 7).

9. Sosa (1991: 278).

10. Cohen (1988: 106–7).

11. My claim is not that standards contextualism cannot explain the lottery case in principle. Rather, I restrict myself to the weaker claim that Cohen's contextualism does not in fact explain it. What are the prospects for other versions of standards contextualism? The trick, of course, is for the standards contextualist to explain why S does not have knowledge in the lottery case, while at the same time preserving the intuition that S does have knowledge in other cases of inductive reasoning. But this will be hard to do. For example, Keith DeRose argues that S has knowledge if her belief matches the truth out to the nearest world where a salient alternative possibility is actual. However, the matching requirement ensures that DeRose's account rules incorrectly in the garbage chute case and in the rookie cop case from n. 5. This is because these cases are designed so that not-p worlds are very, very close, and so no matter how weak the standards for knowledge are being set, S's belief will not match the truth far enough out into alternative possible worlds. In other words, no matter how close the nearest world where a salient possibility is actual, S's belief will not match the truth out to that world. See DeRose (1995).

12. The example is from Lehrer (1965: 169–70).

13. I first suggested a solution to Gettier problems along these lines in Greco (1994). Linda Zagzebski develops the idea in a different direction in Zagzebski (1996) and (1999a), and Keith Lehrer develops a similar idea in Lehrer (2000). Earlier than any of this, Sosa writes that in cases of knowledge one's belief must "non-accidentally reflect the truth of P through the exercise of . . . a virtue." However, he does not suggest that this idea can be used to address Gettier problems. See Sosa (1988: 184). See also Sosa (1991: 277).

14. Feinberg's discussion takes place over three papers, "Problematic Responsibility in Law and Morals," "Action and Responsibility," and "Causing Voluntary Actions," all of which are collected in Feinberg (1970). My account of Feinberg's account of blaming is a reconstruction—I have taken parts of what he says from each of his three papers and put them together in a way that suits my present purposes.

15. It is tempting to follow Feinberg and to put things this way; when we say that Y occurs because X occurs, or that Y's occurring is due to X's occurring, we mark out X's occurring as a particularly important or salient part of a sufficient condition for Y's occurring (Feinberg 1970: 177). This assumes, however, that all causes can be understood as sufficient conditions. Since I do not want to deny either (a) the pos-

sibility of agent causation or (b) the possibility of indeterminate causation, I employ the looser language above.

16. Another example: sports fans will argue endlessly over why we lost the big game. Was it because we gave up too many points or because we didn't score enough? Obviously, the outcome of a game is a function of both points allowed and points scored. The real argument here is over what was the most important factor in the loss. And *that* is a function of what one can normally expect, what could have been done differently, etc.

17. Feinberg (1970: 126).

18. Some recent work in social psychology suggests that common sense is flawed in this respect. For example, see Ross and Nisbett (1991). For a persuasive argument against such a conclusion, see DePaul (2000).

19. Feinberg's own discussion is at times aimed at other kinds of blame.

20. This point is made in Cohen (1988).

21. This kind of case is discussed in Cohen (1988) and in Harman (1974).

22. Cohen and DeRose have both argued that contextualists need not run into closure problems. See Cohen (1988) and DeRose (1995). For an early discussion of relevant issues, see Stine (1976).

23. This sort of case was raised by Phillip Quinn in discussion.

24. See Greco (2000) and (1999).

25. What is a Gettier case? Zagzebski has argued that all Gettier cases are ones where bad epistemic luck is cancelled out by good epistemic luck. For example, in Case 3 S's evidence is deceptive (bad luck), but someone else in S's office owns a Ford (good luck). This analysis suggests that we can treat Gettier cases in the same way that we treated the lottery problem above—we can say that Gettier cases involve salient luck, and salient luck undermines credit. In my opinion this assessment is correct, but it is not as informative as we would like. This is because in Gettier cases, to say that S believes the truth because of good luck is very close to saying that S believes the truth for some reason other than her own abilities. And although that seems true, it is not more informative than what we already have—which is that clause (3) is violated. (In the lottery case, we said that the clause is violated because of the role of salient chance. That explanation is informative, however, because we have an independent grasp of what we mean by chance in a lottery.)

26. Sosa (1991: 281–2).

27. The example is from Goldman (1976). Reprinted in Goldman (1992).

28. The example is from Sosa (1995).

29. The example is quoted from Chisholm (1977: 105).

30. The watch example is due to Bertrand Russell (1948). The example is cited by Chisholm (1977: 104–5), where he points out that it is a Gettier case.

31. The distinction employed here is similar to Mylan Engel's distinction between verific and evidential luck, in Engel (1992). I thank Michael Bergmann for pointing out to me that Engel's distinction is helpful in the present context.

32. In this regard, see Nagel (1979), Walker (1991), and Greco (1995).

33. We can imagine Gettier-type cases, for example, where the problem is not abnormality in the way that S comes to believe the truth, but the interference of another agent, such as a 'helpful demon.' Here, as in other cases, credit for true belief and hence knowledge is undermined. And, here again, this seems to be a general phenomenon regarding credit. So, for example, the influence of a helpful demon would undermine moral credit as well. I thank Daniel Nolan and Tamar Gendler for raising this kind of concern.

34. Zagzebski raises the problem in (1996: 300–2), and in a more extended way in (1999a), reprinted in expanded form in Axtell (2000). See also Zagzebski's contribution to this volume.

35. Riggs takes a similar approach to the value problem. He writes, "When a true belief is achieved non-accidentally, the person derives epistemic credit for this that she would not be due had she only accidentally happened upon a true belief. . . . The difference that makes a *value* difference here is the variation in the degree to which a person's abilities, powers, and skills are causally responsible for the outcome, believing truly that *p*" (Riggs 2002: 93–4).

References

Axtell, G. (2000). *Knowledge, Belief and Character: Readings in Virtue Epistemology*. New York, NY: Rowman and Littlefield Publishers.

Chisholm, R. (1977). *Theory of Knowledge* (2nd ed.). Englewood Cliffs, NJ: Prentice-Hall.

Cohen, S. (1988). "How to be Fallibilist," *Philosophical Perspectives* 2: 91–123.

———. (1998). "Contextualist Solutions to Epistemic Problems: Scepticism, Gettier and the Lottery," *Australasian Journal of Philosophy* 76: 289–306.

DePaul, M. (2000). "Character Traits, Virtues and Vices: Are There None?," in B. Elevitch, ed., *Proceedings of the Twentieth World Congress of Philosophy, IX: Philosophy of Mind and Philosophy of Psychology*. Bowling Green, OH: Philosophy Documentation Center, 141–57.

DeRose, K. (1995). "Solving the Skeptical Problem," *Philosophical Review* 104: 1–52.

Engel, M. (1992). "Is Epistemic Luck Compatible with Knowledge?," *The Southern Journal of Philosophy* 30: 59–75.

Feinberg, J. (1970). *Doing and Deserving: Essays in the Theory of Responsibility.* Princeton, NJ: Princeton University Press.

Goldman, A. (1976). "Discrimination and Perceptual Knowledge," *The Journal of Philosophy* 73: 771–91.

———. (1992). *Liaisons: Philosophy Meets the Cognitive and Social Sciences.* Cambridge, MA: MIT Press.

Greco, J. (1994). "Jonathan Kvanvig's *The Intellectual Virtues and the Life of the Mind*," *Philosophy and Phenomenological Research* 54: 973–6.

———. (1995). "A Second Paradox Concerning Responsibility and Luck," *Metaphilosophy* 26: 81–96.

Harman, G. (1974). *Thought.* Princeton, NJ: Princeton University Press.

Lehrer, K. (1965). "Knowledge, Truth and Evidence," *Analysis* 25: 168–75.

———. (2000). *Theory of Knowledge* (2nd ed.). Boulder, CO: Westview Press.

Nagel, T. (1979). "Moral Luck," in *Mortal Questions.* Cambridge: Cambridge University Press.

Nozick, R. (1981). *Philosophical Explanations.* Cambridge, MA: Harvard University Press.

Riggs, W. (2002). "Reliability and the Value of Knowledge," *Philosophy and Phenomenological Research* 60: 203–6.

Ross, L. and Nisbett, R. (1991). *The Person and the Situation.* New York, NY: McGraw-Hill.

Russell, B. (1948). *Human Knowledge: Its Scope and Limits.* New York, NY: Simon and Schuster.

Sosa, E. (1988). "Beyond Skepticism, to the Best of Our Knowledge," *Mind* 97: 153–89.

———. (1991). *Knowledge in Perspective: Selected Essays in Epistemology.* Cambridge: Cambridge University Press.

———. (1995). "Perspectives in Virtue Epistemology: A Response to Dancy and BonJour," *Philosophical Studies* 78: 221–35.

———. (1999*a*). "How Must Knowledge Be Modally Related to What Is Known," *Philosophical Topics* 26: 373–84.

———. (1999*b*). "How to Defeat Opposition to Moore," *Philosophical Perspectives* 13: 141–55.

————. (2000). "Skepticism and Contextualism," *Philosophical Issues* 10: 1–18.

Stine, G. (1976). "Skepticism, Relevant Alternatives, and Deductive Closure," *Philosophical Studies* 29: 249–61.

Vogel, J. (1987). "Tracking, Closure, and Inductive Knowledge," in S. Luper-Foy, ed., *The Possibility of Knowledge*. Totowa, NJ: Rowman and Littlefield, 197–215.

Walker, M. (1991). "Moral Luck and the Virtues of Impure Agency," *Metaphilosophy* 22: 14–27.

Zagzebski, L. (1996). *Virtues of the Mind: An Inquiry into the Nature of Virtue and the Ethical Foundations of Knowledge*. Cambridge: Cambridge University Press.

————. (1999*a*). "From Reliabilism to Virtue Epistemology," in R. Coff-Steven, ed., *Proceedings of the Twentieth World Congress of Philosophy* (Boston, 1998) v: *Epistemology*. Bowling Green, OH: Philosophy Documentation Center, 173–9.

————. (1999*b*). "What Is Knowledge?," in J. Greco and E. Sosa, eds., *The Blackwell Guide to Epistemology*, 92–116. Oxford: Blackwell.

13 Why Epistemologists Are So Down on Their Luck[1]

Wayne Riggs

Abstract

It is nearly universally acknowledged among epistemologists that a belief, even if true, cannot count as knowledge if it is somehow largely a matter of luck that the person so arrived at the truth. A striking feature of this literature, however, is that while many epistemologists are busy arguing about which particular technical condition most effectively rules out the offensive presence of luck in true believing, almost no one is asking why it matters so much that knowledge be immune from luck in the first place. I argue that the best explanation for the consensus that luck undermines knowledge is that knowledge is, complications aside, credit-worthy true believing. To make this case, I develop both the notions of luck and credit, and sketch a theory of knowledge in those terms. Furthermore, this account also holds promise for being able to solve the "value problem" for knowledge, and it explains why both internal and external conditions are necessary to turn true belief into knowledge.

1 Introductory Remarks

Much of the recent literature on knowledge seems to focus on notions like "safety" and "sensitivity." These are technical notions designed to capture the right sorts of counterfactual conditions under which a true belief should count as knowledge. The usual explanation for why these notions are appropriate conditions for knowledge is that each serves to rule out certain classes of "lucky" true belief. It is nearly universally acknowledged among epistemologists that a belief, even if true, cannot count as knowledge if it is somehow largely a matter of luck that the person so arrived at

Reprinted from Wayne Riggs, "Why Epistemologists Are So Down on Their Luck," *Synthese* 158 (2007): 329–344.

the truth. Thus, conditions like safety and sensitivity are posited to rule out these sorts of lucky instances of true belief.

A striking feature of this literature, however, is that while many episte-mologists are busy arguing about which particular technical condition most effectively rules out the offensive presence of luck in true believing, almost no one is asking why it matters so much that knowledge be immune from luck in the first place. After all, the immunity-from-luck requirement is virtually the only thing in the theory of knowledge about which we can claim consensus. Surely this fact alone renders it worthy of explanation. Why do we care so much about the presence of luck in putative instances of knowledge? I think answering this question can tell us more about what knowledge is and why it matters to us than the usual technical collection of necessary and sufficient conditions. This is not to deride the project of providing such conditions for knowledge, but my project here is different. I would like to explain the place knowledge holds in our value system in a way that will both help us understand the phenomenon we are trying to capture with our technical theories, as well as account for the fact that knowledge is, at least sometimes, something of great value.

So the gauntlet has been thrown down. It is now up to me to give an enlightening account of why we care so much about luck-free true believ-ing. Before settling down to this task, there are several misunderstandings prevalent in discussions about so called "epistemic luck" that I wish to forestall. First of all, luck can enter into a situation in a variety of ways. Luck varies both in degree and in kind. If I narrowly avoid being crushed by a falling safe because of a freakishly strong gust of wind, everything I believe truly afterward is a matter of luck, simply because it is a matter of luck that I am alive to have any beliefs at all![2] But it is uncontroversial that luck of this sort does not undermine one's ability to know things. The tricky part, of course, is figuring out how to distinguish the undermining from the non-undermining sorts.

Philosophers have also pointed out that an anti-luck epistemology is doomed to failure because our ability to accomplish anything, whether it be to cross the street safely or to believe truths rather than falsehoods, is always and inevitably due in part to luck. We frail and causally inept hu-mans are never 100% responsible for anything we "accomplish," so any theory that requires the total absence of luck for knowledge is a recipe for instant skepticism. Agreed. But rather than obviate the possibility of an anti-luck epistemology, this merely demonstrates the need for a bit of sub-tlety in one's view. Knowledge is not incompatible with luck full stop. It is incompatible with luck of certain kinds to a certain degree. Further elucidation of this point will have to wait until more has been said about the nature of luck and the role it plays in undermining knowledge.

Why, then, are we so united in our opinion that knowledge is incompatible with luck of certain kinds to a certain degree? Why care about the presence of luck at all? After all, epistemologists are always saying that what we *really* care about is something to do with having true beliefs and avoiding false ones. If so, what difference does it make whether our proficiency at producing such results is due to luck or not? As I have indicated elsewhere,[3] I think the best answer to this question is that luck matters because knowing is an accomplishment. It is something that one deserves credit for. Analyses of knowledge all attempt to ensure that no putative instance of knowing actually counts as such if the believer was too lucky in coming to believe the truth. This unanimity can be explained by the conceptual connections among a family of concepts that includes credit, responsibility, attribution, and luck. In this paper, I will argue briefly for this claim, though the stronger case for it comes from the explanatory power afforded by the hypothesis that "knowing" is credit-worthy true believing. The latter part of the paper will be devoted to articulating this explanatory power, which includes the ability to explain the role of luck in the theory of knowledge, the value that knowledge has over and beyond the value of mere true belief, and, perhaps surprisingly, the reason for the persistence of the longstanding debate over internalism and externalism about epistemic justification.

So, the next two sections of the paper will articulate what I mean by "credit" and "luck," and how I take these to be related, both in general and specifically with regard to knowledge. Following that, I will address a pair of objections to my account of luck due to Duncan Pritchard, which threaten to derail the account of knowledge that I base upon that conception of luck. And the final section will pull together many of the points argued for in previous sections to illustrate the explanatory power alluded to above.

Before turning to these tasks, I want to acknowledge that I am not the first person to propose and defend a theory of knowledge in terms of credit-worthy true believing. Greco (2003) has made a persuasive case for his version of such a theory in his aptly titled paper, "Knowledge as Credit for True Belief." Although our views are quite similar in many respects, I will be developing and defending my own view independently of the arguments he gives in that paper. I believe that we are working toward similar goals, and I take my defence in this paper of a "credit-theory" of knowledge to be complementary to the arguments he gives, rather than either opposed to or in rivalry with them. Ideally, interested readers will find the combined case for a credit-theory of knowledge all the more persuasive.

2 Credit: Moral and Otherwise

The task of this section is to defend my claim that theories of knowledge are designed to eliminate luck from putative instances of knowledge because of our intuitions about the credit-undermining effect of luck. This, if true, would at least suggest that we are intuitively committed to the idea that knowing is an accomplishment—the kind of thing that one deserves credit for.

To begin, it might help to consider another area of philosophy that takes luck to be importantly detrimental to a certain kind of accomplishment. I am speaking, of course, of ethics and the "problem" of moral luck. The classic literature on moral luck originates with two papers on the subject, one by Nagel (1976) and the other by Williams (1976). Both were concerned with the fact that the correct moral evaluation of a person could vary, even when nothing within that person's control varies. This has the implication that our moral standing is not entirely up to us, but is sometimes at least a matter of luck. In particular, it seems that judgments of a person's moral responsibility for certain outcomes, whether good or bad, are undercut by the presence of luck. To take a famous example, suppose two people drive home drunk and veer onto the sidewalk. In one case, there happens to be a pedestrian on the sidewalk, and she is struck and killed. In the other case, there is no pedestrian, though had there been she would have been struck and killed. Here it seems that there is no difference between the two drivers that should make a moral difference. It is purely a matter of luck that one encountered a pedestrian and the other did not. But one is responsible for killing someone and the other is not, despite their apparent moral equivalence.

Ethical theorists have been worried about these sorts of cases because of the plausibility of the Kantian intuition that "ought implies can." If an outcome is due to something beyond our control, we cannot be held accountable for it. When we compare the two drivers, it is clear that the only difference in the two situations is one that is beyond either driver's control—the presence or absence of a pedestrian on the sidewalk at the precise time and place that the driver lost control. It appears that we cannot judge the two drivers differently since the only difference in their situations was beyond their control.

As anyone knows who has even a passing familiarity with this literature, there are many different responses to this problem. I am not suggesting that one is forced to agree that the two drivers must be evaluated identically. My purpose is simply to point out what motivates philosophers to worry about moral luck in the first place: a concern that the presence of luck undercuts responsibility. To the extent that some event is due to luck, it is not due to anything attributable to me. Indeed, that is what "luck" means in these cases. To say that it was a matter of luck that the pedestrian happened to be in that particular place is not to say that the event was metaphysically "random," or uncaused or any such thing. It is not to say that the pedestrian did not have clear reasons for being there or didn't intend to be there. AH of this is perfectly compatible with the (un)luckiness of the pedestrian's presence. All we mean by saying that the pedestrian's being there was a matter of luck is that her being there was in no way due to the *driver*. So, in cases of moral luck, the luck is significant because it appears to defeat what would normally be an attribution of moral responsibility.

How does this help us make sense of the importance of luck in epistemology? One possible lesson to draw from the consideration of luck in ethics is that luck plays the same role in epistemology. In other words, perhaps we care so much about eliminating luck from cases we are willing to call knowledge precisely because we consider knowing to be something attributable to the agent, in much the same way as acting rightly or wrongly is something attributable to the agent. Of course, I have already tipped my hand and made it clear that this is precisely the lesson that I draw from the analogy between moral luck and the kind of luck that undermines knowledge.

Resting one's case on an analogy is always risky, and I would like to have a more convincing and direct argument for the claim that knowledge is credit-worthy true belief. But in the absence of such an argument, I will offer two compensatory considerations.

First, if the significance of luck in the analysis of knowledge is not due to the conceptual connections among the notions of luck, responsibility, attributability, and the like, then to what is it due? (A rhetorical question rushes to the aid of an analogy. Perhaps my argumentative strategy is going in the wrong direction! Nevertheless . . .) I cannot think of any situation in which we actually care about the degree of luck involved in producing some outcome in which the reason for our concern is something other than our desire to determine whether, and if so to whom, to credit that outcome. Given that unanimity about anything in epistemology cries out for explanation, having one for the unanimity among epistemologists for the debilitating effect of luck on knowledge should surely count in favour of my view—at least until an alternative explanation is proposed.

Second, in the remainder of the paper I will explain in more detail what I mean by "luck" and "credit" and show that an account of knowledge in terms of these notions allows us to better understand some important issues in epistemology.

3 The Anatomy of Luck and Credit

Let's consider some simple cases in which we would unhesitatingly attribute an event or outcome to luck. (1) Sam wins 1 million dollars in a fair lottery. (2) Fran throws the basketball across the entire court to make a last-second shot, and it goes in. (3) Three people who operate a small department in a corporation are given promotions for the terrific work of the department. This includes Jerry, who is a complete slacker and rides completely on the coattails of his two talented workmates. (4) Barbara is walking through her house and stumbles on a piece of carpet that has just come loose. Alas, uncontrollably she falls against a table holding an expensive and treasured antique lamp. It falls and shatters.

I take it to be uncontroversial that luck plays a large role in the outcomes in each of these four scenarios. Sam's case of winning the lottery is probably the purest case of luck there is. In Fran's case, it is important to keep in mind that nobody is able consistently, or even more than rarely, to make a basketball shot from across the entire court. It simply is not within normal human abilities to do such a thing. Thus, it was almost entirely due to luck that Fran made the shot. If you need more convincing, imagine that Fran is not even a basketball player, but an enthusiastic (but untalented) fan who rushed onto the court after the game and throws the ball in her exuberance. And Jerry's case is definitely one of undeserved reward. But more importantly, the promotion was undeserved because it was awarded for a performance that Jerry had virtually nothing to do with. Jerry simply lucked out that he had such talented co-workers. (More on Barbara and the final example in a moment.)

There are several points I wish to draw from these examples. The first is that what we mean by "luck" in all these cases is that the agents in question did not bring about the events in question by their own agency. These events were out of the agents' control. We don't mean that the events were uncaused, undetermined or even necessarily random in any important sense. Even the lottery case, which we might suppose to be one that has a random element to it, can be changed to make this point. We might imagine that, unbeknownst to Sam, the lottery was fixed by a crime syndicate boss. The boss made the winning number the birthday of his girlfriend. In this case, it isn't even random which number is picked, but it is just as lucky for Sam that his number was a winner. So it is not the element of randomness in a lottery situation that makes winning it lucky for Sam—it's the fact that the event (Sam's ticket winning) is not Sam's doing.

The same holds true for the other three cases. Since no one has the ability to consistently make a full-court basketball shot, it is not something Fran has control over. It is not something she can *do*, even if she throws the ball and it goes in. That's why we call it a "lucky shot." Barbara, by hypothesis, cannot control her fall and thus the shattering of the lamp. And as I have already explained, Jerry is lucky that his co-workers are so good at their job and that his boss does not realize what a slacker he is. Again, we can modify the case to see that it is the lack of control or agency doing the work. Suppose that Jerry is quite crafty, and always looks busy when the boss is around. He also manages to claim credit for work that he does not do, and convinces the boss that his co-workers' claims to the contrary are the result of envy. Perhaps he even manipulated himself into this department because he knew that his co-workers would do good work that he could claim. Would we still say that Jerry's promotion is "lucky"? Undeserved, yes, but not lucky. His promotion in this case is due to his own efforts and cunning, though not due to his work ethic or competence at the job itself.

The second point to draw from these examples is that luck comes in degrees—it is not an all-or-nothing concept. This is especially clear in the basketball case. As we change the example, bringing the shot closer and closer to the basket, the degree of luck involved when someone makes the shot diminishes. Although there is always *some* element of luck in any basketball shot, there is no question that the degree of luck it is appropriate to attribute to a successful shot varies with the difficulty of the shot for the individual.

The third point is the obvious one that luck comes in both good and bad varieties. In other words, "luck" is itself value-neutral, and needn't imply that the event in question is either good or bad for anybody. It was a matter of luck for Sam that he won the lottery, but it was also a matter of (bad) luck that Barbara broke her favourite lamp. This goes slightly against common usage, since when we talk about "luck" *simpliciter* we tend to mean good luck, as in "he is a lucky guy." But it is also common to use it value-neutrally, as in "if it weren't for bad luck, I'd have no luck at all." In this paper, I will use "luck" value-neutrally.

The final point I wish to bring out with these examples is that there are two importantly different ways in which an event can be lucky for us. It comes down to two importantly different ways in which an event can fail to be something we "do." The first three cases highlight situations in which the event is not due to the agents' control because their actions simply have no significant effect on the outcome of those actions. Merely buying a lottery ticket is not a causally efficacious way to win the lottery (though it's better than not buying a ticket!). Nor is throwing the basketball the length of the court an efficacious way to make a basket (though, once again, it's better than not throwing it at all). Note that merely being in the causal chain that leads to the event, even being a necessary element of the causal chain leading to the event, is not sufficient to make an *agent* causally efficacious in bringing something about. So one way for an event to be lucky for agent *A* is for the agent to be causally inefficacious in bringing about the event.

But there is another way that an event can be a matter of luck for someone, and it is illustrated by the fourth example. In this example, Barbara is unlucky enough to stumble and break her lamp. Here, the main reason this event is unlucky for Barbara is *not* that stumbling into a lamp is not a causally efficacious way to break it, but rather that her stumbling (which caused the breaking) was inadvertent. She did not *mean* to stumble. She had neither the intention nor the desire either to stumble or to break the lamp. To make it plain that it is the inadvertence that is doing the work here, we can again change the example. Suppose that Barbara finds herself through no fault of her own in a room full of delicately balanced, expensive antiques. There is very little room to move, and any misstep will be very likely to cause something valuable to crash to the concrete floor. In this case, it is fairly clear that stumbling is a highly efficacious way to bring about something's destruction. But if Barbara stumbles in this scenario, it is still bad luck when something breaks (so long as she is being sufficiently careful).

So in the realm of action, to say that an outcome or event is "lucky" for someone is to say that it was, to some important degree, out of his or her control—it is not something that the agent brings about. But it is also important that there are two significantly different ways for an outcome to be lucky. It can be a matter of luck because you, the agent, were insufficiently causally efficacious is either of two senses: (1) the outcome was not causally due to the agent's *abilities*, or (2) the outcome was not intended by the agent.[4] The basketball example shows one way that these two kinds of luck can come apart, and the example of the room full of antiques shows another.

I have argued for this distinction elsewhere, so I do not want to bela-
bour the point.[5] But this distinction is important for two related reasons. First, in order for an agent to be fully responsible for some positive
event, and thus deserve full positive credit, her connection to the event
must not be undermined by the presence of either kind of luck just distinguished. With respect to her, the event must be neither causally indiffer-
ent to her abilities nor inadvertent. Interestingly, there is an asymmetry
here between what is necessary for positive credit and what is necessary
for negative credit. One can be held fully blameworthy (negative credit)
for something one did not intend, if one's inadvertence was due to something like culpable ignorance. But one can never be granted full positive
credit for bringing about some good end if one was not aiming to bring
about that end. Fortunately, I need only consider the simpler case—that
of the conditions for positive credit. Since my claim is that knowing is
credit-worthy true believing, the credit involved will always be positive
credit.

Second, there is an epistemic analogue to both these kinds of luck, and
so any definition of knowing in terms of luck must take both into account.
Here is a rough sketch of what I have in mind:

S knows that p iff:
(1) S believes p,
(2) p is true,
(3) S is sufficiently deserving of credit for the fact that she has come to
      hold a true belief in this instance.

Clause (3) must be spelled out in terms of avoiding both the kinds of luck
mentioned above. So,

S is sufficiently deserving of credit for the fact that she has come to hold a
true belief in this instance iff
(a) S's coming to hold a true belief in this instance is the product of S's
      actual abilities and
(b) S's coming to hold a true belief in this instance is not inadvertent.

Putting these two definitions together, we get:

S knows that p iff:
(1) S believes p,
(2) p is true,
(3a) S's coming to hold a true belief in this instance is the product of S's
      actual abilities and
(3b) S's coming to hold a true belief in this instance is not inadvertent.

Again, roughly speaking, in order for an agent's true belief that p to meet condition (3a), it must be the case that forming true beliefs of the sort that p is something that S is ordinarily able to do. One way to fill this out more specifically is to say that condition (3a) is met when and only when S's belief that p is the product of a reliable belief-forming process. Since I want to keep my analysis of knowing at a general enough level to be compatible with a variety of more specific theories of knowledge, I will refrain from committing myself to any more specific formulation of condition (3a).

Condition (3b) is a little trickier to explain. When is S's coming to hold a true belief in this instance inadvertent? It is not necessary that S have the conscious intention of forming a true belief when coming to believe p. Ordinary folks rarely, if ever, meet such a strange condition. But something like a "desire for one's beliefs to be true rather than false" must be sufficiently operative in regulating S's doxastic performance in the production of p for S to be credited with knowing, rather than merely believing p. The classic example of a failure of this sort of regulatory influence is wishful thinking. When someone believes something mainly because he wishes it were true, he does not have the intention of believing something false. Nor does he have the intention of believing something because he wishes it were true. What has happened is that the psychological mechanism of wishful thinking has short-circuited his normal belief-forming mechanisms, and so has screened off the influence of his desire for truth. He still has the desire, but it is not exerting its usual causal regulatory influence in the production of the belief that p. If the belief happens to be true, he is due no credit for it because his believing something true in this case was inadvertent.

4 Whose Luck, Which Credit?

Before going on to argue for the advantages of construing knowing as true belief for which one deserves credit, I want to address an objection that strikes at the very heart of my project. As I have made clear, there are deep conceptual connections between the notion of credit, as I am using it, and the notion of luck. I have argued that our distaste for lucky true belief is what motivates our contemporary analyses of knowledge, and in particular motivates the analysis that I prefer. If my account of luck is wrong in a substantive way, then the analysis of knowledge which I motivate in terms of that notion of luck is similarly cast into doubt. In my discussion and my examples, I have consistently treated "lucky" events as those events that are outside the control of the agent for whom they are lucky. And the intuitive connection between luck and credit depends upon this feature of luck. But Pritchard (2005), in one of the very few philosophical discussions of luck in the literature, considers a conception of luck in terms of this sort of lack of control, and concludes that it will not do. He argues that an adequate account of luck need not impose a "lack of control" condition at all. He prefers a modal conception of luck according to which

(L1) If an event is lucky, then it is an event that occurs in the actual world but which does not occur in wide class of the nearest possible worlds where the relevant initial conditions for that event are the same as in the actual world.

and

(L2) If an event is lucky, then it is an event that is significant to the agent concerned (or would be significant, were the agent to be availed of the relevant facts). (Pritchard, 2005, pp. 121–125).

Both (L1) and (L2) express only necessary conditions for luck, but while he admits these conditions are somewhat vague, Pritchard seems to be committed to taking their conjunction to amount to a set of necessary and sufficient conditions for an event's being lucky. I want to defend my "lack of control" thesis against Pritchard's objections, as well as point out a few problems with his own modal analysis of luck.

Pritchard gives two arguments against the "lack of control" account of luck. The first reiterates a point made by Latus (2000, p. 167) that, while the Sun's coming up this morning was an event that was out of my control, we would not ordinarily consider its rising to be *lucky*. Thus, lack of control over an event can at best be a necessary condition that allows in all kinds of events that are not intuitively counted as lucky. But he denies lack of control even this role in an analysis of luck, arguing instead that his modal account captures all the intuitive force of the lack of control provision, without being subject to its flaws.

Pritchard's second objection addresses *epistemic* luck directly, by considering the status of beliefs, and in particular simple perceptual beliefs. We do not have any sort of "direct control" over these beliefs, and so it would seem that our having these beliefs is always out of our control, hence lucky. But if that is the case, on my view one would never have perceptual knowledge, because the having of such beliefs would always be a matter of luck for me, and hence never creditable to me. I will address these objections in order.

The first thing to ask about Pritchard's appeal to Latus's example is whether we do, in fact, ever consider the rising of the Sun to be lucky. I think there are cases where we do, but I must admit that as a general rule, we do not think of the Sun's rising in the morning as a matter of luck. Given that the rising of the Sun is beyond my control, I must also admit that my lack of control over event E is not a sufficient condition for the occurrence of E being a matter of luck for me. But neither of Pritchard's two conditions (L1) and (L2), is sufficient by itself for luck either. The question is, why does Pritchard abandon lack of control as one of the necessary conditions that are jointly sufficient for luck? The closest he comes to giving an answer to this is in the following passage:

A further motivation for employing (L1) as a condition on luck is that it can explain why . . . lack of control [is] closely related to, but not essential to, luck. This is because if one has control over a certain event, such that one is able to (typically) determine that a certain outcome obtains, then that is naturally understood as implying that in a wide class of relevant near-by possible worlds that outcome is realized and therefore not lucky (just as (L1) would predict). (Pritchard, 2005, p. 123)

Here, Pritchard seems to argue that his condition (L1), which requires that the lucky event be absent in a wide class of relevant near-by possible worlds, will do a better job of ruling in and out the right cases than a lack of control condition. Furthermore, Pritchard seems to believe that we think that a lack of control is somehow constitutive of the luck relation between an individual and an event because we are conflating "having control" with "high likelihood of occurrence." It would then be natural to conflate "lack of control" with "unlikelihood of occurrence." Thus, we come to think that lack of control is necessary to luck, when really it is unlikelihood that matters.

But a brief consideration of some examples suffices to show that Pritchard's two conditions on luck are not themselves sufficient, and moreover that it is precisely the lack of control condition that is missing. Indeed, the lesson of these examples is that Pritchard has gotten the significance of unlikelihood and control precisely backward. In an admirably clear paper Coffman (2007, DOI: 10.1007/s11229-006-9046-8) offers an example that purports to show that an account of luck that fails to incorporate a "lack of control" clause is insufficient. In fact, it is an entire class of examples.

Suppose that, at time t, S performs a morally significant action such that there was just before t a large chance that S would not perform that action at t. For concreteness, suppose that S chooses at t to make a large donation to Oxfam, where there was just before t a large chance that S would not so choose at t. [Pritchard's account of luck] entails that S is lucky with respect to her choosing at t to make a donation to Oxfam [. . .] More generally, [Pritchard's view] entails that any morally significant action such that there was a large chance its agent would not perform it is such that its agent is lucky with respect to its occurrence. (Coffman, 2007, DOI: 10.1007/s11229-006-9046-8)

This looks like a class of counterexamples to Pritchard's view, if we agree that an agent who chooses on the spur of the moment, against her ordinary inclinations, to do a morally significant action is not, in fact, lucky to have done so. While I am inclined to agree with this diagnosis, I think that Pritchard has a response that threatens to pull the teeth of this purported set of counterexamples. Recall that Pritchard's principle (L1) states that a lucky event is one that occurs in the real world, but "does not occur in wide class of the nearest possible worlds *where the relevant initial conditions for that event are the same as in the actual world*" (*emphasis added*). It seems that Pritchard has only to insist that the circumstances, whatever they were, that led our reluctant philanthropist to donate the money are part of the "relevant initial conditions" that must be the same in the nearest possible worlds in which the lucky event must not occur. But if the prompting events are present, then the action will be present. So, the event will not count as lucky on Pritchard's account, thus saving his view from the purported counterexamples.

Yet we cannot let Pritchard off so easily. After all, why should we grant that the relevant initial conditions include the prompting events of the donation? It seems that Pritchard owes us some account of how we determine the relevant initial conditions. If it were not for such purported counterexamples, perhaps we could make do with a rough and intuitive account of these conditions, but here some precision and objectivity are called for. Pritchard acknowledges this shortcoming of principle (L1), and is uncomfortable relying on bare intuition to provide us with the specification of which conditions are to be preserved in the cross-world comparisons. But, he concludes that the problem is not fatal, because the "relevant initial conditions" clause can be jettisoned if need be.

There are, of course, problems with this partial specification of luck, one of which is the inherent vagueness involved in the demand that the relevant initial conditions of the event should be the same in all the near-by possible worlds under consideration [. . .] One way around this problem could be to drop this clause and simply consider the (unrestricted) class of near-by possible worlds, on the grounds that this class of worlds will tend to be dominated by worlds in which the "relevant initial conditions" as we intuitively understand them are the same [. . .] Given this possible escape route, the objection is no longer fatal. (Pritchard, 2005, pp. 124–125).

But if this clause is jettisoned, then Pritchard has no reply to Coffman's example.

But it is instructive to consider how we would intuitively determine which initial conditions are relevant to the determination of the "luckiness" of an event for an agent. To do this, I think we need a slightly different example. Imagine a young basketball player who has tremendous natural and developed skills and displays them proficiently every day in practice. Unfortunately, he also has a terrible fear of failure which causes him to "choke" when he is actually playing a game against an opposing team. A typical performance during a game would be for him to take, say, 20 shots and miss all 20. And this is due to his fear interfering with his ability to deploy his impressive skills. But every once in a while, for no reason the player has ever been able to determine, he finds himself confident and calm for a moment or two during a game. One night he happens to have the ball in his hands when this occurs, and he shoots the ball. Absent his usually crippling fear, he makes a skilful shot, which goes in.

Are we tempted to say that this was a "lucky shot"? I don't think so. If he had taken the shot under the conditions of his typical fearfulness, and it had gone in, we would be tempted to call it a lucky shot. But in this case, the ball went in by virtue of his skills and abilities. Thus, we give him credit for making the shot, rather than calling it lucky. This looks like another case in which Pritchard's principle (L1) goes wrong. In a large class of nearby possible worlds (now unrestricted), our player misses the shot because he doesn't happen to have his moment of calm right then. If there were some principled, non-question-begging way to determine that the relevant initial conditions that had to be the same across the possible worlds we are comparing included whatever produced the calm confidence that the player experienced, then Pritchard might still have a way out. But in the example we are not even given an account of what causes the player's occasional periods of calm confidence. So it's very hard to imagine how we could be making any kind of intuitive judgment about whether that cause, whatever it is, is among the relevant initial conditions of the event. Yet I submit that we are in no similar uncertainty about whether the event was lucky. Our judgment about the luckiness of the event is conditioned on our judgment that the player was in control of the event, not on some nuanced understanding of what conditions are or are not included in a cross-world comparison.

Now this does not mean that a principle like (L1) is not still necessary in an adequate analysis of luck. It simply shows that such a principle, even in conjunction with (L2), is not sufficient. What is needed is a third principle:

(L3) If an event E is lucky for S, then E was either:
    (1) not the product of S's actual abilities, or
    (2) inadvertent with respect to S.

Notice that this principle incorporates the elements of the account of epistemic credit offered previously. Principle (L3) says, in short, that if E is lucky for *S*, then *S* does not deserve credit for *E*. This is precisely the relationship I think holds between luck and credit in general.

If we add this principle to Pritchard's first two, then we have a more adequate analysis of luck. In short, Pritchard was wrong to have abandoned the lack of control condition on luck. But if we add (L3), why do we still need (L1)? It seemed as if they were rivals to be decided between, not independently necessary conditions. But the initial objection raised by Pritchard shows why we must keep something like (L1). Even though the Sun rising this morning was not under my control, it was nonetheless not a matter of luck with respect to me. Pritchard is right to point out that lucky events must be modally remarkable, though I disagree with him on the details of what (L1) should look like. I think that the proper condition (L1) should be capturing is actual probabilistic unlikelihood, rather than his more sophisticated condition involving "close" possible worlds. But that is beyond the scope of this project. For now, I will rest content with having shown that Pritchard's account of luck is unsuccessful without the addition of a principle that incorporates the lack of control on the part of the lucky agent.

Pritchard's second objection to the "lack of control" thesis about luck is that we seem to lack precisely the kind of control over our beliefs that would be necessary for them to fail to be lucky with respect to us. He takes perceptual beliefs to be particularly problematic, because we seem to get them "willy nilly," without any sort of control at all. I recognize that this is one of the most difficult objections facing an account of knowledge in terms of credit. Responding adequately to it would require at least a paper of its own. However, I will offer two brief responses to indicate how I think such a response should go.

First, it is important to realize that perceptual believings are not as passive as epistemologists sometimes try to make out. Sosa (1991) has pointed out that we do not automatically believe everything that our senses report. When there is a cue in our environment that something may be abnormal about our current perceptual situation, we do not take our sensations at face value. Rather, we check to see what the abnormality is, and we compensate as best we can for it in what we believe. Thus, even knowledge that flows more or less directly from our faculties of perception, memory or introspection is still what Sosa calls "reflective knowledge," rather than a more brutish, non-reflective kind he aptly calls "animal knowledge."

Note that no human blessed with reason has merely animal knowledge of the sort obtainable by beasts. For even when perceptual belief derives as directly as it ever does from sensory stimuli, it is still relevant that one has *not* perceived the signs of contrary testimony. A reason-endowed being automatically monitors his background information and his sensory input for contrary evidence and automatically opts for the most coherent hypothesis even when he responds most directly to sensory stimuli. For even when response to stimuli is most direct, *if* one were also to hear or see the signs of credible contrary testimony that would change one's response. The beliefs of a *rational* animal hence would seem never to issue from *unaided* introspection, memory or perception. For reason is always at least a silent partner on the watch for other relevant data, a silent partner whose very *silence* is a contributing cause of the belief outcome. (Sosa, 1991, p. 240, *emphasis in original*)

Sosa is arguing that beliefs resulting from perception, memory or introspection are categorically the product of reason, though there are differences of degree between these beliefs and more deliberative beliefs in terms of how large a role reason plays in their production. But even if we grant this, Pritchard may still contend that beliefs in general are not the sorts of things that one can have control over. Thus, the more general issue of "voluntarism" is still to be addressed, which leads me to my second brief response to this line of objection.

It is important to understand the kind of control that is required for me to be able to make my case. It is not necessary that we have so-called "direct control" over our beliefs in order for my account of knowledge to be successful. It is a commonplace that we cannot choose to believe that *p* in the same way that we can choose to raise our arm or close our eyes. But such direct control over events is not necessary for one to deserve credit for them. All that is necessary is that one has the kind of control over one's beliefs that one typically has over other kinds of happenings that we rightly attribute to individuals. For example, we might attribute the success of a debate team to the hard work and brilliance of its coach, and credit her for that success. Yet having a successful debating year is not something the coach has direct control over.

I take the problem of "doxastic voluntarism" to be one of the most important objections to the analysis of knowledge in terms of credit that I offer here, and it deserves a paper unto itself. Although I cannot address this issue as effectively as I would like here, I will at least point out that a number of philosophers writing on this subject have argued that we do have the kind of control over our beliefs necessary to make them something for which we are rightly attributed credit. Interestingly, these philosophers come at this issue from a variety of perspectives, some from moral psychology, some from the free will debate, some from more traditional philosophy of mind, and some from mainstream epistemology.[6] I will have to settle for a promissory note that sense can be made of our having the requisite control over our beliefs necessary for the analysis of knowledge I provide. The promise, however, is at least backed by the support of the influential philosophers who have made similar cases recently.

I conclude that Pritchard has not succeeded in making the case that we can leave out a "lack of control" condition from our account of luck, at least as a necessary condition. This is crucial for my account of knowledge, because I have argued that knowing that p depends upon one's having control (of certain specified kinds) over the fact that one came to hold a true belief in the circumstances, and this part of the account of knowing explains the widely held intuition that knowing is incompatible with (certain kinds of) luck. If an event's being lucky for S did not imply that S lacks control over E, then this explanatory function of my account of knowing would fail.

5   The Payoff

Having laid out in somewhat more detail what luck and credit amount to, and how an analysis of knowledge can be given in terms of these notions, I want to point out some of the advantages of such an analysis. To begin with, I have already shown that this analysis can account for the significance of luck in putative instances of knowledge. As far as I know, no other account of knowledge has a good answer to the question, "Why must knowledge be (sufficiently) immune from luck?" unless it concedes, either implicitly or explicitly, that knowing is an achievement for which the knower deserves credit.

There are two other major problems in the theory of knowledge that this analysis sheds light on. First, there is what has been variously called the "value problem," the "Meno problem," and the "swamping problem."[7] All of these amount to the problem of accounting for the value that "knowing that p" has over and above the value that "believing-p-when-p-is-true" has. Several epistemologists have addressed this problem recently,[8] mostly with an eye towards showing that certain theories of knowledge (usually reliabilism) cannot solve the problem. But others have argued that a view much like my own *can* solve the problem. Greco (2003) defends an account of knowledge that, like my own, is given in terms of credit-worthy true belief, and he claims that this view can solve the value problem. And I have argued· that a version of reliabilism, suitably revised to reflect the notion of credit, can also make some progress toward solving the value problem.[9]

The reason that credit-worthiness views of knowledge can solve the value problem is that they introduce a new vector of value: credit. Traditional reliabilist theories have trouble accounting for the extra value knowledge has over true belief because the only elements of the theory are true belief and reliability. But the value of reliability derives entirely from the product that is reliably produced. Thus, any value that reliability might have is "swamped"[10] by the value inherent in any true belief. A true belief is not made more valuable by being produced reliably. But if knowing that p always entails that one deserves credit for having achieved a true belief, then this introduces something besides true belief that is valuable. Even though deserving such credit requires that a belief be produced by a reliable process, deserving credit for the thing so produced is a further fact that confers additional value on the state of affairs of which it is a component.[11]

This point raises obvious and important questions about the nature and source of the value of credit, and these are questions that the credit-worthiness account of knowledge should address and, hopefully, satisfactorily answer. But for now, I will have to make do with the intuitive pull of a representative pair of examples.

Scenario 1 Suppose that a small child has fallen into a raging river, and will soon drown if not rescued. I leap into the dangerous waters, swim to the child and bring her safely to the shore.

Scenario 2 Once again, a small child is in danger of drowning in the river. I leap into the dangerous waters, but I'm unable to reach the child, despite exerting just as much effort and displaying just as much courage and skill as in Scenario 1. It simply is not enough in this scenario to allow me to reach the child. However, in leaping into the water, I dislodge a fallen branch which falls in to the water. The swirling current carries it to the child, who is thereby able to stay afloat until she is carried ashore further downstream.

In both scenarios, the good outcome comes to pass—the child survives. But I would prefer Scenarios 1 to 2, because in Scenario 1 the good outcome is attributable to me. Of course, the difference in value between the two scenarios pales beside the value of the child's survival, but the difference is nonetheless there.

Besides offering hope of solving the value problem, the credit-worthiness account of knowledge also explains both the source of the internalist/externalist controversy and the fact that neither side has ever achieved victory. The controversy arises because, while proponents of each side agree that "knowing" must preclude lucky true belief in some way, they focus on different *kinds* of luck that undermine knowledge.[12] Until it is understood that an adequate account of knowledge must preclude both kinds of knowledge-undermining luck, these approaches will be seen as rivals rather than complementary elements of a single account of knowledge.

But if we see that knowing is an achievement, and that for S to achieve X is for S's abilities and intentions to be sufficiently credit-worthy for bringing X about, then it is clear why both internalist and an externalist conditions on whatever is needed for knowledge in addition to true belief are necessary. An agent cannot be said to be credit-worthy for having a particular true belief, p, unless the process, method, habit, trait or what have you that produced it is objectively reliable. That is because objective reliability is a mark of having an ability. This may need to be suitably indexed to an environment, as Sosa (1991) does on his version of reliabilism, but the fact remains that it is an externalist, objective condition that must be met for an agent to be sufficiently credit-worthy for her belief.

Furthermore, the credit-worthiness account of knowing explains why S's desire or intention to have true beliefs must also be operative in the production of the true belief as well. This ensures that S is employing her own best epistemic standards in coming to believe p—that she is being epistemically responsible. While meeting one's own best epistemic standards (or being epistemically responsible) is not a universally accepted condition of internalist justification, it is at least a common one. So the credit-worthiness account of knowing demands both external and internal conditions to be met for an agent to be sufficiently credit-worthy to be said to know that p, and does so in a way that ties those conditions to what makes knowing more valuable to us than merely being right.

So the credit-worthiness account of knowing has the advantages of explaining the relevance of luck to knowledge claims, of showing promise in solving the value problem, and of explaining the need for both internalist and externalist conditions on whatever turns true believing into knowing. I think these are powerful advantages and warrant taking seriously this view of knowing. Admittedly, it is an analysis at a very high level of abstraction. As I have pointed out at several points, this rubric for knowing is compatible with a variety of different specific theories of knowledge. Yet, at the same time, it does impose a substantive constraint on such theories.

Notes

1. The arguments and ideas in this paper have been in development for a while, and I would like to thank a number of people for their contribution to that development. For many helpful discussions on these topics, I'd like to thank Steve Ellis, Linda Zagzebski and the students in my graduate epistemology seminar—Mary Gwin, Ben

Hagy, Matthew Hodge, Robert Johnson and Shyam Patwardhan. And thanks to Karen Antell for her comments on an earlier draft.

2. Unger (1968), p. 160.

3. See Riggs (1998, 2002a, b).

4. I don't mean to suggest here that the agent must have formed a conscious intention to do X in order for her to be creditable with X. But if there is nothing even remotely intentional involved in bringing about the event (e.g., an intention, desire, practical reason), then the event is lucky in an important respect with respect to the agent.

5. See Riggs (1998).

6. For a representative sample, see Hieronymi (2006), Raz (1999), Adler (2002), Owens (2000) and Audi (2001).

7. See Kvanvig (2004) and Zagzebski (2000).

8. See Kvanvig (1998, 2004), Jones (1997) and Zagzebski (2000).

9. Riggs (2002b).

10. Kvanvig (2004).

11. For a defence of this claim, see Riggs (2002b). For a more extended defence of a similar claim, see Sosa (2003).

12. See Riggs (1998) for a fuller defence of this claim.

References

Adler, J. (2002). *Belief's own ethics*. Cambridge, MA: MIT Press.

Audi, R. (2001). Doxastic voluntarism and the ethics of belief. In M. Steup (Ed.), *Knowledge, truth, and duty* (pp. 93–111). Oxford: Oxford University Press.

Coffman, E. J. (2007). Thinking about luck and making it pay off. *Synthese*. DOI: 10.1007/s11229-006-9046-8 (this issue).

Greco, J. (2003). Knowledge as credit for true belief. In: M. DePaul, & L. Zagzebski (Eds.), *Intellectual virtue: Perspective from ethics and epistemology* (pp. 111–134). Oxford: Oxford University Press.

Hieronymi, P. (2006). Controlling attitudes. *Pacific Philosophical Quarterly, 87(1)*, 45–74.

Jones, W. (1997). Why do we value knowledge? *American Philosophical Quarterly, 34*, 423–439.

Kvanvig, J. (1998). Why should inquiring minds want to know? *The Monist, 81,* 426–451.

Kvanvig, J. (2004). *The value of knowledge and the pursuit of understanding.* Cambridge: Cambridge University Press.

Latus, A. (2000). Moral and epistemic luck. *Journal of Philosophical Research, 25,* 149–172.

Nagel, T. (1976). Moral luck. *Proceedings of the Aristotelian Society, 76,* 136–150.

Owens, D. (2000). *Reason without freedom.* London: Routledge.

Pritchard, D. (2005). *Epistemic luck.* Oxford: Oxford University Press.

Raz, J. (1999). *Engaging reason.* Oxford: Oxford University Press.

Riggs, W. (1998). What are the chances of being justified? *The Monist, 81,* 452–472.

Riggs, W. (2002a). Beyond truth and falsehood: the *real* value of knowing that *P. Philosophical Studies, 107,* 87–108.

Riggs, W. (2002b). Reliability and the value of knowledge. *Philosophy and Phenomenological Research, 64,* 79–96.

Sosa, E. (1991). *Knowledge in perspective.* Cambridge: Cambridge University Press.

Sosa, E. (2003). The place of truth in epistemology. In M. DePaul, & L. Zagzebski (Eds.), *Intellectual Virtue: Perspective from ethics and epistemology* (pp. 155–179). Oxford: Oxford University Press.

Unger, P. (1968). An analysis of factual knowledge. *The Journal of Philosophy, 65,* 157–170.

Williams, B. (1976). Moral luck. *Proceedings of the Aristotelian Society, 76,* 115–135.

Zagzebski, L. (2000). From reliabilism to virtue epistemology. In G. Axtell (Ed.), *Knowledge, Belief and Character* (pp. 113–122). Lanham, MD: Rowman & Littlefield.

14   Knowledge and Credit

Jennifer Lackey

Abstract

A widely accepted view in recent work in epistemology is that knowledge is a cognitive achievement that is properly creditable to those subjects who possess it. More precisely, according to the *Credit View of Knowledge*, if S knows that *p*, then S deserves *credit* for truly believing that *p*. In spite of its intuitive appeal and explanatory power, I have elsewhere argued that the Credit View is false. Various responses have been offered to my argument and I here consider each of these objections in turn. I show that none succeeds in undermining my argument and, thus, my original conclusion stands—the Credit View of Knowledge is false.

A widely accepted view in recent work in epistemology is that knowledge is a cognitive achievement that is properly creditable to those subjects who possess it. More precisely, according to the *Credit View of Knowledge*, if S knows that *p*, then S deserves *credit* for truly believing that *p*. So, for instance, Ernest Sosa claims that "[b]elief amounts to knowledge when apt: that is to say, when its correctness is attributable to a competence exercised in appropriate conditions" (Sosa 2007, p. 92). Similarly, John Greco argues that ". . . knowledge attributions can be understood as credit attributions: when we say that someone knows something, we credit them for getting it right" (Greco 2007, p. 57). And Wayne Riggs holds that "S knows that p only if being right about p in this instance is attributable to S as a cognitive agent" (Riggs forthcoming, p. 1 of ms.).[1]

But what exactly does it mean for a subject to be deserving of credit for a true belief? Different answers to this question are provided by the various proponents of the Credit View. According to Sosa, ". . . we might

Reprinted from Jennifer Lackey, "Knowledge and Credit," *Philosophical Studies* 142 (2009): 27–42.

understand success due to an agent's competence as success that *manifests* that competence, a special case of the manifestation of a disposition" (Sosa 2007, p. 80, original emphasis). In contrast, Greco understands credit in causal/explanatory terms, such that a subject deserves the relevant kind of credit when she believes truly *because of* her reliable cognitive faculties. More precisely, S deserves credit for her true belief that p when S's reliable cognitive faculties are the most salient part of the cause explaining why S holds the true belief in question. And Wayne Riggs claims that "Knowing that p . . . requires truly believing p in a way that is neither veritically lucky nor accidental. Under those conditions, one is creditworthy for having come to a true belief" (Riggs forthcoming, p. 3 of ms.). Veritic luck, according to Riggs, is what is present in a lucky guess, and "one avoids accidental true belief when something like a 'desire for one's belief to be true rather than false' is sufficiently operative in regulating one's doxastic performance in the production of the belief" (Riggs forthcoming, pp. 2–3 of ms.).

Despite these different conceptions of credit, however, all proponents of this view of knowledge agree that credit is deserved for those true beliefs that qualify as knowledge, but not for those acquired in Gettier or Gettier-type situations. Such a claim has a great deal of intuitive appeal, which is often emphasized by considering other kinds of achievements: when Allen Iverson, for instance, makes a much needed 3-point shot in a basketball game, this is a success that is due to his impressive athletic ability. Now compare this to my making a 3-point shot, which would undoubtedly be purely the result of good luck. In both cases, the ball ends up in the basket after being shot from behind the 3-point line, but only in the former is the player deserving of credit for this success. Similarly, according to proponents of the Credit View, true belief acquired in a case of knowledge is a success that is due to the subject's cognitive ability, but true belief in Gettier or Gettier-type situations is a success that is due to good luck. Thus, while true belief is acquired in both cases, it is only in the former that the subject is deserving of credit for this cognitive achievement.

It should be clear that the Credit View, if correct, has enormous explanatory power. First, it provides an explanation of the widely accepted thesis that knowledge is incompatible with luck. If a subject's true belief is the result of good luck, then this success is not properly attributable to her cognitive faculties and is, thus, not an instance of knowledge. Second, and related, such a view sheds light on what is absent in Gettier and Gettier-type cases: when a success, cognitive or otherwise, is disconnected from a subject's ability, then it is not an achievement creditable to the subject herself. And, finally, it explains the additional value that knowledge has over justified belief that is merely accidentally true: just as a basket made through athletic ability is more valuable than one made via good luck, so, too, hitting upon the truth through cognitive ability is more valuable than doing so via good luck.

In spite of its intuitive appeal and explanatory power, I have elsewhere argued that the Credit View is false.[2] One of my central arguments against this view relies on the following type of case:

CHICAGO VISITOR: Having just arrived at the train station in Chicago, Morris wishes to obtain directions to the Sears Tower. He looks around, approaches the first adult passerby that he sees, and asks how to get to his desired destination. The passerby, who happens to be a lifelong resident of Chicago and knows the city extraordinarily well, provides Morris with impeccable directions to the Sears Tower by telling him that it is located two blocks east of the train station. Morris unhesitatingly forms the corresponding true belief.

I have argued that while Morris clearly knows on the basis of testimony that the Sears Tower is two blocks east of the train station, he does not deserve the requisite kind of credit for truly believing this proposition, thereby showing that the Credit View of Knowledge is fundamentally incorrect. In a nutshell, I argued that whatever notion of credit the proponent of the Credit View invokes, it has to be robust enough to rule out subjects in Gettier and Gettier-type situations from deserving credit for their true beliefs, yet weak enough to allow subjects in testimonial cases, such as Morris in CHICAGO VISITOR, to be deserving of credit for their true beliefs. And this, I argue, is a task that is doomed to failure.[3]

Various responses have been offered to my argument and I shall here consider each of these objections in turn. I shall show that none succeeds in undermining my argument and, thus, my original conclusion stands—the Credit View of Knowledge is false.

1   Credit and Knowledge Go Hand in Hand

One of the more common responses to CHICAGO VISITOR can be put in the form of a dilemma: either Morris doesn't deserve credit for the truth of the belief that he acquires on the basis of the passerby's testimony, but then neither does he acquire the relevant testimonial knowledge; or Morris does acquire the testimonial knowledge in question, but then so, too, does he deserve credit for the truth of the belief about the whereabouts of the Sears Tower. Either way, credit and knowledge go hand in hand.

The first horn of this dilemma is defended by Riggs in the following passage:

The first task . . . is to call into question the attribution of knowledge to Morris in Lackey's example. I am surprised that it is offered as an uncontroversial example of testimonial knowledge. Why on earth would we say that Morris knows where the tower is when he has picked a stranger at random, and unhesitatingly (and, one assumes, unreflectively) accepted what that person said? On the face of it, this is terrible epistemic practice. Intuitively, more is required on the part of the hearer than simply opening his brain and putting into it whatever some random stranger has to say. (Riggs forthcoming, p. 10 of ms.)

According to Riggs, then, since Morris does not acquire the testimonial knowledge in question in CHICAGO VISITOR, it clearly fails to provide a counterexample to the Credit View of Knowledge. The second horn of the dilemma is advanced by Greco. He begins by arguing that his preferred virtue-theoretic view provides a unique approach to analyzing testimonial knowledge. He writes:

Often theories of testimonial knowledge are divided into two camps. On the first kind of theory, what is important for testimonial knowledge is that the source of testimony is in fact reliable. On the second kind of theory, it is also important that the believer knows, or at least justifiably believes, that the source is reliable. From a virtue-theoretic perspective, however, a third kind of theory becomes plausible. Namely, testimonial knowledge requires that the *believer* is a reliable *receiver* of testimony. (Greco 2007, p. 63)

Given this conception of testimonial knowledge, Greco argues that if Morris indeed possesses the relevant testimonial knowledge in CHICAGO VISITOR, then he must be a reliable receiver of testimony, which in turn requires ". . . reliable capacities for discriminating reliable sources of testimony from unreliable sources" (Greco 2007, p. 63). According to a virtue-theoretic account of testimonial knowledge, then, if Morris knows the whereabouts of the Sears Tower, he *does* deserve credit for this true belief. In particular, "his success is grounded in his ability to discriminate good from bad testimony and is therefore attributable to him" (Greco 2007, p. 63).

By way of response, there are several points I shall make which, together, address both horns of this dilemma. Let me begin with Greco's purportedly alternative, virtue-theoretic conception of testimonial knowledge. Now, the first point to notice is that his claim that the acquisition of testimonial knowledge requires a reliable receiver of testimony is neither novel, nor unique to virtue-theoretic accounts. Indeed, in my own work on testimony,

I have argued that a "properly functioning or reliable recipient of testimony" condition needs to be added to *any* plausible account of testimonial knowledge, regardless of whether it is non-reductionist, reductionist, virtue-theoretic, and so on.[4] While I have argued that such a requirement involves a hearer's exercising the capacity for being appropriately sensitive to defeaters and possessing minimal positive reasons,[5] Greco argues that it involves reliable capacities for discriminating reliable sources of testimony from unreliable sources. The point I wish to emphasize here, however, is that if a virtue-theoretic approach opens new doors in the epistemology of testimony, requiring that testimony be reliably received is not one of them.

This leads to my second point: given my own requirements on testimonial knowledge, I certainly never presented CHICAGO VISITOR as involving a hearer who is "simply opening his brain and putting into it whatever some random stranger has to say," much like a robot would. On my view, testimonial knowledge requires that Morris exercise the capacity to be appropriately sensitive to defeaters—if, for instance, he would accept the passerby's testimony even if he appeared highly intoxicated or told him that the Sears Tower was in France, then he would clearly not acquire the knowledge in question. In addition, I require the presence of minimal positive reasons for rational acceptance of testimony—if Morris had no relevant beliefs about humans' general testifying habits, or about the reliability of humans when offering directions, or about Chicago, and so on, then, once again, I would deny that testimonial knowledge has been acquired. If these rudimentary abilities are what Greco means by ". . . reliable capacities for discriminating reliable sources of testimony from unreliable sources," then we agree on whether Morris acquires knowledge in CHICAGO VISITOR. However, this is not sufficient for creditworthiness. For surely Morris's being reliable at discriminating between the intoxicated and the sober, and between those who believe that the Sears Tower is in France and those who believe that it is in Chicago, does not explain in any substantive sense why he ends up with a true belief about the precise whereabouts of the tower. Instead, it is the *passerby's* familiarity with the city of Chicago and *her* experience with the Sears Tower that explains *his* true belief. In other words, Morris's knowledge is not success because of *his* cognitive ability but success because of the *passerby's* cognitive ability.

But what if Greco means something more robust by ". . . reliable capacities for discriminating reliable sources of testimony from unreliable sources" than the rudimentary abilities I require for testimonial knowledge? What if he instead means that, relative to a given domain, I am able to reliably discriminate between the competent and the incompetent, the sincere and the insincere? For instance, I have enough experience with stories in *The New York Times* being confirmed by multiple other independent sources, and with the ludicrous cover stories of *The National Enquirer*, to deliberately choose the former and avoid the latter in my consumption of news. In this way, I am playing a significant role in the acquisition of these testimonial beliefs. What if something similar were required of Morris in CHICAGO VISITOR? If Greco generally requires this sort of reliable discrimination for testimonial knowledge, he will be forced to embrace a limited form of skepticism regarding our testimonial beliefs. To see this, let us ask: what does an honest, competent passerby look like that would enable Morris to reliably distinguish her from a dishonest or directionally challenged one? Sure, when asking for directions, most of us would reliably choose an adult passerby rather than a toddler, a sober person rather than one who appears intoxicated, one with a native accent rather than one with a camera and a guidebook, and so on. But among adult, sober, humans not carrying guidebooks, there can be substantial variation in the competence and sincerity of their testimony. Thus, on any ordinary reading of CHICAGO VISITOR, Morris could have plausibly approached a competent-looking liar or a directionally challenged speaker in much the same way that he did an honest, knowledgeable, Chicago resident when asking for assistance in finding the Sears Tower. But if Morris's behavior is equally compatible with all of these outcomes, then it is clear that he is not reliably discriminating reliable sources of testimony from unreliable ones in the robust sense under consideration. Hence, Greco will be forced to deny that knowledge can be acquired in the sort of scenario envisaged in CHICAGO VISITOR.

Some may think that it is not necessarily a problem if we deny that knowledge is acquired when we find ourselves in new cities asking for directions. But situations similar to that found in CHICAGO VISITOR arise with respect to countless other areas in which testimony is not only frequently accepted, but is also intuitively acceptable. Most of us, for instance, are not very reliable at discriminating reliable testimony from unreliable testimony when people whom we first meet report their names, occupations, family histories, and so on. For in such circumstances, liars and incompetents typically fail to have identifiable marks announcing their deception and incompetence, and those who are honest and competent in such matters rarely can be picked out as such. To put this more concretely, how on earth would you be able to tell that the woman next to you on the airplane is lying when she tells you that her name is Amanda, or that she is a nurse, or that she has 3 children, or that she lives in Albuquerque? Similar considerations apply when we find ourselves confronting entirely new areas of inquiry for the first time. How, for instance, would a high school student learning U.S. history for the first time be able to tell that her teacher is slightly off with respect to most of his dates about wars? And would the student who is taking physics for the first time be in any position whatsoever to assess the reliability of his teacher? Moreover, infants and young children often engage in even less discriminatory behavior on a wider range of topics than many adults do. For instance, many 3-year-olds would not be able to reliably discriminate reliable preschool teachers from unreliable ones, or reliable televisions programs from unreliable ones, or reliable books from the public library from unreliable ones. Thus, the Credit View of Knowledge may be saved by making the requirement about what the reliable reception of testimony amounts to extremely demanding, but it does so at the cost of embracing a limited version of skepticism about testimonial knowledge. I, for one, think this price is far too high to pay.

Thus, I have argued for three central conclusions: (1) on any plausible conception of testimonial knowledge, Morris can be said to know the whereabouts of the Sears Tower in CHICAGO VISITOR; (2) Morris does not deserve the requisite credit for the truth of this belief; and (3) denying Morris knowledge in CHICAGO VISITOR leads to a limited form of skepticism about testimonial knowledge.

2 Credit Can Be Shared

A second general response offered to CHICAGO VISITOR is that my argument implicitly relies on assuming that credit for true belief cannot be shared. For instance, Greco argues that:

. . . credit for success, gained in cooperation with others, is not swamped by the able performance of others. It's not even swamped by the outstanding performance of others. So long as one's own efforts and abilities are appropriately involved, one deserves credit for the success in question. (Greco 2007, p. 65)

In a similar spirit, Riggs argues:

Why do we suppose that someone has to get *all* the credit? Why not just say that both the parties involved get some credit for the recipient's true belief? It is vanishingly rare for any human being to accomplish anything completely on the basis of his own powers and abilities alone. And yet, even in many of those cases, we unhesitatingly attribute such accomplishments to people. (Riggs 2009, p. 215.)

Thus, once it is acknowledged that credit can be shared by both speaker and hearer, it is thought that there is no longer a problem posed by CHICAGO VISITOR for the Credit View of Knowledge.

By way of response, let us begin by examining the second part of Greco's claim above; namely, that so long as one's own efforts and abilities are appropriately involved, one deserves credit for the success in question. Now, the crucial task for Greco, and indeed for any proponent of the Credit View, is to flesh out the precise sense in which a subject's own efforts and abilities must be "appropriately" involved for creditworthiness. But there is a serious problem lurking: a subject's own efforts and abilities are often importantly involved in the acquisition of true beliefs in *Gettier-type cases*, which stand as a paradigm of the sorts of true belief that are supposed to lack creditworthiness. The sense in which a subject's own efforts and abilities must be "appropriately involved," then, must be strong enough to rule out deserving credit in Gettier-type cases, yet weak enough to render subjects deserving of credit in ordinary cases of mundane knowledge, such as that found in CHICAGO VISITOR. The prospects for successfully striking this delicate balance are, I suggest, bleak.

To see this, consider the following familiar Gettier-type case: while driving from Iowa to Illinois, Fiona looks out her window, sees a barn in the distance, and forms the corresponding true belief. As it happens, the barn she sees is the only real one, completely surrounded by barn façades that the local farmers have erected to make their community appear prosperous. Now, in this Gettier-type case, Fiona's own efforts and abilities are surely importantly involved in her truly believing that there is a barn in the field: she trusts her reliable faculty of vision and she forms her belief on the basis of her veridical perceptual experience of a barn. Yet, according to the proponent of the Credit View—who maintains that deserving credit for holding a true belief is what renders knowledge different from and more valuable than those beliefs that are true merely by luck—Fiona *does not* deserve credit for truly believing that there is a barn in the field. In contrast, Morris, whose own efforts and abilities have very little to do with why he has a true belief about the whereabouts of the Sears Tower, *does* deserve credit for his true belief. Here is the problem: Fiona's own efforts and abilities are far more intimately and importantly involved in the true belief that she acquires than Morris's are in the true belief that he acquires. For Fiona's reliable vision and veridical perceptual experience shoulder much of the explanatory burden for why she formed the true barn belief, while Morris's ability to choose a conscious, adult human to ask for directions shoulders very little of the explanatory burden for why he formed a true belief about the whereabouts of the Sears Tower. Sure, Fiona is lucky to have looked at the one real barn, but Morris is also lucky to have chosen a Chicago resident who knows the city extraordinarily well when asking for directions. The central difference in luck in these two cases is that Morris's *environment* is far better suited than Fiona's is to the formation of true beliefs. But this difference has *nothing* to do with the epistemic effort, virtues, or faculties of the respective subjects, and hence it has nothing to do with whether they deserve credit for their true beliefs.

To my mind, this is the central problem afflicting the Credit View of Knowledge. Let us formulate this objection even more precisely as follows:

Creditworthiness Dilemma: Either the notion of creditworthiness operative in the Credit View of Knowledge is robust enough to rule out subjects from deserving credit for the truth of their beliefs in Gettier-type cases, but then neither is credit deserved in CHICAGO VISITOR-type cases; or the relevant notion of creditworthiness is weak enough to render subjects deserving of credit for the truth of their beliefs in CHICAGO VISITOR-type cases, but then so, too, is credit deserved in Gettier-type cases.

As should be clear, either horn of this dilemma undermines the Credit View of Knowledge at its core. For, on the first horn, credit may be adequately blocked in Gettier-type cases, but only at the expense of also blocking credit in countless cases where testimonial knowledge is intuitively present despite minimal work being done on the part of the hearer. And, on the second horn, credit is secured in cases of testimonial knowledge where such minimal work is done by the recipient, but only at the expense of also securing credit in Gettier-type cases. Either way, the Credit View not only fails to shed light on what is absent in Gettier-type cases, but it also fails to explain the additional value that knowledge has over merely accidentally true belief.

It should also be clear that my argument against the Credit View does not at all depend on assuming that credit for true beliefs cannot be shared. Surely, there are all sorts of ways in which this can happen. You and I may jointly work on a scientific experiment and thus both be equally responsible for the truths that we uncover. Or you and I may collaborate while bird watching and, through our combined ornithological knowledge, together correctly identify the bird in the distance as a golden eagle. There are also cases of testimonial knowledge where shared credit between speaker and hearer does not seem entirely misplaced. If I do extensive research on your background in medicine and choose to consult you because of your outstanding credentials, it may be appropriate to say that I deserve some credit for the truth of the belief I form on the basis of your medical testimony because my cognitive faculties were so intimately involved in my choice of source. None of this, however, addresses in any way the fundamental problem that the Creditworthiness Dilemma poses to the Credit View of Knowledge.

3 Sosa's Response

A third response to CHICAGO VISITOR can be found in recent work by Sosa, where he takes up the problem that testimony generally poses for the Credit View of Knowledge. He writes:

> Any belief that is knowledge must be correct, but must it be correct due to an epistemic competence? That seems strained at best for knowledge derived from testimony. . . . Others no doubt made the relevant discovery—perhaps a historian, or a detective, or a scientist, or a physician—and the information was then passed on, resulting in some later recipient's belief, whose correctness then owes little to his own individual accomplishment, if all he does is to receive the information. (Sosa 2007, p. 93)

By way of answering this problem posed by testimonial knowledge, Sosa argues that despite the minimal role played by the epistemic competence of the hearer in the acquisition of a true testimonial belief, such a subject still deserves *partial credit* for the correctness of her belief, and this suffices for the relevant notion of creditworthiness operative in the Credit View of Knowledge. For instance, a quarterback may exercise a competence by throwing a touchdown pass, but this individual accomplishment is part of a broader competence in the whole offensive team. Thus, while the individual player certainly deserves credit for this great pass, it is only partial given the crucial role of his other teammates. Similarly, Sosa argues that in the case of testimonial belief, the individual hearer exercises a competence by receiving the testimony in question, but this individual performance is part of a broader competence in a collective social group. Hence, "[t]he correctness of one's belief is still attributable in part to a competence seated in oneself individually, but the credit that one earns will then be partial at best" (Sosa 2007, p. 95).

But if partial credit is sufficient for the Credit View of Knowledge, then doesn't Sosa face the second horn of the Creditworthiness Dilemma? In particular, while partial credit may be weak enough to render subjects deserving of credit for the truth of their beliefs in cases of testimonial knowledge, won't credit likewise be deserved in Gettier-type cases? Sosa provides a threefold response to this question. First, he distinguishes among at least two different kinds of Gettier cases. On the one hand, there are what we may call *traditional Gettier cases*, a paradigm of which is the following:

NOGOT/HAVIT: Anya has ample evidence supporting her belief that Nogot, who works in her office building, owns a Ford. She has, for instance, repeatedly seen Nogot driving a Ford to and from work, Nogot frequently wears a T-shirt that boasts, "Proud owner of a Ford," Nogot showed Anya sale papers that indicated that he had purchased a Ford, and so on. From her justified belief that Nogot owns a Ford, Anya draws the existential conclusion, "Someone in my office building owns a Ford." It turns out that Nogot does not in fact own a Ford—he has been driving his sister's car and forged the sale papers he showed to Anya. But the existential conclusion that Anya drew from her false belief is nonetheless true because Havit, who also works in her office building, does indeed own a Ford.

On the other hand, there are what we may call *extended Gettier cases*, a paradigm of which is the barn façade case discussed in the previous section. What is the precise difference between these two kinds of Gettier cases? Various proposals have been offered in the literature. Duncan Pritchard, for instance, argues that "intervening luck" is found in traditional Gettier cases, where this is understood as "luck that intervenes between ability and success, albeit in such a way that the success is preserved" (Pritchard 2008, p. 16). In contrast, Pritchard claims that extended Gettier cases involve "environmental luck," where this is understood as luck that ". . . concerns the environment in which ability generates that success" (Pritchard 2008, p. 16). For our purposes, we can simply grant at this point that there is a difference between traditional and extended Gettier cases without settling what exactly it amounts to. Now, given this distinction, Sosa moves to his second point where he argues that not even partial credit is deserved for the truth of the beliefs acquired in traditional Gettier cases. To this end, he distinguishes between a competence explaining the *existence* of a belief and a competence explaining the *correctness* of a belief. For instance, consider again the NOGOT/HAVIT case. According to Sosa, "[t]he reasoning by way of Nogot does of course help explain why the believer has that belief, but it does not in the slightest help explain its correctness" (Sosa 2007, p. 96, emphasis in the original). Finally, Sosa grants that, because extended Gettier cases involve apt belief that is correct in a way that is sufficiently

attributable to the exercise of the subject's competence in its proper conditions, knowledge is indeed acquired in such cases.[6] Thus, with respect to
extended Gettier cases, he essentially accepts the second horn of the CRED-
ITWORTHINESS DILEMMA.

In response to Sosa's view, I shall raise three concerns and offer one main
argument against this sort of defense of the Credit View of Knowledge. Let
us begin with the concerns. First, Sosa introduces the problem as one involving testimonial knowledge in general. But to my mind, focusing on the
issue of testimony at this level of generality misses the force of CHICAGO
VISITOR-type cases in particular. There are countless ways in which we go
about choosing our testimonial sources and forming beliefs on the basis of
what they say. For instance, in seeking an answer to one's question about
World War II, one may thoroughly investigate all of the expert historians
on this topic, evaluate their reputations, credentials, and areas of special-
ization, and then deliberately choose the best to consult on this matter. Or
when choosing one's source of news, one may do extensive research on the
reliability, backgrounds, and experience of the writers for all of the major
newspapers and then specifically choose *The New York Times* as one's regu-
lar newspaper. In such cases, it does not seem strained to say that such
recipients of testimony deserve some credit for the truth of the relevant
beliefs that they acquire, and thus it is not clear that they even pose a problem for the Credit View of Knowledge. At the other end of the spectrum,
however, is a case such as CHICAGO VISITOR, where the hearer in question chooses the first conscious adult passerby that he sees in a new city
to ask for directions. Here, the absolutely minimal work being done by
the recipient of testimony casts serious doubt on the plausibility of him
deserving credit for the truth of his belief. And, of course, there are all sorts
of cases in between, where more than the minimal work in CHICAGO
VISITOR, but less than that involved in the WWII and *New York Times*
beliefs, is done by the hearer in a testimonial exchange. Thus, I think that
treating the problem posed to the Credit View of Knowledge as one involving testimonial beliefs in general groups together under a single category
importantly different epistemic phenomena.

This leads to my second concern: it is not clear that even partial credit is
deserved by Morris of the true belief that he acquires in CHICAGO VISI-
TOR, nor is it obvious that most of the credit in such a case is due to a
"complex social competence" (Sosa 2007, p. 97). To see this, recall that the
analogy that Sosa relies on in elucidating the notion of partial credit at
issue is that of the quarterback who throws a touchdown pass but shares
credit of this accomplishment with the other members of his team. It is

quite intuitive that credit is shared in such a case: the quarterback is exercising his competence as a football player in successfully throwing the ball to one of his teammates, and yet the touchdown pass would not happen without the other players, one of whom must actually catch the ball in order for it to even be a touchdown pass. But what competence does Morris exercise in asking the first adult, conscious passerby that he sees for directions that justifies granting him partial credit for the truth of the belief in question? Of course, as already noted, he knows not to ask a toddler, an obviously intoxicated adult, and so on. This minimal cognitive work, however, seems more analogous to a quarterback who knows not to throw the football to a member of the opposing team or to the fans watching the game, but is quite unaware that the player who in fact catches his pass is well-situated to do so. In other words, just as Morris is not at all responsible for choosing a lifelong resident of Chicago who knows the city extraordinarily well, the parallel situation in football would be that of a quarterback who is not at all responsible for choosing a player who is in an excellent position to catch his pass. But then attributing partial credit in either case for the respective successes seems misplaced. Moreover, why is the correctness of Morris's belief primarily creditable to a complex social competence rather than simply to the individual passerby's competence? After all, it is the passerby's extensive experience with the city of Chicago, and with the whereabouts of the Sears Tower in particular, that shoulders most of the explanatory burden for Morris's true belief. Indeed, everything could be exactly as it is in CHICAGO VISITOR, except Morris asks a passerby who always confuses the Sears Tower with the John Hancock building and thus ends up conveying incorrect directions to him. The broader complex social competence is the same in both cases, yet Morris acquires a true belief in only one, depending on whether the passerby in question knows the layout of the city of Chicago. To my mind, this casts serious doubt on attributing creditworthiness to a broader social competence in CHICAGO VISITOR rather than simply to the individual testifier.

Third, granting knowledge in extended Gettier cases is arguably an unwelcome concession. While defending this claim at length lies beyond the scope of this paper, it is worth pointing out that such a conclusion flies in the face of some deeply held intuitions in epistemology. For instance, the barn beliefs of a subject who is surrounded by barn façades will fail to be both sensitive and safe; that is, such a subject would still believe that there is a barn even if she were in fact seeing a barn façade, and such a subject would believe that there is a barn without it being so that there is one. Thus, granting knowledge in such cases is incompatible with any epistemological view that includes as a necessary condition for knowing either sensitivity or safety.[7] Moreover, it is a widely accepted thesis that subjects who are unable to discriminate among relevant alternatives in a given domain do not possess the knowledge at issue.[8] For instance, if I am completely unable to distinguish between a Siberian Husky and an Alaskan Malamute, then it is quite plausible to conclude that I do not know that the dog next door is a Siberian Husky even if in fact it is one. Once again, then, granting knowledge in extended Gettier cases is at odds with a deep commitment in epistemology since subjects in barn façade cases are unable to discriminate between the one real barn and the many surrounding fakes.

At this point, I have focused on some broad concerns with appealing to partial credit to vindicate the Credit View of Knowledge. I shall now turn to my direct argument against Sosa's defense of this view. To begin, consider the following:

TWO SHEEP: While taking a walk in the country in late October, Nolan stops in front of a farm to admire the animals. After seeing what appear to be two sheep grazing in the field next to a large rock, he forms the belief, "There are two sheep in this field." It turns out that while one of the sheep Nolan sees is real, the other is a goat that the farmer has dressed up as a sheep for Halloween. However, behind the rock and out of Nolan's sight, there is a second real sheep, thereby rendering his belief that there are two sheep in the field true.

Notice, first, that, by all accounts, TWO SHEEP seems to be a traditional Gettier case. If one wishes to adopt Pritchard's distinction, for instance, the luck involved is of the intervening rather than the environmental sort; that is to say, the luck at issue intervenes between Nolan's perceptual ability and his success in acquiring a true belief, albeit in such a way that the success is preserved. This stands in contrast to the barn façade case, where the luck is in the environment in which the subject's cognitive ability successfully acquires a true belief. But, however, one wishes to cash out the difference between traditional and extended Gettier cases, TWO SHEEP seems to clearly fall in the former camp.

Moreover, if one wishes to quibble about this conclusion, it is certainly not difficult to construct a modified version of one of Gettier's own counterexamples along lines similar to those found in TWO SHEEP. Consider, for instance, the following:

TWO HIRES: Bennett's office is currently in the process of hiring two new employees, and he has excellent evidence for believing that the jobs will be offered to two of his friends, Smith and Jones. For instance, Bennett overheard his boss saying on the phone that Smith and Jones will get the positions, he knows that they are both exceptionally well-qualified for the jobs, and he saw employee papers on the secretary's desk with the names of Smith and Jones written on them. Bennett also has excellent reason for thinking that Smith and Jones each have ten coins in their respective pockets, having seen both of then empty the contents of their pockets, count the coins, and then place them back in their pockets. From this, Bennett concludes that the two men who will get the jobs have ten coins in their pockets. It turns out that while Smith will get the job and does have ten coins in his pocket, the boss misread the name of the other applicant when he spoke on the phone and had the secretary write up the employee papers—in fact, the job is going to James not Jones, who also just so happens to have ten coins in his pocket.

As was the case in TWO SHEEP, Bennett's belief about the new hires is true, justified, and yet not an instance of knowledge. The similarity of TWO HIRES to Gettier's own cases, however, completely precludes trying to deny that it is a traditional Gettier case.

The second point to notice about TWO SHEEP is that Nolan clearly deserves partial credit for the truth of his belief that there are two sheep in the field in question. For at least part of the justification for his belief—namely, that involving the first real sheep—is grounded in a veridical visual experience, which in turn results from the exercise of a competence in proper conditions. Otherwise put, part of Nolan's true belief is successful precisely because of his cognitive ability. Similar considerations apply in the case of TWO HIRES: Bennett clearly deserves partial credit for the truth of his belief that the two men who will get the jobs have ten coins in their pockets since part of the justification for this belief is based on excellent evidence that appropriately grounds a justified inference. Of course, in both cases, part of the belief in question is not creditable; namely, that part that is riddled with accidentality. But the thesis under consideration is whether "[p]artial credit might hence suffice for aptness, and so for animal knowledge, without risk of Gettier refutation" (Sosa 2007, p. 97). And this conclusion is precisely what is called into question by TWO SHEEP and TWO HIRES.

It is worth pointing out that the conclusion here defended can be applied to a response offered by Pritchard on behalf of the Credit View of Knowledge. According to Pritchard, while proponents of this conception of knowledge are right about intervening luck—which he claims is incompatible with achievement—they are wrong about environmental luck—which is compatible with achievement.[9] According to Pritchard, then, if one is in a traditional Gettier case, one is denied credit for successfully acquiring a true belief and this, it is urged, goes some way toward explaining the value that knowledge has over accidentally true belief. But, as we have seen above, there can be traditional Gettier cases, such as TWO SHEEP and TWO HIRES, that involve true beliefs properly regarded as achievements that are nonetheless riddled with intervening luck. Pritchard's strategy, then, fails to vindicate even the spirit of the Credit View of Knowledge.

But, one might argue, there are two different senses in which one might be said to deserve partial credit for the truth of a given belief. On the one hand, this may be understood in terms of *part of the correctness* of a given belief being *fully attributable* to a competence seated in the subject. On the other hand, this may be understood in terms of the *full correctness* of a given belief being *partially attributable* to a competence seated in the subject. For instance, it may be argued that in TWO SHEEP, part of the correctness of Nolan's true belief is fully attributable to a competence seated in him—namely, the part grounded in the veridical experience of a real sheep. In contrast, the model of the football analogy employed by Sosa to explain testimonial knowledge may be understood as suggesting the latter sense, in which the full correctness of a testifiee's belief is partially attributable to a competence seated in her and also partially attributable to the individual testifier or to a broader social competence. Given this, it may be argued that TWO SHEEP and TWO HIRES fail to provide relevant counterexamples to Sosa's view since the notion of partial credit at work in these cases is not the same notion at work in his view.

By way of response to this objection, there are two central points I should like to make. First, it is questionable whether the distinction between these two notions of partial credit can be rendered clear enough to underwrite this defense of the Credit View. For instance, let us take an ordinary case of testimonial knowledge: I come to believe that the bird on the tree is a Harris's hawk, in part because I am able to identify it as a hawk—rather than, say, an eagle or a falcon—and in part because your expert ornithological testimony enables me to specifically classify it as a Harris's hawk. There is a perfectly reasonable sense in which the truth of my Harris's hawk belief here seems to involve partial correctness that is fully attributable to me. The generic hawk part of my belief is fully attributable to me, and the Harris's part of my belief is fully attributable to your expert testimony. Yet, according to the objection under consideration, this notion of partial credit is not relevant to the notion at work in the Credit View of Knowledge, and thus the proponent of this view will be forced to maintain that all cases of this sort exemplify full correctness that is partially attributable. This, I take it, will strike many as *ad hoc*. Moreover, it is questionable whether sense can be made of full correctness being partially attributable to a subject. Doesn't the truth of our beliefs nearly always rely in part on non-attributable features of our situation, such as the epistemic suitability of our environments? Given this, is the *full* correctness of our beliefs ever partially attributable to us?

Second, and more importantly, even if a tenable distinction could be made between partial correctness being fully attributable and full correctness being partially attributable, there are still problems for the Credit View of Knowledge involving instances of the latter kind of partial credit. To see this, consider the following:

TWO JOKES: Isabella has been working on a complicated and lengthy mathematical proof in her college dorm room for several days. After she stopped working on the first day, her roommate, Catherine—who happens to be a bit of a jokester—tiptoed over to Isabella's desk and removed a negation sign from one of the steps of the proof. After Isabella finished work on the second day, Catherine again crept over to her desk, but this time she added a negation sign to one of the steps of the proof. It just so happens that Catherine's two jokes—the removal of a negation sign and the addition of a negation sign—offset one another, and thus enabled Isabella, who was completely unaware that her work had been tampered with, to correctly proceed with her proof and ultimately end up with a true conclusion at the end of her third day of work.

There are several features of this case that are worth noting. First, TWO JOKES is clearly a traditional, rather than an extended, Gettier case. The good luck involved in Catherine's two jokes offsetting one another intervenes between Isabella's ability and her success, but in a way that preserves the truth of her belief. This stands in contrast to the luck involved in extended Gettier cases, where the environment is ill-suited for success, but the subject in question just so happens to arrive at a true belief. Second, Isabella clearly deserves partial credit for the true mathematical belief that she comes to accept as a result of completing her proof. For arriving at the true belief in question involved successfully working through numerous steps of a complicated and lengthy proof over the course of 3 days. Indeed, without all of Isabella's meticulous and competent work, she never would have arrived at the true mathematical conclusion that she ends up holding.

Given this, the correctness of her belief is surely at least partially attributable to an individual competence seated in her. Third, the sense in which Isabella deserves partial credit for the true belief in question does not involve partial correctness being fully attributable, at least not in the sense found in TWO SHEEP and TWO HIRES. In these latter two cases, the subject at issue holds a complex belief whose justification is in part grounded in a veridical experience that results from the exercise of a cognitive excellence and in part the result of good luck. The composite nature of this belief may be what underwrites the intuition that such a case involves partial correctness being fully attributable to the subject. In TWO JOKES, however, Isabella's mathematical belief does not in any sense have such a nature. She holds a simple belief that owes it correctness to various sources, including her own competence, Catherine's two offsetting jokes, and good luck. Thus, to the extent that a distinction can be clearly made between partial correctness being fully attributable and full correctness being partially attributable, TWO JOKES is an instance of the latter, thereby ruling out a defense of the Credit View that relies on rejecting the former notion of partial credit.

Of course, the proponent of the Credit View of Knowledge may argue that partial achievement is not good enough for creditworthiness; full or complete achievement is necessary for properly deserving credit for success. But then the question arises: how does a testifiee, whose belief is true almost entirely because of the competence of the testifier, deserve credit for the truth of the belief that she acquires via testimony? And this brings us right back to where we started.

Acknowledgement

I am grateful to Marian David, Sandy Goldberg, members of the Northwestern Metaphysics and Epistemology Reading Group, audience members at the 2007 Midwest Epistemology Workshop at Northwestern University, and, especially, Baron Reed, for helpful comments on an earlier version of this paper.

Notes

1. See also Sosa (1991, 2003), Zagzebski (1996, 1999, 2003), Riggs (2002), Greco (2003), and Neta and Rohrbaugh (2004).

2. See Lackey (2007).

3. It should be noted that I include several kinds of counterexamples to the Credit View of Knowledge in my (2007), some of which do not involve testimonial knowledge.

4. See Lackey (2003).

5. See Lackey (2003, 2008).

6. It is only what Sosa calls animal knowledge that is acquired in extended Gettier cases; he still denies that subjects in such cases acquire what he calls reflective knowledge.

7. See, for instance, Nozick (1981), Sosa (2000, 1999, 2002), Williamson (2000), and Pritchard (2005).

8. For an early discussion of this thesis, see Goldman (1976).

9. See Pritchard (2008).

References

Goldman, A. I. (1976). Discrimination and perceptual knowledge. *The Journal of Philosophy, 73*, 771–791.

Greco, J. (2003). Knowledge as credit for true belief. In M. DePaul & L. Zagzebski (Eds.), *Intellectual virtue: Perspectives from ethics and epistemology* (pp. 111–134). Oxford: Oxford University Press.

Greco, J. (2007). The nature of ability and the purpose of knowledge. *Philosophical Issues, 17*, 57–69.

Lackey, J. (2003). A minimal expression of non-reductionism in the epistemology of testimony. *Noûs, 37*, 706–723.

Lackey, J. (2007). Why we don't deserve credit for everything we know. *Synthese, 158*, 345–361.

Lackey, J. (2008). *Learning from words*. Oxford: Oxford University Press.

Neta, R., & Rohrbaugh, G. (2004). Luminosity and the safety of knowledge. *Pacific Philosophical Quarterly, 85*, 396–406.

Nozick, R. (1981). *Philosophical explanations*. Cambridge, MA: The Belknap Press.

Pritchard, D. (2005). *Epistemic luck*. Oxford: Oxford University Press.

Pritchard, D. (2008). A defence of quasi-reductionism in the epistemology of testimony. *Philosophica, 78*, 13–28.

Riggs, W. D. (2002). Reliability and the value of knowledge. *Philosophy and Phenomenological Research, 64*, 79–96.

Riggs, W. D. (2009). Two problems of easy credit. *Synthese.*

Sosa, E. (1991). *Knowledge in perspective: Selected essays in epistemology.* Cambridge: Cambridge University Press.

Sosa, E. (1999). How must knowledge be modally related to what is known? *Philosophical Topics, 26,* 373–384.

Sosa, E. (2000). Skepticism and contextualism. *Philosophical Issues, 10,* 1–18.

Sosa, E. (2002). Tracking, competence, and knowledge. In P. Moser (Ed.), *The Oxford handbook of epistemology* (pp. 264–287). Oxford: Oxford University Press.

Sosa, E. (2003). The place of truth in epistemology. In M. DePaul & L. Zagzebski (Eds.), *Intellectual virtue: Perspectives from ethics and epistemology* (pp. 155–179). Oxford: Oxford University Press.

Sosa, E. (2007). *A virtue epistemology: Apt belief and reflective knowledge* (Vol. 1). Oxford: Oxford University Press.

Williamson, T. (2000). *Knowledge and its limits.* Oxford: Oxford University Press.

Zagzebski, L. (1996). *Virtues of the mind: An Inquiry into the nature of virtue and the ethical foundations of knowledge.* Cambridge: Cambridge University Press.

Zagzebski, L. (1999). What is knowledge? In J. Greco & E. Sosa (Eds.), *The Blackwell guide to epistemology* (pp. 92–116). Oxford: Blackwell.

Zagzebski, L. (2003). Intellectual motivation and the good of truth. In M. DePaul & L. Zagzebski (Eds.), *Intellectual virtue: Perspectives from ethics and epistemology* (pp. 135–154). Oxford: Oxford University Press.

E   Visions for Epistemology

15   Epistemic Injustice and a Role for Virtue in the Politics of Knowing

Miranda Fricker

Abstract

The dual aim of this article is to reveal and explain a certain phenomenon of epistemic injustice as manifested in testimonial practice, and to arrive at a characterisation of the anti-prejudicial intellectual virtue that is such as to counteract it. This sort of injustice occurs when prejudice on the part of the hearer leads to the speaker receiving less credibility than he or she deserves. It is suggested that where this phenomenon is systematic it constitutes an important form of oppression.

There is a growing sympathy with the idea that epistemology should look to ethics for conceptual tools to use in solving traditional epistemological problems. My aim here is to identify a role for virtue in accounting for both the rationality and the ethics of what must surely be our most basic and ubiquitous epistemic practice—the practice of gaining knowledge by being told.

I shall try to argue that a central difficulty in the epistemology of testimony is best handled by reference to a notion that belongs in the first instance to ethics, the notion of a *sensibility*. To this end I shall advance the idea of a *testimonial sensibility*: something that governs our responsiveness to the word of others so that, given the sensibility is properly educated, we may gain knowledge that p simply by being told that p. Next, on the assumption that such a sensibility incorporates a variety of intellectual skills and virtues that govern how much credibility the responsible hearer will attribute to different sorts of speakers in different sorts of circumstances, I shall identify a phenomenon of epistemic injustice with a view to homing

Reprinted from Miranda Fricker, "Epistemic Injustice and a Role for Virtue in the Politics of Knowing," *Metaphilosophy* 34 (2003): 154–173.

in on the particular virtue whose role it is, or should be, to pre-empt such injustice. The form of epistemic injustice in question happens when a speaker receives the wrong degree of credibility from his hearer owing to a certain sort of unintended prejudice on the hearer's part. The virtue I shall try to home in on, whose role it is to safeguard against such operations of prejudice, embodies a special sort of *reflexive critical openness* to the word of others. The possession of this virtue is presented as an important regulator in the politics of testimonial practice, though I shall suggest ultimately that its powers are limited.

1 Avoiding Intellectualism: The Word of Others

There is a certain impasse to be detected in a traditional approach to the epistemology of testimony.[1] When we try to account for what goes on in an informal discursive context when someone comes to know that *p* by an interlocutor's telling him that *p*, it can seem as if we must plump for one of two epistemological stories. It can seem as if we must either endorse the idea that the hearer gains knowledge just by being uncritically receptive to the speaker's word, so long as there are no explicit signals that scepticism is in order, or else endorse the idea that the hearer gains knowledge only in virtue of rehearsing an appropriate inference—an argument whose conclusion licenses believing what he has been told. Thus the choice of philosophical pictures can seem to be between sheer uncritical receptiveness on the one hand and intellectualist argumentation on the other.

The shortcoming of each is the allure of the other. The uncritical-receptivity model surely leaves us too open to believing anything people tell us, so that, in the absence of signals of untrustworthiness, we are licensed to be entirely uncritical.[2] Philosophical accounts of testimonial knowledge will require the speaker to be both competent and honest with respect to her assertion that *p*. But the experience of everyday life leaves us only too aware that human beings cannot systematically be relied on in respect of either. Crudely, people often get things wrong, out of innocent error, or perhaps because they fancy they know when really they don't. And of course people can also succumb to the temptation to mislead deliberately—for instance, because it is in their interests to do so. When these two types of unreliability are compounded with the obvious fact that such mundane things as haste, or misunderstanding the inquirer's purposes, or simple carelessness can lead a speaker to mispronounce even on something he is perfectly competent and ready to be honest about, it becomes clear that a blanket policy of accepting the word of others unmediated by any critical filtering would be justificationally lax. The mere absence of explicit signals for doubt is not enough to justify a general habit of uncritically accepting what other people tell one.

This shortcoming in the uncritical-receptivity model might draw one's sympathies towards the inferential model. As C. A. J. Coady (1992, 122–23) describes it, this common picture of testimony has it "that all knowledge by testimony is indirect or inferential. We know that p when reliably told that p because we make some inference about the reliability and sincerity of the witness." In an alternative formulation, John McDowell presents the inferentialist model as resting on the following assumption:

If an epistemically satisfactory standing in the space of reasons, with respect to a proposition, is mediated rather than immediate, that means the standing is constituted by the cogency of an *argument* that is at its occupant's disposal, with the proposition in question as conclusion. (McDowell 1998, 415)

On either formulation the inferential model is clearly invulnerable to accusations of justificational laxity, since it precisely requires that the hearer go in for a piece of reasoning that provides a justification for believing what she has been told. Inevitably this will usually be some sort of inductive argument—for instance, an argument about the individual speaker's past reliability on these matters, or about the general reliability of people like that about things like this. But the trouble now is that this requirement that the hearer avail herself of such an argument seems too strong, because too laborious intellectually. It simply does not match our everyday phenomenology of informal testimonial exchange, which presents learning something by being told as distinctly *un*-laborious and spontaneous. Surely an epistemic practice as basic to human life as being-told-things-by-someone-who-knows cannot possibly require all that *activity* at the level of propositional attitudes. If the hearer were genuinely supposed to consider (in however rule-of-thumb-ish a way) the likelihood that she has been told a truth, that would take at least a moment's hard-nosed assessment of a sort that simply does not tally with the effortless spontaneity characteristic of so much of our everyday testimonial exchange.

The advocate of the inferential model will naturally respond by emphasising that the mature hearer will normally rehearse her argument very readily and easily. But the more he is at pains to emphasise that such justificatory argumentation can be so swift as barely to be noticed, and might even be altogether unconscious, the more the model strikes one as a piece of intellectualism in a tight corner.

This problem with the inferential model now leads one back again to the picture on which the hearer is entitled, other things being equal, to be uncritically receptive to what she is told, for this picture of things can now be seen to retain something rather strongly in its favour: it more faithfully represents the phenomenology of our everyday exchanges. In the absence of explicit cues for doubt we do seem simply to accept most of what we are told without going in for any active critical assessment. An ordinary case might be that, as I make my way hurriedly to the train station, I ask a stranger what the time is, he tells me it is 4:30, and I simply, unreflectively, accept what he says. This unreflectiveness is underlined by the fact that if I do pick up on some cue for doubt—such as his saying it is 4:30 when I already know it cannot be later than four o'clock—then I experience a sort of intellectual shift of gear, out of that unreflective mode and into some more active one of critical assessment. It is only with this shift of gear that I might start to bring some argumentation to bear on the matter of my interlocutor's trustworthiness.

But now we may feel that the intuitive relevance of the evidence of past experience in how we are conditioned to receive the word of others has gone missing from the ordinary unreflective case. Surely one's knowledge of a particular speaker's track record, or one's general background assumptions about how likely it is that someone like this will speak the truth about something like that, must be somewhere in the offing? If such inductive considerations are wholly absent from our unreflective exchanges, imposing no constraint whatsoever upon what the hearer is entitled to accept, then this does seem to leave our ordinary unreflective exchanges in an unacceptable rational vacuum. This thought, then, casts the inferentialist model once again in a more favourable light. And so, perhaps, the oscillation continues.

The conclusion I suggest we should draw from these brief considerations is that what is needed to provide a suitable exit from the impasse is a picture of informal testimonial exchange that honours the everyday phenomenology of unreflective transparency between speaker and hearer, while none the less avoiding justificational laxity. We need a positive account of how the responsible hearer may spontaneously and non-inferentially give an appropriately critical reception to the speaker's word. This critical reception must be such that, reliably, when the hearer simply accepts what he is told by someone who knows, he is justified in simply accepting it. The reception will be one of openness to his interlocutor's assertions, yet critical too—the hearer's normal stance needs to find a philosophical characterisation such that it constitutes a *critical openness* to the word of others. Such a characterisation will be able to explain how, when we are told things, we are indeed able to acquire knowledge, and as effortlessly as the phenomenology suggests.

2   The Responsible Hearer

McDowell argues for the view that a hearer gains knowledge by testimony in virtue of exercising "doxastic responsibility"; and what it is to exercise doxastic responsibility is explained in characteristic Sellarsian terms of a "sensitivity" to one's place in the "space of reasons." As I understand this way of putting things, the idea of a "mediated standing in the space of reasons" is the idea of a state—a state of knowledge, for example—that has been arrived at by way of an appropriate sensitivity to the reasons for and against the proposition. This sensitivity need not manifest itself in the making of inferences or arguments—precisely not. As McDowell says:

What I am proposing is a different conception of what it is for a standing in the space of reasons to be mediated. A standing in the space of reasons can be mediated by the rational force of surrounding considerations, in that the concept of that standing cannot be applied to a subject who is not responsive to that rational force. (McDowell 1998, 430)

So, if the standing in the space of reasons is "knowing that p," then McDowell's proposal is that this knowing that p has as a background precondition that the knower has somehow exercised a sensitivity to surrounding reasons for and against taking it that p.

If one accepts this eminently acceptable proposal, then it is natural to move to the next question and ask, If not by our usual faculties of argumentation and inference, then by what rational capacity *is* the hearer able to be responsive to the rational force of surrounding reasons? The idea that the fulfilment of doxastic responsibility need not require argumentation is surely crucial to explaining how testimonial knowledge can be mediated yet direct (or, as I am putting it, critical yet non-inferential), but something further needs to be said to explain how the hearer does it. If she is not exercising her capacity for inference and argumentation, what rational capacity is she exercising?

McDowell is minded to say there is nothing to be explained here:

If we are not to explain the fact that having heard from someone that things are thus and so is an epistemic standing by appealing to the strength of an argument that things are that way . . . do we need some other account of it? I would be tempted to maintain that we do not. The idea of knowledge by testimony is that if a knower gives intelligible expression to his knowledge, he puts it into the public domain, where it can be picked up by those who can understand the expression, as long as the opportunity is not closed to them because it would be doxastically irresponsible to believe the speaker. That idea seems obvious enough to stand on its own epistemological feet; the formulation makes as much sense of the idea that knowledge can be transmitted from one subject to another as any purported explanation could hope to confer on it. (McDowell 1998, 437–38)

But I am not sure that nothing more is needed here. One does not have to be an advocate of inferentialism to think that something more is called for in order to explain how a hearer can count as exercising doxastic responsibility if her acceptance of what she has been told is not based on any sort of inference or argumentation.

Let me be clear that the non-satisfaction I am registering is not about what doxastically responsible behaviour *consists in*, as if I were demanding that some rule-like norms or principles be explicated. No doubt there are a number of norms general enough to be expressed as guiding principles of a hearer's doxastic responsibility, but we don't need them in order to have a reasonably firm idea of what that responsibility requires. Indeed, those of us sympathetic to virtue-theoretical accounts of responsibility might be quite happy with the possibility that there were no such principles available at all. The question of what constitutes doxastic responsibility for a hearer, then, is not my worry. The worry is rather that the claim that a hearer exercises such responsibility without making any inferences leaves one wondering *how*—by what capacity of reason—she is supposed to do it.

If we look to Coady, we find tacit support for the view that something is needed on this score, since he does make a brief suggestion, albeit rather too brief to provide more than a pointer. He asserts we have a "learning mechanism" that operates critically though non-inferentially in the hearer to determine the balance of trust. He says:

What happens characteristically in the reception of testimony is that the audience operates a sort of learning mechanism which has certain critical capacities built into it. The mechanism may be thought of as partly innate, though modified by experience, especially in the matter of critical capacities. It is useful to invoke the model of a mechanism here since the reception of testimony is normally unreflective but is not thereby uncritical. (Coady 1992, 47)

This seems exactly right, but as it stands the metaphor of a learning mechanism remains philosophically and psychologically mysterious. So much so that we are not much better off with this idea of a mechanism than we were with the non-metaphorical but equally elusive idea of a hearer's doxastic responsibility exercised non-inferentially.

It is time to take stock. What we are looking for is some mode of rational sensitivity that yields spontaneous, non-inferential judgements. And we are also looking for a mode of rational sensitivity that is learned, and learned in an ongoing way so that it is constantly developing and adjusting itself in the light of experience and critical reflection. I propose that at this point epistemology should turn to ethics for sustenance. For in ethics we find a notion that seems to me to fit the bill: the notion of a *sensibility*. An ethical sensibility yields genuine *judgements*—interpretative judgements, such as "That was cowardly," or immediately practical judgements, such as "I ought to confess"—yet these judgements are not conclusions to arguments. (They may permit of reconstruction as conclusions to arguments, but that is quite another thing. A rational reconstruction of a human practice does not automatically constitute a proper characterisation of it.) A well-trained ethical sensibility will presumably incorporate a range of relevant conceptual and social-perceptual skills, but most importantly it will comprise ethical virtues. The central place of virtue explains how a sensibility issues in non-inferential judgements. The virtuous person does not have to *work out* that an act was cowardly, or that the culprit should own up; he just sees that this is the case; he just knows. Continuing in this broadly Aristotelian vein, we might add that the virtuous person is able to perceive the moral colourations of things spontaneously in this way in virtue of his sensibility being formed by a proper ethical training or upbringing.

This idea of ethical training will be important for present purposes, but we shall need a more historicist or socially situated conception than we find in Aristotle. Let me suggest, then, that we think of the training of a sensibility as involving at least two distinct streams of input: social and individual—in that order. One develops an ethical sensibility by becoming inculcated with a historically and culturally specific way of life—or as Alasdair MacIntyre puts it, an ethical "tradition"[3]—where this is to be construed as a matter of ongoing ethical socialisation. There again, it is from an irreducibly individual life experience that one gains a particular sentimental education, and in that respect the ongoing formation of one's sensibility is something distinctly individual. Together these two streams of input—collective and individual—continually generate a person's sensibility.

The deliverances of an individual's sensibility, then, are shaped by a set of background interpretative and motivational attitudes, which are in the first instance passively inherited from the ethical community but thereafter actively reflected upon and lived out in one way or another by the reflective individual. Ethical responsibility demands that there be an appropriate critical link between the traditional moment in which the individual gains her ethical socialisation and the experiences life offers her—experiences that may sometimes be in tension with her ethical socialisation so as to prompt critical reflection on the sensibility which she has otherwise simply inherited.[4]

This idea of a sensibility gives us a picture of how judgements can be rational yet unreflective, critical yet non-inferential. It presents us with a rational capacity that is comprised of virtues, that is inculcated in the subject through a process of socialisation, and that permits of ongoing correction and adjustment in the light of experience and critical reflection. Thus we are confronted with a rational capacity unlike anything commonly entertained in epistemology, and a version of it seems to me to fit the bill as the explanation of how a hearer might be able to give an unreflective yet critical reception to the word of another. With this in mind, we must now ask what the epistemic analogue of an ethical sensibility would be like for testimony. I would like to think that this is not only a worthwhile philosophical question in its own right but also an important question at the level of epistemic practice. For if one wants to know how to improve one's performance as a receiver of the word of others—if one wants to become more responsible and successful as a hearer—then one had better know what, if not one's skills of inference and argument, one should be trying better to develop.

3   Testimonial Sensibility: Critical Openness to the Word of Others

We are setting our sights on the possibility that responsible hearers in unreflective testimonial exchanges exercise a *testimonial sensibility*. This possibility introduces the idea that our responses to the testimony of others are learned and internalised through a process of *epistemic* socialisation—a social training of the interpretative and affective attitudes in play when we are told things by other people. We might think of it as part of our epistemic "second nature."[5] Here, again, I suggest there is in the first instance a passive social inheritance and then a sometimes-passive-sometimes-active individual input from the hearer's own experience. Together these two streams of input mean that our normal unreflective reception of what people tell us is conditioned by a great range of collateral experience. Just as the experiences pertinent to the training of ethical virtues are internalised in the sensibility of the virtuous person, so the body of collective and individual testimonial experience is internalised by the responsible or virtuous hearer, rendering it immanent in her testimonial sensibility.

It is through the inductive influence of this body of experience that we may learn, reliably enough, to assume trust when and only when it is in order. Our perception of speakers and their assertions comes to be informed by an inductive conditioning relating to what sorts of people are likely to convey the truth about which sorts of subject matters, just as in the ethical case our perception of agents and their actions comes to be informed by a motivational conditioning relating to what sorts of actions are ethically called for in which sorts of situations.

There is more to be said, however, about what sorts of experiences properly feed into a testimonial sensibility. They will chiefly be experiences of testimonial exchanges had by the individual and the wider community. But it must be acknowledged that these experiences can only have a rational impact on sensibility under a socially rich description. This is because the only way they can have inductive significance is by being such as to support or undermine existing habits of response concerning what sorts of people are trustworthy in what sorts of situations; which sorts of incentives to deceive are likely to be acted upon by which sorts of people; and so on. A testimonial sensibility, then, needs to be shaped by collective and individual experiences of testimonial encounters described in rich, socially specific terms relating to the trustworthiness of speakers of different social types in different sorts of contexts. These descriptions cannot but involve common cultural stereotypes of intellectual authority or its lack, perhaps by way of related characteristics, such as openness or inscrutability, steadiness or flakiness, rationality or emotionality, dependability or deviousness, logicality or intuitiveness. . . . I use *stereotype* neutrally, but of course stereotypes are fertile ground for prejudice, so it is easy to see how a testimonial sensibility may come to embody the prejudices of the day. Where a testimonial sensibility is informed by stereotypes that are unfair—that is, where they are empirically unfounded—the sensibility will be both epistemically and ethically defective.

We shall return to this theme, but for the moment the point is rather that such elements of the social imagination as stereotypes of authority can be a perfectly proper part of a testimonial sensibility, for the necessary social richness of the body of testimonial experience which informs sensibility means that stereotypes are positively needed to oil the mechanism of our day-to-day exchanges. Hearers need spontaneously to perceive their interlocutors in a socially fine-grained way so that they can be appropriately responsive to all the subtleties of the interaction. Without this richness of social perception, many epistemically relevant cues will be missed. Consider, for instance, what complexity there can be in cues indicating how far one should interpret an interlocutor as *taking seriously* what he is asserting. Perhaps the hearer sees the speaker as entirely competent in all relevant matters, yet still her perception of him has to be responsive to all sorts of features of social location and discursive style that would not figure in any but the richest of social-psychological descriptions of the encounter.

If these remarks provide a reasonable working idea of *which* experiences feed into sensibility, is there something further we can say about *how* an individual takes them on in sensibility? Here again the task is to develop a parallel with the ethical case. An individual's testimonial sensibility will in the first instance be passively inherited. This passivity is justified, firstly, for the a priori reason that the body of judgements and attitudes which comprise a sensibility constitute the basis *from which* a hearer's doxastic responsibility emerges. And, secondly, for the empirical reason that even a minimally successful epistemic community must be operating with a broadly functional testimonial sensibility. But once light has dawned for a hearer, she will come to find that sometimes her experiences of testimonial exchange will be in tension with the deliverances of the sensibility she has passively taken on, in which case responsibility requires that her sensibility adjust itself to accommodate the new experience.

This might happen spontaneously, without active critical reflection on the part of the hearer, but it is more likely that she will need actively to bring critical thought to bear on her internalised habits of hearer response in order to shake them up sufficiently to effect the adjustment. If, for instance, a hearer is a teenager whose testimonial sensibility has contracted the defect of not taking seriously what old people say, and if this teenager finds himself one day struck by the veracity of his grandfather's stories of the war, he may experience a small epistemic revolution that requires some significant deliberative follow-through in terms of how he receives the word of the elderly quite generally. In so far as this teenager is doxastically responsible, he will effect an adjustment to his testimonial sensibility either directly, by way of a shift of social perception, or indirectly, by way of critical reflection. If the adjustment is direct, then he will undergo a Gestalt switch in how he perceives elderly speakers so that the adjustment to his testimonial sensibility is more or less instantaneous. If it is indirect, then active critical reflection on his habits of hearer response will first produce some sort of corrective policy external to the hearer's sensibility. (Perhaps this teenager disciplines himself when in conversation with the elderly, "Don't be dismissive. . . .") Given time, and all being well, such a corrective policy will become internalised as an integral part of his sensibility, so that it comes to be implicit in his newly conditioned perception of elderly speakers.

Whether direct or indirect, then, we can see how the responsible hearer's sensibility matures and adapts in the light of ongoing testimonial experience. Its claim to be a capacity of reason crucially depends on this adaptiveness, for otherwise it would be little more than a dead-weight social conditioning that looked more like a threat to the justification of a hearer's responses than a source of that justification.

This model for how inductive rationality can be embodied in sensibility shows that the making of an explicit inferential step is not the only way that the justificatory force of induction can enter into the hearer's reception of a speaker's word: an appropriately trained testimonial sensibility enables the hearer to respond to the word of another with the sort of critical openness that is required for a thoroughly effortless sharing of knowledge.

To sum up this section, then, the idea of a testimonial sensibility has in its favour not only that it represents a way out of the impasse with which we began (where we were stuck oscillating between the uncritical-reception model and the inferentialist model of testimonial knowledge) but also that it retains those features of each model that explained its attractiveness. Testimonial sensibility, as I have characterised it, pictures inductive rationality as the basic source of justification for hearer response, and this was the main thing we found attractive in the inferentialist model. Yet it also pictures hearer response in such a way that where knowledge is gained it is usually non-inferential. This means that the idea of a testimonial sensibility honours our everyday phenomenology of spontaneity and unreflectiveness, thus incorporating the non-intellectualism we found attractive in the uncritical-reception model.

Perhaps enough has now been said to show that the idea of a testimonial sensibility is able to explain how everyday testimonial knowledge can be non-inferential. But more needs to be said about what constitutes such a sensibility. I would like to think that introducing the notion opens up some new terrain for work of a virtue-ethical kind in exploring which virtues are properly incorporated into such a sensibility—work that could be regarded as either replacing or complementing more technical, probabilistic approaches to these matters. My next task here, then, will be to home in on one virtue in particular, which—although it is in a certain way thoroughly familiar—does not have a name. The role that this virtue has to play in testimonial practice comes into view only if we follow through the implications of our historicist, socially situated conception of the epistemic socialisation that forms testimonial sensibility. More particularly, it comes into view if we return to the role of social stereotypes in how a sensibility determines habits of hearer response. I have said that such stereotypes, where empirically founded, are a perfectly legitimate heuristic and a necessary determining factor in how a hearer perceives a speaker. But we must also confront the fact that in any actual human society, human societies being what they are, it is inevitable that such speaker stereotypes are susceptible to distortion by the prejudices of the day. Stereotypes informing testimonial exchange will tend to imitate relations of social power at large in the society. Our everyday, face-to-face testimonial encounters bring to bear a whole social consciousness in an instant, and this creates a deep structural liability to prejudicial dysfunction in our testimonial practices.

4   Epistemic Injustice: The Word of *Others*

Broadly speaking, prejudicial dysfunction in testimonial practice can be of two kinds. Either the prejudice results in the speaker's receiving more credibility than she rationally deserves—*credibility excess*—or it results in her receiving less credibility than she rationally deserves—*credibility deficit*.[6] Consider the immediate discursive impact of accent, for instance. Not only does a speaker's accent carry a great deal of baggage in terms of how a hearer perceives the speaker socially; I would suggest that part and parcel of this social perception are implications for how the hearer perceives the speaker epistemically. Accent can have a significant impact on how much credibility the hearer affords the speaker, especially in a one-off exchange. I do not mean that someone's accent is especially likely to lead a hearer, even an intensely prejudiced one, simply to *disbelieve* some perfectly believable assertion, or simply to *believe* some otherwise incredible assertion. Given that it is overwhelmingly in the interests of hearers in general to believe what is true and not believe what is false, it would have to be an unusual prejudice to be strong enough to have that sort of effect. (We should note, however, that social contexts structured by relations of systematically unequal social power do have a habit of generating situations in which a hearer with the greater social power is in a position such that it costs him nothing to disbelieve a manifestly believable speaker, as one of my examples will demonstrate.)

More usually, however, power will influence hearer-response in a less obvious way. Rather than turning belief into non-belief or vice versa, it will surreptitiously raise or lower the hearer's *degree* of belief, by inflating or deflating the credibility he affords the speaker. Epistemic trust, like other kinds of trust, has an affective[7] aspect that is influenced—sometimes rightly, sometimes wrongly—by how the hearer perceives the interlocutor. Its key affective aspect is a kind of minimal interpretative sympathy with the speaker that allows signs of her trustworthiness to be picked up on in the hearer's perception of her. Even such a minimal sympathy will be signally uneven across differences of social identity and especially where those differences of identity are characterised by dramatically unequal relations of power. Both of the examples I shall present illustrate how the social "otherness" of the speaker is fundamental to the prejudiced reception their word is given—the hearers re-enact their general social advantage in the reception they give the speaker's word.

To the examples, then. Both present cases of credibility deficit (rather than credibility excess), since that is the phenomenon that most urgently calls for the specific anti-prejudicial virtue I aim to identify. My first example is drawn from a novel, *To Kill a Mockingbird*, by Harper Lee (1974); the second is drawn from a screenplay, *The Talented Mr Ripley*, by Anthony Minghella (2000).[8] I offer the first as an example in which the epistemic failings on the part of the hearer (or rather hearers) is clearly culpable, the second as an example in which it is plausible to suggest that the hearer inflicts the injustice non-culpably. Each presents an instance of epistemic injustice in testimony—an instance, then, of *testimonial injustice*.

First example: The year is 1935, and the scene a courtroom in Maycomb County, Alabama. The defendant is a young black man named Tom Robinson. He is charged with raping a white girl, Mayella Ewell, whose family's run-down house he passes every day on his way to and from work. It is obvious to the reader, and would be obvious to any relatively unprejudiced person in the courtroom, that Tom Robinson is entirely innocent. For Addicus Finch, our politely spoken counsel for the defence, has proved beyond doubt that Robinson could not have beaten the Ewell girl so as to cause the sort of cuts and bruises she sustained that day, because whoever gave her this beating led with his left fist, whereas Tom Robinson's left arm is disabled, injured in an accident when he was a boy. The trial proceedings present a fairly clear-cut struggle between the power of evidence and the power of racial prejudice, with the all-white jury's sympathies ultimately succumbing to the latter. But there is a great complexity of social meanings at work in determining the jury's perception of Tom Robinson as a speaker. In a showdown between the word of a black man and a white girl, the courtroom air is thick with the do's and don'ts of racial politics. Telling the truth here is a minefield for Tom Robinson, since if he casts aspersions on the white girl he will be perceived as a presumptuous, lying Negro, yet if he does not publicise Mayella Ewell's attempt to kiss him (which is what really happened), then a guilty verdict is even more nearly assured. (This discursive predicament mirrors his practical predicament at the Ewell's house when Mayella grabbed him. If he pushes her away, he will be found to have assaulted her; yet if he is passive he will equally be found to have assaulted her. So he does the most neutral thing he can, which is to run away, though knowing all the while that this action too will be taken as a sure sign of guilt.)

At a pivotal moment during the prosecution's interrogation, Tom Robinson makes the mistake of being honest about his motivations for stopping off at Mayella Ewell's house as regularly as he did to help her out with odd jobs. The scene, like the whole story, is reported from the point of view of Scout, Addicus Finch's little daughter, who is secretly surveying the proceedings with her brother Jem from the "Negro gallery." Mr Gilmer, the prosecutor, sets him up:

"Why were you so anxious to do that woman's chores?"

Tom Robinson hesitated, searching for an answer. "Looked like she didn't have nobody to help her, like I says—" . . .

Mr Gilmer smiled grimly at the jury. "You're a mighty good fellow, it seems—did all this for not one penny?"

"Yes suh. I felt right sorry for her, she seemed to try more'n the rest of 'em—"

"*You* felt sorry for *her*, you felt *sorry* for her?" Mr Gilmer seemed ready to rise to the ceiling.

The witness realised his mistake and shifted uncomfortably in the chair. But the damage was done. Below us, nobody liked Tom Robinson's answer. Mr Gilmer paused a long time to let it sink in. (Lee 1974, 201)

Here the "damage" in question is done to any interpretative sympathy the white jury has so far been human enough to feel towards the black defendant. For *feeling sorry for* someone is a taboo sentiment if you are black and the object of your sympathy is a white person. And the fact that Tom Robinson has made the sentiment public raises the stakes in a way that is disastrous for justice, disastrous for him. The trial is a contest between the word of a black man against that of a white girl, and there are those in the jury whose testimonial sensibility is such that the idea that the black man is to be trusted and the white girl distrusted is virtually a psychological impossibility—Robinson's expressed sympathy for a white girl only reinforces that impossibility.

As it turns out, the members of the jury stick with their prejudiced perception of the defendant, formed principally by the racial stereotypes of the day. Addicus Finch challenges them to dispense with these stereotypes, to dispense with the "assumption—the evil assumption—that *all* Negroes lie, that *all* Negroes are basically immoral beings, that *all* Negro men are not to be trusted around our women" (Lee 1974, 208). But when it comes to the verdict, the jurors go along with the automatic distrust delivered by their corrupted testimonial sensibility. They find him guilty. And it is important that we are to interpret the novel so that the jurors really do find him guilty. That is to say, they do not privately find him innocent but cynically convict him anyway. They really do fail to do what Finch in his summing-up describes as their duty: they fail to *believe Tom Robinson*. Given the evidence put before them, their immovably prejudiced social perception of Robinson as a speaker leads at once to a gross epistemic failure and an appalling ethical failure.

Second example: It is the 1950s, and we are in Venice. Herbert Greenleaf, a rich American industrialist, is visiting, accompanied by a private detective he has hired to help solve the mystery of the whereabouts of his renegade son, Dickie. Dickie Greenleaf recently got engaged to his girlfriend, Marge Sherwood, but subsequently spent a great deal of time travelling with their "friend" Tom Ripley—until Dickie mysteriously disappeared. Marge is increasingly distrustful of Ripley because he seems to be obsessed with Dickie and suspiciously bound up with his strange disappearance. She also knows very well that it is unlike Dickie—unreliable philanderer though he undoubtedly was—simply to do a bunk, let alone to commit suicide, which is the hypothesis Ripley is at pains to encourage. Ripley, however, has all along done a successful job of sucking up to Greenleaf senior, so Marge is entirely alone in her suspicion—her correct suspicion—that Tom has in fact killed Dickie.

Herbert Greenleaf has just asked Ripley to be as helpful as he can in "filling in the blanks" of Dickie's life to Macarron, the private detective, and Ripley responds:

Ripley: I'll try my best, sir. Obviously I'll do anything to help Dickie.
Marge looks at him in contempt.
Herbert Greenleaf: This theory, the letter he left for you, the police think that's a clear indication he was planning on doing something . . . to himself.
Marge: I just don't believe that!
Herbert Greenleaf: You don't want to, dear. I'd like to talk to Tom alone—perhaps this afternoon? Would you mind? Marge, what a man may say to his sweetheart and what he'll admit to another fellow—
Marge: Such as? (Minghella 2000, 120–21)

Here Marge is being gently, kindly, sidelined by Greenleaf senior, who pathologizes her disbelief that Dickie would kill himself as a sweetheart's wishful thinking. He also seems to assume that Marge is generally innocent of the more tawdry facts of Dickie's life, so that his primary attitude towards her on the one hand and the-truth-about-Dickie on the other is that *she* needs protection from *it*. Greenleaf's everyday theory about what a man may say to his sweetheart, et cetera—though in itself quite possibly true enough—has the effect of undermining Marge as a possessor of knowledge about the lover she had been living with for some time. Greenleaf is only too aware how little he knows of his son—pathetically enthusiastic as he is at the prospect that the private detective might help make good this ignorance—and yet he fails to see Marge as the source of knowledge about Dickie that she manifestly is.

This attitude has the knock-on effect that Greenleaf fails to trust one of Marge's key reasons for her correct hypothesis that Dickie has died at the hands of Ripley. Even when Marge finds hard evidence back at Ripley's place, coming across a ring which she had given Dickie and which he had sworn never to remove, still she receives no credibility. Ripley's deliberate tactic is to dismiss her as "hysterical"—a line he continues to peddle in front of Greenleaf in order to get him to share this interpretation. The tactic works, not only on Greenleaf but also on her friend Peter Smith-Kingsley, so that the result is a collusion of men against Marge's word being taken seriously. The theme of knowledge ever to the fore in the dialogue, we at one point hear her off-screen, soon after she finds the ring, saying emphatically to the incredulous Greenleaf, "I don't know, I don't know, I just know it," and Greenleaf replies with a familiar put-down: "Marge, there's female intuition, and then there are facts—."

A number of these sorts of exchanges build up to the scene in which Marge, being taken back to America, is ushered on to a boat but breaks away to lunge at Ripley, saying, "I know it was you—I know it was you, Tom. I know it was you. I know you killed Dickie. I know it was you." Macarron, the private detective, comes out of the waiting boat to restrain her, and the stage direction reads: "Ripley looks at him as if to say: What can you do, she's hysterical. Macarron nods, pulls her onto the boat." As the viewer is aware, however, Marge was right: she did know; she knew Dickie well; and she knew Ripley had killed him. Her suspicions should have been listened to; *she* of all people should have been given some credibility. But Ripley cynically exploits the gender attitudes of the day so that the kindly and well-meaning men around her effectively collude with him to make her seem epistemically untrustworthy.

What both these examples present us with, in their different ways, is a case of a hearer failing to correct for one or another sort of prejudice in his testimonial sensibility. Both Greenleaf and the members of Maycomb County's jury fail to distrust their own distrust[9] of the speaker. They fail to adjust for the way in which their testimonial sensibility is badly trained. In the formal courtroom context of Tom Robinson's trial, they have ample opportunity to sense the dissonance between the distrust that their defective sensibility spontaneously delivers and the trust that attention to the evidence ought to inspire. Even if members of the jury were to be forgiven for the way their sensibility is saturated with the prejudices of the day, they remain starkly culpable in failing to respond appropriately to the new testimonial experience afforded by the trial. In the case of Herbert Greenleaf, he fails to correct for the way in which his habits of hearer response are saturated with the sexist constructions of gender—notably, ideas of women's innocence concerning the truths of men, and their need to be protected from such truths; ideas of feminine intuitiveness being an obstacle to rational judgement; and even ideas of a female susceptibility to hysterics.

But it is not simply a matter of failure properly to accommodate the speaker's social identity. In both examples, the hearers fail to adjust for the way in which their *own* social identity affects the testimonial exchange. The jury fails to account for the difference it makes to Tom Robinson's "performance" as a speaker (in the wide sense of performance, to include both what he does and how the audience responds) not only that he is black but equally *that they are white*. What Greenleaf fails to account for in his sceptical responses to Marge is the difference it makes to her performance not only that she is a woman but also that *he is a man*. The relation—a relation of power—between the social identities of hearer and speaker influence both how the speaker expresses herself and how the hearer responds.

Our two examples, then, demonstrate that testimonial responsibility requires a distinctly reflexive critical awareness. Had Marge shouted her accusations in the presence of Mrs Herbert Greenleaf, one speculates that she might have received from her some greater degree of credibility. That things would have gone differently at Tom Robinson's trial if the members of the jury had been black goes without saying.

Thus we have arrived at the final feature of the anti-prejudicial testimonial virtue we have been looking for: it is essentially reflexive. Its possession means that the hearer reliably succeeds in correcting for the way testimonial performance can be prejudiced by the inter-relation of the hearer's social identity and the speaker's social identity. In testimonial exchanges, for hearers and speakers alike, no party is neutral—everybody has a race, everybody has a gender. What is needed on the part of the hearer, then, in order to avert an epistemic injustice (and in order to serve his own epistemic interest in the truth) is a virtue of *Reflexive Critical Openness*. This is

the virtue we have been aiming to identify by attending to the phenomenon of testimonial injustice.

5   The Virtue of Reflexive Critical Openness—Historicism

The virtue of Reflexive Critical Openness is an especially hard virtue to
achieve at the best of times, inasmuch as prejudice is a powerful visceral
force, functioning less at the level of propositional attitudes and more at
the level of the social-imaginative and emotional commitments that colour
one's perceptions of speakers. (Even if one were only faced with correcting
for prejudice at the level of belief, this can still be very hard while those
beliefs are propped up by motivational attitudes in this way. As Christopher Hookway [2001, e.g., 182] has argued, there is the usual room for
akrasia in the practical business of managing one's epistemic habits.)

Clearly, however, it is in principle achievable, and the virtue will be an
integral part of any well-trained testimonial sensibility in so far as the risk
of prejudice-induced credibility deficit is an inevitable feature of epistemic
life. The human condition is a social condition, and social relations inevitably create space for prejudice.

Yet, there are circumstances under which the virtue cannot be achieved,
for it is a notable and ethically significant feature of this virtue that it displays a special sort of cultural-historical contingency. In order to explain
this, let me follow Linda Zagzebski's (1996) definition of virtue such that
virtues have both a motivational component and a component of reliable
success in bringing about the end of that motivation. In the case of intellectual virtues there will always be a motivation to achieve truth, but usually there will also be a more proximal aim to achieve something that is
conducive to truth—notably here the aim of ensuring that one's levels of
trust are untainted by prejudice. As a matter of definition, then, the intellectually virtuous subject will be reliably successful in fulfilling that proximal aim of ensuring against prejudice, and she will succeed in this by
achieving reflexive critical awareness of the prejudicial distortions in her
existing testimonial sensibility and by correcting for those distortions.

It must now be acknowledged, however, that the ability to do that is
dependent upon the cultural-historical setting. A setting in which there is
little critical awareness of gender is a setting in which no-one is in a position to possess the virtue of Reflexive Critical Openness *vis-à-vis* gender
prejudice of any subtle kind. While the Herbert Greenleafs of this world
were always at fault in failing to exhibit the virtue, I would suggest they
were not *culpably* at fault until the requisite critical consciousness of gender
became available to them. They were not culpably at fault until they were

in a position to know better. Now there will of course be no precise answer to the question of at what point a Herbert Greenleaf comes to be in a position where he should know better than to overlook the possibility that Marge was right. But no doubt someone like him will be in that position long before he actually lives up to it by taking on board the gender-critical insights newly available to him. Thus there will tend to be some period of historical transition in which a Herbert Greenleaf, well-intentioned and paternal as he may remain, moves from innocent fault to culpable fault. He lacked the virtue of Reflexive Critical Openness with regard to women speakers all along, but the relevant advance in collective consciousness will mean that this shortcoming in his epistemic conduct, and in the testimonial sensibility behind it, will have become blameworthy.

This shows that the power to possess the virtue of Reflexive Critical Openness depends upon the social-historical context. The case of Herbert Greenleaf, as I have characterised it, exemplifies the idea that one cannot be blamed for failing to do something one wasn't in a position to have reason to do. Essentially this is an instance of the maxim that "ought" implies "can," since in our example the "can" part is a matter of whether Greenleaf could reasonably be expected to *achieve* the critical perspective on gender that would have given *him* a reason to cast doubt on his lack of trust in Marge's word. More specifically, and more controversially, we might think of ourselves as having arrived at an insight into the structure of responsibility that is advanced by Bernard Williams (1995, 35) in terms of the internality of practical reasons. It would not be right to blame someone for an action or omission unless there existed a "sound deliberative route" from that person's actual motivational set ("the set of his desires, evaluations, attitudes, projects, and so on"). Whatever one thinks about the disagreements between so-called internal and external reasons theorists, it is worth noting that our intellectual case could not be controversial in anything like the way the ethical case is. This is because it could not be controversial to presume that all epistemic subjects possess in their motivational set a general motivation to aim at truth, and *a fortiori* to aim at more proximal ends which are in the service of that general motivation (such as correcting for prejudice in one's habits of trust, for instance).

Given this, it is clear that not just Herbert Greenleaf but even the most virulent, dyed-in-the-wool sexist version of Herbert Greenleaf possesses a motivation (the motivation to truth) from which there might be a sound deliberative route to distrusting his lack of trust in Marge. It is not the lack of a motivation, then, that explains why Greenleaf "cannot" do what he ought—cannot exhibit the appropriate virtue. It is rather the unavailability to him of a sound deliberative route from that veridical motivation to the conclusion that he should doubt his lack of trust in Marge. There is no such sound deliberative route available to him, in as much as the critical concepts in which that deliberation would have to be couched are genuinely not yet available. On this (perhaps rather charitable) interpretation, then, Greenleaf is unlucky, epistemically and morally. His non-culpable inability to exhibit the virtue of Reflexive Critical Openness not only means that he misses out on a truth that he is especially interested in acquiring (Marge is right; Ripley is Dickie's murderer) but also means he inflicts a significant injustice on Marge. She is treated as a hysterical female who cannot handle the truth, someone who deserves protection and sympathy but not epistemic trust. If one's rationality is an essential part of one's humanity, then Marge is gently undermined in her very humanity.

Evidently testimonial injustice will tend to imitate the broader structures of power in society, and where it is systematic we should recognise it as a face of oppression. In an essay on the nature of oppression Sandra Lee Bartky (1990, 30) quotes Frantz Fanon's notion of "psychic alienation," where the alienation in question consists in "the estrangement of separating off a person from some of the essential attributes of personhood." I take it that basic forms of epistemic agency, such as functioning as an informant on everyday matters, is indeed one of the essential attributes of personhood—it is part and parcel of being accepted as a compatriot in the community of the rational. If this is so, then an epistemic climate in which some people suffer systematic testimonial injustice must be regarded as seriously defective both epistemically and ethically. It is the site not simply of error and frustration, advantage and disadvantage, but of a distinctively epistemic kind of oppression. We have seen that the virtue of Reflexive Critical Openness (and doubtless many other virtues besides) has an important role in combating this sort of oppression. But as something possessed of mere individuals whose social-historical situation can deprive them of the very resources they need in order to attain the virtue, its anti-oppressive power remains hostage to the broader social structures in which our testimonial practices must take place.

Notes

1. For an account of how the impasse is merely an artefact of a certain misguided conception of the philosophical options, see McDowell 1998.

2. See Elizabeth Flicker 1994, and also 1987, in which she presents a powerful case against the idea that we have a "presumptive right" to believe what we are told in the absence of countervailing evidence.

3. See MacIntyre 1981, especially chapter 15.

4. I have tried to develop this theme in my 2000.

5. I echo John McDowell's use of this term, which he finds "all but explicit in Aristotle's account of how ethical character is formed," and which he extends to apply not simply to our ethical upbringing (Aristotle's "practical wisdom") but also, more generally, to our epistemic upbringing (McDowell 1994, 84).

6. Someone might ask how far the idea of a credibility excess or deficit depends on there being some exact degree of credibility which the speaker is due. I share Coady's scepticism about there being any precise science here, any precise credibility ratio to determine what degree of belief the hearer is entitled to. As Coady says, people are not like coins, exhibiting quite general tendencies to be right and honest about things (see Coady 1992, 210). And I see no reason to think this difficulty can be made good by building a sensitivity to subject matter into one's calculations, for the likelihood of speaker veracity is always dependent on which of an indeterminate number of discursive contexts the interlocutors happen to be in (including maximally contingent shifts of context that depend, for instance, on whether the speaker is in the mood for being undetectably sarcastic, and so on). This dependence on such finely differentiated contexts seems not merely to indicate that if there is a precise probability available then it can hardly be available to the hearer. Rather, it would seem to indicate that there is no such precise probability available at all, and that the matter is in some significant degree indeterminate.

7. See Jones 1996.

8. Minghella's screenplay is closely based on Patricia Highsmith's novel, though, crucially for present purposes, the character of Marge Sherwood and her relationship with Dickie Greenleaf is developed differently.

9. I borrow this formulation from Jones 2002, in which she explores the themes of power and credibility specifically concerning astonishing reports.

References

Bartky, Sandra Lee. 1990. "On Psychological Oppression." In *Femininity and Domination: Studies in the Phenomenology of Oppression*, 22–32. London: Routledge.

Coady, C. A. J. 1992. *Testimony: A Philosophical Study*. Oxford: Clarendon Press.

Fricker, Elizabeth. 1987. "The Epistemology of Testimony." *Proceedings of the Aristotelian Society* (supplementary volume) 61: 57–83.

———. 1994. "Against Gullibility." In *Knowing from Words*, edited by B. K. Matilal and A. Chakrabarti. Dordrecht, The Netherlands: Kluwer.

Fricker, Miranda. 2000. "Confidence and Irony." In *Morality, Reflection, and Ideology*, edited by E. Harcourt, 87–112. Oxford: Oxford University Press.

Jones, Karen. 1996. "Trust as an Affective Attitude." *Ethics* 107: 4–25.

———. 2002. "The Politics of Credibility." In *A Mind of One's Own: Feminist Essays on Reason and Objectivity*, edited by L. Antony and C. Witt, 154–76. Boulder, Col.: Westview Press.

Lee, Harper. 1974. *To Kill A Mockingbird*. London: Pan Books.

Hookway, Christopher. 2001. "Epistemic *Akrasia* and Epistemic Virtue." In *Virtue Epistemology: Essays on Epistemic Virtue and Responsibility*, edited by A. Fairweather and L. Zagzebski, 178–99. Oxford: Oxford University Press.

MacIntyre, Alasdair. 1981. *After Virtue: A Study in Moral Theory*. London: Duckworth.

McDowell, John. 1994. *Mind and World*. Cambridge, Mass.: Harvard University Press.

———. 1998. "Knowledge by Hearsay." In *Meaning, Knowledge, and Reality*, essay 19. Cambridge, Mass.: Harvard University Press.

Minghella, Anthony. 2000. *The Talented Mr Ripley*. London: Methuen.

Williams, Bernard. 1995. "Internal Reasons and the Obscurity of Blame." In *Making Sense of Humanity and Other Philosophical Papers*, chapter 3. Cambridge: Cambridge University Press.

Zagzebski, Linda. 1996. *Virtues of the Mind: An Inquiry into the Nature of Virtue and the Ethical Foundations of Knowledge*. Cambridge: Cambridge University Press.

16   Recovering Understanding

Linda Zagzebski

I

There have been radical changes in epistemology in recent years, although not always in the same direction. The naturalistic epistemologists treat it as a branch of psychology, whereas I treat it as a branch of ethics. Still others gleefully pronounce the field dead on the grounds that the central epistemological questions are based on defective assumptions. In the first part of this essay I want to look at what we can learn from the death-of-epistemology camp because I think that the lesson of their argument is that epistemology ought to be reoriented in a direction I believe is desirable for many other reasons. In particular, I want to focus on the neglect of the epistemic value of understanding. Recovering understanding requires an approach like the virtue approach I have endorsed elsewhere. It also may alter the way we respond to skepticism.

The death-of-epistemology theorists claim that epistemology is primarily concerned with demonstrating that knowledge is possible, and that project arises only if we take the threat of radical skepticism seriously. But the peril of skepticism is not perennial. It is only because of certain historical contingencies that it has assumed so much importance in the last three hundred years. And the danger arises only within the context of a certain set of theoretical ideas—ideas that can and must be challenged.

Beyond this, the death-of-epistemology theorists do not agree on the particular set of ideas that are at fault. Richard Rorty (1979) blames skepticism on the "representational" conception of belief and the correspondence theory of truth, while Michael Williams (1991) blames foundationalism.

Reprinted from Linda Zagzebski, "Recovering Understanding," in *Knowledge, Truth, and Duty: Essays on Epistemic Justification, Responsibility, and Virtue*, ed. Matthias Steup (Oxford: Oxford University Press, 2001), 235–251.

But they agree that the demise of the presuppositions behind the skeptical challenge undermines its danger and makes the attempt to answer it pointless. Since answering skepticism is reputedly the major job of epistemology, it makes epistemology pointless as well, and to the extent to which the rest of philosophy is built on epistemology, philosophy itself is allegedly in danger of collapse.

I have no interest in pointing out the many defects in this line of reasoning. Instead, I want to start with what I think is a worthwhile contribution to philosophy from this argument, and that is the way it reminds us how the questions that we consider central to epistemology change over time and are not presented for our reflection singly, but in clusters. An important way in which questions bunch together is around the issue of skepticism. There have been significant periods of philosophical history in which skepticism was thought to be a serious threat, and other periods in which it was not. In those eras in which it *was*, philosophers gave preeminence to the epistemic value of certainty and focused on the nature of justified belief. In those eras in which it was not, the questions that assumed most importance were quite different. Philosophers gave most of their attention to the value of understanding and focused on the nature of explanation rather than on the nature of justification. We may be ending a period in which radical skepticism is taken in full seriousness, but whether or not that is the case, we should admit that the questions of most significance to epistemology in the askeptical periods have been neglected. It is time we cease the obsession with justification and recover the investigation of understanding. At least, that is what I intend to propose.

My position is that (1) the death-of-epistemology theorists are right that the danger of skepticism has been perceived quite differently in different periods of philosophical history, and one reasonable conclusion to draw from that (but not the only one) is that skepticism does not arise from the pure a priori use of presuppositionless reason, but only within a context of certain substantive philosophical positions.[1]

But (2) the death-of-epistemology theorists are mistaken if they think the seriousness of skepticism is a peculiarly modern phenomenon. There are, in fact, revealing similarities between the modern skeptical period and the post-Aristotelian skeptical period, both of which are significantly different from the askeptical periods that make up most of the rest of philosophical history. But I am not interested in the theoretical presuppositions of skepticism for the purposes of this paper. My point is just that many epistemologists are ready to put skeptical worries aside, although not all for the same reasons. This is not to say that most of them accept the claims of the death-of-epistemology theorists. In fact, they clearly do not. But many now agree that epistemology is stultified if the issue of skepticism is allowed to dominate epistemological inquiry. It is perfectly legitimate to pursue epistemological issues that leave the skeptical challenge to one side.

But what are the questions that should then capture our attention? A good way to answer that, I propose, is to look at the questions that dominated epistemology during askeptical periods. Since I believe this opens up an important range of neglected issues involving the epistemic value of understanding, I conclude that (3) the death-of-epistemology theorists are quite wrong that there is nothing left for epistemology to do. In what follows I will look at the work of some historians of philosophy for interpretations of the epistemological enterprise in previous eras. This will lead to some suggestions for the future of epistemology. But, unfortunately, it is not enough to announce that skepticism should be treated independently and then continue to use the approaches that are most common in Anglophone epistemology. Most of the dominant theories make it almost impossible to undertake an investigation of understanding. I will then argue that virtue epistemology has the greatest promise of giving us a new and useful way to approach the neglected value of understanding.

II

Understanding and certainty are two epistemic values each of which has enjoyed pride of place for long periods in the history of epistemology, but rarely, if ever, at the same time. In Hellenistic philosophy and much post-Cartesian philosophy, certainty was given more attention than understanding, while in Plato and Aristotle, in the long medieval period, and even in some of the major modern philosophers such as Spinoza, it was the reverse. Usually whichever one of the two concepts dominated was the one connected with the concept of knowledge, so Plato comes very close to identifying knowledge with understanding, while Descartes comes very close to identifying knowledge with certainty.[2] Historians have attributed this difference in focus to differences in the way skepticism has been handled. The rise of skepticism is accompanied by the concern for certainty, and that brings with it a batch of questions, most of which focus on propositional belief and the process of justifying belief, since justification is what is needed to defend the right to be sure. In contrast, the askeptical periods have been mostly concerned with understanding, and the questions accompanying it show little concern for justification, often not even much interest in propositional belief, but instead, an interest in the process of explanation, since explanation is what is needed to defend a claim to understand. The understanding/explanation orientation is much less atomistic and more social than the certainty/justification orientation. This is noteworthy in the present climate of opinion, since these features of the understanding approach are the very things that would meet some recent criticisms of contemporary work in epistemology.[3]

So the rise of skepticism led to a move from a concern with understanding and explanation to a concern with certainty and justification in ancient epistemology. As Stephen Everson points out in the introduction to his book on ancient epistemology (1990, p. 7), "It has become generally accepted . . . that what marks off post-Aristotelian epistemology from what went before is a novel concern with justification . . . and that this concern was elicited by the onset of scepticism." In contrast, the central epistemological aim of Plato, as Julius Moravcsik has argued (1979, 1992), was the delineation of what it means to understand something (1979, p. 53). Propositional knowledge was of secondary interest (p. 55) and derivative from it:

The only propositional knowledge that will be of interest will be that which is derived from the kind of theoretical understanding that Plato envisages. Mere knowledge of truths is of no interest to Plato; propositional knowledge figures in the dialogues only insofar as this may be, in some contexts, evidence for understanding, and needed for practical activity. (p. 60)

Gail Fine (1990) has a similar interpretation:

On the account [of Plato] I have proposed, one knows more to the extent that one can explain more; knowledge requires, not a vision, and not some special sort of certainty or infallibility, but sufficiently rich, mutually supporting, explanatory accounts. Knowledge, for Plato, does not proceed piecemeal; to know, one must master a whole field, by interrelating and explaining its diverse elements. (p. 114)

Gail Fine translates the word *episteme* in Plato as "knowledge," but in a sense that includes understanding, whereas Moravcsik translates it simply as "understanding."[4] Either way, understanding is a central epistemic value in Plato. But not justification. Occasionally, a contemporary philosopher such as Chisholm (1966) will claim to find the origin of the idea of epistemic justification in Plato's *Theaetetus* (201c–210b), where Socrates proposes and then rejects the suggestion that knowledge is true belief plus a *logos*. But both Burnyeat (1980, pp. 134ff) and Fine (1990, p. 107) have disputed the idea that Plato's notion of a *logos* can be identified with justification, maintaining that a *logos* is an account or an explanation, and as already mentioned, Everson says that the historians agree that the concept of justification was a new idea in Hellenistic philosophy, associated with the rise of skepticism.

In examining Plato's early theory of knowledge, Paul Woodruff argues that Plato distinguished expert from nonexpert knowledge,[5] where he indicates expert knowledge by *techne* and its cognates, and, in many contexts, also by *episteme* and *sophia*. To be expert at a *techne* is therefore associated both with knowledge/understanding and with wisdom. The expert, Woodruff says, is a person on whom others may rely in difficult or highly technical matters (p. 68). What makes the expert reliable is that he knows the essential nature of his product (p. 76). Whether he has that knowledge is revealed in his ability to give a Socratic definition of the good produced by his *techne* (p. 74). Woodruff then argues that it turns out that the same basic knowledge is essential to *every techne*—knowledge of the good. It follows that the person who is the most reliable source of knowledge for other people is someone who has mastered a skill and in doing so has a basic knowledge of the good shared by all experts.

Aristotle's notion of *episteme* is also one that is far removed from a concern with justification arising out of the threat of skepticism, and for that reason, I have heard some scholars remark that they have trouble finding his epistemology at all. But that reveals more about the contemporary philosopher than about Aristotle. Consider what C.C.W. Taylor says at the beginning of a paper on Aristotle's epistemology:

While Aristotle was certainly aware of sceptical challenges to claims to knowledge, whether in general or in specific areas, the justification of knowledge claims in response to such challenges, which has been central to most epistemology since Descartes, is at best peripheral to Aristotle's concerns. On the whole, he does not seek to *argue* that knowledge is possible, but, assuming its possibility, he seeks to understand how it is realised in different fields of mental activity and how the states in which it is realised relate to other cognitive states of the agent. In particular, the central problem of post-Cartesian epistemology, that of showing how our experience may reasonably be held to be experience of an objective world, is hardly a problem for Aristotle. The problem for the post-Cartesian philosopher is how, once having retreated in the face of Cartesian doubt to the stronghold of private experience, he or she can advance sufficiently far beyond that experience to recover the objective world. Aristotle, never having made the retreat, does not have the problem of the advance . . . (1990, pp. 116–117)

And Burnyeat:

All through the Hellenistic period, both positive philosophy and the negative attacks of scepticism take their starting point to be the problem of perceptual certainty. Aristotle does not. But not because he is unacquainted with sceptical arguments for conclusions which would undermine his enterprise, nor because he does not think (some of) them worth extended discussion. He is simply very firm that he is not going to let them structure his inquiries or dictate his choice of starting-points. (1980, p. 138)

Like Plato, Aristotle was particularly interested in understanding, either as a form of knowledge or as a special cognitive state.[6] The dispute about the connection between understanding and knowledge in Aristotle is reflected in the fact that *episteme* in Aristotle is variously translated "science," "scientific knowledge," or "scientific understanding," but sometimes *nous* is translated as "understanding" instead. I will not investigate Aristotle's rather complicated notion of understanding, as it has been discussed in the literature. My point is merely that Aristotle's epistemological interests were quite different from ours, concerned with a complex of ideas associated with understanding rather than with justification, and that those concerns can be explained in part by his lack of interest in skepticism.

So the practice of epistemology in the ancient world was quite different when menaced by skepticism than when no such peril was perceived. The rise of skepticism in Hellenistic philosophy is both the source of and the explanation for the shift from the Platonic/Aristotelian concern for understanding to the post-Aristotelian concern for certainty, and that shift was associated with the emerging dominance of the concept of justification. It would be interesting to investigate how philosophers went about the return to the askeptical epistemic values of understanding and wisdom in the early medieval period, since our situation is similar. We also live at a time in which the focus of epistemological investigation is the individual belief state. For decades, epistemologists have concentrated on justification, and scarcely a word is said about understanding. There is not even an entry for "understanding" in the new Routledge *Encyclopedia of Philosophy* nor in the recent Blackwell *Companion to Epistemology*, and rarely is there an entry for "understanding" in the indices of scholarly books in epistemology.[7] On the other hand, justification is given even more attention than knowledge, notwithstanding the fact that the term "justification" may sometimes be explicitly rejected, as in Plantinga's recent work on warrant. In Plantinga's case, he rejects it because of the ambiguities he finds in the concept of justification. Notice that this means that justification can direct the inquiry, even when the theorist refuses to use the word "justification."[8] But if I am right that the concept of justification is associated both historically and conceptually with the perceived danger of skepticism, and if I am also right that epistemologists are now prepared not to let skeptical worries direct their inquiry, it follows that it is advisable to give up the preoccupation with justification and perhaps even with the propositional belief and to turn instead to an investigation of understanding.

III

So far we have only hints about the nature of understanding from its use in ancient epistemology, particularly by Plato. But we need much more than hints if we are to have reason to attempt to recover it. If understanding is a notion peculiar to Plato's philosophy, it is unlikely that very many contemporary philosophers believe it exists at all. It is always problematic to use a single term to apply to the object of study of philosophers from completely different historical periods and with completely different background theories. This occurs whether we are talking about knowledge, freedom, causation, the human person, justice, the good, or many others. So when we discuss Plato's theory of knowledge, can we be sure that it is a theory of the same thing as Chisholm's theory? Are they giving two different accounts of the same thing or accounts of two different things? I am not convinced that this question has a determinate answer, but it can be finessed to some extent if we find a common ground between us and Plato. What I will try to do in this section is to find the common ground in the concept of understanding.

There is another problem that makes it hard to find our target. A consequence of the neglect of understanding as an object of philosophical investigation is that the word "understanding" is used loosely, with a wide variety of meanings, and usually without any notice of ambiguity. When Alston (1993) and Plantinga (1990) detected ambiguities in the concept of justification, they both treated that as a serious problem and concluded that the concept must be disambiguated before there could be further epistemological progress. In contrast, even when people notice that "understanding" is ambiguous, they do not consider that a real problem, since they assume that all they have to do is to stipulate the meaning they want before proceeding. The fact that so little contemporary literature depends on any given sense of understanding seems to make the choice inconsequential. This situation makes it very difficult to even identify the value that needs recovering. One of the consequences of scholarly neglect is fragmentation of meaning. And the more that meaning is fragmented, the more reason there seems to be to neglect it since there no longer seems to be any "it" that is being ignored. This vicious circle of neglect has probably occurred before in philosophical history with other concepts.[9]

Let us see, then, if we can find some commonality between us and Plato's notion of *episteme*. From Moravscik's and Woodruff's work, we see that understanding (*episteme*) in Plato has something to do with *techne*—practical human arts or skills. These include such complex activities as medicine, hunting, and shipbuilding, two of which are no longer widely practiced, but they also include more-specific practical skills, such as cooking or even pastry-making. Understanding is a cognitive state that arises from *techne*, and since *techne* includes certain practical activities that are by no means wholly cognitive, it follows that understanding in Plato is a state that arises from practices that are not purely cognitive. The person who has mastered a *techne* understands the nature of the product of the *techne* and is able to explain it. She also knows the good in a sense that gives her a common understanding with the practitioners of other *technai*.

This seems to be the case even when the *techne* in question is an academic field. Fine says in the passage quoted above that to have *episteme* one must have mastered an entire field. One does not have *episteme* of an astronomical fact[10] without interrelating and explaining its relation to diverse elements within the field of astronomy. And one can do that only by mastering the *techne* of being an astronomer. In other words, one does not understand a part of a field without the ability to explain its place within a much larger theoretical framework, and one acquires the ability to do that by mastering a skill. Similarly, one does not have *episteme* of some feature of human psychology without the ability to explain how that feature fits into the larger framework of human psychology, and that requires having mastered the *techne* of the psychologist. Assuming that epistemology is also a *techne*, it follows that one does not have *episteme* of some object of epistemology, such as having *episteme* of what knowledge is, without the ability to explain how knowledge fits the other objects of study in the field, and one cannot do that without having mastered the skills of the epistemologist.

So far, two ideas about understanding have emerged from the Platonic notion of *episteme* that are live options in the contemporary milieu. One is that understanding is a state gained by learning an art or skill, a *techne*. One gains understanding by *knowing how* to do something well, and this makes one a reliable person to consult in matters pertaining to the skill in question. This way of looking at understanding makes it unlikely that understanding is achieved by a single mode of reasoning, but it involves more-complex processes, including, perhaps, processes that are noncognitive. This leads to the second idea, which is that understanding is not directed toward a discrete object, but involves seeing the relation of parts to other parts and perhaps even the relation of part to a whole. It follows that the object of understanding is not a discrete proposition. One's mental representation of what one understands is likely to include such things as maps, graphs, diagrams, and three-dimensional models in addition to, or even in place of, the acceptance of a series of propositions.

The formal structure of some states of this kind have been examined by John Etchemendy and John Barwise.[11] They have investigated the complex reasoning involved in problem solving that they call heterogeneous reasoning. This form of reasoning would be used in such situations as planning the layout of a group of offices that meet certain requirements, designing a cellular telephone, a computer, or an airplane, or figuring out a food distribution system that maximizes utility. In the cases Barwise and Etchemendy consider, there is no unique solution to the problem, but the goal is to find *any* solution that meets the requirements, and these could include cost, efficiency, safety, style, aesthetic quality, as well as probabilistic considerations. The reasoning involved is not only complex, but often collaborative. The process uses diagrams, graphics, and other representational forms in addition to sentential reasoning.

People who make discoveries or solve problems often do so by a process of visualization, sometimes even in dreams. One of the most famous examples of this was the discovery of the structure of the benzene molecule by Auguste Kekulé. While working on the problem, he dreamed of a snake biting its own tail. Upon awakening he realized that the benzene molecule had a ring structure. There are many other examples of this in science. The American mathematical geneticist, Sewall Wright, used the metaphor of a landscape with hills and valleys as a way of explaining adaptive genetic mechanisms. Selection drives populations up the slopes, he argued. Scientists who think that populations seek the closest lowest level have suggested turning the image upside down. Either way, people find that the image gives them an understanding they would not have had otherwise and it has become well known.

We now have identified three features of understanding: It is acquired through mastering a *techne*; its object is not a discrete proposition but involves the grasp of part/whole relations; and it involves representing some portion of the world nonpropositionally. Let us look more closely at this last feature.

I take it for granted that reality has a structure or structures and that the comprehension of these structures is an important epistemic goal. I also take it that it is unlikely that propositional structure exhausts the structure of reality. This point raises deep metaphysical questions about the relation between mind and reality. Whether or not propositions exist independent of the mind, and whether or not something sentential in form is the bearer of truth value, we can all probably agree that there is a form of knowledge that is mediated through a sentential structure, leaving aside the question of whether the mind imposes such a structure or whether it is *there*—independent of the mind. But I think it is consistent with theoretical neutrality to maintain that reality has a propositional structure as long as we are not committed to the position that propositional structure is the only structure it has. In fact, I want to claim now that it is very unlikely that propositional structure exhausts the structure of reality, and it is even unlikely that propositional structure exhausts the structure of what is intelligible to us.

I propose that *understanding is the state of comprehension of nonpropositional structures of reality.* In this sense of understanding, we can understand such things as an automobile engine, a piece of music, a work of art, the character of a human person, the layout of a city, a causal nexus, a teleological structure, or reality itself—this last being the object of the science of metaphysics. There is no reason to think that any of these things has an exclusively propositional structure, if indeed it has a propositional structure at all. I am not denying the possibility that all of reality can be represented propositionally, but I am denying that the proposition is the only form in which reality can be made intelligible to the human mind.

The structures of music include harmonic structures and rhythmic structures extended in time as well as formal patterns, such at the sonata form and structures that blend ingredients simultaneously to produce a sound with a certain color, such as the simultaneous blending of many distinct instruments in the creation of a single note in a musical composition.

The structure of works of art is also quite obviously nonpropositional, and for this reason it is very difficult for interpreters of art to translate their understanding of that structure into a propositional form. Understanding literary figures is probably easier to achieve than the understanding of paintings or sculpture, since it is probable that the aesthetic sense of many persons is not very well developed, whereas understanding a literary character is an extension of understanding oneself and one's friends, something that is presumably more common. Some, but not all, literature has a narrative structure. The pieces are propositional, but the structure of the whole is not. Narrative structure is relatively easy to understand because it is the same as the structure of our own lives.

The *technai* of art, music, and literature can produce a state that has epistemic value. The arts enable us to penetrate reality more deeply than we could without them. Understanding works of art and literature is probably one step removed from understanding basic features of reality, since the arts are in part an attempt to understand reality. That is, to understand a work of art is to understand something that is itself the product of an attempt to understand something else, although this is, of course, arguable. But it is much less arguable that the state we get from the successful creation or appreciation of works of art is understanding, and it has much in common with the *episteme* discussed by Plato. I have said that I think it is likely that academic fields are *technai* also, although that is more controversial. But it is uncontroversial that one can have understanding of an academic field and only somewhat more controversial that understanding some part of an academic field may require understanding how that part relates to other parts of it.

Philosophy aims to understand the whole of reality, not simply that portion of it or aspect of it that is successfully represented by propositions and their constituent concepts. An enormous advantage of language is that we have rules codifying the logical relations among propositions, and these are very useful in comprehending a certain kind of structure. What we do not have is a set of rules codifying the relations among pieces of the structures that make up an artwork or a piece of music or the motivational structure of a person, although metaphysicians have sometimes proposed rules of a sort for the deepest structures of reality, as in Plato's theory of Forms. Of course, there is little chance that we can reach agreement on any of these matters, and that is no doubt one of the reasons that so few people attempt to figure things out in these areas. It is probably also a reason for the lack of prestige of the attempt.

There is one form of understanding that epistemologists have not given up, and that is the understanding we get from a theory. Philosophical theories these days are considerably less grandiose than Plato's, of course, but despite their modest pretensions, they often attempt to do what Plato did in the respect we have been considering: to represent the objects of epistemological inquiry nonpropositionally. For example, the two main models of justified doxastic structures for some time were the coherentist raft and the foundationalist pyramid.[12] Even though many epistemologists have given up these models, they look for alternatives that serve the purpose of the raft and the pyramid—to represent the structure of an entire system of beliefs when it is epistemically good. So even when one way of attempting to give us understanding of the whole of a good belief system is unsuccessful, nobody rejects the point of the attempt.

IV

What is the relationship between understanding and knowledge? As we have seen, understanding in Plato is closely connected with knowledge, since *episteme* is a state in which the two are not clearly distinguishable, and the same word is variously translated as "knowledge" or "understanding." But since knowledge these days almost always means propositional knowledge, and since I have proposed that understanding has a non-propositional object, understanding differs from knowledge as it is normally understood. I argue elsewhere (1996) that we should not assume that propositional knowledge is the only kind of knowledge. Nonetheless, I think that knowledge and understanding differ. We can have both understanding and knowledge about the same part of reality. Understanding deepens our cognitive grasp of that which is already known. So a person can know the individual propositions that make up some body of knowledge without understanding them. Understanding involves seeing how the parts of that body of knowledge fit together, where the fitting together is not itself propositional in form.

Moravscik uses the example of understanding a mathematical theorem to make the same point. A proof of a mathematical theorem is a sequence of propositions, but understanding the proof involves seeing the relations between the propositions, and that is not itself the knowledge of a proposition (1979, p. 55).[13] It is possible that understanding a theorem is just a different kind of knowledge, but it differs from knowledge in the usual sense and it often cannot be attained until after knowledge in the usual sense is reached. In some cases, then, understanding is a stronger state than knowledge.

On the other hand, understanding does not always build on a base of knowledge. It may be achieved in more than one way about the same portion of reality. More than one alternative theory may give understanding of the same subject matter. This makes sense if we think of a theory as a representation of reality, where alternative representations can be better or worse, more or less accurate. But more than one may be equally good, equally accurate.[14] This form of understanding does not presuppose knowledge or even true belief, and if we assume that two competing representations of the same part of reality cannot both constitute knowledge, it cannot be a form of knowledge.[15]

Another reason for thinking that understanding is not a form of knowledge is that in some cases, truth can actually be an impediment to understanding, as Catherine Elgin (1996) has pointed out. Her example is propositional. "Objects in a vacuum fall toward the Earth at a rate of 32 ft/sec^2" is not strictly true, since it ignores the gravitational attraction of everything except the earth, yet it gives more understanding for most purposes than the vastly more complicated truth (p. 123). The same applies to Boyle's Law (p. 124). The strictly true (that is, accurate) law can be grasped, but only at high cognitive cost.

These considerations suggest that understanding is achieved partly by simplifying what is understood, highlighting certain features and ignoring others. This process compensates for our cognitive limitations. Understanding aims at comprehensiveness, not exactness, and we usually need to sacrifice one for the sake of the other. As van Fraassen has noted in a different context, a more informative theory is less likely to be true, but I would say it is more likely to produce understanding.[16] In each of these instances, understanding aims in a different direction than knowledge, and yet it does not necessarily have a lesser status.

At the beginning of this essay, I observed that many epistemologists are willing to put the skeptical threat aside, but that is not because they all agree that knowledge can be taken for granted. Some do think that, of course, but many others merely think that the need to answer skepticism should not direct all epistemological projects, but that skepticism can be put aside while other questions are addressed. In proposing that the value of understanding ought to be recovered, I do not mean to imply that we can take for granted that the object of understanding is also something known or even that it is true. We can leave aside questions of knowledge and threats to knowledge in addressing understanding, but as we will see in the next section, a form of skepticism arises anyway.

Truth is a thin epistemic goal, and knowledge is derivative from it, since believing the truth is a component of knowing. Understanding is a thicker goal, and its connection with truth is often indirect. When we want an expert about a problem, we consult a person who has understanding of the subject matter, since such a person is likely to be a reliable problem solver. A reliable problem solver ordinarily will also be a reliable source of propositional information, but her reliability is not limited to being a reliable truth-bearer. The problem solver may use something like the complex process of heterogeneous reasoning investigated by Etchemendy and Barwise, but whether she does or not, what enables her to figure out the solution to the problem is her understanding of a complex chunk of the world, not simply her knowledge or true beliefs about that portion of the world.

This suggests another feature of understanding that links it with a *techne*: Understanding makes its bearer reliable in carrying out the goals of the *techne*, some of which are not epistemic goals. It enables him to produce a flakey pastry, repair an automobile, design a bridge that will not collapse, or figure out why the vintner failed this year. This means that understanding is a property of persons. It is not carried by propositions or states of belief. This consequence is important because so many contemporary theories in epistemology focus exclusively on the proposition or the state of believing a proposition. We will get to that in section VI.

If understanding is a goal worth pursuing, there ought to be criteria for success in reaching it. We do have such criteria, but they are not as clear as we would want. We expect students to demonstrate their understanding of a text or a conceptual point by reconstructing it in their own words. Understanding in some areas may be displayed by drawing a diagram. We attempt to give understanding to others by constructing models of what we want them to understand. If they can construct their own models, we take that as a sign of their understanding. In Plato, understanding is demonstrated by successfully passing the *elenchus* test. A person demonstrates *episteme* of the product of the relevant *techne* by giving a definition of its essential nature that withstands attack. Problem solving of the sort examined by Etchemendy and Barwise is an attempt to understand the relations among a given set of requirements. Finding a solution is a matter of figuring out how to make them all compossible. So more than one solution is permitted. Any solution that meets the specifications is successful.

V

Once we bring up success, we implicitly bring up failure, and that means there is a danger of skepticism. Skepticism about understanding is as real as skepticism about truth. Skepticism threatens whenever there is a goal that is such that we cannot tell for sure whether we have attained it even after we think we have done so. It is a threat to our motivation because motivation to reach X requires both the belief that reaching X is possible and some way of telling how well we have done after we have made the attempt. So skepticism about our ability to get knowledge or true beliefs is not unique. It arises for understanding because success in gaining understanding may be illusory. It may seem to me that I clearly understand something even when I do not. It might even appear to me that I have demonstrated my understanding by passing the *elenchus* test or constructing a model or producing a solution to a problem even when I have not. But unlike truth skepticism, understanding skepticism has never had a significant hold on the philosophical imagination. That is because the test for success is largely within the practice, the *techne*, itself. Reliably carrying out the goals of a *techne* can be verified within the *techne*. One's understanding of an art work can be proven by successfully giving that understanding to others by teaching it in an art history class, and success in teaching is defined within the practice of teaching. Success in problem solving is proven by the workability of the solution produced. Again, success is defined within the confines of the *techne* that gives rise to the problem to be solved.

In each of these cases, of course, the test for success is not infallible. It is still possible that failure has occurred. But skepticism about infallibility is not the most serious form of skepticism. As we have seen, justification is associated with the response to skepticism because it is the state we want to defend our right to be certain we believe the truth, but the justification test was never an infallible test for certainty. In recent epistemology, foundationalism and coherentism have been treated as alternative ways of answering the challenge of truth skepticism by describing the conditions for having a justified belief structure. But there are many ways fallibility creeps into both kinds of structure, and certainty is never guaranteed. There always has been considerable slippage between justification and certainty. So the fact that there is also slippage between explanation and understanding is not a special problem. Skepticism at the level of infallibility arises within any epistemological framework. The most threatening form of skepticism occurs when it takes away the motive to even *try* to reach an epistemic goal—at the level of motivation. At this level, understanding skepticism is less serious than truth skepticism. That is because, as I have argued, success in understanding is demonstrated within a practice.

Understanding has internalist conditions for success, whereas knowledge does not. Even when knowledge is defined as true justified belief and justification is construed internalistically, the truth condition for knowledge makes it fundamentally a concept whose application cannot be demonstrated from the inside.[17] Understanding, in contrast, not only has internally accessible criteria, but it is a state that is constituted by a type of conscious transparency. It may be possible to know without knowing that one knows, but it is impossible to understand without understanding that one understands. To repeat, this does not eliminate every form of skepticism. Skepticism can appear at the second-order level. Nonetheless, there is less reason to doubt my understanding than there is to doubt other internally accessible states, such as the justifiability of my beliefs even on strong internalist theories of justification. That is because for most of my beliefs, the belief is justified only if a long string of other beliefs are justified, and even if I have cognitive access to the entire string of beliefs, I cannot cognitively access them simultaneously and probably cannot consciously go through them one by one. In contrast, understanding is a state in which I am directly aware of the object of my understanding, and conscious transparency is a criterion for understanding. Those beleaguered by skeptical doubts therefore can be more confident of the trustworthiness of putative understanding states than virtually any other epistemic state. Ironically, then, even though understanding dominated epistemology in askeptical periods, there is good reason for the skeptic to recover it as well.

VI

The recent interest in virtue epistemology makes the recovery of understanding more likely, but it is difficult to reclaim it within the other theories that have the most influence. Epistemology is dominated by the information model of knowledge. This is even true of many theories that are commonly called forms of virtue epistemology, such as process and faculty reliabilism. Almost all contemporary theories agree that to know is to believe a true proposition plus something else. A true proposition is treated as a piece of information that can be passed from one person to another. One of the critical issues in this model is how the original informant obtains the information. Knowledge is akin to a physical object that is discovered in some basic way by one person and is then passed from person to person through the epistemic community. There is little attention in the contemporary literature to this part of the theory, since almost all of the competing theories agree with that part of it. The disagreement arises over the "plus something else" component of the definition. In evidentialist theories, a true belief is an instance of knowledge, just in case it is based on the appropriate evidence.[18] Defeasibility theories maintain that to be knowledge, a true belief must also be justified in certain counterfactual circumstances—if certain other pieces of information (defeaters) were also known.[19] Process and faculty reliabilism and the proper function theory maintain that it is not a true belief's justificatory relations that make it knowledge, but the epistemic process or faculty by which it was acquired. That process or faculty must be a reliable truth-producer, or alternatively, a properly functioning faculty.[20] The earlier causal theory maintains that to be knowledge, a true belief must be properly caused by the fact the belief is about.[21]

All of these theories focus on propositional objects, and none of them can be reinterpreted as theories about valuable epistemic states that have a nonpropositional object. That is, in each case, the "something else" that is a component of knowledge in addition to true belief is something about the proposition believed or the state of believing a proposition. The theory does not make sense when applied to anything other than a propositional object, and it has nothing to say about epistemic states that do not have propositional objects. Consequently, they have nothing to say about understanding.

Epistemologists presumably think that their own theories have positive epistemic value, yet these theories generally do not meet the criteria for the epistemic concepts they address—justification, warrant, or knowledge. In other words, most theories of justification are such that the theory itself does not pass its own criteria for justification, and similarly for warrant and knowledge. This is not an objection to these theories because most of them are couched in terms that make it clear the theory is not intended to be self-referential. The theory aims at giving an account of justification or warrant for beliefs of a certain kind, often empirically based beliefs, and the account itself is not a belief in the category it addresses. Even so, epistemologists must think that their own theories are better than competing ones, which means that they must think, at least implicitly, that there are valuable epistemic states other than the ones they address in their theories. I propose that understanding is one of those goals and that most epistemologists tacitly aim at achieving understanding through the theories they advance. Since understanding is an epistemic state they implicitly value, it would be a good idea to investigate it.

Virtue theories make the "something else" in the definition of knowledge a property of the knower.[22] Since theories of this kind identify a property of the knower as the value-conferring property of epistemic states, they not only have the advantage of not being committed to the view that justification, warrant, and knowledge have propositional objects, but they have the additional advantage of making a recovery of the investigation of understanding much easier to do. Valuable epistemic properties of agents produce valuable epistemic states of agents. The states produced need not be limited to justification or knowledge. Some of them may not have propositional objects. They may be states of understanding.

In *Virtues of the Mind*, I propose two definitions of knowledge that differ only in the way the object of knowledge is identified. In both definitions, knowledge is a state that is the result of acts of intellectual virtue, where I define "act of intellectual virtue" in a way that is intended to capture the idea of an intellectual act that is good in every respect.[23] The definition of an act of intellectual virtue is unimportant for my purposes here. My point is that I give two definitions, and they differ only in the way the object of knowledge is specified. That is because I do not address the issue of the object of knowledge in that book except in passing. The first definition is neutral on the issue of whether knowledge has a propositional object. To maintain neutrality I propose that knowledge is cognitive contact with reality plus something else. I take it that everyone can agree on that. The issue is what that entails and what else has to be added to it. I have proposed that the something else is that it is the result of an act of intellectual virtue, but, as I say, that is not important for the topic of this essay. The second definition follows the contemporary convention of defining knowledge as true belief plus something else. That definition presupposes that the object of knowledge is a proposition. It is important to notice that this definition of knowledge can remain neutral about the object. In contrast, most other definitions do not make sense unless the object is a proposition. Since understanding has a nonpropositional object, it is easier to connect it with knowledge in the kind of virtue theory I propose than in those that define knowledge by looking at properties of propositional beliefs or the processes that produce them.

I am not going to propose a definition of understanding in this paper that is as specific as my definition of knowledge, but I think that a definition can be generated by looking at those intellectual virtues that aim not at truth, but at understanding. The virtues I have previously examined were in the former category. An investigation into the latter would be very interesting. I suspect that understanding arises from special and unanalyzed, even unrecognized, virtues. It follows from what I have said that we educate people in these virtues when we teach them a *techne*, but what we do, exactly, is very hard to pinpoint. I think there is a form of teaching that can produce these virtues so they are not simply natural talents—but even their names are elusive.

There is a difference between the kind of understanding a person has who acquires it from a teacher and the kind that a person has who has figured it out for herself. Good teachers learn how to give their students understanding of difficult subject matter by the use of diagrams, vivid examples, and explanations of the way the new subject matter connects to things the students already understand. Understanding can be taught, like knowledge; and like knowledge, there is probably a qualitative difference between the state one gets from another and the state one gets on one's own. Recovering understanding as an object of epistemological investigation should include an investigation of these differences.

What about wisdom? Is there any hope of recovering that also? I have claimed that the neglect of understanding is associated with the fixation on certainty and justification and the accompanying focus on the propositional belief, a complex of interests associated with pessimism about the possibility of knowledge. But unlike the neglect of understanding, the neglect of wisdom is probably the result of another kind of pessimism as well—pessimism about the concept of the good life, the life a wise person understands. This pessimism is primarily an ethical one, and leaving aside radical skepticism will not be sufficient to make wisdom the object of inquiry. The task of recovering wisdom, then, will be more difficult than the task of recovering understanding, but I believe the latter is a necessary condition for the former.

VII

The epistemologist asks what knowledge is and how it can be acquired. The skeptic suspects that knowledge as the epistemologist defines it cannot be acquired at all. The two have been locked in a battle that has lasted many centuries. Paul Woodruff remarks in response to this situation: "Which came first, the sceptic or the epistemologist? The answer is, 'Neither: Plato came first'" (p. 61). The philosophical inquiry into understanding came before the philosophical inquiry into propositional knowledge and doubts about the latter. Epistemology should not only make the investigation of understanding one of its aims, but if epistemology is itself a *techne*, it should aim to understand how understanding relates to knowledge and the other objects of epistemological study. And if Plato is also right that the ultimate object of a *techne* is some good and all the forms of good are related, we can deepen our understanding of understanding and other epistemic goods by inquiry into the good itself. With luck, that might give us a glimpse of what wisdom is.

Notes

1. The reason I say this is not the only possible response is that it is still possible that there is progress in philosophy, and the lack of concern for skepticism in some previous eras might just be a mistake destroyed once and for all by Descartes. I believe this is Richard Foley's view.

2. Roger Florka has argued that even though Descartes was interested in certainty, his concerns were more metaphysical than epistemological. Florka (1997) addresses Descartes's view of reasoning according to which the reasoning faculty attempts to follow the metaphysical structure of the universe. He claims that what Descartes wanted to achieve in gaining certainty was close to what I mean by understanding.

3. See, especially, Kvanvig (1992), 181–2, and Code (1987) for the complaint that contemporary epistemology is too atomistic and insufficiently social.

4. See also Everson (1990), 4–5.

5. The distinction between expert and nonexpert knowledge is important for the consistency of Socrates's position since, according to Woodruff (1990), it is only expert knowledge that Socrates says he lacks.

6. Taylor (1990), 116.

7. See the *Routledge Encyclopedia of Philosophy*, edited by Edward Craig and Luciano Floridi, Oxford: Routledge 1998, and the *Companion to Epistemology*, edited by Jonathan Dancy and Ernest Sosa, Oxford: Blackwell 1992. Even when the term "understanding" is used in the title of a work on epistemology, that often means nothing when it comes to an account of the nature of understanding. I am pleased to find that one recent book on epistemology does not neglect understanding and is even concerned to reclaim it. See Elgin (1996).

8. Note that Plantinga's use of the word "warrant" is a replacement for one of the meanings for "justification" that he says he has identified (1990). Large sections of this essay appear in (1993a).

9. I suspect that this happened for a time with the concept of virtue and the concepts of some of the individual virtues.

10. I am using the word "fact" as a placeholder, since we have not yet identified the object of *episteme*.

11. Etchemendy and Barwise have a number of papers on this. For a good overview and bibliography, see Hammer (1995).

12. See Sosa (1980) for these analogies.

13. This is also the moral of Lewis Carroll's famous paper, "What the Tortoise Said to Achilles," (1895). The tortoise keeps trying to turn a logical inference of the form of *modus ponens* into another premise. The effort leads to an infinite regress.

14. This way of looking at it forces us to make a decision about an issue I left up in the air earlier. There I wanted to be neutral on the question of whether understanding gives us a grasp of nonpropositional structures that are actually there in reality, or whether it gives us a way of *representing* reality nonpropositionally, where there is no commitment to the idea that the structure of reality and the structure of

the theory are isomorphic. A theory seems to give us understanding in the latter sense.

15. This point raises deep metaphysical questions that I cannot address here. For those who disagree with me, I can only say that nothing of importance in this paper hinges on the point. If it turns out that all forms of understanding are forms of knowledge, that actually strengthens my main point, which is that understanding has been neglected and ought to be investigated.

16. van Fraassen (1991), 3.

17. A priori knowledge is an exception, of course, but most of our most interesting knowledge is not a priori.

18. See, for example, Conee and Feldman (1985).

19. For the strong defeasibility theory, see Lehrer (1990) and Klein (1971), 471–82.

20. For reliabilist theories, see Goldman (1986) and Sosa (1991). Plantinga gives his theory of warrant as proper function in (1993b).

21. See Goldman (1967).

22. In addition to the virtue theory I endorse, John Greco's agent reliabilism is a form of virtue epistemology in which properties of the knower are the focus of the theory. Sosa's faculty reliabilism is arguably a form of agent reliabilism also.

23. Zagzebski (1996), 264–73.

References

Alston, William. 1993. "Epistemic Desiderata." *Philosophy and Phenomenological Research* 53 (3): 527–51.

Burnyeat, Miles. 1980. "Aristotle on Understanding Knowledge." In *Aristotle on Science: The Posterior Analytics*, edited by E. Berti. Padua, Italy and N.Y.: Editrice Antenoire.

Carroll, Lewis. 1895. "What the Tortoise Said to Achilles." *Mind 4*.

Chisholm, Roderick. 1966. *Theory of Knowledge*. Englewood Cliffs, N.J.: Prentice Hall.

Code, Lorraine. 1987. *Epistemic Responsibility*. Hanover, N.H.: University Press of New England for Brown University Press.

Conee, Earl, and Richard Feldman. 1985. "Evidentialism." *Philosophical Studies* (48): 15–34.

Elgin, Catherine. 1996. *Considered Judgment*. Princeton, N.J.: Princeton University Press.

Everson, Stephen, ed. 1990. *Epistemology.* Vol. 1 of *Companions to Ancient Thought.* Cambridge: Cambridge University Press.

Fine, Gail. 1990. "Knowledge and Belief" in *Republic* v–vii. In *Epistemology.* Vol. 1 of *Companions to Ancient Thought,* edited by Stephen Everson.

Florka, Roger. 1997. *Descartes' Metaphysical Reasoning.* Los Angeles: University of California Press.

Fraassen, Bas van. 1991. *Quantum Mechanics: An Empiricist View.* Oxford: Clarendon.

Franklin, R. L. 1981. "Knowledge, Belief and Understanding." *The Philosophical Quarterly* 31 (124): 193–208.

Goldman, Alvin I. 1967. "A Causal Theory of Knowing." *Journal of Philosophy* 64 (12): 357–72.

———. 1986. *Epistemology and Cognition.* Cambridge: Harvard University Press.

Greco, John. 1999. "Agent Reliabilism." In *Philosophical Perspectives,* edited by James Tomberlin. Atascadero, Calif.: Ridgeview Press.

Guerriere, Daniel. 1975. "The Aristotelian Conception of *Episteme.*" *The Thomist* 39 (2): 341–48.

Hammer, Eric M. 1995. *Logic and Visual Information.* CLSI.

Hankinson, R. J. 1995. *The Sceptics* (The Arguments of the Philosophers series). London: Routledge.

Klein, Peter. 1971. "A Proposed Definition of Propositional Knowledge." *Journal of Philosophy* 67 (16): 471–82.

Kvanvig, Jonathan. 1992. *The Intellectual Virtues and the Life of the Mind.* Lanham, Md.: Rowman and Littlefield.

Lehrer, Keith. 1990. *Theory of Knowledge.* Boulder, Colo.: Westview.

Moravscik, Julius. 1979. "Understanding and Knowledge in Plato's Philosophy." *Neue Hefte für Philosophie* (15/16): 53–69.

———. 1992. *Plato and Platonism.* Oxford, U.K.: Blackwell.

Plantinga, Alvin. 1990. "Justification in the Twentieth Century." *Philosophy and Phenomenological Research,* 50 suppl (Fall): 45–71.

———. 1993a. *Warrant: The Current Debate.* New York: Oxford University Press.

———. 1993b. *Warrant and Proper Function.* New York: Oxford University Press.

Rorty, Richard. 1979. *Philosophy and the Mirror of Nature.* Princeton, N.J.: Princeton University Press.

Sosa, Ernest. 1980. "The Raft and the Pyramid." In *Midwest Studies in Philosophy*, Vol. 5 of *Studies in Epistemology*.

―――. 1991. *Knowledge in Perspective*. Cambridge: Cambridge University Press.

Sosa, Ernest, and Jonathan Dancy. 1992. *Companion to Epistemology*. Oxford, U.K.: Blackwell.

Taylor, C. C. W. 1990. "Aristotle's Epistemology." In Everson 1990: 116–42.

Williams, Michael. 1991. *Unnatural Doubts*. Cambridge: Blackwell.

Woodruff, Paul. 1990. "Plato's Early Theory of Knowledge." In Everson 1990: 60–84.

Zagzebski, Linda. 1996. *Virtues of the Mind: An Inquiry into the Nature of Virtue and the Ethical Foundations of Knowledge*. Cambridge: Cambridge University Press.

17 Selections from *The Intellectual Virtues and the Life of the Mind: On the Place of the Virtues in Contemporary Epistemology*

Jonathan Kvanvig

When we think about the cognitive aspects of the life of the mind, what we want from epistemology is an evaluation of this life from the point of view of getting to the truth and avoiding error. We want to know when the quality of that life is adequate for epistemological purposes and when it is not. We want to know which ways of organizing, structuring, or arranging this cognitive life will be most fruitful from an epistemic point of view. If we think of the epistemological enterprise in this fashion, it is far from obvious that the Cartesian answer is right. That answer tells us that the best way of structuring a fruitful cognitive life is to concentrate on the individual time-slices and whether knowledge or justification is possessed at each such time-slice, and let the totality of that life get generated by cementing together these time-slices. This is, of course, not an argument; it is rather a picture intended to convey a feeling of dissatisfaction with the Cartesian perspective. The arguments will come later.

In recent years, several epistemologists have signaled an interest in avoiding the Cartesian perspective on epistemological matters, and some of these epistemologists are among those whose work is either a version of, or strongly suggestive of, virtue epistemology. Goldman, for example, holds that the epistemological enterprise needs for its success an account of justification and knowledge which is radically different than the Cartesian heritage that has dominated much of recent epistemology.[1]

However, once one understands fully the implications of the Cartesian perspective for an account of the intellectual life of the mind, these rejections of the Cartesian perspective can be easily seen to involve significant Cartesian elements which go unrejected. What is rejected is the reflective

Reprinted selections from Jonathan Kvanvig, *The Intellectual Virtues and the Life of the Mind: On the Place of the Virtues in Contemporary Epistemology* (Lanham, MD: Rowman and Littlefield, 1992), 165–178 and 181–186.

standpoint involved in Cartesianism, a standpoint in which the important epistemological issues are addressed by considering that which is accessible to the individual *cogito* reflecting on those issues. Appropriately so, this element of Cartesianism has been abandoned by many in recent years, for even if justification, for example, were solely a matter of what is "in one's head" at a particular time, it is an unfortunate and certainly pre-Freudian attitude to assume a transparency thesis about the contents of one's mind (the thesis that a mental state is present only if simple reflection by the person in question would reveal its presence).

My objection here about the reflective standpoint is not that the notion of justification does not involve such a standpoint. My point is, rather, that wedding such a view of justification to the Cartesian perspective generates a picture of the cognitive life that is unduly abstracted from the temporal flow involved in the cognitive life. It suggests that we concentrate on the time-slices and not worry about the connections between these time-slices. This view is mistaken in two respects. First, there are stages of life at which such advice is wholly inappropriate, for there are stages of life at which reflective capacities are severely limited. So the first point is that the Cartesian picture is one geared toward adult human cognitive ideality, and my complaint is that, however important such an account might be, it cannot be the whole picture. Second, even as adults, we simply do not and need not behave cognitively in accord with what this Cartesian approach suggests in order to be cognitively ideal; in particular, a cognitively ideal cognizer will often display immense concern about the way in which one's past affects one's present. For example, most of us adjust for intellectual weaknesses, whether acquired or inherited, in reflectively considering various problems and puzzles that confront us, and a failure to do so, whether one is aware of the weakness or not, can lead to a lack of ideality in a cognitive life.[2] This is the insight I believe we should take from reliabilists.

In addition to rejecting the appropriateness of the reflective standpoint for determining the epistemic status of belief, several reliabilists have attempted to incorporate cross-temporality into their accounts of justification or knowledge. Goldman, for example, calls his version of reliabilism "historical reliabilism," for in it, information about how an employed method of belief acquisition was acquired is relevant to whether the use of that method generates justification for the beliefs it produces.[3]

From the present perspective, the reliabilists' objections have hit on something important, but reliabilists have located the problem in the wrong domain; they have claimed that the problem was with a reflective standpoint about the nature of justification and knowledge, and they have thought that the problem was a time-slice view of justification which pre-cluded consideration of any other points of time in determining whether a belief is justified or not. The fundamental flaw of the Cartesian perspective, however, is not its reflective standpoint nor its time-slice approach to the nature of justification and knowledge; nothing I have said to this point suggests that either aspect is to be rejected. In fact, I believe both aspects are correct if suitably formulated. Instead, the fundamental problem with the Cartesian perspective is the assumption that an account of the life of the mind is to be generated by cementing together the time-slice accounts of justification and knowledge for each moment of an individual's life. Given this difficulty with the Cartesian perspective, the rejections of the Carte-sian perspective described in the last paragraph seem quite ancillary to the heart of the matter. Of course, one might say, the reflective standpoint runs the risk of over-intellectualizing the life of the mind in its possession know-ledge and justification; and, one might continue, of course a time-slice view of knowledge and justification has inherent limitations. But attempt-ing to patch up the Cartesian perspective by introducing a historical ele-ment into the accounts of knowledge and justification is like trying to make a continuous and adequate concrete foundation by joining two dis-connected pieces with a superficial patch of the joint: a connection now exists that did not beforehand, but the foundation cannot bear any weight. The heart of the problem is not the time-slice account of knowledge and justification, but rather the attempt to cement together the disjoint pieces into a unified account of the cognitive life of the mind.

A more accurate picture of the life of the mind recognizes that an inquiry into that life at any point in that life will, of necessity, have recourse to much of the rest of the life of the individual. Consider some examples. Some persons see deep connections between apparently unrelated domains of knowledge; others equally intelligent (by certain measures, at least) lack the capacity to concentrate for any extended period of time and so miss these connections; still others lack the discipline to approach any topic with carefulness and also fail to achieve much understanding. How are we to understand these phenomena? Clearly, all of them are related in inter-esting ways to how much a person knows, and whether or not that person is rational in believing what they believe. But that is not the place to begin; rather, that is the result of a much deeper kind of understanding, an under-standing which pays attention to the history of each individual. And the history in question will not be one that pays attention only to what a person knows or justifiably believes at each instant in the past. I will say more about this later, but for present purposes it is enough to note that the history in question will have to pay attention not only to one's native cognitive endowments but also to what kinds of teachers one has had and to whether one's intellectual models were adequate.

Seen from this perspective, the rejections of the Cartesian perspective that have appeared over the last two decades seem quite superficial rejections of that perspective. What they do well is point out where epistemology has gone wrong; what is needed, however, is a full-blown rejection of that perspective rather than an approach that seems wedded to the very perspective that is problematic, wedded by approaching the entire epistemological enterprise by beginning with the question of when an individual person knows or is justified in believing an individual proposition at an individual point in time.

Of course, nothing said or implied by the contents of these recent anti-Cartesians commits them to holding to a fundamentally Cartesian perspective regarding the relation between questions and knowledge and justification and the cognitive life of the mind. For we should not conclude that time-slice questions concerning knowledge and justification cannot be formulated sensibly nor that they are unimportant in a complete account of the life of the mind. The difficulty, however, is that if one realizes the true nature of the Cartesian perspective, one will not begin by asking questions concerning the time-slice nature of knowledge and justification. For it is of the nature of perspectives that questions important in one perspective are unimportant or subject to a new twist of some sort in another perspective. Thus, if an epistemological theory is conscientiously anti-Cartesian in outlook, it would be a serious mistake to begin epistemological theorizing by asking and answering those questions central to the Cartesian perspective.

The objection I am raising to the Cartesian perspective concerns its construal of the life of the mind. Now, die-hard Cartesians will find little persuasive quality to my complaints at this point, and I believe that response to my complaints is a fair one. For whatever importance is to be attached to what I have claimed is to be found in the way it leads to an alternative perspective. In the absence of such an alternative, the simple response to my complaint is that the Cartesian perspective merely distorts reality a bit as a matter of necessity in order to pursue a formal, abstract approach to epistemological inquiry. In the absence of an alternative to this perspective, the Cartesian would seem warranted in claiming that the demands of formality and abstraction are regrettable, but that serious investigation in matters epistemological cannot be pursued otherwise; hence, the alternative to the distortion contained in the Cartesian perspective is an abandonment of any attempt to understand in a systematic way the cognitive life of the mind.

So, in order to drive home my complaint against the Cartesian perspective, it is important to consider what alternatives there might be to that perspective; in effect, I want to claim that the force of what I have claimed against the Cartesian perspective is to be found in the power and insight to be found in the alternative perspective to be outlined. I want to suggest that perhaps a better picture of an ideal cognitive life is one which does not emphasize individual propositional warrant, knowledge-that, and the cementing of time-slice relations between warrant, the individual, and belief. Perhaps, instead of beginning from the Cartesian perspective, we should think more realistically of what human beings are like without abandoning the attempt to understanding systematically the life of the mind. Instead of beginning from the assumption of an ordinary, competent adult isolated from the flow of time in studious contemplation of evidence, warrant principles, and argument forms having individual propositions as their (warranted) conclusions, we should think of human beings in terms of potentialities in need of socialization in order to participate in communal efforts to incorporate bodies of knowledge into corporate plans, practices, rituals, and the like for those practical and theoretical purposes that ordinarily characterize human beings.

What I am suggesting is meta-theoretical advice about how theory construction in epistemology should begin. I am not suggesting that our theories must include such information, or that it is a necessary truth that all cognitive beings begin with limited cognitive resources in need of development. Should a world contain cognitive beings completely fitted for the search for truth from the moment of birth, our theories can still apply. For the advice is not that we should construct theories only for the less advantaged from birth, but that our theories must not be constructed so that they cannot accommodate anything less than full outfitting at birth. I am suggesting, that is, that our theorizing can be educated to possibilities that are frequently ignored within the Cartesian framework by paying some attention to the feeble beginnings of human cognitive capacities. Cognitive ideality is possible for such beings, but we cannot account for this possibility by concentrating only on beings who begin life already in full command of the proper procedures and methods for beginning the search for truth. These cautionary remarks are intended to prevent the misunderstanding that the approach I am suggesting presumes some knowledge of what actual human beings are like. Instead, it only advises a meta-theoretical appreciation of the range of possibilities for cognitively ideal lives, and paying attention to what types of possibilities there are in a given domain is always appropriate advice for any theorizing about that domain.

What I am arguing for is an approach that pays attention to the possibility of finding cognitively ideal mental lives in the case of individuals who depend on a social structure to become competent in the search for truth. Such a perspective would foster an initial wonder concerning how human beings come to be competent truth-seekers, in much the same way that they become competent language speakers. In both cases, appreciating the contingent facts about human beings shows that proper inquiry needs to begin in the arena of know-how, whether regarding the search for truth or proper grammatical understanding. Instead of beginning the epistemological inquiry from the assumption that the search proceeds by accessing evidence that is tied to belief by adequate epistemic principles, we would instead ask how it is that cognitive individuals come to know how to conduct themselves in the search for truth, how it is that human beings come to master the tasks crucial for the acquisition of knowledge. This question would be important even if human beings were born knowing how to acquire knowledge, for our theories must be sensitive not only to what actual beings are like but to what they might be like as well. In this case, however, the fact that human beings are not born fitted for the search for truth lends even greater significance to the project of epistemologically theorizing about how one might achieve cognitive ideality from such frail beginnings. Perhaps what is needed is a paradigm shift, a shift from the perspective which takes "when does S know that p?" to be the foundational question of epistemology to a perspective that begins by asking how the know-how which is at the heart of the cognitive life is acquired.

Suggesting a paradigm shift is treacherous business, one in which the temptation to insecure inferences is great. In the present domain, once the fecundity of the new perspective comes to be appreciated, there is the danger of a wholesale condemnation of the old perspective. In particular, there is a danger of either claiming or being construed as claiming that knowledge and justification, those cherished concepts within the Cartesian perspective, have no place at the foundations of epistemological inquiry. Of course, such a conclusion would be unwarranted, for nothing in the paradigm shift entails or even supports the claim that small children have no justified beliefs about the world or beliefs that constitute knowledge about the world. The point of the paradigm shift is not to reject the claims of the prior perspective, but rather to open up new possibilities by allowing epistemological investigation to take us where the new perspective naturally inclines. Thus in the remainder of this final substantive section of this final substantive chapter, I want to pursue in a very programmatic way the out-lines of this new approach to epistemological inquiry. The ultimate point of this inquiry is to make room for the guiding premise of this work, that the heart of epistemological inquiry involves an account of the intellectual virtues. In order to accomplish this goal, I want first to suggest what the foundational inquiry in genetic epistemology might look like. I have al-ready shown that this alternative approach to the cognitive life of the mind requires that genetic epistemological inquiry be the foundational form of inquiry, and that these first epistemological issues be from a social perspec-tive on epistemological inquiry. Once the new direction is appreciated, there may be a tendency in some readers to question the necessity of wandering in the wilderness of the previous seven chapters of this work. Though my remarks on genetic epistemology will of necessity be program-matic, they will involve sufficient content to foster an appreciation of the claim I made in the Preface that the only way out of the maze of con-temporary epistemological discussion is through the maze itself. Thus, in addition to the ultimate aim of making room for the guiding premise of this work, the present section has as an ancillary goal accounting for the necessity of this work in breaking the grip of the Cartesian perspective.

In addition to genetic questions, however, it is also important that we address structural issues as well, if only out of fairness to those contempo-rary epistemologists attracted to versions of virtue epistemology. For my aim is to suggest that the social perspective offers a strong vindication of the guiding premise of this work, the premise that the virtues ought to be the focus of epistemological inquiry. If virtue epistemology is wrong, then, it is not because its heart is in the wrong place, and so it will be useful to consider just what happens in the domain of structural epistemology on the new, social perspective. As we shall see, the most radical implications of the new perspective are to be found in this domain. First, though, we turn to genetic issues.

Genetic Epistemology and the Social Perspective

Should we make such a shift in perspective, the important question in ge-netic epistemology concerns how one progresses down the path toward cognitive ideality. The manner in which this progress is achieved concerns the social patterns of mimicry and imitation, and has much less to do with the explicit internal representation of rules and principles. In sum, this new perspective would place an emphasis on the role of *exemplars* rather than on epistemic principles and evidence, and on the importance of training and practice in learning how to search for truth rather than on mastering a body of information about how to draw inferences. As such, the rules, procedures, and principles would be conceptually secondary to the cognitive life, for the heart of the cognitive life involves mimicking and imitating our parents and teachers (and perhaps at more advanced stages, at times dissenting from them as well) in the process of coming to know how to conduct ourselves in the search for truth. As this process becomes more rigorous, disciplined, and formal, attention turns to propositional knowledge in formal schooling settings. The more fundamental knowledge the social perspective is interested in, however, is revealed in the early stages of development in which "why?" questions predominate. One construal of this activity of questioning is that the child is seeking and finding propositional information about the world. Of course, that is partially true, but the fundamental importance of this activity concerns the acquisition of knowhow: the child learns to know how one goes about looking for explanations and when the task of seeking explanations is done (that is why this activity is found exasperating by some adults, for children have a way of asking such questions beyond the point of sensibility). By asking and receiving answers, those endowed with adequate basic cognitive equipment come to internalize approaches to the world by mimicking their models.

This basic point about the secondary character of explicit epistemic rules can be misunderstood. I am not saying that there are no rules that characterize the early stages of knowledge acquisition by children. Nor am I saying that these rules are not internal, in the sense in which hardwiring in computers is internal to the functioning of the computer. What I am denying is that figuring out what the world is like is not a matter of consulting and following rules, and I am also denying that whatever hardwired principles we are born with are insufficient for competence in the search for truth. Without the know-how acquired in mimicking and imitating one's models, the hardwired epistemic mechanisms of nature would leave us dramatically inept in our search for truth. So any realistic account of the purely cognitive aspects of the life of the mind cannot afford to begin elsewhere than by paying attention to this process of mimicry and imitation.

To repeat cautionary remarks made earlier, I am not saying it is not possible for a cognitive being to have less feeble beginnings. The danger of epistemological theorizing is not that of failing to provide an account of an ideal life of the mind for individuals more fully outfitted at birth, perhaps both linguistically and epistemically. Rather the danger is that we theorize with no attention paid to less blessed beginnings, pretending that cognitive ideality always requires a full grasp of the correct set of epistemic principles and reflective abilities to determine which principles to apply in a given case. A complete theory must address the nature of cognitive ideality for superhumans as well as humans; my remarks are intended not to dismiss the possibility of those better endowed from birth, but to prevent the ignoring of less charmed, and therefore more realistic, entrances into the cognitive sphere.

A more realistic account of the cognitive life gives an answer to the foundational question of how we come to be full-fledged cognizers, an answer given in terms of the social arrangement involving interaction with other persons. But not just any kind of person; the persons are conceived of as *exemplars*. Of course, such an account does not presume success of outcome; the skeptic still has the option of claiming that the mimicry and imitation is inadequate or that there really are no exemplars. The point, however, is that a successful answer to the skeptic will involve an appeal to the intellectual character of our teachers and parents and to the native ability to mimic and imitate those same parents and teachers in the process of coming to be like them.

Compare this role for skepticism with the role for skepticism in the Cartesian perspective. The classic Cartesian worry concerns how one gets from the inner world to the outer; for the Cartesian, the inner world of the mind is epistemologically unproblematic, while the connection between inner and outer world—the external world of common experience—occupies the central position of concern. Once we shift perspectives to the social, anti-Cartesian perspective, this question hardly makes sense any longer. For one thing, appearance-state statements appear to exploit outer world concepts in their very formulation: for example, to be appeared to birch-treely appeals to the notion of a birch tree in its very formulation. Further, there are strong reasons concerning the individuation of mental states to think that external world factors infect the individuation of such mental states. If, for example, the stuff that is H_2O were to have a functional equivalent in another world with a different chemical constitution, a belief by English-speakers in that world represented by the sentence "water quenches thirst" would be a different belief than that represented for English speakers in this world by the same sentence.[4] Yet if these outer world propositional contents differ because of the chemical nature of the substance in question, then surely the related appearance-state statements expressed by the sentence, "I am appeared to water-ly," would express different propositional contents in the two worlds as well. The cost of denying this symmetry between ordinary object statements and appearance-state statements will be quite high, for if the symmetry of content is denied, it is difficult to see what account can be given of the evidential support relation between the two. For if the symmetry of semantic content is denied, then *I am appeared to water-ly* bears no more intimate an internal connection to *there is water in front of me* than does *I am appeared to red-ball-ly*. One will have introduced a "sense-data" language (though perhaps without ontological commitments to sense-data) in which the propositional expression of the contents of appearances is semantically unrelated to the propositional contents expressed by ordinary discourse, and doing so makes any evidential connections between the two kinds of propositional contents extremely remarkable.

Once this difference between the two perspectives is noted, certain skeptical concerns seem more like psychological ailments needing therapy than significant epistemological worries. In particular, a skeptic whose primary concern centers on how to get outside of the inner world of private experience to knowledge of the public, external world has a more difficult time being taken seriously once the Cartesian foundation is rejected. The foundations of knowledge are not found in appearance-state statements, independent of the external world, for the dependence between the two is shown to obtain by the anti-individualism considerations above regarding the content of "water"-beliefs.[5] If the skeptic is to avoid a psychiatric diagnosis, he or she will first have to convince those adopting the social perspective that there is a problem; whereas, within the Cartesian perspective, his concerns about the inner-outer connection needed no defense.

Skeptical concerns are still of importance in the new perspective, however, for the social perspective allows the possession of knowledge in a way which appears to involve quite a bit of luck: one must be lucky enough to be in the right community, one in which exemplars reside; one must be lucky enough not to fasten onto those which are anti-exemplars, and one must be lucky enough to be endowed by nature with sufficient simulation capacities to allow the conditioning necessary to become proficient in cognitive tasks.

In describing the quality of progress toward proficiency, virtue notions will come into play. We will want to describe some individuals as abnormal and others as exceptional; some as retarded in their development or deficient in basic cognitive equipment and others as exceptionally bright or as having superb native endowments. Each such description is a description of an intellectual virtue, and since the notion of an intellectual virtue relies on that of justification, each such description would seem to involve the notion of justification as well. So the social perspective, like the Cartesian perspective, will involve formulating a theory of justification as one of its basic projects.

There is no reason at this point to believe that the project of constructing a theory of justification will look the same for each perspective. At this point, we know that the theory developed for the social perspective will have to involve certain subjective, internalist features in order to be able to function properly in the account of a virtue. For the lesson of evil-demon concerns implies that such internalistic features are necessary. But beyond this point, nothing more is fixed. Just what is left open is a topic in the next section.

The important point to note in this section, though, is the central role that the virtues play in epistemology done from the social perspective. This perspective shares with the Cartesian perspective the need to provide a theory of justification, but from the social perspective, the point of the theory is to provide a complete understanding of the central notion of a virtue. The main focus is not on the theory of justification, but rather on that which the theory of justification can illuminate.

Structural Epistemology and the Social Perspective

So much for the genetic viewpoint. What if, however, we determine to address structural matters? If we take a realistic view of the cognitive activities of human beings, we will be careful to engage in abstractions only when there is good reason to do so. If we find a good reason to abstract enough to address structural issues, a minimalist approach in this abstraction to structural epistemological questions will leave unabstracted the social nature of human cognitive activity and the corporate nature of bodies of knowledge. Thus, in addressing structural issues, our first questions will concern accounting for the superiority from an epistemological point of view of certain communities and the bodies of knowledge they generate. In order to answer these questions, we might go on to abstract from the social nature of knowers and ask what makes certain organized claims to truth epistemologically more significant than others. If we abstract in this fashion, we might ask what makes physics better off than, say, astrology; or what makes scientific books, articles, addresses, or lectures somehow more respectable from an epistemological point of view than books, articles, addresses or lectures regarding astrology. On the other hand, we might abstract from the concerns of subject matter to ask what makes certain communities epistemically better off than other communities of inquirers.

For example, what makes the scientific community superior to monastic communities for purely epistemic interests?

Finally, we might abstract from both the corporate nature of knowledge and the social nature of those who search for truth. This final level of abstraction takes us as close as we will come to the Cartesian perspective, and it is possible that the questions involved at this point revolve around the question, "When does S know that p?" However, there are a couple of reservations I wish to note about this final level of abstraction, one concerning whether there is cause to undertake the questions at this final level of abstraction and one concerning whether the questions at this level revolve around the issue of when a person knows a particular proposition.

A point I have been emphasizing is that epistemological questions worth addressing arise from concerns internal to the epistemological enterprise itself and the perspective from which that enterprise is addressed. Thus, it is poor motivation for epistemological inquiry that the questions addressed are central to epistemological inquiry from a different perspective. So, the mere fact that the question of when a person knows an individual proposition is central to epistemological inquiry from the Cartesian perspective should not lead those engaging in epistemological inquiry from a social perspective to undertake to answer the very same question. In order for this issue to warrant attention, there must be issues arising from within the social perspective that call for this issue to be addressed.

The question for this final level of abstraction, the level at which the social perspective comes closest to displaying concern over those affairs foundational from the Cartesian perspective, is how concern over the issues raised at this level is conceived to arise out of the social perspective and its concerns. Since this level of abstraction involves an abstraction to the individual person and the individual proposition, let us consider each aspect in turn.

There does seem to be some warrant for considering structural aspects of the cognitive life of an individual mind if we engage in epistemological inquiry from a social perspective. For one thing, our ontology has to be individualistic with regard to persons and, more importantly, in order to account for advances in the shared knowledge of a culture, we will have to have recourse to what is going on in individual minds. For example, original and creative ideas ordinarily are not the product only of a particular individual mind, though it is true that such ideas arise first in a particular mind. In addition, the results of the last section show that a notion of justification applicable to individuals is needed in the context of a genetic account of the cognitive aspects of the life of the mind. Further, even the most community-oriented perspective must allow for notions such as leadership and division of labor, and once these notions are introduced into a perspective which takes the social nature of human beings seriously, we need to be able to address questions concerning the individual person as well as questions concerning the community. Intellectual leadership is as important as other kinds of leadership, and the intellectual division of labor has borne immense fruit in the total storehouse of knowledge humanity has generated; thus, there is good reason to address questions concerning the life of the individual mind, in both structural and genetic epistemology.

A note of caution is also in order, however, about the abstraction to the level of the individual, for if we take the social perspective seriously, we should never begin to think that the deepest epistemological questions concern the isolated intellect. Instead, as is clear from the above motivation for considering questions concerning individual intellects, such questions arise on the rockbed of social concern, for the notions of leadership and division of labor have no purchase outside the social domain. One is reminded here of the attempt to do ethics by beginning with "desert island" cases; even if such cases are possible, it is absurd to think that we can come to be enlightened about the nature of the moral life we share by focusing on such cases. Just so in the epistemological case: divorcing epistemological concern from the realities of social interaction generates an epistemology built on answers to questions as relevant to the life of the mind as "desert island" cases alone in ethics.

Thus, though there are some qualifications on the importance of the abstraction to the individual person, there is motivation to be found within a social perspective for addressing issues surrounding the life of an individual mind. I believe, however, that the abstraction to the level of the individual proposition is fraught with difficulty, and I wish to make a few remarks about why the final level of abstraction in the social perspective will not best be addressed only or primarily by considering when a person knows an individual proposition.

Propositions, it would seem, behave in discourse more like mass nouns than they do count nouns. For example, consider one encounter between an individual and a certain environment—Joe's looking carefully at a particular portion of the Grand Canyon, and acquiring information about it. It makes no more sense, it would seem, to ask how many individual propositions Joe has come to believe or be aware of in this encounter than it does to ask how many little heaps there are in one big heap of dirt. In each case, the acquired information can be divided up in a variety of ways to yield answers to the question, but no answer counts as the real or correct answer to the question in itself. Given particular interests, we can attribute to Joe particular propositional contents, but in doing so, we should note carefully that it need not be an intrinsic characteristic of Joe (one which is independent of our concerns) to have that particular proposition as an object of belief.

Furthermore, treating propositions like we do mass nouns can help explain some puzzles about belief. In the Grand Canyon case, consider asking Joe whether the canyon is longer than it is wide. Now, certainly Joe has information acquired during his experience of the canyon that gives him knowledge that the canyon is longer than it is wide; but it is doubtful that he ever considered that very proposition. Yet it is implausible to suppose that, if asked, Joe would have to infer the truth of this claim from other claims he already believes.

The informational chunk view suggests an alternative. According to it, sentential expressions of informational content need not reflect an aspect of the architecture of the mind, and, hence, need not express propositions that are explicitly represented. There is, perhaps, a representational structure in the mind that, if structured by a query in a certain way, yields the proposition or a representation of the proposition that the canyon is longer than it is wide. Yet, on the informational chunk view, it is implausible to describe a certain informational chunk as involving a definitive number of propositions or to describe a certain informational chunk as in itself containing a precise particular propositional constituent. In sum, the representational architecture of the mind is much more amorphous than this propositional view requires, and it is this fact that accounts for our ambivalence in ascribing particular propositional contents of belief in cases where the particular propositional content has never been explicitly considered.

Of course, I am not arguing that a person cannot have a particular propositional content as the object of belief—Joe might consciously hold before his mind the proposition *the depth of the gorge is breathtaking*. The point is rather that experience conveys information only *en masse*, and the individuation into propositional form often imposes structure rather than conforming to it.

An epistemology sensitive to the representational structure of the mind will begin the tasks of structural epistemology from a different point than that of asking when a particular person knows or justifiably believes an individual proposition. Instead, it will begin with the issue of the adequacy of a representational structure to the world, where this question is not a question concerning what individual propositions are believed. In fact, it may turn out that a representational structure elicited from an encounter with the world, such as the one above in which Joe examines a particular portion of the Grand Canyon, stands or falls together so that the structure is either adequate as a whole or inadequate as a whole. If so, it is easy to see how a kind of coherence account of the adequacy of a representational structure might result from a more realistic appraisal of the architecture of the mind than that assumed by approaches which take the fundamental question of epistemology to be, "When does S know that p?" Regardless of the force of these points about the representational nature of the life of the mind and the question of the adequacy of a propositional approach, the point I want to emphasize is the remoteness of such issues from the central epistemological concerns that arise from the social perspective. The question that is fundamental from the Cartesian perspective is the most ethereal question from the social perspective; thus the landscape of epistemological theorizing would be quite different if the social perspective were taken seriously, both in the domain of genetic epistemology and in the domain of fundamental epistemology.

The final question we need to address here concerns if and how these structural issues from the social perspective make a place for the virtues at the foundational stages of epistemological inquiry. We have already seen that the encroachment by the virtues at the foundational stages of genetic epistemology is significant; I want to suggest that we find the same significance in structural epistemology as well. In particular, I want to suggest that a virtue account of superiority of informational structure is a plausible account of what makes a particular organizational structuring of informational content superior to another. We have already noted that knowledge comes in bodies and information in chunks, but it would be misleading to suggest that the bodies or chunks are simply amorphous wholes. Instead, these bodies of knowledge and chunks of information come structured, with paths or routes built in between compartments in the body or chunk. Noting these features raises the issue of when one structured chunk of information or one organized body of knowledge is superior to another, and a natural account here is that a structured chunk of information is superior to another when it is at least in accord with what the intellectual virtues possessed corporately would have produced in the circumstance of acquisition and/or sustenance. What makes us count a certain structuring or organizing of information as superior is that it is the kind of structuring or organizing which a person of superior intelligence, insight, perceptivity, wisdom, etc. would come to possess in the appropriate circumstances.

Note that this account has added advantages apart from its explanatory power in the epistemological domain. One puzzling question that philosophers of science and epistemologists have worried over is why those characteristics of scientific theories which lead to their acceptance over rivals are of epistemological significance. For example, scientific theories win out over rivals on the basis of such factors as simplicity, fecundity, the power to explain apparently unrelated data, etc.; and none of these characteristics seem necessarily connected to the epistemic goal of finding the truth and avoiding error. A virtue approach to structural questions, though, provides a natural account in this matter: the reason these features count in favor of the superiority of one theory over another is that *they mirror the cognitive behavior of exemplars of intellectual virtuosity*. In other words, theories with these characteristics are direct analogues of informational chunks and bodies of knowledge which are structured or organized in a way that makes them superior to alternative structuring and organizing.

A virtue approach within the social perspective has another advantage over traditional approaches within the Cartesian perspective as well. Both approaches assume that the epistemic goal is to find the truth and avoid error. It is typical, however, to find those within the Cartesian framework positing other goals as well. The most important of these is that one's beliefs cover a broad variety of topics and issues with sufficient depth. Yet within the Cartesian framework, it is not clear how this emphasis is to be explained, for it certainly cannot be explained solely with reference to the epistemic goal: from the point of view solely interested in finding truth and avoiding error, no advice can be forthcoming to distinguish between those who secure the truth by repeated applications of the logical process of addition and those who aim at being Leibnizian polymaths. Yet there is quite a bit of discomfiture in maintaining that when epistemological concerns alone are in question, the issue of breadth and depth of knowledge never arises.

A virtue approach has a better answer, one which explains the importance of breadth and depth on the same grounds as it explains the superiority of structuring of informational chunks. Note first that any person who, in a particular situation, fastened onto an individual propositional element from which inferences were drawn by the operation of addition would be clearly inferior in the structuring of informational content to what one would expect of an exemplar of intellectual virtuosity. In sum, once a virtue approach to the structure of informational content is accepted, an emphasis on breadth and depth of knowledge falls out naturally in a way that is internal to the epistemological project—for the emphasis falls out of the notion of what an exemplar of intellectual virtuosity would know.

In the foregoing discussion of this section and the previous one, I have emphasized strongly the role that exemplars play in a complete epistemology. I have also been emphasizing the lack of purchase that traditional skeptical questions have on such an approach. Skeptical worries cannot be completely avoided however, for the emphasis on the role that exemplars play is subject to the distinction between appearance and reality which is so central to the history of epistemology and which gives rise to skeptical concerns. For one's mentors may be exemplars, but then again they may only appear that way. I cannot pursue here what this implies about the nature of cognitive ideality and its connection to the reliability of our representation of the world, but it is important to note the importance of these issues even if addressing them must be postponed for now.

Given even the advantages described above concerning the way in which the importance of breadth and depth of informational content falls out of a virtue approach to epistemological inquiry, the important question of how the notion of justification fits into the picture persists. For it is not only important to ascertain what counts as a superior structuring of informational content, it is also important to bring the virtue approach to bear on the epistemic goal of finding truth and avoiding error. And, as I understand the notion of justification, it is just this notion that is at stake in this endeavor.

There is nonetheless a difference within a social perspective concerning how a discussion of the notion of justification will go, for within the social perspective we will not begin a discussion of the notion of justification with respect to an individual proposition. We may come to need such a discussion, but the foundational issue will be the justificatory status of informational chunks rather than individual propositions. In addressing the nature of justification from within this perspective, it seems fairly obvious that some kind of coherence relation will play a distinctive role, and thus the answers here may impact some of the discussion of the nature of justification by traditional epistemologists from within the Cartesian perspective. We need not pursue that issue here, though, for all that is needed here is an explanation of the centrality of investigation into the nature of justification within a social perspective.

To sum up, in this new perspective, the social and cross-temporal nature of the cognitive life establishes the foundational domain of epistemological inquiry. Note that, in such a context, the important epistemological aspects come grouped: bunches of people rather than isolated individuals, bodies of knowledge rather than individuated propositions, and experienced, processual chunks of time rather than abstracted, individual time-slices. The question "When does S know that p?" is at the highest level of abstraction, in this perspective. What the community has come to know in its communal life is the first issue once we begin the process of abstraction to structural issues. The abstraction to the individual is natural, for human beings form ontic units on their own. In the realm of bodies of knowledge, however, the abstraction is singularly unnatural; the natural home (if there is one at all) for such an abstraction, I want to suggest, is the mathematician seeking a proof for a proposed theorem. Perhaps adopting this social perspective would lead one to ask, not when a particular proposition is epistemically better off than a competitor, but rather what makes some books, for example, better examples than other books of what the life of the mind can yield when properly conducted (say, books on science versus books about astrology). This is not to say that we cannot abstract to such a level that we do inquire into the relationship between individual propositions and individual persons, but only that such a level of abstraction would not be the nearest to the foundational, core issues for such an epistemology.

Of most interest in the context of this work is the fact that the social perspective is pregnant with implications for the role of the virtues in matters epistemological. For, if such a paradigm shift is undergone, there will be room for the view that the intellectual virtues should provide the focus for epistemological inquiry. Recall that in the social perspective, the notion of an exemplar is foundational to the epistemological project, and if it is, an investigation is called for into the nature of those characteristics which combine in such an exemplary fashion. In addition, when we turn to structural epistemology, an emphasis on the virtues is required as well, in that one of the initial question which arises is what makes one structuring of informational content superior to another. The answer, I have suggested, is that such a structuring mirrors the kind of structuring that an exemplar of intellectual virtuosity would display. Thus, in both domains of epistemological inquiry, the social perspective relies on the notion of an intellectual virtue.

Notes

1. Alvin Goldman, "Epistemics: The Regulative Theory of Cognition," *The Journal of Philosophy* 75 (October 1978), pp. 509–523; "Varieties of Cognitive Appraisal," *Noûs*, Vol. 13 (1979), pp. 23–38.

2. It is a different, though important, question whether this lack of ideality infects the justificatory status of beliefs at the moment in question. I happen to think not, but will not defend that view here. Let me just register, however, that not all intellectual sins count as breaches of the canons of justification or rationality, just as not all moral failures count as breaches of the canons of the kind of rationality appropriate in that domain. Hitler could have been perverse, depraved, degenerate, corrupt, ignoble, or whatever and still have displayed no faults in terms of rationality.

3. Goldman, *Epistemology and Cognition*, pp. 76, 78.

4. Some theorists distinguish between narrow and wide semantic content, claiming that wide content is outer-world-infected whereas narrow content is not. See, for example, Jerry Fodor, *Psychosemantics* (Cambridge, Mass.: MIT Press, 1987). This distinction, however plausible and useful it might be in other contexts, is of little use in the present context. For propositional knowledge is knowledge of what the world is like, and to be that, the contents of such knowledge must be broad contents.

I discuss the relevance of this distinction between broad and narrow content to the social perspective in "Structural Epistemology and the Social Perspective," later.

5. I borrow the term "individualism" from Tyler Burge. His arguments against individualism are contained in the following articles: "Individualism and the Mental," *Midwest Studies in Philosophy*, Vol. 4 (1979), pp. 73–121; "Other Bodies," in Andrew Woodfield, ed. *Thought and Object* (Oxford: Clarendon Press, 1982); and "Two Thought Experiments Reviewed," *Notre Dame Journal of Formal Logic*, Vol. 23 (1982), pp. 284–93.

Index